THE PROVING GROUNDS

THE PROVING GROUNDS

*A Journey through the Interior of
New Guinea and Australia*

BENEDICT ALLEN

HarperCollins*Publishers*

HarperCollins*Publishers*
77–85 Fulham Palace Road
Hammersmith, London W6 8JB

Published by HarperCollins*Publishers* 1991
1 3 5 7 9 10 8 6 4 2

A catalogue record for this book
is available from the British Library

ISBN 0-246-13633-2

Set in Pilgrim

Printed in Great Britain by
HarperCollinsManufacturing Glasgow

To Sue Kennett
friend, patron and landlady extraordinaire

CONTENTS

Map 1   Showing the location of the Gibson Desert in Western Australia and relative position
of New Guinea

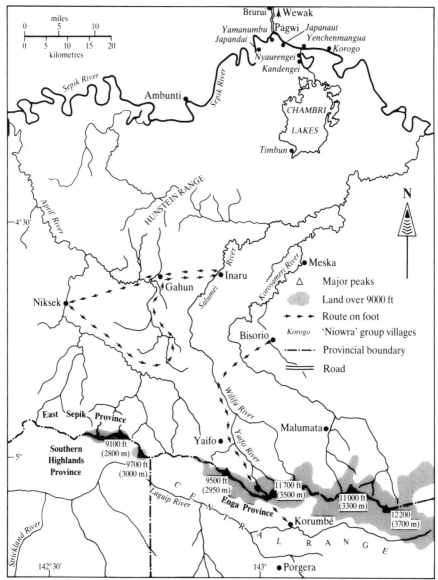

Map 2 The Middle Sepik and the route taken by the author into the Central Range of
Papua New Guinea

AUTHOR'S NOTE

I n my childhood I had a dream, to cross the land of El Dorado, the forest between the Orinoco and Amazon deltas; and years later, finishing university, I decided to do just that. I had little money and next to no knowledge of the forest, and from the moment I arrived on the Orinoco shore and found myself facing the mangroves, I had to learn to rely solely on the skill and goodwill of local Indians. Months went by as we paddled our dugouts and hunted our monkey suppers, and I began to get to know some of my guides. But however close to each other we grew, somehow I was always 'Louco Benedito', always 'Mad White Giant'. To them the venture was pointless – and, I began to suspect, much worse. By cutting through the forest, their home, or merely as a scientist trying to define it, I was imposing an outsider's will on the land, seeking to conquer it. It was something alien, this tendency to rationalize, this urge to expand man's control of the world. So I decided to record this and future expeditions – the intention was to write four Rain Forest books, each taking one different mood – in a way that played down scientific observation, our rationalizing slant on life. Recollection of day-to-day incident and detail would be of secondary importance; the emphasis would be on exploring ideas as they were shaped by the journey. This became 'concentric' exploration, building up ideas from the place, using it as a nucleus and probing horizons outwards – not extending principles from the West in traditional, 'linear' exploration, a form based on our rationalizing groundrules.

Mad White Giant, the story of that first independent journey, became a story of the imperialism that was its main feature – the Mad White Giant of the title being not only myself but the encroaching Western world represented by missionaries, scientists, miners and loggers. After completing three books, during a return trip to New Guinea I found the chance to bring together my experiences, and, within a community I had already been 'adopted' by, take a considerable step further, actually starting an expedition from within the 'forest'.

The events of the book centre on this return visit (May 1988–February 1989) to the Middle Sepik village of Kandengei, Papua New Guinea, where in 1985 I had been privileged to go through an initiation ritual by which boys traditionally gain manhood status. A description of that ceremony forms a major part of *Into the Crocodile Nest*; in this account I have changed the names of the major Kandengei characters – also those of two very minor characters in Wiluna. Where there are other changes from the earlier book, for instance in spellings, it is because I now favour the later version. The dated extracts from notebooks which begin and end the text I've smoothed out and elaborated to avoid continual use of square brackets. Everywhere else, I've told the story by simply reliving the journey from notebooks and memory, without 'background' reading or other external sources. The various notes were added after completion of the draft manuscript and serve to put what I have written in a more objective context, or simply to provide considered information, travelogue-style. I think it will quickly become clear to the reader that, with the extent of my involvement, any attempt to stand back, to write the fairly objective account that most travel books claim to be, would have been only a pretence of honesty. I learned through experiencing – I was never a spectator, always a participator. I was always vulnerable, immersed in the place, often out of my depth; at other times, perhaps, succeeding in looking at the world outwards, from through the trees, as it were.

I would like to thank the Moresby staff of Air Niugini for their friendly and efficient help, also the Institute of Papua New Guinea Studies for their co-operation and kindness once again. I'm also indebted to Matthew and Serena Jebb and their generous friends at Pacific Helicopters; 'Geoff' at Indaba, Jakob, Laurie, George, the two Bobs and the various members of NTM who helped me on my way. In Australia, Richard and Linda Douglas-Henry, the Ngangganawili Community and Herbie Stewart, who was always sympathetic, often with little cause, Peter Burns, and, of course, Charles and Nola Stewart-Robinson for resuscitating me so many times. Above all, to all the numerous indigenous guides and advisors, many of whom would not expect or want thanks, at Wiluna, Kandengei and along the route between. I must also thank some of those who propped me up back in London while I was sunk deep inside the manuscript – in particular Candida Julian-Jones, David Livesley, Gail and Andy Hinkinson, Kate and James Henry, Vivien Green; also particularly Jita Singh and family and as usual my own extended family – especially Kate Allen and Paul Pestille. Finally, everyone at HarperCollins, especially Ian Paten,

Stuart MacDonald in Australia and my editor Richard Johnson who has been so very understanding all along.

The island of New Guinea was originally settled by successive waves of peoples – principally those related to the present-day aborigines of Australia; Negritos; 'true Papuans' and Melanesians – when, as a legacy of the Ice Age, lower sea-levels considerably aided navigation. In general usage the label 'Melanesian' is an overall one attached to the peoples of the archipelago that begins in the west with New Guinea and extends eastwards to New Caledonia and Fiji.

New Guinea's awkward topography – the coastal mangrove swamps, the thick freshwater nipa and sago palm forests, and the central mountain ranges – inhibited communication between peoples and they became culturally introspective; no change from stone-tool technology came about.

Early in the sixteenth century a Portuguese explorer, Jorge de Meneses, became the first European to set foot on New Guinea. He called it the *Ilhas dos Papuas* because of its 'fuzzy-haired' people. In the 1540s the Spaniard Yaigo Ortiz de Retez named the island after the Guinea coast of Africa. During the next three centuries New Guinea's terrain discouraged exploitation of the island by European traders and governments. The Dutch, however, wishing to reinforce the eastern flank of their lucrative East Indies trading empire (today's Indonesia), recognized the claim to New Guinea of their vassal the Sultan of Tidore and so in the early nineteenth century themselves became rulers by proxy. Britain acknowledged the Dutch claim west of the 141° meridian, but in 1884 took the southerly portion of eastern New Guinea to provide Australia with a buffer against other European powers. Within days the Germans laid claim to the remainder, along with the Bismarck Archipelago. In 1906 British New Guinea was renamed 'Papua' and control was transferred to the new Commonwealth Government of Australia, which also seized the weak German colony during the First World War.

After the Second World War the Dutch were ousted from the East Indies by the pre-war independence leader Sukarno, who won sovereignty for an Indonesian Republic in 1949, securing their thoroughly suspect claim to western New Guinea, later 'Irian Jaya', in 1962. In 1975 Australia launched their island half to independence as Papua New Guinea, with a democratic parliamentary government and an economy based on Australian fiscal support, copper mining and plantation crops such as coffee and cocoa. When I visited PNG ten years later and went through Kandengei's initiation ceremony, copper and gold were becoming increasingly important and reliance on Australian finance was lessening (from half PNG's budget at independence to 20 per cent), though lack of infrastructure and therefore jobs for an increasingly educated population was leading to frustration.

The Kandengeis, with their satellite village Timbun, consider themselves the most senior of the Niowra group of seven major villages which compose about the most westerly of the 'Iatmul' people, who occupy the marsh margins of the Sepik (one of the island's two very major rivers) extending from 250 to 150 miles from the mouth. Niowra, a dialect of Iatmul, is the language of the village, but Pidgin is spoken fluently by nearly everyone and, though school is conducted in English, serves as the lingua franca between peoples here as in much of PNG. Sago is the staple food, the main source of protein is fish, though each family keeps a forest garden plot of sweet potatoes, yams, bananas and so on. Regular hunting trips are also made into the forest and *kunai* and waterside *pitpit* grasses for birds and cuscus (a marsupial related to the Australian opossum).

There are six major clans in Kandengei. As you approach the village from the forested channel that connects the lake with the Sepik they are, along the lake front: Smaark, Yaark, Posago, Yargoon, then Gama; Niowra, a founding clan, lies behind the main spirit house, backing on to the forest. Each clan has its own god-like spiritual figurehead(s) and each clan also holds responsibility for a portion of the world's beings, be they the stars, prawns or banana palms. To the spirits of these each clan member has allegiance; they must also maintain harmony with the spirits of their dead ancestors. The society is ostensibly a patriarchy, traditionally men running religious and political affairs from the spirit house, from which women and children are excluded – the village houses are considered their domain. However, the most traditional institutions, such as the practice of polygyny and also the moiety – the political division of the village into two balancing halves – are showing marked decline. Only the central spirit house of the three is operative, and the village converts of the Catholic church have at least nominally recruited the young at their (Smaark) end of the village; the 'hard-line', evangelizing Assemblies of God converts are working in from their far, Gama clan end. Since the completion of this book, in July 1990, over a year after my return to England, the elders appear to have further loosened their control of affairs; in the power vacuum the village has become increasingly embroiled in minor disputes with other Niowras, the disillusioned young back from towns and other parties with interests. It is not clear whether the hard-line Assemblies of God – with their penchant for evangelically head-hunting potentially the strongest tribe in the place – have yet taken the initiative.

Prologue

NOTES, LONDON SW17

June 1989, Tooting

Sentimental, I know, but I'm glad I brought my 'regalia' back with me – my shell earrings, the old pig tusk to put through my nose, the belt of cowries, the headdress of cassowary plumes. 'Your uniform', they said as I backed out of the spirit house. 'For ceremonial use only!' the old men yelled. 'Keep them in your house for ever!' What? I thought. My top floor room in Tooting? My landlady might not approve! 'They are your *entitlement*, Benedix,' said Wallace, my 'Brother', walking with me through the village palms.

No, I thought. Not an entitlement, exactly – more like a compulsory promotion, another reminder of my place in your people's hands.

Next morning, I had opened my eyes to find a handful of cousins assembled around my mosquito net, as I lay inside, naked. Wallace's eyes had a predatory lustre and they flicked from me to my 'entitlement' lying in a heap where I'd chucked them – the cowrie belt, the earrings. He was waiting . . . I remembered, moaned, and braced myself to fork out for the traditional return gesture. (Two small-sized pigs, as things turned out – could have been worse.)

Now, back in London, I keep them with me, this plumage of rank, not because I promised but because I like to. You might argue that it's romance on my part, something to do with the 'love of glamour of strangeness' that Lawrence of Arabia warned about. But how can a lanky Westerner pretend to be New Guinean? You should see the photos: six foot four inches of pallid cream flesh daubed in clashing reds and yellows. Even the clay they made me wear didn't stick. And when they beat me – part of the initiation ritual – my skin simply split open. Not much good for the jungle. But that, I suppose, was the point. *They* were at home in the 'Rain Forest' I was trying to understand.

So I went there with my low-grade skin, and began suffering under their suffocating village taboos – not forgetting the women. And, after only a couple of weeks, I was thankful (in the nicest possible way) that once I'd seen what it was like to grow up their way, become a man as strong as a crocodile, I could leave the forest and write about it in Tooting, an up-and-coming area of South London.

But it didn't work out as simply as that. I went back.

From the notebooks of the second expedition:
Kandengei village, July 1988
The two women they send me I've always found enchanting – and I mean the word to be taken literally. It isn't their personalities that I like about them, because I've hardly spoken to either. Nor their bodies – I've hardly seen them. (And, I should say, I haven't touched them.) If pressed, I'd honestly say that attraction in the Western sense doesn't come into this; the attraction is something imposed on us – nothing chemical or physical but something beyond ordinary sensual calculation. I hesitate to use the word magical.

If there is magic worked, it is an overall one of silent, sparking forest energies. On a cousin of mine, for instance, who hears her sister 'Nightlight' – her feet in the grass as she comes to my house. Then hearing the creak of the ladder; catching the scent of her sister or the other girl, 'Stars on the Water', as they pass, feeling the vibration of their feet on the long palm floors. Sensing it all – and keeping her eyes closed.

Stars on the Water they only send for companionship – she's from my world. Sometimes I lie next to her and contemplate the town upbringing which has not coated her in fat, as it has most, but instead strapped her with muscle; I ponder on the way she entrances the men with her Western patina – and also distances them with it. This is the difference between Nightlight and Stars. Stars carries the urban mystique. So much forest, and it has yet to embrace either of us!

Nightlight, it does embrace. And the community, working in one coherent force, steered by the ancestral urge to unite, are using her to bring me in. They are seizing the opportunity of a bond with the triumphant West; all available power – all the male, all the female directed at me.

It comes down to this: we hold a quite different degree of magic, the handful of Western-educated – Daniel, myself, Stars, the Catholic or Assemblies of God Christians. We offer the West, another world, an illusion of heaven, one of mastery over nature. Here's a man-centred future. A promise which sounds rather like security. So the village wants us. The initiation was only ever a lesson in the workings of power, and so they know what to do. They use every fibre of their forest zeal to gain a foothold, kick back the vines, welcome the West in. Ranks close – not a word being passed as the instinctive operation runs its course; the clans unite, bonds fasten. They want us all – stray spirits from the flip side of the world . . .

7 June 1989, Tooting

Each time I want to make a start on describing my return to the village, I abandon the expedition notebooks, pace my room and look at the headdress, bone dagger and the other bits and pieces – even a letter, the envelope in my PENDING tray sent by Daniel, a friend out there. I go into a kind of stupor, running my hands over the feathers and cowrie shells, trying to conjure up that world.

To tribal art dealers the objects are worth quite a bit. But to me they are worth – what?

A man on the flight home offered me 2000 American dollars for the lizard-skin drum. Sometimes I like to think that I'll send it to Sotheby's, auction it off. I say to myself, they're like some backpacker's trophies. They don't mean that much to me. I had friends out there, I like to say; I'm not being an imperialist, gathering up their culture, claiming them.

The honest answer is that I'm not sure what I feel. I'm too far away to judge. The only way to remember truthfully is to plunge right back to their forest on the other side of the world – dive down and, eventually, retrieve . . .

9 June 1989, Tooting

The women. They, not some new insect species or unknown river, left the greatest impression. As important in my mind as the initiation ritual I had undergone on the first stay were the courting intrigues of the lovers. Over half of Kandengei's population were women, and whatever power they wielded, usually so well hidden, showed a chink here – in the etiquette of their secret assignations.

For the moment I will just say this. That by daytime, lovers couldn't even risk a fond glance, a cryptic gesture. They waited for darkness, when the last children had stopped running around with the bats, youths had retired to the high benches of the spirit house, where they'd talk, kicking their feet in the fire smoke to clear mosquitoes. Then, and only then, boy and girl came together. And girl became woman . . .

I should explain that for discretion's sake lovers had to wait for the darker phases of the moon. (In this way the courting occurred in monthly cycles, and even here nature seemed to be trying to put the ball in the woman's court.) That it was the boy, not the girl, who was pursued with a bush knife if their assignation was discovered. So, in a boy's first assertion of his masculinity, it was in the girl's power to control him. It was another kind of initiation ceremony, an initiation into womanhood: at puberty, this female learned whether or not to let the male slip quietly out of her embrace, into the night, free . . .

Take my case – on the second visit just last year when I was given those cumbersome gastropod earrings and all the dance paraphernalia. That night, for the first time Stars on the Water, the towngirl they'd like me to take, called by. (I say Stars 'called' as if she just popped in – but if you only knew how long they took to set up these midnight rendezvous! It tires you just to think about it – and all to no avail, because I wasn't taking either her or the other girl, thank you.) Anyway, she came and I told her to go – the risk of being caught was too great. This despite most of the village being in on it. Almost everyone except me . . .

But I am digressing. Let me just say that whenever I have tried to conjure up the village in the past, I first picture the strident men with their speeches and flashy dance prowess; but it's the voices of the unseen women that I hear.

10 June 1989, Tooting
Morning

You'll have noticed. I'm still not getting along very fast. My efforts at recounting my experiences have so far only produced a vague impulse to turn to the women. Maybe it's admiration at their quiet power as they were buzzed by the swarms of truculent men, or maybe it is a natural affinity – the men, despite their very best endeavours, never did get rid of all my female blood in the initiation.

But I think it is because I went in among them – and they lie within a closed circuit of time. The place by its very nature was inaccessible. The forest was enclosed, composed only of cycles – its near timelessness begins to account for the tendency to have life stages so clearly marked by ceremony. Life was too much in the present; the future hardly existed at all, and the past was eaten by the forest – all except a few stone hand-me-downs and their verbal history, which became sacred. Your best chance of remembering becomes when you are extracted from the forest cycle altogether, briefly joining with the victims at the moment of their ceremonial or actual death. Here I'm thinking of our symbolic death and rebirth – all female blood removed – at the initiation, and also of the real death of a woman I knew.

4.30 p.m.
I've brought Daniel's letter out onto my desktop, for a closer look. His writing style is schoolboyishly dramatic – the envelope is emblazoned with GOOD LUCK!

He must be out there *now*, sleeping. Kandengei is the obverse of this world; they get darkness while we get light, and vice versa. But there is a greater difference – we fence nature out, while they are fenced in by it. It's a big jump that I have to make – adjustment to the complex taboos which kept their world in a state of everlasting balance with nature, adjustment to the sleepy afternoons hiding from my forest-bred cousins, their eternal gift 'exchanges' which robbed me blind, the five hundred possessive eyes, the forest power struggles – leaf politics. But I am getting there, slowly . . .

In the notebooks I've found a quote recalled from the previous visit, a speech given by my wau, my Guardian Uncle, during the initiation.

> Always so eager to learn. WHY? Why not our Niowra men? Why has this [whiteman] in you not died? Well, all to the good. LEARN NOW THEN: THAT OUR INCANTATIONS TO YOU HAVE LONG SINCE BEGUN. While you are gone, MEN STAND WITH YOUR SPIRIT, WOMEN LIE WITH YOUR SPIRIT. TOGETHER, AS BEFORE, WE INVOKE YOUR PRESENCE HERE . . . THIS WAY WE MAKE YOUR SPIRIT STRONG. While we do this you [i.e. your body?] can journey from here to Heaven or even as far as England. But your spirit can never die.[1]

11 June 1989, Tooting
6 p.m.

MEN STAND WITH YOUR SPIRIT, WOMEN LIE WITH YOUR SPIRIT. TOGETHER, AS BEFORE, WE INVOKE YOUR PRESENCE HERE . . .
Sometimes I leave my notebooks. I go weightlifting or for a brief run up our terraced road, along the pavement with all the 'For Sale' signs. (Why *are* people always selling up? Perhaps I'm forgetting we're not quite the tribe I'm used to. Or is it simply there's a lot of death about this summer – accounting for the discarded possessions in the council skips: no one wants to keep their granddad's death bed.) I take a route round the ridiculous pond on Tooting Common – Coke cans bobbing with the geese. The sun on the tarmac path cooks the duck-squeezed mud, and whiffs of the pond across it are those of the Sepik marshlands.

The Sepik, Papua New Guinea – Kandengei's lotus-studded lake. Don't ask me how this can be.

Often memories catch me unawares – the odour of oppressed commuters in the Tube. (Though maybe it's a particular musk aftershave – who knows what they've invented in my absence? Last time it was little yellow message stickers which you post around the office to remind you to buy a pint of milk on your way home.) Or there's something in the chemical composition of the oak leaves as they burn in a park keeper's heap – that same fusion of compost oils as when sago fronds crackle under new canoes, cooking the wood hard.

Naturally, after each expedition I can't wait to settle down to life back here – an 'explorer' in lodgings near the end of the Northern Line. I say I can't wait to settle down, but after the first New Guinea trip, ending in the initiation, some things were a little different. For instance, each time I went to visit my parents in Hampshire, my mother gave me a firmer hug than any I remember as a child, as if tomorrow or the next day a spirit – some giant ancestral crocodile in the swamp – might charm me away to the airport again.

If I had left it at the initiation in Kandengei. But then, after a short journey to Sumatra, again, unexpectedly, I seemed to be returning to New Guinea . . .

8.30 p.m.
WE INVOKE YOUR PRESENCE HERE . . .

I've now pulled Daniel's letter from its envelope. It's signed off with 'BEST WISHES – I YOUR BEST FRIEND. WUMVUNNAVAN THINK OF ME IN ARE HOT COUNTRY'.

Your hot country . . . It's eight-thirty p.m. Our dusk, your dawn.

On the first visit, I trusted Daniel because he was 'safe' – he was a fellow initiate, a *wanbanis*, and also obliged to me as a Smaark – which was my clan, my other clan brothers including the stars, moon, egret, and various fauna and flora. After my departure he would always reply to my letters, unless pressure had been placed on him, such as when I asked for an opinion about the death of a woman I knew – a matter I'll be coming to, no doubt.

The day we first met, my first day in the village, I was, of course, struck by Daniel's ability to speak English, but also by his fingers – those of a nervous academic, and as soft as mine. He also had a librarian's gait – a sort of bookworm's stance. He wore glasses bought by his father, who, he said, had been recruited as a policeman and come to a sticky end whilst on duty. Daniel had received pots of money in compensation, and it helped our relationship in those first vital hours – where else but

12

among the financially secure could a young whiteman, turning up one day to ask to go through a sacred ceremony, know that he had a true friend? White is, of course, the colour of money in New Guinea.

Once the old men had agreed, for no very obvious reason, to hold the ceremony, my canny Brother Wallace moved quickly to adopt me into his household. From then – and it was a welcome surprise at first – all his sisters and brothers began acting as mine; his cousins, including Daniel, mine. I'd known them for only a couple of weeks, I only knew their missionary names, but they cried when Wallace's wife had to snip off my hair. Antonia, while watching a cooking pot; Errol, Imelda and Rowena cried while they chased a chicken to put in it, Teresa, in a very white blouse from a missionary with the usual Victorian dress-sense as she sat bent and cross-legged, scraping out a coconut for our last treat. In the dark, the men began invoking the crocodile ancestors with their whoofing, slapping, chanting dance, calling the women to give up their boys. Daniel, Spencer, Johnson and I looked at each other's shorn babyish heads. The women began to cry again. We felt very cold suddenly.

The men danced exactly as their forefathers, the half-human crocodiles, had danced. The taboos that kept things as they were had been obeyed. Time had not moved on, and the ancestors were with them again. We lay in our mosquito nets, trying to sleep, but instead feeling the ground thump to the old pulse.

Suddenly, we are being pulled from our beds by the women. Still half asleep, we find we are being led through the village. We notice that the grass is wet and flattened from dancers' feet. We are being hauled up into one of the largest houses. The light from the lamps is sharp. The room is empty, apart from a few men talking loudly, sitting around the edge. They wear leaf aprons; sweat is bubbling on their greased black faces. They tell us to leave space. They laugh at us as we blink and look around. We notice that we are shivering, though the air is warm.

We hear the dancers coming – the slap of their feet on the mud. Now they are so precisely in the traditional step that they *are* the forefathers. We are crawling forward through the legs of the long line of men – sweat and paint smearing our shoulders – and, at the end of the long crocodile line, sago mixed with ancestors' bones is put in our mouths.

We lie down again, dazed, wondering how much has been a dream; we wait for the cold of dawn, when it's time to go to the Crocodile Nest.

*   *   *

10 p.m.

Late at night, here in England, and now their day must be under way, the dawn fisherwomen slipping out in their canoes, taking to the water with the first light . . .

At first light, Daniel took me by the hand, and like little schoolboys we went leaving our mothers crying behind us. We were joined by the other Smaark initiates, *bandees* – Saun, Johnson, Spencer. Wallace gave us leaves to wear, and coconuts and chickens to give as presents to the spirits; we clutched them like school satchels; it was good to hold on to something. I looked around and again was struck that some of the crying was for me; so much misery about a gangly stranger with white knobbly knees sticking from his untidy grass dress. I began to cry too.

We stood there with tears flying around us, waiting to have our 'female' weakness extracted. From either side of our navels, up over the breast, down arms and back and thighs they'll cut and cut the skin that will soon rise up in crocodile-scale ripples. We pictured blood running down us from the blades. At last, our waus, our Guardians, came. They'd be the men holding us when the crocodile came to bite, we were told. We'd rise between their legs for our re-birth, and they'd comfort us during the beatings. After it all, and for the rest of our lives, they'd advise us; we wouldn't need our mothers any more.

Nightlight, Songbird, Imelda and Rowena must have gone away quietly at that point, paddling in a flotilla of Smaark canoes, trying their best to concentrate on spearing and netting the day's fish, while we bled away our childhood connection with them, the female. We walked into the Crocodile Nest for the initiation; our waus held us by the shoulders in case we made a bolt for it. No one did, not under the eyes of the women – mothers or sweethearts or, in my case, a woman I'd only seen once.

11.30 p.m.

It's strange. Now that I'm at last on the brink, so to speak, I'm reluctant to jump in.

I said that I find my first instinct is to turn to the women. As if in such a timeless place, and one with so much display – the birds of paradise, the tattoos, the dance masks, the woodcarvings – I need to grasp something that is obviously a sure foundation to a village I can hardly believe actually exists. Rituals of birth and death and real death itself provide a moment of possible entry into that world for me; women, however, were the providers, the feeders. They were at the base of it all, and the surest actual target for this 're-entry'. I have in mind this one woman in particular and in point of fact all my fragmentary notes above have been leading to this brief mention of her, someone I hardly knew.

We met at Pagwi market, where she sold home-grown tobacco, *yargee*. I would never talk to her again, yet somehow, to the memory of my departure from the village – a memory so fixed by her act of death – has become attached my whole memory of the ageless community of Kandengei.

The weeks before the initiation, when Daniel was almost as much a Westerner as I, and nature was still pretty, something to look at: that was when I met the *yargee* woman. It was in the market. She sat cross-legged in the line, some women smoking cigars, some pipes. Flies played on the bananas and smoked fish. Babies sucked and cried or stared at me. The *yargee* woman and I hardly exchanged a word – I think I said a word or two as I chose the tobacco. But she wouldn't accept the money, and her insistence wasn't spoken, it was in her glance – and also, oddly enough, her teeth. They expressed the certainty in her smile, giving it a steely intent. There I was, about to be hurled into a masculine world. She was a stranger, but in that moment I saw the feminine I was leaving. As she handed me the tobacco leaves, coming at me through the lightly resting tips of her fingers, the press of her eyes, was a homely type of strength, a type of tenderness in power. I realized then that I was becoming like the others – just like one of the boys about to be taken away.

The shock was still with me as our hair was cut off and we prepared ourselves for the Nest.

Then, not before time, we are inside. We are listening for the sound of girls' bare feet on the paths or secretly telling each other the names of our favourite girls – mine's Augusta, I say to Daniel, referring to a towngirl who has ambitions to be a secretary. But secretly it's Yargee I like best; I think of her out there, selling her produce. She begins to take on fundamental, earth properties – she is a provider and a healer, and begins to have stillness and wisdom from so much intercession with Mother Earth. And while the Senior Men are beating us, beating the outside world from us, it's the memory of her silent rainbow of electricity, the current of her fixed intent, which I fight hardest to keep from them.

But fear is tiring. We become disoriented for longer and longer periods. It is not just after each beating, but all night as we shiver, and the daylight hours in between, heads bent and waiting for orders and more beatings. The force-feeding and the beating and the cold nights naked on our stomachs are breaking us. Finally, all the secret places we've reserved for women are given up.

We are detached; we are floating because we have nothing from the outside world to hold on to. No sweethearts, no mothers at the fireplace. We are lost from reality. We become scared. We clutch at the only things left us now – things from this male kennel. We are given this world of male dominance, shown a hierarchy and made to climb onto the bottom rung. We are forced onto a second rung. Now the bottom rung is knocked from under us. We have nowhere to go but up the ladder of patriarchy. We set our sights on being *geenjumboos*, junior men; as a reward we will regain our freedom, and our women, who we are told are no longer trustworthy. From now we'll have our waus to replace our mothers.

I am taken from the nest a few days before the others. The village wants my whiteman's medicine – a woman is dying. I recognize her as she lies with her head in Augusta's lap. The Catholics say prayers to their God at her feet, the rival Assemblies of God rant to their God at her head, an old man chants from the left. I go to the only spare side, and take Yargee's failing pulse.

I leave with the cortège, over the lake to the burial. Her departure, mine. The wailing of the women echoing off the lake – *that* is my exit from Kandengei village after six weeks of initiation: tears stinging on my face as the canoe cuts slowly out through the breeze.

Some say she's been poisoned; the old men, *avookwaarks*, that it's a sign the village has broken the laws – it accounts for other, more to be expected deaths as well. And, sure enough, an Assemblies of God man admits having bribed a man not to kill a special gift pig for the spirits. None the less, the ceremony *has* been accomplished. It is a minor victory for nature's insiders, as crocodile tribalism falls along the inevitable road to the West, and their crocodile spirit dies and their forest world crumbles. And, as the village fades in my tears, the women sobbing on the bank call that they are happy, because I, like the others, am the beginnings of a man . . .

12.30 a.m.
During the following two years or so, I dreamed of the return. Of making the effort and plunging back, right through to their lake on the underside of the world. In the daytime my world was the doggy-splashed kerbs, flourishing privet and mown parks of Tooting, the natters over pub beer, or a bottle of wine with friends. But often, towards night, my mind switched to Kandengei, surfacing in New Guinea with their sunrise.

Then, one day last year, wide awake, I did return. You might say it was the natural consequence of submitting to such a momentous exercise in brainwashing – the stress, the theatre. Or you might even say that for over two years the crocodile magic had been niggling away inside me. WE INVOKE YOUR PRESENCE HERE . . .

But I was in a muddle. *Still* in a muddle. I wanted to know about the forest, but exploration was something that people who knew the forest didn't do. They didn't take flags and conquer mountains and rapids. They didn't draw up maps and classify species, expanding a rational grip on the world. They got on with living and accepting what their ancestors had done, having found a way that worked. They were not racing with each other to the poles, they were not naming mountains after each other, they were not giving each other medals, congratulating each other on expanding world knowledge.

I'm confused that the villagers have told me one thing, my heritage another. My heritage says I must claim to be the first man to travel between the Orinoco mouth and Amazon mouth, to be proud to have 'discovered' eight new species of fig wasp and to have had one named after me – something *alleni*. I'm in a muddle. Out there in the forest this had been irrelevant – none of this had rung true. I feel tricked by my own culture.

But perhaps I got it wrong. Anyway, first things first – I'm off to New Guinea, it seems. I say goodbye, first to friends, then down in Hampshire to my family. I tell them not to worry. I'll be back. On a last walk with the two dogs in the beech woods I reassure my mother; I'm not going there for good – after all, my crocodile markings are fading. She could have stopped, there on the path with the dogs, then turned and let me see her eyes and the unspoken plea – 'Do you *have* to go?' But she says nothing – as she said nothing every time my father went, driving away in his airline captain's uniform, his cap on the back shelf of the car. She makes me a Marmite sandwich as I get out my old backpack and begin squeezing in the presents for the Kandengeis.

I mustn't be put off by silliness – that some of my sweet dreams have, on occasion, curdled. That some nights I have found myself groomed as champion of the old men's dwindling Niowra tradition. Then in my dreams I've found myself the wrong side of a religious war; whether king or pawn, a white piece in a black game.

There is no doubt about what's on my mind – a woman died during the ceremony I started. Poisoning, magic, angry Assemblies of God God, unhappy ancestral spirits – I don't know. The Crocodile Nest is a threshold into adulthood, it isn't a lesson in the spirits.[2] I only know that people shaped by Nature maintain a balance with their surroundings; the missions, towns, scientists and schools believe in progress. The sides are drawn, and the conclusion of the battle seems inevitable – the balanced side will be smashed. And when the bonds of a tight, closed society break, the release of energy is by all physical laws great and unpredictable.

To put it plainly, one day it might be me, not the *yargee* girl, lying in Augusta's lap, rocking on the long dark floors of a family house, an Assemblies of God man whacking his Bible at one end of me, a Catholic at the other, an *avookwaark* murmuring over my chest, Daniel fumbling to find my pulse like a whiteman, professionally murmuring sweet nothings.

As I have a last cup of instant coffee, Mum watches, occasionally trying to be useful with luggage labels. I tell her again that I'll be back. I'm a whiteman, not a Niowra crocodile thing.

She asks if I've remembered my maps.

'But Mum,' I say. 'You know what I feel. If I go with a map I'll only ever get a better defined version of the one I set out with.'

'That's what the experts say, is it? At the Royal Geographical Society, that's what they say, is it?'

'Well, no. That's not what they say, actually. But I'm sure you'll agree, it's worth a go.'

She doesn't. I feel her eyes on me. I concentrate on strapping up my backpack. The old men were kind, even though I turned up as a stranger. If their rituals are good enough for them, they're good enough for me.

She says, 'They were head-hunters until recently.'

I tell her she mustn't worry. 'They're friends.'

'So are *we*.'

All the way to the airport, I'm feeling torn inside. Do I have to go *there* again? Get even more tangled up with them? But I say to myself, I'm meant to be an 'explorer', for heaven's sake. And I reassure myself – I remember how Daniel used to go around Kandengei, explaining my involvement: 'Actually,' he said, knowingly, 'it is only normal for a man of his position.' My exact position being, he meant, that I'm an Allen and all that went with it – including, I suppose, the faulty gene which resulted in wanderlust. The villagers listened as he told them my family tree – a great long string of wandering ancestors. After one of Daniel's sessions, the Kandengeis went away fingering the names like worry beads, working through the Allens, Staffords and Gores, to me. Why *did* he do our ceremony? they asked. So did just about everyone else.

But the Allens *et al.* and the tropics – Daniel had got it about right. They mapped the tropical belt, they fought in it, they built bridges across it, they edited newspapers and invited Kipling out for his first job in it, they flew over it, they wrote books about colonial aspects of it, they planted tea on hills of it. Riding a mule, they bought a rug from a villager in the arid north of a fringe of it.

My father was the one who flew over it, being a young pilot then and taking missionaries into the Nyasaland bush. Later, as a test pilot, he brought back weaver birds' nests, dance masks, a stuffed crocodile that Toffee the corgi chewed a leg off. Carvings of elephants, the whole lot. This was my world: not cricket or football or stamps but walls and shelves lined with foreign objects. At any moment, looking round about me, I saw the tropics. Naturally it began to look like home.

I grew up, and because of the family inheritance – wanderlust – my heroes were places, not people. Burton, Cook and Stanley to a boy seemed no greater than the family around me. Scott was no good – he had failed. Sir Walter Raleigh I recognized for what he was, an imaginative pirate. But I made a note of his independent life-style and pencilled in El Dorado – somewhere the wrong side of the labyrinthine mangroves of the Orinoco Delta – as my first major objective.

My first expeditions were along the blue cliffs of the south coast; I converted the garden shed into a home for my finds, laying the damp cement floor with old carpets from the attic. The fossils perched on shelves of elm, rows upon rows of them that waited for me during term time at the end of the flagstone path, under the damp chestnuts. I scraped and scratched them clean and some I varnished from a spare pot I found in the garage, all the while dreaming of what lay ahead for me.

'The dreamers of the day are dangerous men,' said T.E. Lawrence, and I was a dreamer, all right. The dreamers were dangerous because they acted their dream 'with open eyes, to make it possible' and that was fine by me. I was thirteen years old – not a top stream schoolboy but one with an independent eye. I also had my destiny.

I read more about El Dorado, between the Orinoco and the Amazon: knotted mangroves, the hothouse creepers, bottled-in air, Indians who ran without raising leaves. I looked forward to the future with excitement: one day I'd be joining in.

Six generations in India on one side, and my mother's side not all that much better – Grandfather awarded an MC in the Arras trenches. Now the ammonites were not enough. The red carpets in my fossil shed grew a white mould, and came out in tufts like the corgi in moult, and I went to university and read Environmental Science. I learnt that the forests were called ecosystems. They were the lungs of the earth, and we talked about genetic pools, and the flux of competing populations – all of them threatened by us, the West, because we had a consumer economy, and were consuming the world. In my final year I went on two expeditions and led a third. And there began my confusion. In exploration, the procedure seemed to be that you used guides to show you around, because the forest was their home and they knew it intimately. But the maps which the guides helped you fill in, they didn't use; the plants and animals which you classified according to 'science' were their clan brothers and sisters. To them, the *magic* that we, faintly amused, smiled at, was as powerful as the bark and berry medicaments we took away to examine.

But it was time to go to El Dorado. I worked in a warehouse to earn the air ticket, packed my rucksack and left. Secretly I was expecting a welcome. It would be a home from home. But, though bits looked familiar close-up, the Orinoco Delta was a disappointment. It was overcrowded and impatient – making you feel an outsider with its self-contained battles and mannered sophistication.

I watched the Indians – drawing bows, skinning monkeys, getting sick. The simple truth dawned on me: I and my kind *were* outsiders and, ecologically speaking, the Indians were as much a part of the forest as the trees themselves. They alone knew nature's inside story; I wondered what it was . . .[3]

So, on 17 May 1988, travelling at 70 mph up the M3 towards the airport, I take comfort in Daniel's explanation. Perhaps he was right: it is inevitable that a man of my position – someone with a dodgy gene – wanted to try growing up again, this time within natural means. Maybe I was just nostalgic for an 'unspoilt' place – who isn't nowadays? But places, not individuals, were my heroes and, by any definition, a characteristic of heroes is that they inspire emulation . . .

At Immigration, I wave a final time. I feel terrible, gutted. All very well putting the blame on genes – my home is back there, in the departure hall, making its way back to the car. My home is the fossils I found at Lyme Regis and lugged back in the little rucksack bought by saving up Green Shield Stamps. Specimens treasured in the garden shed at the end of the flagstone path – *that* is home. As well as – at a pinch – the grey skies of Tooting. Yet I'm digging myself deeper into a New Guinean society and we all know that societies work through excluding loyalties to others.

Aeroflot flight to Moscow, delay, Aeroflot flight to Bangkok, delay; but my mind is settling. I will find somewhere en route to pause – clear my mind before I do anything. I relax into my seat. Yes, I'll feel better with a stepping stone – any place in the world that isn't Kandengei but has its natural balance. Some place where I have no loyalties, and which therefore won't have to be banned by the Kandengeis – in the sly way that they do these things.

Gold temple domes and green tiles in warm rain; I take my shoes off to approach a temple Buddha – light a candle, reach out and touch gold foil on to the figure, offering it a lotus. Thailand; the stepping stone. Time is going by and I let it, leaving for the other side of the world, where I'll eventually emerge through the waters of the crocodile lake.

Continuing by bus up north, my knees in a child-sized peasant's back. On a trailbike, through bamboos and hillside maize crops, to a Hmong village. Pan, the English-speaking teacher at the school, takes me away up the hill. He shows me into an empty hut. He leaves me.

The warm air that I brought in through the tilting doorway cools around me. I feel it settle.

The man I want comes in from the sloping fields. We talk. He agrees. It will cost me nothing. I'm to come back the next day, with candles please. A live chicken – his son would bring it. In the teacher's room, sharing my baked beans with the teacher. He admires my motor-bike, but again, says he wants nothing for his services. He leads me back. It is dawn. We have all day. Myself on a stool, Pan on a stool, the son on the stool with the chicken between his small knees. He has missed his school for this. He must learn here: the sorcerer's apprentice.

This child has probably seen only as much as I have – the wailings, pauses and murmuring of a religion based on natural laws and their use in magic – that out-of-fashion word for energy. One day, he'll go into the spiritual dimension and discover how to set the world's forces back to their balance – or, where it suits, create imbalance. It must be a complicated business, learning to ride off into the machinations of the cosmos, but I envy the boy his task . . .[4]

The shaman is on his back in a plank-walled room, opium smoke clouding the rafters. Come out blinking from the smoke. Proceeds: three stages of a magic ritual.

Preparation. Paper beaten into circles with a round punch: cash payment for the spirits. Rice from the wife in her best silver – another offering to the spiritual forces which, in the balanced nature of things, will get us something in return.

Purification. Incense at the wall altar, the candles banishing dark, but tightening shadows.

The ritual. The boy squats, attending to the man. The wife rises and fire-builds. The two outsiders – Pan, the schoolteacher, and myself – are still. Daze-faced, the man proceeds: sudden, indiscreet nonsense-calling and gong-banging; the satin trousers gleam in the vertical sun-shafts. His trance disturbing school maths classes below. Gone from this world, as the boy watches, doing the same as his friends in the classroom, learning the mathematics of life. But no Western-style teacher's talk of progress; just the basic laws: every force has an opposite. No missionary talk of forces of good and evil, the world divided into God and Satan. Just opposing natural forces which keep our world balanced – as natural as the poles of the earth. Studying the natural powers is a job of pure maths – *every action has an equal and opposite action.*

Give your right arm, Pan is saying. The priest ties tough yellow cotton three times around my wrist. Now I can let myself go; I can put my feet up and relax; it's a little token from nowhere very special to me, something to tell the Kandengeis – and they'll notice it all right – that I'm not committed to them for ever.

The boy holds the chicken – his large cheeks no longer smiling apart; turns away, squeezing his eyes closed to avoid the sight of blood, which now runs quickly from the bird's throat. The wife, sweaty from fire stoking, plucks the feathers with thick thumbs, thin fingers. Boiled, knifed, the bones can talk.

We wait.

In the dim light and sandalwood incense, the Hmong shaman is calm. He speaks: I'll be all right, the chicken bones say. He gives the results without emotion, as orderly as a computer print-out. One man may be trouble; but you'll be safe. However, do try to keep clear of water.

There are many things you can escape in tropical rain forest, I think to myself nearing Kandengei in the canoe, but water happens not to be one of them. In this part of the world, New Guinea, water laps houses, water runs daily from the sky, water settles on your skin and encourages the healthy growth of unhealthy fungi.

We pass a couple of fishing women from Nyaurengei, the Niowra village before Kandengei, slowing the outboard engine so that the wash running the channel banks won't tip them. They are at home, afloat in marsh gravy, setting their traps in the reeds without a ripple, showing no recognition, but slipping back into their canoes wet, glossy-skinned, with the remote silence of cold-blooded, aquatic creatures.

This is a watery place; my 'brothers and sisters' are descendants of the crocodile – supreme being of forest water, the top predator. And even if they no longer believe in their crocodile heritage, they are certainly water-bred. Their house might be up on stilts, but those stilts run deep into the marsh, roots into the watery bed which feeds them their swamp sago, lake fish. In this wet neck of the woods, if toddlers don't learn to paddle, they don't grow up; here, natural selection favours amphibians.

The channel opens up, the shade retreats. I have a sense of imminence; I'm about to arrive; I can feel it in the way my mind opens out. It's as if I'm resurfacing. This image stays with me – I have just swum up through the muds, up from the other side of the world, and I am breaking the surface. I begin remembering the thick smell of their skin, the weight of their rain on the thatch. I have arrived at the other side of the world, and it seems as if I'm waking to some task or other I've become committed to.

The lake is spread ahead – warm and silent and shifting; plains of water which seem livelier the nearer they are to the rubble of forest on the banks, and the thicker the drapes of roots dragging in the flow. Ahead, low blue smoke is leaking from the forest, and nearer, the forest steps back. It hasn't been forced away, it is providing a space. This felled area which holds the village is a niche, a nest – part of the forest, not an encroachment.

I look at the coconut palms, and the dun thatch of the village houses. They can't have seen me yet. There'll be children running along the bank when they do.

But the canoe owner, from Pagwi, looks mystified. He's waiting for me to get the welcome Father George gets. So am I. We wait for the clap of excitement – so far nothing has broken the village's parochial fug. The breeze that a second ago riffled the water now stirs the palm fronds. But the village is making no movement of itself.

Not to worry. They still haven't noticed me.

The canoe slides through the lake, over the waters of their ancestral crocodile. Nearer and nearer, creasing lily pads, away from the Sepik river and to these back marshes, reptile retreats. Rafts of lake grass spin away as we go further in. We watch for children streaming from the houses, eyes alight. Very soon now. The return of their most famous prodigy – not to boast, but the only outsider to have gone through the Niowra ceremony.[5] A surprise arrival. There'll be jubilant smiles on the lakeside, milling children in Wallace's house as I sit on a stool being stuffed with food while the Smaark boys come in to shake my wrist – because my hands will be greasy from the smoked fish – the girls having to wait until after I've eaten, heads down, shaking my hand with as much arm's length as they can muster. Later, a token presence of the old men in the spirit house to greet me – from my wau a decent-sized pig tonight.

Running crowds, any moment now. But I don't really believe it any more, and the driver no longer has a smile across his face. Not even the welcome Father George gets?

Needing something to occupy myself – just a wave, *please?* – I check the presents. A penknife for Wallace, wristwatch for my wau. Necklaces, bangles – all the glittering objects they insist on, and which I hate, as well as the traditional bunches of betelnuts for the old men.

Is that going to be enough? The New Guineans have taken the charm out of present-giving. The country is so tribalistic – 765 languages! No wonder every gift has the weight of a peace offering. Each present has power. The act of giving is an act of magic – a directing of energy, a change brought about by unseen means. If the gift is reciprocated, so is the current. If the act is not repaid, you've left an imbalance. 'Payback' – an eye for an eye. That's why, coming to meet the New Guineans, you remember to bring along a little something.

The lakeside is empty. The running crowds – absent. No one is coming to greet me. There isn't even a child to chuck a line to. From the excitement my arrival is causing, you would have thought I'd been away fishing for the day. I've been absent just under three years. Five seasons. Two rainy, three dry. Maybe I've just come at a bad moment – perhaps Kandengei is in mourning. But this isn't an absence of everyday village life, it's a continuance of it.

Were they now blaming me for the death of Yargee? I'm sure they aren't. But a memory comes to me – a little bubble that has followed me here from home, up through the water.

My brother, sister, parents standing around the car, as we loaded up before going to the airport. A neighbour, out walking her dog, stopped, thrust her hands into her Barbour and sighed. 'I *do* think your mother copes well, with all she goes through.'

The sentence stung me badly.

But, I wanted to say, I was born in Macclesfield because my father had to be near Woodford aerodrome; we moved to Buckinghamshire for Heathrow Airport. We were now in Hampshire, because it was near Farnborough. To put it another way, our ashtrays incorporated models of planes screwed in take-off positions; when we got Christmas cards, you could spot the family ones because they weren't of mangers and angels. They were Japanese prints, or Gurkha regimental issue cards or a piece of frail paper stamped with a Yeti charm from Tibet – a kingdom half-way to the sky, I learnt aged ten, perfect but for the Abominable Snowmen, which left tracks as they ran from mountaineers encroaching on their sacred peaks. In summary, I wanted to say, if I *am* a little excessive in the lengths I go to, you can put it down to my family, not me. None the less, as my father warms up the car, I go back indoors one last time and fetch a large-scale map. An utterly useless piece of extra baggage, but I'll do it for my dear mum.[6]

I trail my hand in the water, and notice it warming as we turn in towards the bank. Nearer and nearer the land – really just a floating forest – the water becomes less and less a cleansing thing, and more and more something of itself, a life-supporting soup.

I pay off the boatman, who hurriedly swings out my luggage into the mud and puts his engine into reverse.

Up in the palms off to my right a boy is catapulting at a bat. A second boy is tucking in his little canoe, another boy hauling ashore a tray of fresh clay pellets, brought from the forest across the lake. I catch this boy's eye and he stares, absently plastering a mosquito to death across his ear. Then he drops his tray and backs into the shade. Further off, girls are playing missionary hopscotch, kicking high with their light legs, planting solidly with their padded feet. These children are laughing excitedly, but it's out of the fun of their games, not happiness at seeing me.

I stand on the lake shore, lonely in the middle of the sound of contained village life – the fireside hubbub, canoe-building thumps, heat-sheared afternoon peace haze. A pet white ibis leans towards my betelnuts, then swings its stick legs away, and flops to a beached canoe. It turns its attention back to the water which has collected there, thickening into a black and tan mousse of leaves.

I pick my bags up from the mud and head along the village front, down the path along the shaded canoes, to Wallace's place. I pass the houses, each resting on giant teeth, the notched posts, wishing I could keep on walking until I'm out of the village.

I hear a girl giggle '*Apinun!*', 'Afternoon!', to me through the slats of a house, up above. It's an uncomplicated childhood expression of joy, with a jingle in her laugh. But she spoke in Pidgin – she's probably new in the village.[7]

Two young women are coming towards me with firewood on their backs. To support the weight of the net bags they have their heads down – a charging posture. From this angle, I vaguely recognize one. She was just a girl last time – the full beauty flush is, it seems, over in a matter of five seasons' exposure to this place.

They aren't stopping. A little way off, there's a man steering a pig with a stick. He mumbles a word. It might be '*Apman nandinya*', good afternoon. It might not.

Then he continues walking. Getting on with his life.

I check, stopping again: no, this is not because I did wrong. Nor is it that I've been away, neglecting them. It's not a cat's sulk.

I leave my bags at the foot of a coconut tree marking Smaark territory. As I walk on, boys gather in, looking greedily at my baggage, standing here and there with shifty feet, not daring to touch the branches of betelnuts meant for the *avookwaarks*, the old men.

I remember the sweet smell on the muds when it hasn't rained. The murmur of a hundred unseen women.

At last. Over in the shade by the water's edge is one of my Smaark cousins – named after an American president, the news of whose election reached here years late, but in time for his nominal christening.

'Johnson, hello!'

He isn't smiling, seeing his old friend. Last time he was covered in grey initiation paint, now I'm watching him chopping out a canoe, tied fast as a member of the community.

'*Apman nandinya*, Benedix,' he says, looking at his watch in the abstracted way a missionary might, wondering if it is quite time for tea. Because I'm less than fluent in their language, he switches to Pidgin. 'Em-nau . . . that's right, they said you'd be coming to the village about now.'

I haven't warned anyone, but that doesn't matter just now. Why isn't he pleased to see me? Then I think to myself: oh, I get it. At least I think I do. They're paying me a compliment, treating me as part of the family.

'How's Augusta, Johnson?'

He loosens his hold on the adze. 'Far gone with a white man.'

Whoops. Poor old Augusta. Last thing I heard she was going to take up a typing course; but she always did like working late a little too much.

'Far gone? How far gone?'

'Very far. Into the Highlands.'

Not as far as I'd thought.

Johnson says, '*Lukim yu bihain* . . . See you later, Benedix.'

But I've come a long way, 12,000 miles. It's good of them not to go to the trouble of acting as if I'm a guest, not having to prove our bonds with hellos and thankyous, but I need a sense of having arrived. It's as if I'm still in the canoe, still on my way. I need to touch land, ground myself.

Johnson begins hitting out with his adze, happily killing further conversation.

'Well, you're obviously busy. I'll come back shall I?' There is a faint mumble. 'Right, I'll come back then.'

I didn't think I would.

At Wallace's house, a young woman's face shines from the dark – I think I see the flash of a smile. Errol comes out offering a cramped grin and then another young boy does the same. They go sheepishly indoors again, having flamboyantly thumped each other. I hear girls whisper quick, tumbling their words, rolling them faster and faster until they are nothing more than a hiss, then suddenly, 'he! heee!'

Errol calls from indoors. 'Benedix!'

'Yes?' I ask, eagerly.

After the one word, the saying of my name, he seems to have run out of things to say.

Then he says, in Pidgin, 'You know the new game?'

'What's that?'

He draws a thumb across his throat and with a grin yells through his blunt teeth, 'Cut throat! *Katim Nek!*'

I do it back. '*Katim Nek!*'

He dives indoors. 'Benedix can do *Katim Nek* too. Only *you* can't do it!'

'Can!' a little voice says, miserably.

Wallace's wife, Priscilla, comes out and leans herself against the doorway, casually. I wait, but she's smiling and nodding. 'Ah yes, you are back, Wumvunnavan.'

Back? I thought. As far as you lot are concerned, I never left.

*　　*　　*

27

An old man was hobbling towards me, forcing boys off the path. He was short, his hair in a high fuzz, nose hole gaping wide.

Errol came up quickly and said to me, 'It's Kumbui.' A warning. But I hadn't forgotten Kumbui, Flying Fox, with the limp he'd got because, he said, a water spirit went up his fishing line one day.

He had worked up a sweat from chewing betelnuts. He skewered me with his eyes, an old codger with a limp and sun-worn skin, who hadn't looked so harmless with a beating stick in his hand. He said, in Pidgin, looking me right up and down, 'You are thin, little man . . .'

Errol breathed, 'Benedix, say "Yes, Kumbui, I am thin."'

'Thank you Errol, I *think* I can manage, don't you?' I said, 'Yes, Kumbui, I'm thin.'

Kumbui turned to Errol. 'You are a big head. Wumvunnavan can speak for himself. He is a man. You are a fugging *manki* brain.'

'Yes, Kumbui.' He crumpled his hands into a ball, putting them away down by his navel. He bent his head a little.

'Shall I beat you at your *banis* [initiation]?'

Errol nodded, made to stand in this submissive stance in broad daylight, his friends maybe watching in the trees along the shore. Seeing the fear in him, I began to feel a little edgy myself – all because of this old chap.

'Yes?'

He said, 'If you like, Kumbui.'

'If I like what?'

'To beat me, Kumbui. If you want to beat me you can.'

'You, long man. You'll beat him?'

'If you say, Kumbui.'

The old man winked at me, and shuffled on. Errol unlocked his hands and snorted. He said, importantly, 'He knows I'm not scared. He's happy. During the *banis*, he won't beat me hard.'

'You think there'll ever be another [initiation] ceremony again?'

'If Kaavon and the top *avookwaarks* live a bit longer.'

Errol followed for a little, and then dropped away, seeing I was on the track to the *geygo*, the spirit house.

No welcoming crowds, only a dog walking with me, just one of a hundred who remembered the sago and fish I slipped in their direction while the village tried to fatten me up.

Somewhere to my right, someone was chopping a log. Than, than, thaack! Than! Then the squeak of the trapped axe wiggling free, and the sweetness of sap coming to me with cool air from under a house.

Yes, gone were the good old days, I thought. Once upon a time I walked like this to the back of the village with Wallace at my side.

Then I had arrived out of the blue and been given a nice welcome – ahead, in the *geygo*, old men craning to look out from under the low roof wing as pigs scattered with the hens, children streaming behind, older girls lifting their hands to hide smiles, running up and down steps, in and out of doors. I hadn't asked for the smiles, the handshakes. Soon I was remembering what, back in Hampshire, the local vicar had once said – that you can tell more about a people by the way they treat strangers than by the way they treat friends. And there I was receiving a reaction warmer than anything provided by the Home Counties – or Tooting, for that matter.

Wallace had still thought he'd heard it wrong; I didn't actually mean to ask to go through a *banis*, did I?

'Yes,' I'd said, not breaking stride. I was wondering whether now was a good time to spout my emerging theory: exploration was not charity – it didn't begin at home. No, Wallace, my experiences in the Amazon suggest that if you go with a map all you'll ever come back with is a more detailed version of the same map. But it was only a theory, certainly not one that had yet been endorsed by any explorer I knew, so I didn't risk spoiling things with Wallace, by taking him aside. I marched on.

But now, a bit less than three years later, I was walking all alone along the same path without even a pat on the back. I came through the palms where once a fence had stood, enclosing the sacred ground and *geygo* at the centre of it, creating the Crocodile Nest for our *banis*, our initiation.

The building, a barn that was low-slung and saddle-roofed, had that DON'T TOUCH quality of a church, the feel of somewhere guarded by its own sense of importance.

I stood at the threshold, looking at the thatch, watching it being sucked away by moss, sawed into portable lengths by wasps, the forest taking it apart. I smelt the cold, heavy air creeping out into the sun. I smelt the smell of a lair.

I walked forward, then stopped and laughed at myself – I was holding my head down, like last time here, like an initiate, a bandee. For the briefest moment, I had my itchy sores again. I was recognizing the sweet smell of the tree oil balm and ash fused with it. I smelt the blood, and tasted the clay we chewed to help our indigestion after the forced meals. Then the sensations were gone.

Who would have thought it: I was now meant to be a Junior Man. I went in, into the cool air that smelt of worms and soil and dank underground things. There was no one here. The long benches running the length of the building were empty. This, surely, was unusual for midday. And – was it my imagination? – the whole place had aged. I meant, in a place that was *ageless*. I couldn't be sure; it was a feeling. Weren't there a couple more cobwebs? And hadn't the logs been allowed to settle a little firmer into their ash?

Here, anyway, I'd stood with Wallace as I put the suggestion that they held the ceremony. I wanted to learn, I said. It would be a record for the future. They weren't good enough reasons for putting young men through a ritual that would entail the death of their prize pigs and chickens, would work their women to the bone and possibly kill their sons – and all for a religion with no future. But they argued among themselves about it, up and down over the heads of these crocodile-carved slit gongs, caged in the dank building on its own territory. Then Lamin, the vocal brother of Kaavon, Crayfish, the head of the *geygo*, spewing his meths breath, said they'd agreed.

I saw Daniel standing at the rear of his house. He was lazily directing young boys as they chopped the grass around the stilts of the Smaark houses, back near the waterfront and the Catholic hut. I was chased by two ecstatic dogs now.

'Daniel!'

Daniel wasn't surprised by my sudden appearance either. He put out his hand rather formally, and we shook as if on a business deal.

'Good afternoon,' he said in English. I asked how he was and he said, cheerfully, 'I am fit to fiddle!' He noticed the dogs – three of them now, sitting at my feet as if I owned them. 'Johnson was making his canoe. He saw you properly?'

'He saw me,' I said, watching the children peel away from us, losing interest, 'but he wasn't very welcoming.'

'It is so funny. You are like us, *that* is why they do not cry out to say "hello again".'

'I couldn't help noticing, the welcome wasn't quite what I was hoping for. Even the children were behaving as if I was like you lot – though I'm obviously white.' I displayed a pallid arm.

He commented, generally, 'It is nice, isn't it?'

Daniel surveyed his work crew of young Smaarks. They were little boys and girls in cloth wraps with wheezing great laughs. 'Henriah, don't stop working. You haven't finished.' He was directing his gaze at a little boy who had caged a tree frog with his fingers. The boy was duly impressed by Daniel's display of English. 'Remember Henriah? He collected eggs with you once, with –'

And he named about seven other boys, all with the fashionable New and Old Testament names.

I said maybe I'd remember later. 'So, how's life in the village?' I asked. 'Still as complicated as ever?'

'There are now Kandengeis who are back from the towns, Ben-ee. There are no jobs and too many *rascols*.' Daniel scratched his chin. And he looked at me. 'When did you leave? Before Lamin died?'

'Lamin has died?'

He was confused. How long had I been away? Six months?

Over two years, I told him.

'Oh. Some of the old men have died, Ben-ee. Lamin has died. And Tovai. And James's father – head of the Smaarks. He has been dead too long.'

'That's very sad.'

'And another man died at the end of the *banis*. After the girl.'

'Yargee?'

He thought about this. '*Yargee*? Home-made tobacco?'

'That's what I used to call her, when we were in the *banis*.'

'Well, the matter is fixed with the spirits, now.'

'Are you sure?'

'Do not be silly – it was not your fault. Anyway, everything is fixed up.'

So, I thought, despite all the West has thrown at it the village is still what it always was, an ordered form of the forest – on the face of it still about as rigid, about as unyielding. Someone had offered a sacrifice to restore the peace of the spirits after Yargee's death, and life was in its natural groove again. That is, the discipline of the taboos had been enforced – they would remain in balance with the forest a while longer. The Assemblies of God converts had not taken hold yet and you could feel the forest in the village's unchanging rhythm – the weight of ecological momentum, grinding wheels working with the steady drone of the humming crickets and cicadas.

Daniel said, 'Things have not broken down yet, Ben-ee, there's Kaavon still.'

I asked him who else could take over if Kaavon died. Kumbui, 'Flying Fox'? Saun, 'White Egret'? Maan, 'Black Diving Bird', Quaark, named after a fine carving wood, Naow, 'Sago'?

He shook his head. It's all hanging on Kaavon, then, I thought. 'Crayfish'.

I said, 'But Daniel, I wish you had written, somehow or other, about the deaths.'

Daniel suddenly tugged his nearest worker into action. I looked around and saw Wallace, my Brother, hovering, trying to listen to us – the crocodile marks running down the unusually light, treacle shade of his canoer's pectorals, the tight diaphragm.

'Sorry about the correspondence, Ben-ee . . .' But Wallace was about to alight on us. He had fistfuls of fresh betelnuts – I looked over and saw mine had gone from my luggage. He said in English, 'Ah yes, good afternoon. Come to my house now, and we will see your other presents please.'

Sometimes I wondered if Wallace was at all my sort of person. I said, 'Good to see you again, Wallace.'

'Yes,' he said.

You haven't changed, I thought. I was hoping you might have.

Those bird of prey eyes, just the same as ever. But his gums were blackened from betelnuts, and where his nose joined his forehead there was now a notch and above it a fold of skin where his eagle eyebrows had amassed somewhat.

He said I would sleep in the small bachelor house belonging to Spencer and Joel, at the foot of his own. It was pitched uneasily on the shore, among the water-licking mosquitoes.

I asked Wallace how he knew I was coming.

Wallace cracked a betelnut and fired the shards from his mouth, at the same time preparing the other ingredients, dipping a pepper into a tobacco-tin of lime. He lobbed it into his mouth and looked amused. 'You think we can know by ourselves? Sorry, we cannot do this.'

'Well,' I said, 'it wouldn't be too hard a guess. It's the dry season – less mosquitoes. You know how I hate the mosquitoes.'

'I hope you are not going to be questioning all the facts of life again,' Wallace said.

Daniel moved to Wallace's side. 'Benedix, you remember the way it works: the old wise mens tell us.'

Wallace looked bored. Daniel hesitated, then carried on. 'In fact it's like when the *avookwaarks* knew something was wrong with custom in the *banis* – their blood started cooking.'

I moved on to more pressing things. 'Wallace, Daniel said some of the old men have died.'

Daniel winced with embarrassment, paddling the space between us with his hand as if to clear the air.

Wallace tutted into my face. 'There are still old men on offer. Kaavon, others. You can talk to them, not the young like Daniel, about matters.'

'It's not too late to talk to the *avookwaarks*, then?'

Wallace said, 'Most *bigmen* are tired all the time. Kaavon is away from the village. I will have to ask your wau to check with him, and I do not know if I have time.' He looked at his watch. It was severely smashed. A new dog, this one with bad dandruff and the bristly, thick spare skin of a pig, leaned against my leg, lovingly.

To my left, walking along the women's firewood-collecting path, strolled a clutch of youths. This was a town gang; they wore brighter rags, and some had shoes. They mooched and milled and might have been out on Tooting Common; if there had been a coconut around, they would have booted it down the path, like a stray Pepsi can.

I commented that there were lots of young here now. It must be good for the village.

Daniel said, 'Some men said they were like fighting pigs in the town, so they made them all come back. But they do not help the village, they are always time-wasting.'

Wallace said, 'And the fanaticals are trying to take them, in case there is another *banis*.'

'You mean the fundamentalists? The AOGs?'

'Benedix,' Daniel said, 'for the good Catholic and also *avookwaarks*, life is unbearable.' He explained, 'There is war here, Benedix.' He added, enthusiastically, 'It's wonderful that you are on our side!'

I groaned. 'What war?'

Daniel said, 'The broad church of Catholics and their friends the *avookwaarks*, versus the fanaticals.'

'And,' Wallace said, raising his finger at my chest, 'the Anglican, versus the fanaticals.'

'Lapsed Anglican, actually,' I said. 'Well, thank you for warning me things have hotted up. Maybe I should potter along and see my wau now.'

Wallace said, 'Firstly, do *not* say thank you. We are your Smaarks, and we do not need to be told thank you. It is a whiteman's habit of lack of trust and it reminds me of the fanaticals – too many smiles and thankyous. Disgustable, Father George says. Second point: You can wait to visit your wau when I have fixed this.'

'I can?'

Wallace said, 'You can. Tonight, next night, or the next night you can wait.'

'Thank you,' I said, doubtfully.

Behind, Spencer and Errol were passing my luggage up to Wallace's house. Some of the bags had been opened. Spencer was wearing Daniel's present, a pair of swimming trunks, on top of his trousers.

'I hope you have remembered to bring the presents for the women,'

Wallace said. 'They fished many fish for you. You were never hungry in the *banis*.'

I thought of the forced feeding – fish and sago, fish and sago every day, four times a day, so that all the gangly adolescents ended up with the barrel bellies of crocodiles, strutting about with a heavy gait. I said, 'I have presents for – let me see – Imelda, Rowena, my sisters. Priscilla, your wife. And those girl cousins.'

'You cannot remember your cousins' names? They can remember your name.'

'There's only one of me. There are five hundred of you lot.'

'These are Smaarks. Smaarks are your clan.'

I tutted. I'd gathered *that* much.

Wallace slapped a mosquito without mercy. 'I hope you have your presents ready. You have Antonia and you have Teresa who is not yet married, and you have Skola the older sister who is also not married.' Wallace was looking at the cotton band around my wrist. Suddenly, rather too late, I remembered that among the Niowras, a string around your wrist was a token from a friend or lover. He carried on, a frown gathering on his forehead, 'And you have not mentioned Errol, your younger brother, and Spencer, who was a bandee with you. And you have . . .' Wallace began walking off, assuming I was coming along behind.

I let him go a few paces. '*Katim Nek!*' I said to Daniel.

'Benedix, yes. Good to see you again. I am sorry for not writing too much information about the happenings.'

I'd been about to turn to catch up Wallace, but now I paused, catching sight of the town rejects again, still wandering lost in themselves. These were the young men who had had 'get up and go'. They'd gone. And come back, fetched here by the old men – whose authority was not going to last. Not with the AOGs about and these stray young looking like such a potentially first-class flock.

I rely on you, Daniel, I thought. I hope you know how much.

I followed in the approved manner: obediently treading in the footsteps of my older Brother. While Wallace droned on, I wondered what else I had to look forward to. No joyous reunion. Hours of everyone comparing their presents. Tonight I'd be quietly laying out bunches of betelnuts in the spirit house, one for each side, shaking hands in the dark and probably tripping over their smouldering logs. My wau might be there. If not, I'd eventually get a formal interview with him, and he'd set me straight about how to learn their forest and its customs.

Never mind for the moment, I thought, yawning, now slowing to the motion of life around me – the lakeside forest, its waterborne people. I've made it. I've made it all the way from Tooting. The duck pond, privet hedges and kerbs are already out of mind and soon I'll be truly dug in here, having a good look at the world from the point of view of nature – in this case, it had to be faced, a swamp. I sighed, happily, already losing sense of time. Good to be back in the natural scheme of things, I thought, and took another look at the lake waters, ungathering, gathering in the easy current, occasional soft billows from the depths, everything lazy and steaming and calming and . . . deceptive.

PART 1

The Nest

Don't say a word more! You have no right to talk about Him. Not one of you has the right. I was His Guardian Uncle: it was on my body that His blood fell. Listen! If any man says otherwise, I'll take his head [off]! HEAR THE TRUTH IN SILENCE THEN:

That I was His Uncle – and His mother. I took Him from the village and gave Him to the Reverend Crocodiles so that they could remove his weak blood. I bore Him between my legs like a mother, while they did this. Afterwards, He was lifted from me and He was the beginnings of a Man. The ancestors put our spirit into His [heart], and if he had died, then I would have cried for Him . . . The women would have rolled in [the earth of] his [fresh] grave. But He did not die, and instead I sang for Him and my women danced for Him. We were happy, because He was the beginnings of a man.

Abridged speech in Niowra to the *avookwaarks*, 'Reverend Crocodiles', by Maan, 'Black Diving Bird', in his role as wau, at the end of the initiation.

Chapter One

IN THE FOREST SPIRIT

I slipped into the workings of the village so easily, it seems, that now I can't distinguish the following day. It was no more special than the third or fourth, here in Kandengei. Things got increasingly complicated, I know that. So I judge the passage of time accordingly, knowing that in the beginning life was simple.

Some people got on with rethatching, some went to Pagwi market to sell fish, some went to Torembi to swap fish, the macaw and nailfish, for sago, some hacked out pretty versions of traditional carvings for tourists and thought up nonsensical prices for them. Here, I was discovering, we each have a function.

Willi, for example. My *wanbanis*, that is, my fellow-initiate, might look a loner, walking about the building site of his new house, silent almost to dumbness, distant and wary, as if on guard duty, with no-man's-land around him. Even in its skeletal timbers his house has managed to take on some of his brooding aloofness. But on investigation, you'll find he contributes the best carvings in the village.

Everyone has a lot and whatever your lot you eventually get on and do it. And after a few days they were expecting me to get on as well, only they'd always said there were no strings to my going through the initiation. Besides, I didn't have much in the way of skills and my most obvious asset was my cash. But I had come to learn from, rather than influence, the culture here so I kept my head down, and listened.

And I watched the Smaarks dipping into my luggage whenever they were in need, and often when they weren't, and I felt the smoothed fingers of young Cousins running over my crocodile marks and I heard their public discussions about how they were failing to fatten me up.

All this strange familiarity had quite an effect on me. It was as if I had missed out a couple of years of my life, and these people had the key to those two years – they had grown familiar with me in my absence. A cast of my personality had stayed out here under the steady shade and extreme, relentless sun, while they developed a relationship to it. I must have been unduly impressed by their grandiose speeches – *while you are gone, men stand with your spirit, women lie with your spirit.* They read like overdone charms, spells aiming to get results through nothing more complicated than a direct threat. However, you have to remember that it's all to do with the Sepiks' oratorical tradition – after all, the country's first Prime Minister came from just down the river.[8] No, you mustn't be too put off, I thought. Kaavon, the elder statesman, did tell everyone I had no further commitment here.

And yet, have no doubt about it, I was used. Years ago, I'd been the sort of schoolboy who waited on the touchline, happy to be the last to be called for a team. And I hadn't changed – I still hated these team games. Each evening, Wallace would escort me back to his house to eat.

'Again? But –'

But it was time for yet another meal.

'You are too thin,' Wallace would say, climbing the back steps up into the glow from the hearth, while Priscilla was already searching for the fattest fish from the smoking rack.

Soon I was craving more personal space. I retreated to make tea – I needed this whiteman's ritual. It worked a kind of magic around me that I could call my own. Daniel as usual joined me, and explained all about it to the women.

Wallace caught us one day. He parted our audience and said to the two of us, 'You are like *womens*. You are time-wasting. A house is for *womens.*'

But Daniel said as he left, 'He is only angry. Priscilla has looked at his treasures again.' (He has an old fish trap full of belongings that have lain there undisturbed, just as he puts them there on top of each other; future ethnologists will come here and ponder on the upsurges in this household's material wealth, the first coinciding with his involvement with the Catholic mission, each of the others coinciding with my visits.) The ladies gathered round again, led by Antonia, my Cousin who was living in the house until full payment was made on her bride price.

We got on with our alien rite. 'Now listen here, sports,' Daniel said, flourishing his English – it was tainted with archaic Australian slang. 'At Tea-time in England, everyone stops his work. He puts down his bush knife, and he stops his car. Whatever he is doing at half past three, he will stop and drink tea.' He held up a steaming tea bag. 'It is the custom.'

The women sighed gently. 'Now, go back to work, you naughty ladies.'

Esau stayed. He's Imelda's new husband from Yamanumbu village, about twenty-five years old, we think. We talked in Pidgin about the problems in the towns, children leaving school for jobs that didn't yet exist and the violence that this was beginning to cause – then Daniel noticed Teresa listening in. Though she couldn't sit in our circle and had her head in her work, she ground out her coconut softly so she could hear.

Daniel said in English, 'What are you making us, Teresa?'

She giggled into the palm of her hand. Daniel said, 'You cannot understand English, you silly girl.'

'Yes,' she said.

Daniel told me to say something to her. '*Katim Nek!*' I said. She pouted, dropped the coconut in the bowl, and ran.

Daniel and Esau laughed. One of them, I can't remember which, said, 'She is frightened of you.'

'But Wallace keeps telling me I can joke with Cousins.'

'She is young,' Esau said. 'She is right to run away from her Older Cousin. You are her hero.'

I looked at two Junior Cousins rummaging around my bags for any spare gilded jewellery. I thought, 'I wish they'd *all* run.'

Wallace came up the steps. 'I find it strange that you are still in the house.'

'I like it here.'

'But all Men like the *geygo* better.'

'Daniel and I don't.' I turned for support. Daniel had managed to escape.

It was hard, this assumption that Wallace now knew my desires. And he wasn't the only one. I had been through the ceremony, certain changes of behaviour and status were always the result. The women rolled with laughter when I quivered and shook, almost tipping over canoes as I got in. But I wasn't joking. And they thought I understood why in the village some young girls ran from me and others – in fact, I know now, those belonging to my wau – tittered with their hands over their faces, braving themselves to do their duty, and say hello. It was a production line mentality; at times I wanted to scream: 'I'm a one-off model!'

And what I remembered of my wau wasn't encouraging. He was a man in the old mould, that of the crocodile cult. Seeing him, his polished leather smoothness, approach you during the initiation, you guarded yourself against something inside. He had an air of impending eruption and he used his potential to effect, combining it with a habit of coming up to you directly and mechanically, silently. He waited until he was in whispering earshot to speak, by which time even if a Senior Man, *jinbungoo*, you'd addressed him first. You felt better, it seemed, once you'd addressed him. He was reluctant to speak much at all, but when he wanted he could stop debates by simply getting to his feet, unknotting his tight jaw muscles, and declaring himself. The other men looked happier then, as if they'd flushed something classically reptilian out into the open.

This was my wau as I remembered him from the admittedly distorting view of the initiation. I started a new page in my notebook, and wrote, 'I need a holiday.'

'Relax,' Esau would say in Pidgin. 'Soon you'll settle down.' He appeared to be a genuine atheist and I wondered what sort of man it was who could withstand the pressure from the red-hot AOGs, give-and-take Catholics, the stubborn, ailing elders. It defied imagination. 'Take a couple of wives, get drunk every week. Live like a townboy – ignore custom. It's a good life.'

But I had come to learn from the inside. I said, 'How do the old men run this village? You never even see them. *Do* they run it?'

'I don't know who runs it – these are secret things. You've been through the *banis*, you know more than I do.' I said it didn't seem to help – I must have missed that lesson. He said, 'I'm sorry, I'm going to be away soon anyway.' He seemed to think this was suddenly all very funny. Perhaps it was the thought of getting out of here. 'Hee! You'll have to find another person to ask. Not Daniel – he's like me, an outsider still. Yes, pity about your wau being away.'

One night – still only the third week! – Priscilla as usual burrowed for the biggest fish in the pot. She heaved it out.

I recognized its eyes. I'd avoided this specimen last time.

I looked for someone to share it with – but Teresa shyly tucked herself away in the corner. Her older sister Antonia crept into her mosquito net to be ready for tomorrow's dawn start.

Supporting its weight with both hands, I lifted the fish to my mouth.

Wallace and I talked in English about our visit to the *geygo*. Imelda, a sister of Wallace, turned the fish that were smoking on a rack over in her corner. Priscilla took a fat cigar of sugar cane in her mouth, softening it for the toddler to chew. The child shook his rubber band necklace, still with its eyes closed to hide from my white skin. Antonia began singing extremely simple Pidgin chorus numbers.

'I do not know why you fell over the fireplaces again,' Wallace said.

I said I was too busy trying to remember the men's names.

'Names are important. I told you before, Benedix. They are like gifts – gifts are important, Benedix.'

While Wallace got up for another fish for me, I deftly squeezed some of my last one down through a crack in the bark floor. Below, the pigs fought loudly for it.

The evening cooled. Everyone did what they liked best – the old men out there in the *geygo*, and back here, Priscilla played at opening and closing her new handbag with her toes, Errol chewed betelnuts, occasionally sweeping the mosquitoes from my feet, the pigs grubbed cheerfully, Antonia warbled, Wallace's two little sons tried to kill each other.

When was I going to see my wau, I asked. Wallace said, 'You must be comfortable first.' But the village'll drive me to the bottle soon, I thought.

'He is too important to waste. He is a mighty man – as mighty as the Pope. He can hear all your confessions, and he can make the world fixed better as well, with things like Holy waters. Why are you too slow at the fish? This one, for example,' he said, prodding the largest, 'is maybe a good fish.' He took it himself and sucked deeply at the white flesh, filtering the bones with his lips. 'He' *was* a good fish.

I listened to Antonia's song. I was sad for her. Soon she would be in residence with her husband's first wife and it's a waste for her to be shared, I thought, as I sat with a stomach ache, her voice floating through the hearthside ash in the wood smoke, quavering awkwardly when there was too much silence from the two of us. I called to her, 'Pretty songbird.' She stopped. I heard a snort from her pillow.

Teresa gave a little shriek of pleasure, but when I looked over, she turned into a side shadow.

'That is nice,' Wallace said. 'You are always such good Cousins to each other.'

No sense in going to see the *avookwaarks* in the spirit house – munching their betelnuts, hunched up with the dry cobwebs – I was a Junior Man. They wouldn't even hear me, under that roof arched over them, in that cool, dark air.

I began to kick out. I was not being allowed to see my wau, this figure whose job it was to advise me. And, if I thought about it, my wau wasn't just the blood-charged predator that I remembered from the *banis*, with a stick concealed behind his back as he prowled between us as we sat naked on the ground. We'd had a meeting as I was about to leave the village on the day of Yargee's death. From what I could remember, and it was a bad moment – the women's mourning wails right outside and my departure imminent – he had been warm, even quite human. Wallace explained that Maan, now to be called 'Wau', 'existed for me' – that was his brief, his job description. He'd said it himself in Pidgin, words to the effect, 'Rest easy. I exist for you.'

Very confident you must be, I'd thought, to pull off this grand talk. But he hadn't needed to be afraid to make claims. He had the authority of the forest – which had, after all, allowed the Niowras a place here because their laws had been invented to suit it. He wasn't any more the dangerous guardian reptile of the initiation; nor the distant religious confessor that Wallace compared him to, a higher type of Roman churchman. He was my Wau, with a capital 'W', a virgin mother, my creator. He would guide me to live safely – that is, in accordance with the rules of the forest. I was his protégé, his offspring, his *Laua*.

But no comfort from him now.

And why had the *avookwaarks* welcomed me on the first visit here? I'd walked into the village, asked if their sons could be put through a dangerous and elaborate ceremony not done for some ten years. They'd agreed. Now, on my return, my old fears were returning. In their excitement at the possibilities – the wealth aura of my white skin – they might be hoping to forget our agreement that they had no claim on me. I appeared to have a talent for integrating and they might be confusing that with heroic upfront leadership. However, I couldn't lead them – I had been a catalyst here before now, but I was not here to impose.

The next day, I found Johnson by my side. I said, 'Haven't seen my wau hanging about, have you?'

He said, 'Gone fishing.'

But it wasn't a joke. Then he leaned over and said, 'Listen. I have something to say. Are you listening carefully? Benedix, if a girl comes to you, never use her name.'

'What do you mean, "comes to" me? At night?'

'Well, she can't come in the daytime!'

'Look. I don't want a girl coming to me. If there's any courting to be done, I'll do it, thank you all the same.'

44

'This *is* the normal procedure, but –'

'This is the first I've heard of there being a procedure. You mean something's organized?'

'Don't you know yet? How long have you been here?'

Seems like years, I thought.

'Anyway,' Johnson said. 'You are different. They must come to you. Your skin is too white – even if her men do not see it, her [clan] spirits will.'

'No girls, thanks. That's my decision. Can you tell whoever it is who does the organizing? Who is it? The *avookwaarks*?'

'Are you sure?'

'Yes.'

'Well, if she does come, call her Stars in the Sky, then no one will know.'

Stars in the Sky? It was a child's Red Indian playname! 'But she's *not* coming, we agreed.'

'No, no, of course she's not coming. But wait, now I remember, don't call her Stars in the Sky.' It seemed that there was one of those already. Johnson said, 'Call her Stars on the Water.'

For goodness' sake. 'Well, it wouldn't be anyone I know – Teresa, Antonia. *They* wouldn't risk doing anything naughty like this. Teresa, for instance. She's sweet: just a girl.'

Johnson's face lit up. He found this very funny. He mimicked what the Aussie carving buyers said, seeing carvings marked with 'First Offer', 'Second Offer', even 'Third Offer' prices. 'You godda be kiddin', mate!'

'She wouldn't,' I said firmly.

Johnson dipped his head down. 'Sorry, I didn't know she was ill.'

'She is not ill. She's just not that sort of person.'

'They *all* are! She's a women now. That is what they *do*.'

That was Johnson's exit line. He was leaving. I said, 'Johnson, please don't tell Wallace about the women plan – the one that's not now going to happen.'

Johnson started laughing. I've never since heard him laugh so loud. 'You think Wallace doesn't know! That is funny. You think he doesn't know what women come and go – and he is your Brother!'

I said, 'Thanks anyway.'

He paused, before turning to go again. 'Benedix, why did you say Teresa?'

'Only the first girl that came into my head. Why?'

'No reason,' said Johnson, looking away too quickly.

I had called Antonia, Teresa's older sister, 'Songbird' not just because of her melodious hymns but because she was flighty but never free; her wings were clipped by her role as a Niowra woman – always with one eye on the pot or on fish being smoked; and now to have second wife status. The imagery frightened me – the tethered bird accepting her fate. All women are songbirds caged by men, I thought, in my innocence. What's more – something I *did* get right – whitemen have stopped the head-hunting and fighting, thereby removing the Niowra men's jobs. And while the men lope around making a nuisance of themselves instead of protecting the village, the women become oppressed even in their homes, their old territories.

I could sympathize. I felt clipped and tagged as well. A Westerner was used to a lot of freedom and I was like a gaolbird myself, joining the women flocking to church on Sundays, just for a bit of freedom of spirit – and it would only get worse.

In the village, another Reverend Crocodile stalked by. These old men would talk, that is, say 'Good afternoon, little man', or 'You have eaten, *saun waark* [white crocodile]?' But that was all. With these pleasantries, and a few more about what I was doing today, they went on their way. They wouldn't converse, and I never heard what *their* plans for the day were. 'What's going on?' I said to myself, looking at Kumbui, with his limp, or Naow, with his pipe – standing there chewing so dreamily. They smile their goodbye and potter into the cool sanctuary, the spirit house, but their necks, I notice, are as tough as vines.

Where *was* my wau?

The children greeted me, the women smiled and scampered, the men called. They were saying they were as happy as sandboys to have me back here. And more. Imperceptibly the village seemed to thicken around me, hardening into a container. At any given moment, it was difficult to think back to home – to Mum and Dad welcoming me off the train at Alton station, to Sue, my faithful landlady in Tooting, to Mrs Simpson, from Jamaica, who came in her black lace-ups to dust the house every Friday, thumping her mop, 'Ever since I was growing up I been a God-fearing person,' clonking her way through the house, leaving every picture in her path at an angle. All this seemed to be out of reach.

Let's be rational about this, I thought. I *didn't* promise them anything on my first stay, did I?

I'd been about to leave the village for England. An old canoe was being converted into Yargee's coffin. As I crouched, saying goodbye to the bandees, I whispered to Daniel, 'The *avookwaarks* really do understand that I can't come back, don't they?' I remember clearly: Daniel nodded.

The men were watching us, alert now because the cause of Yargee's death was not known, and if it was because a taboo had been broken then the ancestors would still be vengeful until a sacrifice was made – the balance of energy restored. However, I was allowed to roll a cigarette for Daniel, so I lit it and put it in his mouth. He breathed the smoke out among the mosquitoes, clearing them. Outside the nest the women were wailing at the death of Yargee, screaming and crying into each other's laps. Daniel said I should try to see my wau and check again. I said, thinking of him, the reptile, 'Oh my God!'

Spencer said, suddenly producing English, 'You *cannot* be fret. You are a man.' Yes, I suppose I am, I said. I went over to Wallace. He said no I couldn't see him. Wallace stayed where he was up on the bench, drawing on a Benson and Hedges, brushing away the smoke irritably as if it were mine. 'You do not want to go into his grim presence.'

But I must sort this out.

'Now!' I said to Wallace, trying out this new manhood idea. He looked a little closer at me, and then got up.

'All right. Find some betelnuts, and we will go.'

We walked fast. Boys parted to let us through. Through the Smaarks, the Yaarks, the Posagos – most of the women drawing in towards Yargee's house, wailing at the sky. We kept on going. This was important to me. I was not just checking how I stood. I was also saying goodbye to someone they called my mother. I almost believed it then; I did believe I was going to see my maker.

Now we were at the steps up to his house, Wallace saying, 'Wau, are you home?'

A woman said yes, he was.

I went straight up behind Wallace, following his feet onto each rung.

The house was big, and we passed by three or four hearths with their clusters of women and children. The far end had suddenly become vacated. All except for Him, sitting on a stool with his back to us, and an empty stool already waiting.

Wallace didn't say hello. Nor did you, 'Wau'. You didn't even look up. Your eyes were hot and hard. You'd had a lot of betelnuts. You were just sitting, as if with a headache, just waiting for peace.

You were everything men had once aspired to. The cold heart, hot blood, the thick skin. But to me you were meant to be more. I thought to myself again: they say you're my 'creator'!

Wallace told me to give the betelnuts. 'I will wait, and then I will go.'

You asked Wallace, did I want to speak or just say goodbye, like a whiteman. Wallace said I wanted to talk. You nodded, and cracked a betelnut. '*Kaikai*,' you said to me. That was your first word to me as your *Laua*. 'Eat.'

I ate a first betelnut, and my vision softened, and I found Wallace had gone. So had half my betelnuts.

We, you and I, looked at each other rarely. We talked to the bark boards, creating more echoes for the empty room. I wondered whether it was like this for the other young men. The silence between us was controlled by you – sometimes a threat, other times flicked back on itself and loosely wrapped around me, softening fears imposed by six weeks of beatings.

'*Laua*, you have some worries . . .'

'I am meant to give you betelnuts. At least, I think I am.'

You looked at the betelnuts. They were rather green.

'Never mind,' you said, staring at them. You lifted your head, turned it aside and called behind you. Your little daughter came up with some redder, hotter betelnuts. She dropped them at your side.

The sight of the girl gave me confidence. It was a family man I was talking to.

'It's the village. I want to know what they *really* expect from me. I know we agreed I had no obligation, but, well, I want it clear in my mind.' I had come fresh from the nest and so was quiet. Yet was breathless. I watched your toes, nails flaky and thick, like flints.

You, a man obliged to be honest to me, said, 'Undo yourself, be at ease. I exist to look after you.'

Which, somehow, didn't sound as if you were overstating the case. I kept talking. You were nodding, as you chewed your *buai* – the betelnuts.

I repeated what I had said to the *avookwaarks* at the outset: I could not settle down in the village. I asked if this seemed ungracious. I make it plain. I'm British. I was born in Macclesfield, Cheshire. I'm not one of your race, I said. My parents live in commuter belt Hampshire, near Alton. My climate is temperate. My blood is predominantly Anglo-Saxon – the blue eyes, the straight fair hair. I'm six foot four.

'Some *avookwaarks* say I should ask why you came here anyway.'

I told him Daniel's recipe – the explanation that blamed all my relatives. An affliction called nomadism. The one who brought back the carpet from the North-West frontier, the African dance mask brought by my father, the yeti charm on the back of the bedroom door, and more.

He raised a hand; strange, but I found myself tensing, thinking I was a bandee again. But of course the hand was held up as a signal, a schoolboy's request in a whiteman's classroom for permission to speak.

'We do not understand each other. You listen to me. It is simple. Kaavon, boss of the *geygo*, says I am to tell you he has had a message from the spirits. It is along the lines: Never, Wumvunnavan, feel bad about taking your body from here. You can go without feeling guilty. The ancestors know you have two homes, maybe three. They will always keep a place for you here.'

This was a pleasant enough idea, but I was suspicious: why *shouldn't* the *avookwaarks* rip me off for what they could, as the whitemen had done to them.

'Kaavon said some more: "In the beginning, some men disagreed. They wanted to capture you. But they are wrong. I have told them, 'Forget his precious white skin. And forget his library head. Pick on another whiteman. Take one sent by the carving buyers, or sent by the God. Or one to study our species. Benedix, you can leave your grubby hands off.'"'

The calibre of this man Kaavon had come through even in reported speech. I asked my wau, 'When can I talk to Kaavon?'

'As you know, he won't talk.'

I said, 'I think he must quite like me. He started the ceremony to help me and so on. What sort of person is he?'

'Listen.' Then my wau, this spiritually empowered man with allegiance to me, said his special line, 'You're a *geenjumboo* [Junior Man] now. Undo yourself, be at ease. I exist to look after you.'

That was my previous visit, two, almost three years ago. I'd been struck by the simplicity of my wau's summary. His earnest reading of Kaavon's intentions had affected me strongly. He might have been a cold fish, but he was sincere. And Kaavon hadn't misunderstood me – maybe he had helped because I'd come prepared to listen, go through what their sons went through. I liked to think so.

But now I'd returned my wau was out fishing all day, every day. Someone ought to tell him to change his hook or bait.

*   *   *

Only one thing signals the passing of time here and that is the weak, town quality drum clonking of the two church slit gongs at service time. Both AOGs and Catholics use cheap imitations of the sacred crocodile slit gong in the spirit house to muster their rival forces to worship. That happens once a week, approximately a Sunday. And it was the third time this sound happened, that Daniel and I were rounding the far end of the village near the Assemblies of God, a tin shed hidden away at the opposite end of the village to the Catholics. An evening celebration was about to begin. I could hear the first warm-up hallelujahs.

And what do *you* do for the village, Daniel? I was wondering as we walked by. You can't paddle, I've never seen you lift an axe. What's your role? Are you just counsellor for stray whitepersons? For all I know, your function is to draw young and gullible whitemen in to boost the village coffers.

A call came at us through the night. 'Yes, Benedict. Good-night.'

'Good-night,' I said. Who's that? I wondered. He'd spoken English and even got my name right. Then a flashlight cut through the dark, lancing the soft structures of the village – the thatch, the banana palms, the grasses – as it zigzagged ruthlessly towards me, cutting uncompromisingly through nature. Then, as we stopped, the hard blade of light found an object nearby that it bounced off – a hard, alien sheet, a metal roof.

Daniel said, 'Watch it! It is Nathan, a friend of Joseph's, the man who tried to stop the *banis*.' It was said he'd bribed a man not to kill a pig for the spirits and there had been a resulting imbalance of energy – or, in everyday speech, the spirits had got angry and taken revenge on the village. The last I had seen of Joseph was him standing over Yargee's body, quoting St Paul. Otherwise he spent much of his time sieving the Bible for advice about his wives, of which he had two, both bought before his conversion. Daniel said, 'Nathan is a very hot AOG, new in from an international Bible-bashing.'

'Mr Benedict Allen, I am glad to meet you,' Nathan said in English. 'I heard that you went through their ceremony . . .'

He said it without an edge. He could afford to be generous – he was speaking from a position of rising power. 'That's right,' I said. 'I learnt a lot.'

'But did you learn the Truth, Mr Allen?'

I was looking for Daniel. Around me, apart from the neon glow now starting to flicker on and off feebly from Nathan's house, there was only blackness. Daniel seemed to have gone.

Nathan said, 'I apologize for the faulty lighting system. I can turn on the generator – we can be up all night, if you like. Not like the poor old-fashioned villagers.'

I said I was quite happy with the dark. I asked if he was angry with me for sparking off the ceremony again after so many years.

'It doesn't matter. If you did the ceremony, then that is Jesus's decision. We can pray that he chooses not to permit this again, but we will see. You can always take comfort that Joseph also made the mistake. He went through the ceremony a time ago when he was a pagan.'

A deep voice, next to Nathan's, made me jerk. 'Hi, Benedict!'

In the dark, Nathan said, mournfully, probably shaking his head from side to side, 'Yes, the old men circumcised him.'

'They did *what?*' From his hiding place in the darkness behind me, I thought I heard Daniel gasp.

'You don't mean circumcised, brother,' said Joseph, tolerantly. 'I just had the crocodile marks made.'

Nathan was too busy thinking of a biblical reference. 'Corinthians 2. No, 2 Corinthians . . . Or is it Philip –' He started afresh. 'Benedict, in your Holy Bible it says: thougheth your body ith circumciseth, it mattereth not. Only that thou's heart ith circumciseth.'

'Well, I haven't got a Bible with me, but we'll have to have a good talk one day.' I started to walk.

Joseph said, 'Wait, brother, I'm trying Galatians.' There was a shuffling of thin pages.

'I'll leave you to it,' I said, going.

'Wait, please,' Joseph said. 'It is not too late.'

'Well, it's past my normal bed time. I get up early like the villagers.' I put in a mention for the forest, for the balanced ways of the old days. 'Each day's exhausting, one big fight, if you kick against nature here.'

Nathan said, 'Brother, he means it is not too late for *you.*'

'Me?' He was appealing to my *self* – the very thing the Niowra tribe wouldn't recognize in anyone here. To those young Kandengeis learning at school to be self-thinking, self-advancing and other things Western, it must have been an exciting message. To me, a Westerner through and through, it was almost irresistible.

I wanted to be helpful, and knowing a few handy quotes myself I said, 'Why don't you give Romans 2: 28 and 29 a go? I think you'll find the reference there.'

Joseph and Nathan joined heads over the book and, as I began my exit, they looked up in astonishment. Nathan said, gratefully, 'Brother, good-night.' His teeth shone. Few men's teeth were that bright – partly because they were red with the betelnut juice that the AOGs banned, and partly because – I could hear Wallace saying it even now – smiling was the dance mask of his religion.

A mask – I remembered the AOGs' implied threat: *It's not too late.*

Once I was away, Daniel reappeared from the dark. 'Everyone is happy to see you.'

'Including your "Fanaticals"? I don't think so.'

'No, they like whitemen. They think you are a whiteman.'

'I *am*! I am, Daniel.'

'Well yes. But they do not know you are also like us. That is why they say hello, jumping up like dogs. They have to say thank you for food and presents, like whitemen.' He spluttered, 'Tee hee! They are like strangers to each other *every* time!'

'Let's go to the forest tomorrow,' I said to Daniel.

'But, Benedix, you want to learn about the customs and please the villagers. You do not want to go to the forest.'

It was *Daniel* saying this – Daniel who was meant to be like me, a Westerner. I had you down as like me, an outsider, a sympathizer, I thought.

Then Daniel's usual earnest, office clerk voice said, 'Sorry. I do not want to boss you. Only, you have plenty to learn about the Niowras.'

I nodded. 'Yes, let's go to the forest tomorrow.'

We were up on our feet during the rising of the early mists, when the hens flap heavily down from their tree roosts, one by one. 'Let's go,' Johnson said, and we pushed off, half a dozen of us. Daniel sat in the front, facing me, with his back to the bow waves, and told me that he had a girlfriend, and he would show her to me one day. It was our secret, but I probably knew the one already. He gave me a clue. 'She is the prettiest.'

I tried to think. Herodias? Rebecca? Ruth with the cheeks tattooed like a casual game of noughts and crosses? Delilah with the eyelashes?

This was a day I would enjoy: one out of the village. We kissed the dawn mist, eye to eye with the low sun. And I was not alone in hugging the unnatural freedom of movement that the outboard provided, a whiteman's means of cheating time; we took the water for all we were worth, full throttle and hacking into the bends.

'Weeee!' Daniel cried out, as we came into the shade of the bank. Then we hit the shore rather too hard. Daniel went overboard.

We walked noisily into the forest – this place was haunted by Wunjumboo, a little naked man with long nails and hair and usually with a filthy belly-button.

I looked up into this forest – overhanging, cloaking – wishing I could be by myself for a while.

The forest is like the village – no freedom for the individual, I thought. I wanted to study it. This was a battleground so efficient that it cleaned and swept its own victims, not leaving a trace in time; unaccountable and uncounting. Just like the nest that lay in its roots, Kandengei village.

Wallace stopped at the front of the line and looked back down the path. 'Where's Benedix?' he said in Niowra. 'Has he been told? Daniel, tell him.' Daniel, who was behind me on the path, said, 'I must tell you this seriously: we are all Smaarks, except Imanwell, the brother of your wau. If you know his village [Niowra] name, do not use it here. All right?'

Daniel had to explain further. Once, he said, when Imanwell was up in a tree, someone used his village name – the equivalent of my own Wumvunnavan. He wasn't a Smaark, but he was on Smaark land, and Wunjumboo became angry and closed the branches of the tree all around him. James, head of the Smaarks, had to plead with the spirits. The tree opened and Imanwell dropped out.

Now we were in a roosting area for the lake fishing birds. Bark was painted with their excreta. The sparse ground plants were splashed in acrid chalk. Plenty of light got in, but the recent growth seemed to be in the creepers climbing the whitewashed poles which had once been trees. The palm trees were like the balding feathers of old birds, and the real birds on them were eagerly awaiting chicks with fluffy plumage. There were half a dozen species nesting here: the saun, egrets which taste a bit too greasy; the kowun, which is dark and curlew-billed; the mamakwa, a freckled bird with a yellow skewer beak that tastes like chicken; the kowopbee, a small blue and white heron-like bird which picked up the fish falling from the beaks and gullets of its neighbours. This was not a normal forest. Fish that were warm and sticky from the birds' bellies were jumping around the floor, chicks poised with featherless wings, ready to jump at their parents, and the tree canopy snowing with scales and spat-out fish bones. Not even snakes lived here. None the less, it was forest. And once I knew the forest, I'd know the Kandengeis, and once the Kandengeis, the forest.

While Wallace and the others went up into the trees and knocked the fledglings to the ground with sticks, Daniel and I were given the duffers' task of collecting up the birds and putting them out of their misery.

Daniel said, 'I do not like this job. The birds are not sure if they are dead or not.'

'You know what? That's because we were brought up in towns or places serviced by towns – not raw forest. We had the security of nature controlled by humans. Hampshire, Washington State, the Rhône Valley, it's all the same.'

'I like you talking this way. You know I don't always understand when you tell me all your student talk, but I like it for answering my questions.'

Daniel must have been waiting for two and a half years, saving up his queries. School had expanded the side of his brain concerned with reasoning, classification. Life in the forest educated the other side of the brain – intuition. One helped you plan, the other helped you sense. You could call one linear, the other spatial. One conception, the other perception. Whichever way you expressed it, I told Daniel, we Westernized ones were the odd ones out here. We were thinkers, in a place for do-ers. 'Ever wondered why life's so tiring here? That's the reason.'

Daniel released one of his questions. 'Do you remember how the Crocodile Nest shook once when the spirits tried to attack us? We were all frightened and our knees knocked together. It was magic, not the earth quaking. But I met a whiteman in Wewak who said that no one who is civilized believes in magic. And not in spirits either. But I know that even Margaret Thatcher and Prince Charles go to church together and believe in prayers – why is that civilized?'

'Christianity is a religion to do with man,' I offered. 'It suits people who live in towns, which are man-made things.'

'But Brian says he is right and he has been to university.'

'All I can say is that whitepeople like to feel they are more advanced. Their whole way of life is about progress; they'd feel very depressed if they found they weren't getting anywhere.'

'Question number two: what *are* spirits?'

Always a tricky one. I said if he really wanted my opinion, then I thought the water spirits and Wunjumboos, like the elves and pixies we used to have at home, were a face of the forest. They personified its mystery, its cloistered oppression. They gave humans, who were so alone in the natural order of unpraying creatures, someone to respond to. In my view – and what right did any outsider have to say? – the forest spirits were hairy angels.[9]

'Hairy *angels?*'

Hairy angels. I could have told him at length about my explanation for the Yeti, Big Foot and the other mystery half-human creatures. Pan, the Centaur. . . All were angels. However, funnily enough, Daniel never chose to ask me about hairy angels again.

In a moment, he said, 'The wise old men say this: they do not like Benedix thinking. They say you brought this faultiness from home.'

'What else do they say?'

'Oh, only that they want to stop you asking questions. I'm afraid they do not like us talking very much. Maybe they'll put me away.'

I said it seemed a bit drastic, just for me. He looked aside, his eyes floating off, sad.

We ran about clubbing the birds, then carried our booty back to the canoe, and took our clothes off and bathed, washing the bark, fish slime and excreta from our hair. Then we made our way home, stopping at Dunguba, a forest belonging partly to the Smaarks that's haunted by both the Wunjumboo, the forest spirit, and Wanjimaut, the water dragon. If you ever lit a fire here, the spirits make it rain. But we lit a fire anyway, for a quick feast. We threw birds into the fire for a singeing, slotted livers and eggs into bamboo tubes and plugged them with palm leaves.

Before we had started eating, gusts of wind came ashore and joined us in the forest, leaves flying with the butterflies, purple and black. The rain was coming.

Did I believe this was the work of the spirits? I certainly believed that the forest possessed them. And after all, belief in something gave it dignity – belief in the spirits stopped you thinking that the forest was just a collection of trees, not actually something that was vital to your tribe. A conviction in the spirits was what had kept the Niowra's balanced existence here. They *did* therefore have a real power over you. Their haunting, while you still believed in keeping at peace with nature, was a real one.

Daniel and I leaned on a tree buttress, away from the smoke and smell of bird gutting. Daniel said, 'Benedix, what is the strings around your hand for? Normally it is the custom only if you have a sweetheart darling.'

He smiled, hearing it was only a charm, not a girl's memento. I felt something that I'd experienced before – an invisible movement – myself being shifted, eased again towards whatever was my place in the power structure. I had to ask. 'Daniel, did Wallace ask you to ask me?'

Daniel all of a sudden looked away at the men working on the birds, then to see if the rain was on the further waters yet.

Then suddenly I said to Daniel, 'I want to get away.'

'Ah yes, good.'

I thought he had misheard, and so I said, 'I want to get far away.'

Daniel nodded. 'The journey.'

'What journey?'

'I'm sure you know. It's the custom, like the olden days of England.

You will go on a journey to slay the dragons. The maidens will be very excited by you.'

'But how many people go head-hunting any more? Like in England, going off to prove yourself has died out, rather. Hasn't it?'

Daniel said crossly, 'Johnson, Lawrence, Spencer, they *all* went after their *banis*.'

'Into *this* forest? A child could do that. Even me.'

'Don't be ridiculous. They went to find danger. They went to the *towns*.'

I snorted. Towns!

Daniel screwed his face up, flustered. 'Benedix, the towns are frightening.'

I said I was thinking of taking a break, getting somewhere right away.

'Yes, that is like the old days,' he said, crossly. 'Not the present day's custom of the towns. But of course we expect this – you will go to the forest after dragons. You were the best bandee.'

He was wrong. You could see it just by looking at this clearing, around us the leaves breathing on us, circling us, up above the roosting bats, and down here the roots to sit on. Of all the living things here, I was the only one questioning whether the rain sent by the spirits would come or not. A biologist could have picked me as the odd one out. I was the one with the questions.

Daniel went on, 'You were the best at old custom. Ask anyone. You remember singing Old MacDonald's Farm? That was very good for us. You made us try to laugh when the spirits killed in the village. You were precisely the best bandee.'

No, no, no! Just an ordinary Westerner – rationalizing and therefore less easily scared by the spirits. That wasn't being the best bandee, that was being the most alien.

'Really, Daniel,' I said, 'kicking Pepsi cans along the gutter instead of going head-hunting. It's not the same, is it?'

'It is the same. The forests were dangerous, and now the towns are dangerous. It is clear to see!' As I laughed, Daniel said indignantly: 'We *knew* you would come back. You had too much crocodile man in you.' The rare sharpness of his tone made me listen a little more seriously. 'The *avookwaarks* said "you will prefer the forest, like the days of old, when you come back."'

The light passing through the heat of the fire was making brown shadows on the forest. Vines above us became flaccid and black.

'That's what they said, was it?' I looked around – here the groping vine fingers, over there broom cupboard crampedness, somewhere else bristle-backed logs or choking satin leaf robes. All this inter- and intra-specific competition, a stewing stable forever mucking itself out.

I said aloud, 'They really *have* fitted me into the mechanics of this, then.' I could see why the AOGs were staying out of village life until the old system collapsed. They were well out of it.

So, what did this all come down to – if I could substantiate it. The old men were saying we, the bandees, had been taught how to become manly, learning their crocodile pedigree so as to take our places in the forest with bravery to the point of total self-sacrifice. The trouble with the ritual was, *anyone* could be brave about death if they'd learnt to play the odds against dying. The real world was less predictable; whether on streets or in forests, you had to show you could be brave about life.[10]

The rain was loud on the trees over the water, roaring breaths that made us run to the canoe. Soon the downpour screened off the village. Rain hit the water and bounced up into the air again, masking Kandengei in a silver powder. Never since have I seen such a rain, drumming the message home to me that the Wunjumboo, the face of the forest and therefore the essence of the Niowra, their doomed pact with Nature, still existed for these people. But for how long? The old men were maintaining a failed structure. There was still natural strength in the Niowras – heavens, hadn't I been experiencing it these last weeks? But it was a residue from the forest days, the crocodile culture; they couldn't last long. Pixies and elves had fled Hampshire, they'd be gone from here soon as well.

But they hadn't gone yet. And, speeding back to the village, through the driving rain, I thought more about this *geenjumboo* journey; it was an expedition that matched my Western heritage, it was the one time a person here acted alone, finding out whether he was brave enough about life. A quest was a time when you *could* ask a question. Here, at last, there might be leeway to explore cleanly, without importing your culture, waving questions at the trees and mountains, a fellow of a learned scientific society. My excitement grew. The lifeblood of exploration had always been imperialism – forwarding the Western idea of knowledge, our scientific frontiers, against nature, against cultures more closely allied to nature: perhaps, as I had always hoped, it need not be like that.

And then, coming ashore, I saw my wau. His sleek presence was defined even from across the water, in the sharp and hard precision of his entry into his house. A little girl ran behind, running in with head down, eyes up, a little fearful.

Chapter Two

DYING WOOD

I've said it already: this village is slow and self-indulgent, as villages are, but it isn't just rural timelessness, a backwater's suspended animation. There's no pasture or copse, not a sign of trim animal husbandry here. The Niowras have subjugated nothing. Instead they've worked out a deal. As long as they do what their ancestors did, first losing their selves in the tribe, and then obeying the taboos that keep that tribe in balance with the forest, then nature grants them what no Westerner has: immortality on earth.

But the West, with its belief in its right to dominion over the earth, has been busily eating up the world. Finally they've turned up in hotter climes – here, in fact, right on Kandengei's doorstep.

Once, I pondered about helping the village – I was, after all, a registered member of their society. I could assist them in their development into Westerners, if that's what they wanted. 'Why not stay [for ever] in K village?' I wrote in my notebook on my return. 'Be the hero of the old man's traditions, filter out some of the whiteman's junk. But,' I went on, 'what good is it me ruling over them? All I can gain is power . . .' And by that I meant power over them.

Power over *them*? Ha! After a week or two, things were looking different. These people might look like 'bush bunnies', as some whitemen call them, they might not have a head for figures, but to state these people need protecting against missionaries, say, is to be a racist. Not this lot. They may be envious and bitter that money isn't coming to them quicker but they are not crushed. No; if the Niowras are starting to drop the Wunjumboos, crocodiles and the rest of their culture you can be sure that the bulk of them have decided that's what they want.

I had been getting an inkling of their hidden power already. Usually I would have been confident that I could adapt. If there was anything good I was noted for in exploration circles, it was my peculiar, if bizarre, success in immersing myself in remote cultures. Orinoco,

58

Amazon, New Guinea, Sumatra, it had all gone remarkably well – certainly better than you'd think, seeing me struggle with a canoe paddle. But here – not even so very remote – I was being squeezed by everyone, even the children, corseted beyond anything I had ever known.

I couldn't win. *They* said my spirit called me back here, I said I was furthering my learning. *They* said my spirit now called me off on a journey, I said it was because I was a Westerner and you Niowras were driving me crazy.

During my evening meal, Songbird was ready with a name for me – the reciprocal gesture; every gift, every act, repaid to restore the balance.

'Nelson!' she stated, proud of this exotic word, harvested from Daniel's naughty colour magazine collection, probably. 'Nelson,' she called in English, clutching Teresa, who shared her stool, 'go to sleep time!' and exploded in piggy snorts, shuffling her feet against her little sister.

But nowadays hearing her, a captured songbird, wasn't funny.

Wallace said, in English, 'Benedix, you are not happy. You want to go on a happy shopping trip to Pagwi?'

'It's okay. I'll stay.'

'Oh . . .' he said, as if his world had fallen apart. 'But if you go, Benedix, buy some Benson and Hedges. The small packets with ten in. They taste better.'

'They don't taste better. I keep telling you. The packets of ten and the packets of twenty are exactly the same. You just don't like losing a big packet's worth when you share them round. Now please leave me alone to write.'

Wallace watched me, whacking my feet, which were embedded with mosquitoes.

'Thanks,' I said as he delivered another zealous blow.

'DO NOT say thank you!'

'You are sick, Benedix?' Songbird asked.

'It's okay,' I said. I just need space, I thought. Then Priscilla began looking at my chest, being encouraging about my crocodile marks, which were rising as my skin tanned.

Rowena, Wallace's tempestuous sister, was visiting for the evening. Now she was with little Cousin Teresa, who was pretty tonight. Her white dress brought out the brightness in her eyes, and the light splashed from the tight black skin of her skull, which had been freshly shaven.

Rowena saw my eyes on Teresa. She smiled, and I felt hot, and looked at my feet. As I poured more water on a tea bag, Rowena called to me in Pidgin, 'You can ask the crocodile to give you new marks, if there's another *banis*.'

Wallace looked up, irritated at the woman's interruption of the evening. 'He is not afraid. If necessary, he'll do it.'

He was waiting, looking at me. I wasn't afraid but anyhow I groaned because they thought it was my duty to say I wasn't, and I felt as though all the weight of the forest was on me. 'Yes, of course I will do what's right.'

Rowena tutted at her brother, not impressed by his show of authority. Wallace ignored her, saying to me in loud Pidgin, 'We can go to Maprik, one day. You can take me shopping.'

'No thanks.' I imagined the financial losses. A shopping trip with Wallace – it was a sort of handy pocket dictionary definition of hell.

'Father George says there are always one hundred and one reasons for not doing something.'

In this case, one hundred and two, I thought.

Rowena hovered closer. She meant trouble. For some reason she was upset with her brother and she was determined to ruin his evening. Mosquitoes were siphoning the life out of me, but I'd forgotten them. I was observing this bated silence.

We waited; even Wallace, though he was chewing and laughing with Esau and Spencer, pretending to dismiss the silly woman's tittle-tattle. But it was Rowena who was controlling the moment. A woman! She stood with her arms fastened across her, playing with her bracelets, which were petrol drum washers. And now Wallace was slowing, becoming self-conscious. She had something she could use against him. He knew it.

We waited there in the house – Wallace, the male, the only one looking hectored here; Rowena, the female, looking stilled by her creation, this moment of power over the apparently dominant male. She stood, poised, like a figurine in satinwood, gold and finely grained, held up in her intrigue, it seemed, by the other women.

I was transfixed by this strange flux in power; looking at Wallace with his teeth astride his fish and Rowena hanging over him like some heavenly agent of disruption, I was recalling another incident: my departure after the Man-making, at the death of the *yargee* woman as I left with the funeral cortège. The men had stayed in the spirit house, with the remaining bandees. The women had moaned and groaned on the river bank as we pushed off, with the coffin. They called out, repeating what the men had said, that they were happy I was the beginnings of a man. It had been a comfort at the time, but only that, a bonus; now, in retrospect, with Rowena's performance going on in front of me, I realized that there'd always been women around at choice moments – they were chief wailers at times of death, they banned men at times of birth, stayed safe when the men were on their head-hunting trips. Now, thinking of it like this, the women looked like agents of the core of things, the men only the arbiters of outer, day-to-day decisions – mending broken taboos. I wondered for the first time if women were merely disguised as caged birds. When the release from the Man-making came and the women ran their fingers like kisses over my embossed chest, arms and back, the neatly harrowed crocodile-skin ridges, just for a moment it had struck me even then that it was as if those women's fingers were confirming their assent. In some way they were adding their own seal of approval to an apparently male-defined culture. They were earthing all that male energy, balancing it with the female.[11] They liked the ceremony not for the obvious reason – they'd get strong, protective men in the village – but because the men were easier handled once inflated with self-importance. Any magical power masculinity might have gained was contained in that earthing touch of their fingers; any effort of the men to prove themselves more powerful than women was negated. I hadn't given it much thought at the time; but I was, of course, newly a 'man' – as disabled by swollen pride as any of them.

And Rowena spoke. She said to everyone, 'Perhaps with new marks, Benedix . . .' – she halted, weighed the words, then dropped them from as high as she could – 'Wallace will have you married to his family quicker.'

I didn't listen to the words, I was watching the weight falling on Wallace. Then it was over. Any power had been given away. The women were embarrassed, taking the consequences for having said something taboo. Songbird tried to sing, but there was still too much silence and it appeared too much a desperate act, a screen. She stopped. Wallace looked to Priscilla, and Priscilla looked quickly over to someone in the shadows, then to me, sharply, and down to the floor.

Suddenly, in the silence, from the same shadows, Teresa got up and left. She rose vertically from crossed legs, unfolding and rising as light as a moth. I sat watching her go, the meaning of what had been said at last striking me forcibly, even painfully.

Antonia began to sing again, and I began thinking along the theme of the captured bird. I'd likened the women to songbirds, but the men themselves were tied up in all their trappings. The prison state was endemic in nature; to a Westerner, everyone was a gaolbird here. That was the Niowras' power. They kept their energy enclosed, away from the world. Only because the culture was dying had I once decided I had the right to go in and ask to live here, releasing the closed knowledge of it, setting the energy, the magic free. But they wanted me caged, just like the rest of them, and so they were lining up Teresa for me.

'I'm going for a breath of air,' I said to Wallace, taking the opposite door out.

Outside under the stars, I wanted to scream. This was going to be my jungle life, was it? My lame attempts at paddling canoes in the approved, standing manner, sago and fish to eat, not allowed to enjoy free female company and no place to hide, and I'm expected to know my rank and to maintain the male collusion against female – if it *is* that – and to remember I have to revere my wau and not talk lightly about forest creatures like birds of paradise that are members of his clan and to remember all the other billion taboos and 'kindly learn our language properly this time, Wumvunnavan' and more than that they still class me a millionaire when I've pinched and saved all year in Tooting to get them these presents and My God on top of all this they are *still* saying the ancestral spirits brought me here – and bang on time – and you still won't let me see my Guardian and I've only been back a few weeks AND I'M A LITTLE SICK OF IT.

Daniel's house was next door to Wallace's, in our territory. It was ramshackle and in my opinion downright dangerous. That was one reason for my not risking the steps up to the cranky entrance. Another was the female complications – inside lived a woman sheltering from her violent husband, and Skola, Songbird's sister who had arrived back one night having run away from the High School under circumstances everyone was trying to forget. There was also Teresa.

Skola came to the entrance with all her easy, town manner. 'You want Daniel,' she told me, and, as if issuing a threat: 'I will produce him.' She called him in a careless, sultry yawn, but Daniel was from the town himself, and waved her away without offence, showing me he understood these matters.

'Hello, Ben-ee.'

A boy popped his head out under his arm. Daniel clipped his ear. 'It's about time he was put in the *banis*, I think. If you are lucky, Benedix, I think the old men will allow you to beat the boys if there is a *banis* again.'

'Oh good,' I said, absently. 'Actually, I have something important to ask you.'

The boy left. Daniel looked around, and ran down the steps to me. He said, quietly, 'Any time, Benedix. I am your best friend.'

'Look, Daniel, what plan have they got for me here?'

'Oh, no special plan.'

But he knew what I was talking about – Teresa had just come flying into his house, I could hear her still flapping about.

'Are they trying to get me married?'

'You must not worry about these things. If you like, you marry. If you do not marry, you do not marry.' We walked up the front of the village towards the AOGs at the far end. Better that they, the AOGs, who were out of village affairs, heard what we were discussing, than anyone else. 'They cannot be angry. Your wau will tell them so, now he is back. And you told me Kaavon has told them they are being too greedy for your money. "Benedix," he is saying, "is not to be taken for grants."'

'That was last time I came.'

A man was in a doorway; an electric lamp made sharp shadows on his face. He was knocking a book on the post. Thump, thump. Nathan, Bible-bashing.

I whispered, 'What are the Smaarks wanting, Daniel?'

The 'thump, thump' got louder. 'Wait.' Then Daniel spoke up. 'Good-night, Nathan.'

A voice sprang from our left. 'Good-night, Benedict. Good-night, Daniel.' Thump, thump, thump.

Nathan was probably thinking, 'Poor old Benedict. You've got my sympathy, mate, you really have.'

Daniel said, 'We *all* have girlfriends, Benedix. I told you.'

The moonlight was shining off Nathan's factory stamped roof – a beacon, a signal of something momentous on the way.

I said, 'And Johnson offered one to me. So what?'

'So you do not worry. If they organize a girl to come to you, that is nice. It is because you are getting to look like a Niowra. It's a no obligation guarantee.'

'Humph,' I said. 'Getting to look like a Niowra indeed.' We walked back along the waterfront. 'No obligation guarantee indeed.' I said, 'Daniel, I'm not going to have anyone in my bed.'

'Shhsss!' he said, though I was whispering. 'I remember now, your wau said that we cannot worry when you say this. It is because you have been away a few months.'

'Years,' I said.

'Your body is returned but has not found your Niowra spirit yet. But when a girl comes, you will know you are arrived and your spirit is settling in. That is what he says.'

Theatre and games, I thought. Right, let's cut through all this. I said I wanted to know who organized it all.

He used a Pidgin word. 'The *bigmen?*'

'You could get Wallace to tell them. Tell them I don't know where I stand. I'm a whiteman. I feel trapped.'

'You are naughty to think the *avookwaarks* want to trap you. They do not. Kaavon wants nothing. He wants your body with your spirit, that is all it is.'

Daniel was an innocent, a romantic. He left me speechless with his calm. Marriage! To someone I didn't know! At Heaven knows whose instigation! 'Daniel,' I said, 'you don't seem to realize this is a crisis!'

The thump, thump. Nathan waiting in the wings to take over the show.

'And,' I said, 'it's going to get harder and harder for us to talk. Wallace keeps saying the *avookwaarks* don't like it.'

'No worrying, please! And do not worry about the girls. Let them come; when they come you will know your spirits are beginning to climb back on board. You are near enough. You are presentable.'

I said, 'What about the girls' feelings? I didn't come here to upset any lives.'

'You know they are not as stupid as whitemen think. They will not wait for you – not like Western girls that have small bride prices.'

'I'm beginning to believe it. The women are very sharp indeed. What a display by Rowena!'

'Remember, I wasn't with you this evening.'

I said, 'The women were all ganged up against Wallace. It was a sort of conspiracy,' I explained, but was Daniel an innocent? He seemed remarkably well-informed for a semi-outsider himself.

Daniel sighed and touched my shoulder, wanting me to stop on the path. Suddenly he had his schoolboy manner; he was saying dramatically, 'Benedix. The girls have *secrets* over you.'

'Meaning?'

'Benedix, the *bigmen* can't allow this to happen many more times.'

The penny dropped. I was still acting as an outsider – and while I held back, the women could embarrass the men by revealing to me what they were up to. Until I committed myself, I was, in fact, a threat. And what if I didn't integrate more? They wouldn't chuck me out of the village, would they?

Daniel told me, 'They will have to treat you like George, who came to study the dances. We do not talk properly to him, as if we are in the bath together.'

Saying I'd be treated like George was putting it mildly. I could see I was a threat that no anthropologist would ever be. I was too involved, just to be able to come and go like this. When it came down to it, I must either join in or leave . . .

Daniel and I agreed to make a sign if we needed a private talk – 'Katim Nek!' Everyone else would think we were joking, Daniel said. 'But we know best.'

'So, I leave you now,' Daniel said. 'You can decide what to do. But stop the worryings and remember this advice from your best friend: the Smaarks can protect you from any village arrangements. You can still leave when you like.'

The Smaarks can protect you. I looked around the territory, the Catholic hut, Daniel's house, Wallace's house, Spencer's bachelor hut, thinking, but it's Smaarks themselves who would arrange this.

I lay awake, feeling captured. '*Katim Nek*.' Ridiculous. Ridiculous and childish.

I went outside to be in the gentle rain, wondering whether to leave the village or stay, surrender myself like lost property.

The moonlight was sponged over the sky, grey. Somewhere eyes must be on me, wondering if I was going back to bed soon. I remembered standing naked in the dark like this as an initiate before sunrise. We used to run to the waterside to wet ourselves, trotting to the Nest before the sun erupted, torn in shreds by the branches of the trees beyond the water. Like this moment in the downpour, it had been a time alone, a sweet flick of freedom.

Spencer came running to me with a torch. He shouted in Pidgin, 'It's raining! You miss the rain and the cold sun of England?'

'Not so as you'd notice.'

'You are walking alone, like a whiteman. You are thinking of Katie and Stew?'

'Who?'

'Katie and Stew – your brother and sister in England.'

'Oh yes, Katie and Stew.' Home, I thought. So far away. The three of us as children: buttered toast as we sat on the Afghan carpet by the fireplace, a picnic – but I stopped myself thinking back and made myself resurface here, crocodile land. I mustn't give up yet.

Spencer said that Alex, a Catholic *wanbanis* who was my age, wanted to give us a meal 'as we don't have wives to cook for us yet'.

It was a sore point, but I asked what we'd be getting.

'*Goo naow*,' Spencer said. Wet sago. 'Yum!'

More rib-encasing food, I thought. Yuck!

He handed over the torch. 'Come back indoors soon. I don't like you to be sad.'

I thought, All very well, but what's it worth calling yourself 'I' here?

In the dark, I walked away from the village, wanting to feel its lifeblood, the forest.

Who was this 'I'? It was not 'I, Spencer.' It was 'I, Spencer, a segment of the Smaarks.' When the Smaarks want you to take a woman, part of *you*, Spencer, will want it, because part of you will be a Smaark. And the same will happen to me if I lose myself here. When she comes to me, I won't even open my mouth to resist. I will let it happen. Just as she will let it.

Near the waterfront, rain cracked from the new tin extension put up by Jimmi – he was doing very nicely selling beer to the townboys. More machine-made roofs, more alien things. The end was close now.

A child's voice, singing a school tune, 'Rainee, rainee, Come back another dayee.'

I could hear Joseph's generator, even above the rain. Soon he'd wire up a neon cross. And me, an outsider like him, what was I doing here? Just tunnelling down until I found the bottom of this village – lake muds; stirrings I could never understand because these people didn't understand either. They were trained to perceive, not conceive; they were sensers, not thinkers.

For a second time I wanted to chuck a line ashore, clamber back home. Maybe I had reached the sensible limit of exploration. I should now step back, gracefully observe, like an anthropologist. Get sponsorship from some industrialist, promote a new walking shoe or line in wristwatches, as I cross and recross the island, mapping it, defining it in Western terms. Give it to the Royal Geographical Society in the hope of earning a medal.

'All you ever get if you take a map is a better defined version of the one you had before,' I'd said to Mum on departure. But it looked like there was no other answer. Trust me to have spent most of my twenties pondering a flawed theory, plodding through forests and participating in ghostly ceremonies and book promotional chat shows.

Might as well pack up, then. Even if I'd been right, the best I could hope for here was to end up in some ethnographer's dictionary of the Niowra language. *'Benedict' = verb. To 'benedict', according to the local usage, seems to mean 'to go about exploring a redundant life-style'.*

It was true; times were changing. Who in the village saw Kaavon and his cronies as offering any future promise? One of the loneliest routes of all the ones I'd travelled in the world was the one right through this village, the path to the spirit house. Unchanged in time, taken only by men, it was a hardened artery to the dying heart. And at the end of it, Kaavon himself, with his strange words, the muscles in his nostrils flexed as he dribbled sacred spit on your forehead, never speaking to you. He offered the village no future, only the present – and now the forest was beginning to rot. The certainty of the AOG dogma would tempt them all, soon. Only a fool would stick with the Reverend Crocodiles fumbling about in the shade, stupid with all their impending loss of authority.

I looked into the night. The muffled paraffin light glowed, the rain now masked the moon. This was a time when crocodiles thrashed and swirled with each other, surging through the water. Somewhere under the cover of this dark, a girl would be leaving her hand stretched out, the way they did, and a boy tying a string around it. Somewhere else a boy's finger working towards a girl, up through a crack in the bark floor. Boys sweating painfully, girls pondering whether to betray them – learning, I was beginning to see at last, the shape and form of their power.

Not that their power ever helped their old men against the West. 'Know how they used to make a slit gong?' I asked myself. Burnt a line of palm nuts on a tree trunk, thumped out the burnt base. Burnt again; then again. One day you ended up with your slit gong. That was Kandengei before the Germans came with their mission boat in Daniel's grandfather's day, the first whitemen smiling at the Niowras' stone axes, or at the standing boulders which the Natives had lugged down from the hills to revere, because the Sepik basin was a land only of roots, leaves and mud and water. And the whitemen had thanked God they had been chosen to bring hope and enlightenment. And now, 1988, here we were, the whiteman having almost destroyed the planet.

With the rain still coming down, I went to the Catholic hut, the nearest to the West I could get in the Smaark territory. I propped the torch on a plank bench and got out my notebook. Then I let my whiteman's mind out and rationalized.

CROCODILE CHARACTERISTICS, I wrote.

Pedigree: 120,000,000 years.
Feeding habits: Carnivorous. Does not chew; swallows whole, or in large chunks. Partly explains why meat is left to rot, before eating.
Position in food chain: Top.
Longevity: Not sure. Same as man?
Intelligence: High relative even to mammals.
Reproduction: High infant mortality. However, strong mothering

instincts. Highly protective and caring of offspring, which are, for instance, led to the water from nest.

General behaviour: Low adaptability to new habitats; restricted to tropics/subtropics, and water environment. A specialist.

Success: V. high. Has survived millions of years without having to adapt.

Present status: In decline.

The rain crackled, and the crocodiles played in the warm rain.

MAN

Pedigree: Only 5,000,000 years.

Feeding habits: Omnivorous.

Position in food chain: Top.

Intelligence: Exceptionally high.

Reproduction: Low reproduction rate, low mortality. Strong family bonding.

General behaviour: Highly adaptable, due to e.g. bipedalism, omnivorous diet, and intelligence. Bipedalism enables adaptation of forelimbs for tool use, making of clothing etc. Complex brain encourages tool use, allows construction of shelters to extend natural habitat. Some groups migrate first from forest/savannah to colder climates, where he is encouraged to store for the winter, therefore plan ahead, therefore 'advance'. In all groups, however, brain capacity has evolved with complex social orders, allowing specialization. Amongst other things, religion serves as cohesive social force and to justify steps that have to be taken to, e.g., maintain balance with habitat – one way might be emulation of successful crocodile species (see above) in Rain Forest environment by basing gods on nature, and using taboos to prevent forward thinking and imbalance. However, cold climate, 'advancing' varieties do not seek balance with habitats, and threaten the remainder, and their own existence.

Success: Very high in short term, but see below.

Status world-wide: Western varieties: growth, which is unsustainable. Indigenous varieties (those integrated with nature, once termed 'savages,' now termed 'primitive' or 'tribal'): threatened by Western, 'modern' varieties.

When I'd finished doing this, I felt better. I'd worked things out in my own culture's terms; afterwards, I could always be comforted by that – it had been a Western decision, not theirs, the clambering Kandengeis, five hundred of them against one. Because, damn it, I couldn't walk out now. These people were worth listening to and I was the only person available here to do it. Furthermore, there was the ritual journey, maybe a chance to explore in terms set by nature, not the West.

My instinct had been to contain my energy, not spread it and lose myself. I'd paced hard against the natural pulse of the Niowras as they tried to draw me in. Now, two nights later, when Wallace said he would take me to my wau, I took the news in my stride. Meeting him had lost all urgency.

And after meeting my Guardian, my relationship with the village changed almost immediately – starting that night, when, having been fitted for an extremely bulky headdress and set of matching earrings they now wanted me to have, I went to bed early, slipping onto my mat in Spencer's little bachelor house and straight to sleep. Later, perhaps an hour after, I woke. I felt the house shudder. Someone climbing the steps. Spencer going to bed? I looked to see his white shirt. But there was only the blackness. Mosquito netting brushed my cheek as it was raised.

Someone was letting mosquitoes in. 'For heaven's sake, who's that?'

'Tsss! *Quietly* talk.'

Help, a female. 'Listen, you must go away.'

But Teresa had lain down alongside me. She was breathing heavily; she had run here, and her heart was knocking against me. Her hand was on my elbow.

'Go! It's taboo if another clan finds out! Someone will come, Teresa.'

She said, '*That* little Smaark girl is coming tonight?'

'But you are a Smaark girl.'

'I am a Yaark girl.'

Oh, my God. I thought, You're not Teresa, are you . . . Not even a Smaark. Yikes! I said, 'It's dangerous to come to Smaark land!'

She was speaking in English. 'It is not nice for me to run and hide from the moon. But it is dangerous for you to come and find me. We think you are too big and white.'

'I can't remember your name.' I peeled off her fingers; they were softly tipped. And her knees had come down heavily to the loose bark floor. Yes, definitely a towngirl.

'It is me!' she said, confidently. 'And remember,' she added in a whisper. 'Tell no one I was here.'

'I wasn't thinking of it.' This was farcical. Any moment we'd get a secret signal telling her someone was coming and she must fly. 'Who arranged this? You said "we".'

'You are too noisy.' She dabbed a finger crossly at my mouth. I swerved and it went in my eye. Outside, under the house, there was a whistle from a forest bird, a *swé*.

I said, drily, 'Must be lost.'

But the girl said, 'Soon I must go.'

I flapped irritably at her mosquitoes. 'Don't let me keep you.'

She was looking me up and down, seeing the light off the pale skin, metre-length limbs stretching from my cotton wrap. 'Eee! You are very long.'

Suddenly she held her breath. Her whole length went taut, her head under my chin, her toes, damp from the grass, splayed against my shins.

Eee! You are very short, I thought.

I heard voices. Young men – two. Three? Then I heard Johnson's voice, intercepting them.

They went on by. When they were gone, she half lifted the net, and waited again. In came a fresh swirl of mosquitoes.

'I am gone,' she said, urgently, and was no longer lying beside me.

Pressing my cheek to the boards, I felt them tremble; down below I heard a sound like the flapping of an alighting hen, then nothing.

I lay awake; I had the warm peace of the freshly arrived. The girl was a sign that I was socially acceptable to the Niowra spirit. I had found my place here. Now I might swim along with everyone, in the same circular current, just occasionally splashing a bit. I had the confidence to make better use of the Niowras' confined space. I had Daniel as a friend and the sanction of my wau, the attentions of 'Stars on the Water' and soon no doubt, Teresa, who'd also be given a professional name.

So, for a while, before my old trouble came back, my inability to accept, to submerge my old, questioning spirit, before that rose up in defiance, everything was fine.

It seemed that I'd never been away – old memories from my first stay at Kandengei interleaved with the present ones, as if the forest had swallowed up the years in between.

Conversations with my wau were terse, but cordial. He was someone to save up for a special day, but when we did meet I didn't come away stunned from the bite of a blue spark from him – the electricity vaulting between our two stations – he, my creator, and me, the newly created. However, by everyone else I was treated as a portion of the Smaark clan, something to be shared, and to my wau I was, as his *Laua* offspring, someone exceptional. It was a feeling familiar to a Westerner. I could forget that I was a whiteman's shape in a blackman's space. I was an individual, a person. In him, I, as a whiteman, found room to breathe.

Then Daniel disappeared. I don't think they really can have taken him away, but it seemed a little like that. On that morning I'd been talking to the little boys playing crocodiles between the moored canoes. Johnson came with a message that I was wanted in the *geygo*. I changed shirts – they always like you to be smart, whether it's leaves or cotton – and went.

I passed Nathan, the AOG. 'So, you are going to the old men again. Did you know they are out of date?'

'That's why I'm trying to understand their forest. Before it's too late.'

I kept walking. But he suddenly shouted after me, 'The awful horror is coming!'

I looked around, genuinely expecting to see a pig snorting, about to charge. But the threat, according to Nathan, was the Bible. 'The Awful Horror,' Nathan said. 'Matthew 24:15–28.'

'Oh,' I said with relief. 'The Bible. You mean the end of the world.'

This time Nathan didn't make a mess of the quote. He read it with his finger. It looked a well-used page. 'For the trouble that time will be far more terrible than there has ever been.'

I sympathized. 'It doesn't sound good.'

'This is the truth. It says so. *This is the word of God.*'

'We don't *know* that, do we? That is the value of faith – not knowing for sure.'

'I do not understand you. You are so loosely minded.'

And you are so fixed, I thought. Nathan said we must talk. But what was there to say? Besides, if I went into his house, I jabbed my foot on the nails of his steps. Anyone who hadn't been to town and bought shoes was penalized.

'Father George, the Catholic head at Brurui, is a collaborator. I am a purer Christian. I do not adore the Virgin Mary and spirits. I do not worship idlers. This way, I believe in the truth only. That is why they call me . . . What? A man of fixed positions . . . Er . . .'

'Dogmatist? Bigot?'

'I remember now –' He quoted a manual, saying something like, 'It's *Knowing the Way* Lesson 32. Benedict, I'm a "Fundamentalist". I believe in the fundamentals.'

'What about Jesus – love, I mean. That's the fundamental essence of his message.' My attention strayed as I thought of Nathan's message, the Awful Horror – the loneliness of the old of thousands of other peoples as the young left for the Western life-style, hastened by the threat of the Awful Horror. 'Love,' I said. 'Isn't that the true fundamental of the Bible?'

71

'I think you are wrong to go out with Wallace. You have been taken by the Catholics – who are anyway followers of Old Nick – and you have talked to their friends, the devilish old men.'

I said I was only bouncing around a few ideas. Nathan was a fundamentalist, but after all, the *avookwaarks* were too. They believed in Man-In-Nature instead of Man-Over-Nature, that was all.

'I am happy to hear you are only bouncing your ideas. You are a useful person here to me.' Useful? I've only just come to terms with the Niowras saying that, I thought. Don't *you* start.

The spirit house was close now, looking old and tired of the fight. Of being polarized by Nathan – labelled evil, something he could fight the good fight against.

'Nathan, what's going to happen?'

Nathan was slowing, pacing himself. He'd have to stop in about twenty steps, at the territorial boundary of the *geygo*. 'This year, or the next year, Kaavon will die. That will be the end of all this.'

We were ten paces away. I wondered how near he would dare go. 'And then?' I asked. Five paces away now, maybe seven if he shortened them. 'What happens when he's died?'

He stopped. 'Then,' he said, pleased at having timed this nicely, arriving on a doorstep soon to be his, 'then that will be the beginning of Jesus's reign. God will be king.'

'You're forgetting the Catholics.' I turned and walked backwards, facing him.

'The Catholics are not certain enough.' He seemed to be reading a manual through in his mind. 'They are not certain enough, except about (a) the infallibility of the Pope, (b) er . . . divine right of kings and (c), I think, yes, (c) contraception.'

'They've brought contraception out here?'

He was jeering a little. 'Yes, Benedict Allen, their so-called "immaculate contraception".'

You're unbelievable, Nathan, I thought. 'Immaculate *conception*,' I said. He said it didn't matter. The young would come to him sooner or later.

'You may be right. Your stance is an easy one; it's security, absolutely black and white.' The AOGs were principled, like the *avookwaarks* they were about to replace.

'Take my words for it,' he said, raising his Bible to his nose. 'When the black magics and spirits are gone, people will want the new rules – the unyielding word of the Bible.' He turned, leaving me with his odd, victorious phrase, 'the unyielding word of the Bible'.

I walked into the cool and the shade and the secrets. In the spirit house there was only my wau. Or so I thought at first. But he told me to go over by the central post, the other side of the flaking crocodile slit gongs. I looked closer at one of the dark low stools by the fireplace and saw it was Kaavon, hunched at the base of a post, head down and panting an incantation onto a spread of leaves.

Kaavon had been back two weeks, and I'd seen him like this before, but hadn't gone up to him – I was a Junior Man. You had to leave him there in a heap, a loose bag of brittle bones, and watching from a little way off, murmuring, chanting, a man who used pliers to open the shells of the betelnut because he was toothless. I sat by his side, noticing he smelt of stale tobacco smoke. Without lifting his head, he reached out his hand and held mine to his lap. His hand was warm, even hot. We stayed like this, hand in hand. I guessed he was feeling my blood next to his – a sort of palm reading.

Then he let go, and called my wau to join us. My wau said in his slow Pidgin, that someone uncharitable might say was pompous, 'We are so careful in the *banis* to remove female blood from the male. It's most important that you do not become infected again.'

Of course not, I agreed. Perish the thought. I must give their tradition a go. I accepted that.

'Men do not talk to women. Luckily, you can accept this for fact. You are a man, not a half man, half woman. And now, I will tell you something. You will have women here, because you are now a man with the Niowras, and men do have them. But whitemen are especially weak for the woman because they have their female blood. It is important that I watch for this tendency in you. BE CAREFUL.'

And he gave me a betelnut to remind me of our bond, and I went outside to go and find Daniel, wondering what this was all about. But he was nowhere to be found. Later, soon after dusk, as I walked with Johnson, he came up from behind. '*Katim Nek!*' I was wondering how to get rid of Johnson, but then I realized he was already dropping back. Something odd was happening. I walked on beside Daniel. But Daniel only wanted to say one thing. 'Benedix: it's grievous news. I am too Western, the old men are saying.' He accelerated away into the thickening dark.

Kaavon was reinforcing his work of Man-making, shaping me up for the journey that everyone had decided I was going on. I was flattered that, having helped me through the ceremony, he thought me worth the effort to go further. He was loading me with energy, pouring the magic of anticipation on to me. I walked over kamuin leaves that he'd spent the whole night talking to, I sat while he breathed on me. He was giving and giving and giving, until I was wanting to expend, give back. I wondered if this was always the procedure in the head-hunting days. Undoubtedly I was getting special attention to make my body – as my wau said – 'feel at home' with the Niowras. But at times Kaavon's commitment to this appeared like a desperate bid to unload himself before the end of his time – perhaps it was my imagination, I don't know.

In the night, Stars on the Water popped in beside me and said in Pidgin, 'Wake up!'

'Oh you. Look, I've had a hard day . . .'

'I am lonely, and so I came to you. I was crying today.'

'Again?'

'Do not behave like that! You are *not* like the other men. There is so little for me to do in the village. Stupid basket-making, stupid fishing. How am I meant to live in this place? It is full of stupid women, and I can't talk to the men.'

'Nothing I can do, I'm afraid.'

'You are a whiteman. You can understand.'

'They tell me not to talk to you. Your blood pollutes mine, they say.'

'But you're a whiteman. These men are too stupid. Can they read and write? Can they send a letter?'

But Nathan could read and write, and what had it done for him? His mind, shaped in the Western classroom, was what people at home called educated: apparently he was no more able to think openly than the *avookwaarks*, those gnarled, lost belongings from the old days.

I said that only this morning the *avookwaarks* had warned me off talking to women.

Stars whispered slowly, 'I can tell you many secrets.'

Then they are right not to trust you, I thought. I told her to be quiet, and to wait for a signal to go. And we waited, as always, never even touching, and we found this silence together painful. She cried to me; I moped secretly, sorry for her and also for myself because I, like her, wasn't fitting snugly into my place here.

In the daylight I tried my best, tossing my empty plates to the women, grabbing the ones they gave full. But I was acting, playing at being a jungle man, and I knew it. I was lonely during those days.

Now Stars was becoming like the Christian devil to me. She tempted me away from Kandengei, made me think of my mother in the kitchen leaning against the Aga. Myself on the red and white chequered linoleum floor, pulling faces at her home-made marmalade. Unlucky Stars; unlucky me. We weren't made for this.

* * *

Daniel had disappeared, probably to Nyaurengei, the next village, and so I turned increasingly to Johnson. 'Shit!' he said. 'It's Stars on the Water again? She's a troublesome girl.'

But I prized her for being real in a place of showmanship. She had the fundamental properties that I'd valued before in Yargee, the market woman who'd died. In the daytime I thought of Stars, a gleaming black boulder laid down alongside me, a cousin of the stones I'd sought as a boy, the Blue Lias boulders in the surf at Lyme Regis. She was solid; I understood her Western tendencies, her frustration at the complacency of the doomed forest heritage.

I know their secrets, she said. She told me this in Pidgin. '*Taim bilong tumbuna* . . . In the old times, the women were in the spirit house. It was not a men's house, it was a woman's house. The men were not allowed in it at all. They lived in the family houses, and cooked fish and carried firewood, and only the women rested on their backs, sleeping in the spirit house. And then, something happened. The men tricked us. They said, "Women, women, please come from the spirit house, because our fires have gone out, and we have no hearths to cook your fish and sago on." So the women came out from the spirit house, and they brought some embers in their [fire] tongs. And they made fires for the men in their family houses. But when they went back to the spirit house, the men had taken it, and they've kept it ever since.'

'It's just that I want to be able to exchange ideas,' I told Johnson. In actual fact the idea in my head was that somehow we might work out a plan to explore together – Stars and Benedix might discover the Niowra female as well as the male.

Johnson said, 'You'll get better. Daniel has the same condition.' He patted my shoulder. 'Be assured. It's extremely common for townboys.'

But I was not assured.

One night – it must have been a Sunday because of the 'clink, clink, clink' sound of the light, easy to carve, Catholic slit gongs – one night under brilliant moonlight, the silver glancing off the palm leaves, Nathan sought me out. He came at me running. 'You know, the *bigmen* talk to Old Nick.'

'The Devil? They don't even believe in him. That's your religion – Pure Goodness versus Pure Evil.'

Nathan applied his alien, hard-reasoning mind, came up with nothing and said he'd pray about it. I said, 'The Catholics say the Niowra stories are based on truth. They have a story of the flood, for example.'

The story of the flood. It went like this. They had a flood. It was a bad one. Everyone in the world drowned – but for a couple of brothers and a woman who had been advised by the mighty crocodile spirit to build an extra large canoe and get collecting two of every species – two banana palms, two mosquitoes, two sago grubs . . . They survived, although the woman got pregnant and as part of the agreement to ensure the waters would go down she had to give her baby girl to the crocodile – who, as chance had it, needed a bride.

'I know the Niowra flood story. A crocodile saves mankind when the Sacred Flood Gates opened. It's badly wrong.'

Unfortunately our discussion didn't end there – the old men had a story of creation, so did the Bible, and so did Nathan. 'In the beginning,' Nathan said, 'there was the world. And the world was made all light. And then there was Man.'

'And woman.'

Nathan frowned at my ignorance. 'In the beginning God made Man come first.' He quoted a few of St Paul's letters. Women should wear veils in church, women were a weaker vessel.

Nathan was more like a disciple of Paul than of Jesus. He wanted a fight, the satisfaction of socking evil in the face. Time was running out fast for poor old Kaavon, only an old head-hunter.

One evening, Wallace said, 'You go and lie down now. Daniel has gone to get you your proper girl.'

'My proper girl, eh? You people amaze me, you really do.' I did what I was told. I found myself waiting in my mosquito net, complying with this. I was trusting but nervous of this first date. The girl was to be called Nightlight, Wallace had said.

I felt the shudder of someone coming up the steps. I listened for the flap of a skirt hem. Then a voice spoke – but it was not a girl, it was Spencer.

'She's here. She wants to talk in English – she's been practising for weeks with Daniel.'

One day I'll have to have words with Daniel, I thought.

'"Talk slowly," she says. I will walk around.' She must have been waiting under the house, moulded to the back of a post. Now she flitted up the steps – hardly a vibration, more like a gentle breeze sound. I opened the mosquito net and saw Teresa's fragile but strong little frame, a tender chick. She lay down alongside, where I had left plenty of room.

'So, Nightlight.'

'Yes, I'm Nightlight.' She spells it. 'N.I.H.T. LIEF, no, LIFH . . . L . . .'

'Never mind,' I said. We played for time, covering silences by asking each other how well we were. This silly, embarrassing talk became repetitious. We stopped to wait every few moments as boys passed. 'Too many *mankis* walk now. I am fret.'

'Don't be afraid.'

'No. I *must* be fret. Too many moonlight.' We had met on a full moon. 'You must be fret too.'

'I did not arrange this,' I said.

She says, 'I can give you my lips only.'

'Listen. I do not want to kiss. I do not want to marry anyone. I'm not staying in the village.'

She sat up a bit, now propping herself on an arm that was slender and soft but muscle. 'It's all all right. Daniel says this to me before you arrived back here even.'

'It's not that I don't like you.' I rubbed her hand as a friend. It became stiff, unyielding.

'You must not talk. The spirits will come from the woods and waters and we will be eaten from the inside.'

'Which spirits?'

'Many of them, or just one of them. Wanjimaut, who has scales like teeth.' I heard a fingernail tap against enamel. 'Horrible Wunjumboo, with his special dirtiness.'

She was scaring herself, saying this. I said, 'It is better for you to leave.'

'Yes, I want,' she said, her head turned away to the slats in the hut and the night outside. 'But oh! There is too many moonlight.' I nodded sympathetically. She drew her feet under her suddenly. She had heard a signal. 'I will talk to you when they next send me.'

Then I found I was alone.

The village was no place to expend energy – females pouring at you by the moon, males by the sun – and more and more my thoughts turned to getting on with this journey idea. Quite honestly, I couldn't wait.

However, I wasn't directed, I didn't know how to spend this 'energy' – this expectation of me – and I did want to do this journey their way, use it to learn.

And while Teresa, 'Nightlight', the traditional alternative, wouldn't talk, Stars was nightly displaying the liberal thinking that had been my heritage; she might have been, with a few minor adjustments, good, liberal, Home Counties stock. I took refuge in her, the nearest available thing to Hampshire, to Tooting, to Melbourne probably, while I continued to bottle the old men's magic in, not sure where to channel it. I thought about making a hike out to the mountains. If I felt like looking back, I could. I could look down at the forest, the village, see how the dark lake looked in perspective – I was picturing the way if you pass light through shallows you see the shadows on the bed from the thicker belts of water, ripples defined.

But days passed by, and the mountains weren't going to be enough. I needed to get right out of here, this thicket. I needed a large empty space – Australia for instance.

'I can tell you the women's magics,' Stars whispered.

'You shouldn't say that,' I said. 'Wunjumboo will get you. Or the water thingy. What's it called?'

She sighed, extremely unimpressed. '"*He*," not "it". He is Wanjimaut.'

'That's right. A dragon. A fiery beast. He probably gave Kumbui his limp.'

I tried to find her eyes and searched the blackness over the ant carapace shine off her shoulder.

She wasn't afraid. Not of the poison that might have killed Yargee – or the magic, the ancestors, the AOGs. She was like me, though not as bad. *I* still had to learn to say 'the spirits are angry', instead of the rationalizing, 'there's an imbalance of energy.'

Once I asked Stars if she knew what had happened to Yargee. 'I was a sweet schoolgirl still,' she said. 'She was very old.' I said she was only about eighteen. Stars drew herself into my sheet, leaving me without it.

More nights of frustration, every other young man running about in the night, their shadows mocking me, my passive role here.

Time went by.

One day I was washing by the canoes at dawn, the sun rising over the trees on the far bank. Over those trees across the lake I heard a soft whoop – a ripping, plaintive cry that stood me still. The sound was coming all the way from Korogo, a Niowra village some ten miles away by canoe. From now on, it would start each day before sunrise: the crocodile spirit chasing through the air, cleaning it for the ancestral spirits, who would, if they were content, guide the bandees to the safety of the sanctified Nest, to learn, if the spirits were still content, all the lessons in submission that I, Benedix, had now – the evidence was overwhelming – forgotten.

Some nights, Stars used to whisper, casually, 'When are you departing for your journey?'

'You know I can't tell you. It's men's stuff.' Besides, I was the last person to know anything around here, she ought to know that by now.

I looked at her. How much did she know? And my Grandmother, my Bambo, an old dear with tortoise eyes and turtle-shell earrings, a bundle of them in each lobe – how much did she know? Living in her shack through the forest where the Kandengeis used to hide from the Japanese during the war. Her visits were never very long – she rarely stayed overnight – and she was happy to be among the Wunjumboos and other spirits that men ran from. There she was, buried among the fishing nets, saying with surprise, 'Egh?' every time a mosquito bit her, slapping her back, swinging her bones heavily at it. What was there to discover here, in this bald old lady? Stars promised so much.

Nightlight hardly ever talked when she came. 'Sssss! I must not. My weak blood will make you weak. If I talk, you will not like me.' And she lay, in silence, and I felt her heat on my neck, on my back, as I faced away, and we waited for the owl they call Ookoon to signal the all-clear, when she could go.

Stars was pushing me still. 'You can take me with you. We could meet outside the village. I could tell you women's things.' I got angry at being tempted and then even felt guilt. I felt as Wallace did on occasion, apparently hogging the confessional at Brurui until, Daniel had said, Father George was feeling woozy.

Kaavon sitting among the cobwebs with his spells . . .

In the middle of the day when we might have been sleeping, this dry-skinned man was blowing over me, or I was crushing more largee and kamuin underfoot, being cleansed.

Afterwards, I would go to the forest and crash around chasing pigs with Spencer. There was another sport – digging for jungle-fowl eggs on another clan's land. The lake was low now. Less rain in the mountains, which fed the lakes that were sustaining the water-lilies, the swordfish, the nailfish, the dull macaw, the crocodile, us. There were fewer mosquitoes in the grass and more lizards – wiggly strings that flicked ahead of us on the paths. Waiting for the all-clear from Waita, Johnson's dog, we'd lie silent among the palm sprouts. I'd notice a *kwandja*, a bat, above us. Or the shadow of a fly squatting and pivoting, silhouetted through a palm leaf; the tubes of bark that lay open, hinged from tree trunks, others suspended twenty feet up, held by palm thorns. But the longer you waited still, the more you saw that everything was moving. The bat shuffled its velvet wings, leaves rose and fell in the draughts of bugs. The silent clay below us was only the cap of an ant-routing system. A fruit ball lifted its studs from the forest floor and was a spider. Very little was what it seemed.

Another night Stars said, 'I have been thinking hard.'

I said, 'Again?'

'A little.'

'You mustn't – the forest isn't a place to think in. At least I don't think it is.'

'I was thinking that if I came on your journey I can be helpful. The Smaark girl is good in one manner. She can fish all day without getting tired and hungry. She can be kind to your headaches and not lazy. But she will not leave the village with you, and I can do all these things *and* do buying for you.'

She was spoiling my nest here. I so much wanted her to go with me, the Westernized female. We could learn both sides of the argument, the complete Niowra person.

But I couldn't face telling my wau. This was not what he had in mind for me at all. So the trouble brewed and stewed inside me, as I heard the Crocodile Nest calls, the dreamy whoops and sighs from the novices, the crocodile initiates at Korogo. Crocodiles – male crocodiles – are merciless. They will eat their young if the female allows. The female stands guard, nest-bound. She can't float free.

I cut myself once – nothing to do with a canoeing accident, this time. At Wallace's house, the women parted from the entrance, looking at the bump on my head.

Priscilla said, 'Blood.'

Errol pranced around. 'Hee-hee! *Katim Nek*, Benedix!' Songbird flicked up a dirty rag with her toes. 'Nelson, you can clean it.' The others, too, were strongly in their roles: Spencer rose for me. Wallace stayed where he was.

I walked around in circles, mopping my forehead. Wallace looked at the clay footprints that I was leaving. 'Wallace,' I said, still walking. 'Let's get out of the village.'

Spencer said, quietly, 'Benedix, I am sorry.'

An accident, I explained. Wallace said, 'Hmm. Stupid.'

Spencer said, 'You'd like to go where? The forest?'

'No thanks.'

'Shopping?' Wallace said, suddenly up off his stool.

'AAGH!'

Wallace took me to our Grandmother, where I now always go when I'm having one of my crises. We paddled over before the sun was too white, then walked through the grasses where the boys dig for clay catapult pellets. We were now well within July, the time of year often devoted to fighting over fishing grounds with Nyaurengei.

We arrived at Bambo's shack, which had recently collapsed, the stilts chewed away by the mud. One post had grown into a tree, but she sat by herself happily in the shade within the walls of fishing netting.

'*Apman gambi!*' I said. Bambo didn't stir her worn stumps but smiled, showing her gums, a juicy pink from her slack black lips. She waved us towards her using her hands as flags. Where the sun was on her skin she was all glassy from the hard rub of her bones against canoes, nets, or the clay bowls they make at Chambri.

She wasn't alone. Nightlight was here, fiddling over by the canoes.

Some scheme or other of Wallace's, I thought. 'Morning, Teresa!' I said briskly. She didn't budge. She perched on the crocodile-headed prow of a canoe, her hand over the snout. Her eyes were on Wallace. She looked as if she was waiting for permission to go. 'Nightlight must have been out fishing. She has called in here,' Wallace said. He turned to me. 'You can talk as much as you like.'

Nightlight turned down her head, her large, girl's face waterlit. In earlier days I'd behaved too much like a Westerner in public – teasing as Daniel did sometimes. But she took my consideration of her feelings as doubt in her, my hesitancy as distaste, my generosity as a pay-off. Nowadays I did my best to behave abruptly, like a proper Man. That way she could react as a Woman. And I wouldn't let her down now in front of her grandmother.

'Cooking?' I said, stiffly.

She said, raising up her head with the confidence of someone who knows her place in the world: 'Yes, some beautiful fish, cousin.'

'I want some.'

'Yes, you may take them.'

She grinned at the water, then up to Wallace, light now dancing on her neck and chin. Wallace smiled with satisfaction. I seemed to be coming along just fine. But how wrong he could be. I was saying to myself, you're no innocent, Nightlight, sitting there with your toes in the water, humble as pie. I see your game. And so do the other men sometimes. Why else are they so scared of you? You're a threat. Much of what we learnt in the *banis* was the means to power. You also learn it – courting, listening. And I'd place a bet that that's why you and other girls are often over here, gleaning it from your old granny – cheeks rolled down her face, teeth fallen in the lake over the years.

Teresa came with a bowl of her fish, and I ate them with the old lady, in the shade of her fishing tackle, thinking of all the things I could learn from her.

Each night as bandees we used to walk – still bleeding, and as fragile as china – through the darkened village, whistling like the bird called *swé*, warning women to hide. But *you* saw us. And in the houses, after eating another meal behind a screen of leaves, when we laid ourselves down on our bellies and waited until the hour before dawn, and the cry from the Crocodile Nest which called us back – you saw all that too. All very well you sitting there as if you're senile. You attended us in the night, with our stomach aches and cramps. You saw the secrets we wore, and held – the objects now buried beneath the spirit house. The old men, younger than you, permitted you this, on the grounds that you are no more female than they. 'The female blood in you has drained off.' That's what they say. 'Your breasts are flat, there is hair on your chin.'

You women get the last laugh, don't you? The men may marry one or two of you each, loaf around all day and exclude you from all official administration, but in the end you live longer and, when they think you're safely neuter, gather up all their secrets anyway.

'Teresa would like to know about your journey,' Wallace said in Pidgin, calling her over. I said we could look from the lakeside.

The three of us stood by the shore. I remembered Bambo and called her. She was fast asleep. I said to Wallace and Teresa, 'See those mountains, up there? Well, I suppose I'm heading that way. No one has told me yet.'

'You are going where the air is blue?'

That's right, into the blue, I thought. We all looked together into the haze and the foothills slouching beyond the pan of calm lily water. I noticed for the first time the way the mountains glower and brood at us here.

'There are naked people there?' Teresa asked.

'Oh. Primitives,' Wallace said. 'They still take heads.' He told us they added them up like Kaavon used to do. They had pretty little tassels, *tambanja*, on their lime gourd containers, so you knew how strong each man was.

'And what is beyond the dangerous primitives?' She was looking out, deep into the clouds, beyond the forest that was, in part, these Niowra people.

'If I carry on that way, I'll come to Australia. Eventually.'

'Your home?'

'No, it –'

'It's where Master Ken comes from,' Wallace said, referring to the store owner in Pagwi. He proceeded with a discourse on Australia. The whitemen lived in the towns, the blackpeople lived in the bush, where it was too hot for trees. There were no leaves, no fish. The white people lived near the seaside, like our town, Wewak.

I didn't know much about Australia myself, but Wallace seemed to be about right. The bulk of the whitemen lived in the 'boomerang', the sweep of coast along the south-east, some more around other bits of fertile area along the coast – that left Alice Springs, Australia's navel. Otherwise, they never much saw the blackpeople.

'The blackpeople have a dry home,' Nightlight said. 'They must be very thin.'

I said I wasn't sure. I'd heard that the black people drank a lot nowadays. Drinking probably made them fat.

'They have snakes?'

'Probably. Certainly spiders.'

'The spiders must be big and strong to live without trees. You are very brave.'

'No, he isn't,' said Wallace. 'It is customary for whitemen to travel. That is why he must travel further than us on his journey.'

'Must I?' I thought. 'The village isn't sending me all the way to Australia, is it?' After a while I said, one interesting thing is that they didn't use bows and arrows. 'Read it somewhere.' Most of the rest of my knowledge about Australia was through friends who'd taken a year off to go sheep farming and come back with stories of flies and 'beach bums'. I told Nightlight, 'They also use a boomerang, a carved bit of wood to spin at the kangaroos.'

'Ah yes,' Wallace said, tapping his fingers contentedly on his chest. 'Father George told me. It can't be as good as our spears.'

'They have those as well, apparently.'

Teresa said, 'Oh, they are sad people. They run in the sun all day and have no fish or sago to eat.'

Wallace said it was time to go. We'd best take Bambo's canoe and do a short cut to the path through the trees to our own canoe. I understood. It would look bad if our arrival back coincided with Nightlight's – even wives alighted in the village at different moorings to their husbands'. I went up to Bambo and said that I'd see her before I left on my journey.

She said, 'Apmanda.' A good thing. And, neither sad nor happy, but as a simple aside, 'Maybe I'll be dead, maybe not.' Over by the water's edge, magnified by the still shield of water, came the sound of Nightlight in tears. Tears for her grandma; how sweet.

Bambo laughed. 'She is a good girl, crying for you.'

'Er . . .' I flustered. 'For you, I'm sure.'

Bambo conceded. 'She is a good girl.'

'Yes, a good girl – she'll make someone a good wife.' I watched her face, but she was happy with what I'd said and I saw she understood. Whatever Wallace thought, she really wasn't expecting me to marry Teresa. Then Bambo said something extraordinary. Her devastated skin flapped from her arms, as she said, forcefully, 'Wumvunnavan. You keep saying you cannot become properly [like us].' Her voice was firm, almost hard. 'But, Wumvunnavan, Benedix, you will see before long that you shall be like us.'

I was shocked. I'd made a guess that the Women had hidden power, but I'd never heard a Woman deliver a policy statement like this. *You keep saying* . . . But I hadn't said anything concerning this to any Woman. *You shall be like us.* Since when did Women make such presumptuous claims to men?

I might have dismissed this as mistranslation of her bad Pidgin. But she hadn't finished.

'The Niowra spirit finds no use in hatching a man of the fireside, but needs you as a man of true men.'

Shaken, I backed off and waved, rather foolishly, to them both – Nightlight wiping her tears with her skirt, Bambo getting on with net weaving, a shuttle in her gums.

The Niowra spirit finds no use in hatching a man of the fireside, but needs you as a man of true men. I knew this, that the Man-making was not designed as an end, that it was a preface, something enabling you to begin, but no one had said it this clearly. From the canoe, I watched Nightlight gather herself up and settle near Bambo. We pushed off with the paddles, blades shaped like the crocodile's amphibian claw.

Their natty phrases did have a way of sticking in the mind, and this one was like a charter from the women. It belittled outsiders, whitemen, who thought women here were necessarily second-class.

Mid-August I thought to myself, though in fact it was still late July. The water was low, the muds exposed, cracked into tiles. This was the time that you saw little flies knitting low in the air over the joints in the clay. The little flies, the *nieniak*, which made a home in the damp nostrils of the crocodiles that were waiting in the mud for water to come again.

Leaving this canoe, we crossed the baked mud – stepping from plateau to plateau, ooze winking from the shafts as we passed over the half-baked crocodile beds.

'You are quiet,' Wallace said. 'Are you now worried about your journeying?' He was asking with genuine concern. I decided then that I was sometimes too hard a judge of Wallace. He said, 'You will not have to kill anyone. The old men do not want that.'

'I do realize that the head-hunting days are over, if that's what you mean, Wallace.'

'If you are ever afraid, you use the special number five, *tambanak* – you remember it from the *banis*.'

I did – the sacred number that measured every dance beat, every ritual. It co-ordinated you with the past, locking you on to the old references.

I'll take her, I suddenly thought. I'd take Stars and she could explore the female while I tried to cope with the male. I'd choose my moment and then tell Wallace.

Later, it seemed to be Nightlight's turn to visit. She said little, as normal, but wouldn't answer me when I asked if she was well. I asked if there was something the matter. After a while she said, 'You can paddle the canoes in the dark?'

Then I knew the trouble. There was a story from Mindimbit, the Seventh Day Adventist stronghold down the river. An English adventurer, Christina Dodwell, paddled near there after dark one night. The rumour down there is, she's what the Adventists call 'a witch'.

I said it was just the way of whitemen. We couldn't sense spirits. It was a handicap. I told her a story. A film crew brought Christina in by helicopter. They'd arranged a Man-making ceremony for the cameras at Kraimbit and then the BBC got Steven, from Yenchenmangua, to take off his sun-glasses, strip off a bit, and, when they'd bought a farm-reared crocodile and tied it firmly down, asked him to whirl his spear bravely into it, making the crocodile kick as much as possible for the cameras. 'You see, whitemen love adventure – they're bored at home, that's all it is.'

Nightlight didn't think the story convincing. She murmured quietly, asking about the best cut of meat, 'Did Steven get the meat from the tail?'

The next day was a Sunday. I went to the Mass, sitting with the group of small boys beleaguered by all the women overflowing from their side. Afterwards, feeling deaf from the screeching congregation, I talked to Wallace. He was having trouble with his surplice, which wasn't designed for his muscle-padded shoulders or best shirts, three of which were underneath.

'Nathan walked into our church once,' he said. 'He wanted to preach and *singsing*. We had to stone him.'

Stone him? 'I know that Nathan is obstinate, but . . .'

'He has a hard head.'

'You scored a direct hit, then?'

'No,' said Wallace, sadly.

Nathan was always quoting St Paul about Christians being forbidden to dabble with magic, and so I reminded Wallace that Nathan said the Catholic stance was unchristian.

'The Bible says, people will come and sit down at the feast of the kingdom of God. Then those who are now last will be first and those who are now first will be last. Luke 13:30. And there's also Matthew 19:30. Father George agrees with what I say about the *banis*. We were strong when we learnt to be like slaves. "Wallace, this is also the Christian way," he says to me. "The rich must pass through the eye of a needle but it's too hard."'

This was the Second Vatican Council in action – 'Inculturalization' I'd heard one stray missionary call it. God, Rome now believed, was everywhere, even among pagans. He was waiting to be encouraged. This was no longer, according to the Catholics, a God-forsaken land.

Wallace wrapped up his surplice. Together we shut the broken cane door.

'Poor equals rich. Bottom equals top. Jesus knows this even when a screaming baby, like Glen. Jesus is very clever. Many times more clever than Nathan. Jesus knew he had to get away from his people into the wilderness. He was like you.'

'Oh, I don't think I'd quite go as far as that, you know.'

Wallace sighed. 'You *big-hed*. I *know* he had a beard. *And* a father that wasn't like yours. But he went to the desert to get away from his people, and talk to the Holy Spirits just like you.'

There wasn't much I could say to that. 'There's something else I was wondering.' I allowed time for a renewed sigh to die down. 'The strength of the women.'

'Kandengei's womens are good.'

'I don't mean just in getting food. You heard Bambo, what she said? They've got it wrapped up, haven't they?'

Wallace was hugging his surplice as if it was a comfort blanket. I could see him thinking, 'Why did I have to choose you as a Brother? It's such bad luck.' Somehow, in the space of a couple of sentences, I'd got to him. 'Your wau told me to expect this, but it is so hard for me.' He had the look of a dishonourably discharged soldier.

'We will find your wau later. Now you must lie down.' Wallace was backing me past his house, off through the village.

My wau wasn't in until the evening. It was raining buckets. People were chewing betelnuts to keep themselves warm – 'they are our cup of winter cocoa,' Daniel used to say.

My wau was eating boiled eggs. Mosquitoes gathered on them, attracted by the heat. Word had got to him already. 'Do not worry, you are meant to be hot-headed before the journey.' But he stood up and, seeing this, the other members of the household got to their feet, and gave him space to pace in. Then, in twos or threes, they left. They had seen this behaviour. It seemed they didn't want to be witnesses.

I looked at his feet again, the faint garters of mud above where he'd washed them. He hung over me; I remembered the unnecessarily silent way he'd done this to me as a bandee.

He sat down and faced me. He closed his eyes and looked utterly peaceful, then snapped his eyes open. '*Laua*, you are learning our custom.'

'I just get the feeling that they –'

His jaw took the light and his face was black. 'Listen. That towngirl will trick you.'

'But maybe I can learn a little – just a little – from the women. *As well*, I mean. For instance, in the same insulting way that whitemen label village houses "huts", outsiders think women don't serve food during their monthly period because they're considered unclean. But that's an over-simplification. It's fear of the *power* of that female blood.' I added, because he had gone so very silent on me, 'Just an idea.'[12]

'We were expecting you to behave unsteady in your stomach.' The stomach, the seat of my emotions, the New Guinean version of the heart. 'But I must enforce the law – too many customs are broken now that the AOGs are trying to throw us away.'

The way the custom went, young Errol, as a member of my clan, could end up taking my punishment for me – no such thing as individual responsibility here. They'd beat him extra hard during his *banis*. There were also other possibilities.

'*Laua*, if you carry on, I shall stand in the spirit house and order Wallace to kill one of his pigs for me.' Not only could he do this, he could call another Niowra village to come and beat up Kandengei as a punishment – it happened to Nyaurengei recently. The women were ordered to hide in their mosquito nets while the men ran around with blackened faces killing anything in their path. Four pigs, three cats, two dogs, Johnson said.

He cracked another betelnut in his teeth and smiled to show it wasn't really my fault. 'I will go to Kaavon and ask what to do with your female blood. Maybe we'll take the girls away so they cannot infect you again.'

'You wouldn't be thinking of punishing Errol, my young Brother, for this? I know it's the tradition, but it's not his fault I'm not fitting in very well. You wouldn't beat him, would you?'

He smiled a little harder. I took this as a yes.

'Maybe you could beat me instead.' Or Wallace, I thought. He wouldn't mind too much, really.

'I have said you have done nothing wrong. You are sick, a little.

It is partly expected. Anyway, there's no problem. We can beat Errol.'

'Yes, but . . . Please?'

'This is not the custom. You can be beaten instead only if Kaavon says.'

Then he looked annoyed with himself, and flicked his eyes to me. '*Laua*, you think too much of yourself.'

I did. And I asked too many questions, and thought too much, and I couldn't really take myself as seriously as he did, calling me *Laua*. I wondered what to suggest next. I'd thought it was quite nice of me to have offered to be beaten.

'But if Kaavon says, you can go to the Korogo *banis* some time to be beaten.'

'Thanks,' I said, and I was grateful. The pain was nothing – I'd been through far worse. No, more important was getting this rationalizing mind thrashed out of me. When could I ever stop it, the questions surfacing, resurfacing, asking 'Why, Why, Why?'

Next morning, Wallace got me out of bed. 'Get up!'

'Why?'

'The *avookwaarks* want you.'

'Oh dear.'

'You have not done anything wrong. It is your body. You are sick. You need fresh magic.'

'Fresh magic, you reckon . . .' We marched towards my purification. 'Kaavon's angry?'

'He cannot be angry with you. You are infected. But I do not know. Try to ask him.'

We were at the *geygo*. Wallace stopped. I stood in its shadow, about to go in, already smelling the cool, slow decay.

Wallace said, 'The *avookwaarks* think you must leave soon.'

'So I'm ready?'

'You are not ready. But it is time to go anyway.'

'And what does that mean?'

'It means I will start proceedings.'

Under the austere cobwebs, I stared at a belly-button stretched over a drumskin waist. Kaavon was mumbling away, raining words with a lot of consonants on me.

'When's this going to end?' I thought. He went on and on, worse than usual, emptying the words from wherever they were filed away with all the other crocodile memorabilia, name after name of ancestor, name after name of *waarkdumba*, the crocodile nests – records going back, presumably, right to the great one, the great crocodile in the swamp. My eyes strayed. I caught sight of the mysterious packages of palm sheath, tying up the stones, the sacred stones brought in from distant forests. I smiled to myself. The Niowras had got their own collection of fossils, I thought.

Kaavon had stopped. And he opened his mouth in my direction and said something. I looked up in surprise and banged my head on the bench above us.

I rubbed my head. 'Did you speak to me?'

His eyes were following my hand, as I rubbed at my scalp. He was looking lightheaded from his trance still.

'Wumvunnavan?' He raised the word from where he sat near the ground, offering it gently. Then he tucked his wrap between his knees, smartening himself into a different, more conversational mode. He spoke Pidgin, a very deliberate style which, not to be patronizing, to me sounded quaint. 'This is not very precedented, but yes, I would like to say words to you.' I remembered that years ago I'd said to my wau that I'd liked the sound of Kaavon, and now I couldn't believe my luck. He was in one of his rare talking moods. This was the man who sat on his low stool, totally ignored, until Senior Man would shout out above the rabble, 'Shut up! I think Kaavon is talking.' 'Of course he isn't.' 'Yes he is!' Men would be peering at him. 'You sure?' 'Yes, he's definitely saying something.'

'I would like to tell you I am not angry with you. You were the best bandee. If a tourist comes here, I tell them, "Mr Benedix Wumvunnavan was the best bandee."'

I wanted to interrupt already. I had *not* been the best bandee. I had learnt to withstand pain, conquering my physical fears like the rest, but that was my body. My other two-thirds, my mind and spirit, were not remoulded by all the bashing. Some part of me had always been rationalizing and independent, closed to the full fear of the spirits.

'And now you go on a journey. Good. It is what Men do. So, we put much magic in you . . .' He looked up, towards the exit. 'But, sadly, this is not a matter for you to consider. Sorry, sorry for mentioning it, Mr Wumvunnavan.'

It seemed that I was meant to leave, though I hadn't got in any questions yet – this was the man partly responsible for making my life a confusion over the last weeks and I had a lot to ask. And I was just beginning to find him a pleasure to be with. He was placing his words so gently. I searched his eyes, which were bright but mostly lost in tired lids. But then Kaavon lowered his hollow-looking rib-cage, and began smoothing his wrap along his thighs. 'Wallace may not have told you. I have had some dealings with whitemen. Master Ken, and some other types.'

I was finding him a civil man; his extraordinarily quiet but distinct presence didn't suggest the word 'head-hunter' at all.

'I know many things about the whiteman. His customs. I have made a special study,' he continued, vaguely, drifting off a bit. He's an old gentleman, I thought, amused at the world and its antics.

But he wasn't in a position to be amused. I said, 'Did you know the AOGs want to topple you from power?'

It didn't seem to be a concern, he smiled deeply – maybe at this, maybe at that – and was then adjusting the tuck of the wrap at his navel. He was rolling a foot-length strip of the *Sydney Morning Herald*, manufacturing a cigarette. 'They're going to act soon,' I said. I put some vim into it, because he was reacting as if it didn't matter. 'You'll be out. The forest and you are about to get the chop.'

I got to the point. His lips fattened, loosening, seeing me tense up. I wanted to understand so much. Before I could stop myself I plunged in. 'The universal laws. Every action has a reaction, they said at school. And they said it in the *banis* as well.'

He said, slowing me, running a finger on a bench strut as if testing for household dust, 'There are only a few rules in the whole world, I think.'

I hadn't actually expected him to agree. What *could* this old killer know of the whole world? But, as he hadn't been baffled by me, I went on. Weeks of repression – I had to let the pressure out. I said, 'Every action causes a reaction. It's physics. Power comes in opposites. You have potential power over someone when you are submissive to them. That's how I learned it at school, that's how Wallace learned it in the Bible, that's how we learned it in the *banis*. As bandees, once we were at last like slaves and under your feet, cowering, we began to have power over you. Because, just as soon as we were fully under your feet and you had, apparently, achieved total mastery over us, resting your entire weight on us, we, in our submissive, totally subservient role, had the power to tumble you off your feet. Do you see what I'm getting at?'

He raised a hand to his mouth. He was silent, but he was definitely chuckling quietly through his fingers. 'Mr Wumvunnavan, you have been thinking so hard about all the world's customs!'

I plunged on, because he wasn't laughing at what I was saying, only at me. 'In the same way, a king like you has to watch out. The top man is sometimes bottom. You are at the mercy of the people at your feet. You are potentially the most vulnerable man in the kingdom. You will fall the furthest. The law of polarity – more elementary physics.'

Kaavon sat there among his cigarette fumes, and became still, his silence calming. Not a man of commanding stature, of long, wise nose, of wizened brow. Just the watchful eyes, hardly showing from dry, wrinkled and soft eyelids. 'The top man is sometimes bottom,' he said. But he was just repeating my words. Then he said, 'I know much about your whiteman's world already. It is an interesting one. Sometimes when I am unconscious I travel to your home.' I had heard this claim from other shaman. In a trance they travel, could become familiar with the grey tarmac of Tooting Bec, the hazardous road bends around Alton, Hampshire.

'What you must know is this business: a whiteman, George, came and asked questions about *sagi* dances and caught them in his notebook and camera. I do not like that in whiteman's custom, this catching – snaps, words. Whitemen like stamping the forest with their shoe footprints.'

Here was the man who perched on his little stool all day, not going even into broad daylight. He was the one you went to when you had an ailment. You sat down with him in the cool, and stayed quiet. You came out with your feet smelling of herbs, and neck stippled with betelnut juice. Fine: it was the local ritual for cleansing you. You were united in mind and spirit, and came out afterwards feeling better, as you would from any mosque or church. But he wasn't speaking here as a priest. He was speaking now with the authority of a traveller, a man who'd knocked about a bit – though he probably hadn't even been to the local town, Wewak. And he was condemning the entire history of Western exploration! Excited as I was to hear him talking on my wavelength, even I wouldn't have gone that far.

He said, calmly, without applying pressure, 'No offence to you, Wumvunnavan, but you come here and catch our knowledge too.'

We both knew this was true – even listening, one way of learning, was a form of capture. You weakened the sealed strength of the tribal unit. But he must face up to it that his culture was dying, and I hadn't come thrusting anything on him, imposing my own power. I told him that – 'I was hoping you might have picked me out *because* of my wanting to listen.'

Suddenly Kaavon laughed. 'Two hundred kina you gave!' He chuckled, rocking his stool – 'It wasn't for the money!'

I settled on my stool.

Kaavon scratched his chin, which was thin, and dry-skinned, like the rest of him: just canopy-covered bones, but somewhere beneath it all, something free, unconfined. He said, 'It is true. You were the whiteman who listened, so maybe we liked you. But you write a book, you sum us up, and you kill us.'

The words hung on. I summed them up. I killed them. We weren't at cross purposes. All seeking of knowledge was taking power. But what could you do other than what I had done, not write all the details of the ritual, and our emotional responses?

He said, 'On the day you came, I said to the men, Benedix is all right. This whiteman is not such a bad whiteman. Niowras are dying by the power of the Christians. He can have our power, if it suits him.'

I said to myself again, Kaavon is meant to be an old, hard-bitten head-hunter. However he has the confidence of someone with what anthropologists call a 'world view'. How can a 'world view' have come from the forest, a place of knotted, thrusting, scampering things? He was trained to kill, I was taught not to. How could we be communicating so well – the common ground rules of the initiation?

I said, 'And presumably it suited the village?' I looked at his concealed eyes – embedded studs of paste jewellery. But not a trickster's; he had power over the villagers but he was not laughing at them. He was not laughing at me.

'In the beginning, we thought you'd bring us money. Then Wallace said he had found only 200 kina in your clothes. What a pity! That was while Andrew took you to wash in the ditch where we take all whitemen. Then we brought you to us and you gave your rude request. We saw you cannot even stand up and give a speech. So it was easy – we were going to dismiss you. But the next thing, the *whole village* wanted the ceremony. You had made us make you a No-obligation Agreement. I laughed. I said to your wau, this whiteman has persuasive qualities.'

This buffer in the sun-pitted skin had always been inaccessible, lost in his own world. Now, seeing the way he was content in his judgement of me, a stranger, I felt as if he had access to that world even while we were talking. There seemed to be so much room within him. I longed for a better idea of all that space.

'You see, I am saying what you know already, but it is a good thought. Mr Wumvunnavan, sum up the forest and you will kill it. I have seen this, I can reassure you. That's all.'

I left him there, below the sacred stones parcelled in sheaths of palm.

Stars on the Water had always been here – rock solid, a reminder of my fossils, bits of ancient sea bed sediment now in cardboard boxes in the attic, each wrapped in newspaper, flakes of our planet, something real and secure around which my thoughts might coalesce. But now I saw the village had its own stones, its own fundamentals, hunks of Earth Goddess if you like a more European metaphor, and Kaavon, sitting silent in the cool all day, had, or so it seemed, taken on something of their properties.

I found myself with a new-found confidence in the Niowras. I still wanted to run away from them – more than ever, because they were rounder characters now. Before they had been a fascinating, highly efficient people of an exotic land – they were ecologically more sound than us, but lacking in the more subtle of the arts and sciences. Now, in Kaavon, I was finding they had a man who was as deeply rooted as the stones themselves. He had a basic wisdom and he was someone deeply set in this infernal village, offshoot of the forest. He was right in the thick of it, maintaining the niche – whether it was to be in the forest or the West, and for the moment still finding no use in house-bound males, but needing true men.

Sometimes I'm lying beside Stars on the Water and my mind wanders; spread out beside her in the heat I think of her again as something more solid than mere flesh; she represents basic values for me again. But since that meeting with Kaavon it's never been the same; afterwards, I was able to place less reliance on her, more on him, sitting there among the real stones of the spirit house. The fossils in my attic, the stones for these people here: they are just about the only objects that won't decay; they are a marker for the villagers – a pivot in circular time, and it's right that they are sacred.

However, the villagers were well aware that I might yet be led astray before the start of my journey. 'Laua, you cannot have trouble with the women. Throw one away, if she talks.'

Another example of the attitude I'm meant to have about women: once I ran to the assistance of a little girl screaming from a doorway. She called even louder when she saw me coming up the steps. And there, indoors, was a little cotton screen, and the different sounds coming from it, a woman panting and the startled cry of a new baby.

'Womenses business,' Wallace said after, and I had to be content with that. I'm a Junior Man, a *geenjumboo*, not like the missionaries or anthropologists who are allowed to see some of both Male and Female ceremonies because they're hermaphrodites, weak in both sexes.

You learn the way things work here, that for a man it doesn't pay to probe about women. I have to stumble across their doings by accident – on that occasion, for example, I noted that while the mother is in labour everything is passed in and out through a window. What the picture is overall, I don't know, but I pay my taxes to enable universities to find objective answers to overall questions and I content myself with learning from somewhere near the inside about specifics – the males, the Smaarks, and occasionally, the secrets slipping from the two women they send through the mosquito-loaded grass.

Bambo has said nothing more. However little warning I give, each time I go, as if by chance, Nightlight is there, waylaid on a fishing trip. Bambo sits in a web of fishing tackle and I ignore Nightlight fidgeting with some basket or other she always seems to be making for me. No one ever expresses their disappointment when I don't walk off with her into the forest. In this matter, they are very patient. She wears a piece of dull purple sheet, bound around and around, or the white Victorian dress that I like.

Wallace escorts me home – taking me to bathe first, as if to train me for a day when I will need to wash her tell-tale scent off. For the moment I take comfort enough from the beginnings of a nest she's building tenderly around me.

Some things I'll never learn. Even now Wallace reminds me of my deficiencies. He sends Smaark boys after me to keep me out of trouble – little squads that keep one eye on me as they play with their toys, often a metallic bug placed on a spindle and whirled buzzing through the air. Daniel, back again now, thinks it a disgrace. 'The little boys follow you like cops and robbers. But you are a *geenjumboo*.'

I'm not so proud. I'm incompetent here and I appreciate my gang of helpers. All these closed faces – how can you deal with them alone? I now see that having been through the initiation helps – every character was laid open. The bullies, the leaders, the warriors, everyone except Kaavon, who stayed apart, and it's another reason why the ceremony is secret – as we've discussed, exclusively shared knowledge is binding, a powerful force.

With all the intrigue, why trust your wau – confide your marriage fears, Brotherly fears? He is meant to tell you whom to trust and you might ask, why have *Him* on the list to start with? Actually, it's a confidence based on his role as Mother; it's the son's birthright. Few mothers will cheat their offspring. That is the way they teach it to us – and I for one swear by mine.

As regards the remaining villagers, I blunder through – Errol accumulating punishments every time I make another mistake. No, Daniel, I'll keep my little entourage, God bless 'em.

I'd been here some two months now. Still the dry season – the water thick and shallow. I now knew Kaavon was on my side; through him I had a let-out clause. But the Niowras were what people call a tribe, and while I was here and still learning, he poured his religion on me, and the village poured their expectations on me, and now I knew I had a valid excuse to get away I couldn't wait for my journey to begin. Any day now, presumably, someone would just say the word, and I'd be off.

The Crocodile Nest at Korogo was still in progress, and one day I was with the other Junior Men, idling by the canoes, trying my best to be interested in their idea for a fight with Nyaurengei – clubs and sticks at dawn. My wau called me to the *geygo* and said, '*Laua*, are you feeling strong?'

'Why?'

'Not sick in any way?'

'Er, no.' This was the first confirmation that I had been chosen to go to Korogo – they were having a big feast there; it wasn't so much the food you remembered from these occasions, it was the violence. Junior Men had to help protect the bandees as other Niowra Junior Men had once helped us, during our time in the Nest.

Then he said, '*Laua*, you were a good bandee.'

Let's be honest about this. He was questioning whether I'd still be any good in the *banis*. Then I'd behaved well, learning to share and also not cry. But since, it seemed, all my independent thoughts had sprung up again and he was wondering if I'd disgrace the village by bursting into tears in front of the Korogo men.

Me? I was as physically brave as the next man; it was being able to fear their ancestors that I wasn't good at.

I told my wau I wasn't scared. Of course I would be a little, nearer the time, but that would be normal and a chance to prove your bravery.

Kaavon beckoned from by the Yaark bench. He said, cheerily, 'We can hope this can be good cleansing. Antiseptic for your journey.'

My sentiment exactly. *This* man had a grasp of the situation. I needed my rationalizing numbness blasted out of me; nearly all Westerners did. I smiled back and left him, reversing, careful not to touch the firewood according to yet another custom – this one that you can't do this until you've killed a crocodile. I trotted over to Wallace's house and started searching everyone's bags for my bandages. I wasn't unhappy to be going – at last I'd be able to tick off some of the vast punishment owed to Errol.

Jackson, a *wanbanis*, came in.

'Are you coming, Cousin?' He was talking to Wallace.

'You're going shopping in Pagwi?'

'No. We are making up a party.'

'A party?' His eyes danced in ecstasy. 'Tinned food?'

'No, the Korogo beating party,' I said.

But it was too late. Wallace was obliged to help me. And soon we had eight young men.

We pushed off in the largest canoe, the *avookwaarks* perched regally on their stools, the rest of us by their feet, having to scoop the blood-bloated mosquitoes out from under our buckled-up legs. Women by the water's edge looked up through the reds and greens of the hunched gooniangra trees to watch us go – Songbird holding up Glen, the little brute, Priscilla washing with a sheet fastened around her, Teresa among soapsuds. More women ran forward as the engine started. They were happy seeing us go away smiling and joking, as if we didn't care.

The air was moving fast against us now, cleaning the mosquitoes away, forcing time, encouraging us to think forward.

Wallace was talking in Pidgin to no one in particular, but meaning to impress the *avookwaarks*, who weren't listening. 'Sometimes I'm asked why Benedix is going to Australia, which is empty. The answer is simple, Jackson. He needs to see the trees from the wood.' He breathed deeply, and reflected on the world. 'You know why whiteman often wear glasses? Because, like Benedix, they have difficulty seeing. Some even have scales on their eyes.'

'Contact lenses,' I said.

Jackson said, 'And Australia is even further than the mountains. Eight miles even.'

We wound out of the lakes, into the river world, into the brown flow of the Sepik and also the bright intensity of the Western doorway. Dug-outs jetted up and down the river, ironclad houses stood rigid on the banks, displacing trees. The Junior Men put on shirts, the Reverend

Crocodiles went silent. The *avookwaark* called Naow held his pipe with gritted teeth, Kumbui ruminated on his betelnut.

'Why are you coming, Errol?' Jackson asked. Errol was sitting facing me, catapulting at the fruit bats which were lumbering back to their roosts, where they'd join the others, garage mechanics' rags dangling from nails. 'You won't be able to go into the *banis*, anyway, and you are just wasting room.'

'I told you. I'm going to the aid post. I am sick. So is Samsonite.'

'Girl!' Samsonite said.

'Monkeynut!' Errol said.

'Clamshitter!' Samsonite said.

Wallace, sitting behind me, his knees under my shoulder blades, said, 'Benedix! Errol is a *big-hed*. Stick him! He is your Young Brother, stick him!'

I biffed his shoulder a little. Wallace did it properly, on his head. Errol let out a sound: 'Ai-ee!'

Wallace was nudging me with his knees, because I hadn't done my bit as Older Brother. To prevent depression setting in – I had failed again – I yelled, startling everyone, 'Monkey-mouth!' Kumbui and Naow rocked on their stools, ballooning out in satisfaction. Wallace said in my ear, 'They are pleased.'

Everyone was laughing, making an effort to forget the beatings coming up. Errol's small face was murderous, and, unfairly, I thought, fixed on mine. He had his catapult flexed in his hands and I felt like Goliath. Wallace nudged me with his knees. I whacked Errol with my mosquito swipe. He mouthed at Samsonite, 'Fig-face.'

Soon we were alongside the high bank of Korogo, and the women were getting out of our way. Kumbui said loudly that Korogo smelt like a town. We all knew he didn't like the way it was cramped against the river edge, all neat and tidy, the grass trimmed to missionary lawn length to keep down the mosquitoes, the women free and easy and every other man a robber. We helped him from the canoe, and Errol threw our mooring rope hard at a Korogo boy. We made our entrance.

From their *geygo*, the hefty beat of the slit gongs announcing us. I was feeling the tension now. My knees were weak. I was glad; I was already a little scared. I would therefore be able to show some physical courage. Some bandees must be fighting off tears now – already, before it had even begun. We walked through the village towards the Nest, the bellowing of the slit gongs, the crocodile spirit himself, coming to us through the mud of the ground, up from under our bare feet.

'Are you nervous?' asked Jackson. 'I'm not,' he added quickly. 'I was just wondering if you were.'

'No, I'm not either,' I said.

The shuddering note of the crocodile voice again.

'Oooh, it's Benedix,' a woman said, sadly. But I didn't look – you weren't allowed to be interested.

The Nest was a little back from the river, at the end of an avenue of houses from where women clung to stilts watching us approach the high screen of leaves.

An awful silence, after the last, the fifth, round of bellowing. I'm definitely apprehensive now. It's the atmosphere, the anticipation in it, and compassion for the poor bandees. I want to protect them, and I'm not scared of the pain, or the spirits. But the spirits – that's the whole point. In order to be brave, be a Junior Man, I must be scared in the spirit as well as the body – and *that's* what I'm scared about. That I might not be scared in my soul.

The *avookwaarks* have gone in already with Jackson. They'll send him out when it's time. We wait – Lawrence, Wallace, a couple of others, conscious of our markings, what we've been told about them – that they do not belong to us. They belong to the spirit that's been given you, like a Wunjumboo dance mask that gives you the spirit of the Wunjumboo when you wear it over your face. It's why tattoos can be drawn bent and squiggly over your face and hands, or why Wewak shop assistants ruin shirts by marking the price in indelible ink. The power is in the possessing, not the artwork.

Some women were coming forward, timidly, behaving like a fish shoal. '*Saun waark!*' they said. White crocodile! Wallace said, 'I am happy. They like you here.' But then he slapped away a woman who tried to touch the marks showing from my short sleeves. They made more fish movements, and slipped to the side. 'Now, tell Errol to go. Properly. Not like Prince Charles.'

'Errol, scram,' I said, limply. What if I'm not scared to the core, I was thinking.

Errol scuttled off, left with his boy's thoughts, the stories that are spread to the uninitiated. At his stage, it was easier to get frightened – you were bewildered, and that was the way the men wanted you to be. Tales of fresh crocodile cuts being scrubbed with the husks of coconuts, of boys taken to the beds of men, of bandees having to eat fresh nettles and their tongues swelling, turning black. Inside the Nest, you found the stories untrue, but they still kept you bewildered. I was scared then, but still not to the spirit.

There was a rustling of the coconut fence. Jackson came out, and smiled. 'Okay.'

'Okay,' I said to Wallace. 'Let's, as the Australians say, party.'

I turned and winked at the crowd. Errol's face was hooked on to mine as I turned to go into the Nest. I had been like him once, watching dumbly, my imagination stirring me into a craze. Yes, Errol, again you'll listen as bandees pound drums and sing to hide the cries of other, weaker bandees, and you'll be out here, feeling helpless but not wanting to show it as the women do. And together you and the women will begin suffering for the brothers and sons in the Nest, clan relations that you are tied to. Little wonder that when pain is offered to you women, you want to accept it – if a hot poker had been handed you, you'd have grasped it. And now the figure appears who *will* relieve you, if you like. He is offering with his stick. Once he was a man; now, with his mask, he is the spirit of the Mai, what the Korogos call the Arvan, wearing a wooden mask of a face stretched in long whites and blacks, a giant in a bale of leaves who runs the avenue between the houses, wielding his rod. You are only too glad to throw yourself at him; your cousins and brothers, part of you, are bleeding inside the Nest.

You feel your forest-honed bonds and one after another you seek relief, bending your torsos to the Mai, throwing open your clothes – all the women and children. This happens five, *tambanak* times. When the bandees are beaten in the *banis*, it must be five times, and when the *avookwaarks* dance in the spirit of the crocodile, they do it five times, when they come out of the Nest and dance, another five, and when the women sob and hurl themselves down to be beaten, they also do it five times.

For the women it is over, the last of the five times; their backs are still stinging, eyes circling in their orbits, and now you little girls bare your lean, tubular bodies for the last time, gripping your hip bones tight for the kick of the stick. Then you can go back indoors smarting, laughing too loudly in your shock; but content, relieved at that unity.

'A load of yobs,' I say in Pidgin to Wallace, coming from the Nest.

'You saw Kumbui walking with us when they were beating? That was good of him.'

'Why did they beat you so hard?' Jackson asks.

'It's complicated,' I say.

'One day, we will hold another Man-making at Kandengei. Then we shall beat the Korogos.'

'That'll show them a thing or two.'

We carry our shirts on our shoulders, not wanting them to stain. The women run behind, secretly comparing our bruises.

'You are good to the bandees,' Naow says, boarding the canoe. He tells me to sit down facing him. Effectively, I am pinned at his feet. 'Tonight, you will eat at my house.'

I'm genuinely touched. Also, I'm ashamed. I'm not as utterly brave as they think I am. Inside Korogo's Nest, I failed again. I wasn't scared of the spirit in the place; I could hardly feel it and I certainly wasn't disturbed by it.

'What's he offering you?' Wallace asks from behind, holding my shoulder and reaching into my ear.

'To eat at his house.'

'Hmmm. Lucky.'

That night I eat with Naow. But my mind isn't on Naow's meal; as we sit on stools without talking, just slurping the fish soup, I notice that Stars on the Water is here in the house. She must be visiting, helping out. She comes and takes my plate and I notice the way a towngirl lifts and lays a plate. It is placed. It lands, it doesn't slide; it takes off without a twist.

'How long have I been here?' I ask Naow.

He calls her name. 'How long has Wumvunnavan been here?'

She stands, her legs firm and apart, holding her skirt taut. There's not a glimmer in my direction. 'Seven, eight, nine weeks something.'

Then it's been seven or eight or nine weeks since my arrival, and I've never seen her close up before in daylight.

Naow carries on eating, saying, 'Soon you will be leaving.' I say to myself, 'So everyone tells me.' Finishing up the fish soup, he says, 'When you come back, you may talk to Kaavon. He is a powerful man, Wumvunnavan. He can make the water rise, he can be rid of the AOGs if he likes. One day you will speak to him.'

He talks a bit more but I am now thinking of the journey, or, more precisely, of the desert, the open space. Like the early days I still want to get right away. Once it was the oppression of the forest, now it's because I see how much I've got to learn. They've chosen Australia for me, and that's perfect. I need living space. I even have a location in mind. It's one of a dozen places which I wrote to from England in case I abandoned the Kandengei project. On the *Times Atlas* at home, in the caramel centre of the continent, a thin red line had run across the page. Then it stopped. For, in the wastelands of Australia, there was a particular bit of waste, a human deposit called Wiluna. Even before leaving England, among all the other remote places – Irian Jaya, Borneo and so on – it had caught my eye. It probably had an excellent view of the Gibson Desert, but I had no idea. Now, in Kandengei, my ignorance of Wiluna made it even more perfect. After this forest, that was its beauty – its emptiness. It was a vacuum.

Often during the next days I look to the mountains beyond the lake, wondering when I'm going to be told it's time to pack. But I get no message to leave and lately my magic sessions with Kaavon have been more and more disappointing; perhaps it is because he feels I don't need them any more, but I know I need all the help I can get; and besides, his chanting seems stilted and sometimes lacklustre. I am worried.

'As others have much implied,' he says one day, 'you are leaving soon.' He strokes the loose, soft folds of his stomach. 'You are going to Australia – which has lots of sunshine?'

I confirm there is, by all accounts. Especially in the deserts. Lots.

He's not getting to the point. He chases a flea through his spring-loaded hair, cornering it with both hands behind an ear, and executing it between his thumb and finger nails. 'I have made killings in the past, you know. Good killings, sorry to say. I send my apologies, now, if you know them.'

I shook my head. He hadn't killed anyone that I knew about. My relatives stuck to India and Africa, mainly.

He tells me the other Junior Men make their journeys to the town, which I already knew. I show sympathy, opening my hands, displaying my palms.

'It is strong magic but it is dead magic.'

'Dead magic . . .' I enjoy the sense of poetry in the old men – dead magic – and I know that I want that phrase later for my notebook, but he's leading up to something.

'Listen while I say this: we Niowras are weak in the forest department now.' I tut along with him, commiserating. Then he says, simply, 'Benedix,' and I'm shocked to hear my Christian name – he wants to be sure of getting through to the whiteman in me. 'Benedix, I cannot help you much.'

'You can't?' I knew he meant it. I didn't argue. It was all too much. *I* was too much.

He adds, 'It is a shame.'

It was more than a shame. I was getting all geared up for this journey to show I've learnt about manhood, how to be brave about life – a journey from out of here, not the West, and all for nothing. I said, 'I'm a problem case, aren't I?'

'We are weak, you see.'

I sighed a bit, then said, 'What now then?'

'You find another place. You are not ready to be hatched here, so leave from another place. The Town – it is not so bad.'

'Dead magic? You don't make it sound very attractive. Anyway, I came to learn about the forest – living magic. And another thing, it's a sense of the spirit that I'm so missing – I won't find that in Wewak. I ask too many questions, and the town will just encourage that in me – I'll be back to my own ways. The town isn't alien enough to me.' I was in a state now – there *must* be a solution to this. 'What about me finding a remoter people, if you really do feel the problem is the lack of something here? I could launch out from there.' I had a nasty feeling that 'there' was going to be in those mountains.

'Wumvunnavan, if you can do this, it is very strengthening in the old way.'

'But it won't be Niowra custom that I learn.'

'It is too late here – the Crocodile Nest is made of dying wood. We cannot make you strong.' *Strongpela* is the word he uses.

Dying wood, I repeat. The Crocodile Nest is made of dying wood. It seems perfectly strong enough to me – Nightlight, Wallace, the other legions. But now it's to the mountains to find a stronger people.

He muses. 'The young man sets out. He needs something from the forest. If he lives, he is stronger – he has something from the forest.'

Naturally, his words – *If he lives* – bounce around my head. And though he must be quoting from the old days, I can't help but feel a little put down. I may be an imbecile, but I'll rally some people to help me up to the mountain villages and they're probably only at 6000 feet. I remind him that there are no head-hunters left.

'Oh?'

He sounds disappointed. I say, drily, I'll let him know for sure. He draws his lips out from around his gums, forming a shy smile. 'Much appreciated.'

But what's the point in all this? I say maybe I should go to the towns like the other Junior Men and do all this proving of myself there. 'The way you're talking, the forest hardly sounds relevant to you any more.'

He raises his bony, flying-fox arms. 'None the less, you will go.'

'And by the time I find that mountain village to launch from, I'll be better prepared myself, I suppose?'

But he is drifting off. 'My wau said when I was a little boy, lost in the forest, "If he lives he is stronger. He has something from the forest."'

On my way back to the Smaarks, thinking over Kaavon's words, 'something from the forest', I see Nathan – something from the town.

'So, Benedict,' he says. 'You're going soon.'

'So everyone keeps telling me.'

'To the forest, *and* the desert, because you need grinding into a proper man.'

'So everyone keeps telling me.'

'In case you do not make it back, let me tell you a story.'

It really was infuriating how little confidence everyone had in my abilities. I said, 'I've things to write in my notebook, actually.'

'This is a story I tell, to illustrate the power of God. It is a video – available now in all good video shops if you want to help me.'

'I can't, sorry. I think you're the only person here apart from Kaavon who hasn't asked for a present already.'

'But let me tell you the power of God. So that when you come back if you find the spirit house burnt to the floor, you will not be surprised.'

'I wouldn't be surprised in the least.'

I'm backing off. He suddenly says, 'A family fell upon bad times.'

I look up, because he has held up his hands, pointing at the sky. But he is only starting a sermon.

'A family fell upon bad times, and the mother of the family died of plague. The children of the family went to the father and said, "Wherefore do we not have a mother when other families have mothers?" And he answered them, "You ask me why you have no mother. It is because the Lord has seen fit not to provide us with one. But when the time is right, the Lord shall provide." But later the children came again to ask him. And he answered them, "I say unto you, the Lord will provide another woman, when he sees fit." And so they went away. But the country fell upon bad times, and many bad soldiers there were who said they would take him away and again the children came to him . . .'

I begin daydreaming: find something from the forest – some people to dispatch me towards Australia, launching me out the old way. And there I'll be, in the simplicity of the open space, losing my whiteman's spiritual numbness. Australia: no shadows, no competition between the living. Elbow room.

Nathan's story must be getting towards the end. I listen in. 'And then, a knock came on the door. The master answered the door, and a stranger said unto him, "I am a lady called Maria from a sacred nunnery. The Lord says you have need of me." And the lady came and stayed amongst them, and her presence was pleasing to them. And when the day came that the soldiers were ready to take the Master and do away with him the lady was forewarned in a dream, and led them away by another route.'

Thank goodness. It's the end. I said, 'You made that up!'

'I did not!'

'You stitched together bits of the New Testament. You can't do that!'

'It is a true story. Our prayer leader, C.K. He said it's on film; soon it will be distributed to all the missions. *The Sounds of Music.*'

I groan. I should have guessed.

'The woman was an angel sent by God.'

'Wrong again. Just a nun played by Julie Andrews.'

'Our prayer leader, C.K. –'

'C.K. and whoever taught you the rest of your theology should be fired.'

My wau calls me.

'*Laua*, Kaavon says you can take a woman.'

But we all know – even I, who am the last to know things – that this is against Niowra custom. My wau explains, 'Kaavon says the spirits will not be too angry if you go to the town with her – not the forest.'

I'm trying to learn traditional ways, I tell him. He is looking at my white skin intently, the freckles on the arms, as if he wants to touch. I get the feeling he is trying to let go of a thought – 'Kaavon says you are allowed to take the towngirl with you.' He winces at some picture in his head – the corruption of a nice traditional journey into the forests – he still has such hope for me, his own *Laua*. 'He says' – another full, medicinal breath – 'he says she will be good for you.'

I decline the offer.

'You do not need to marry her, or have a baby from her.'

'I'd always thought he liked me doing it the old way.'

He lets my comment make its own way through the dust and rafters, out of the wall panel cracks, out of the house. 'It is not for us to question him. You cannot question this.' He stood, squared up to me. 'He says you can go to the town; it's safer. "We are short on forest connections," he says. "Go to the town and take the towngirl."'

'It's all right, I'll do without.'

That night, Stars on the Water comes again. 'Talk to me.'

But I say nothing much, and she goes away without a word, seeing I'm thinking ahead to my journey into the mountains. Now she too knows that I'm leaving any day.

My wau asks if I'm happy. I say I think so and he says, 'When you are launched out from the mountains, it will be a fine, old style of journey. I expect there may be killings.'

'I'm rather hoping not, actually.'

Catastrophes, however, there may well be. A sorry state of affairs, having to scratch and scrape for 'something' from the forest.

I get up to leave. I guess that I won't see Kaavon or my wau again. But he stops me, as I'm by the door, the women queuing up to come back in again. 'Wumvunnavan, I think all white-coloured men travel.'

'In the West, everywhere's like a garden, all under our control. People feel safer, but bored sometimes.'

'And in Tooting?'

Especially Tooting.

As I step out he stops me a second time.

'Let me ask, when I blow a flute. It isn't me waking a spirit to sing by magic? Nathan says it's Jesus.'

I say you could call it magic; at home we called it energy.

'Some *avookwaarks* are thinking of letting their sons become AOGs,' he says.

It is the closest he'll ever come to asking advice from a *Laua*. I feel like a whiteman suddenly. I tell him, 'There was a bloke once, called Virgil. He said that we made our destinies by our choice of Gods.'

'It's safe to ignore the Awful Horror of Nathan?'

'It's difficult to ignore him exactly.'

'One of the *avookwaarks* says he would like the AOGs to be friends with their children, so when we die, they will be safe. I wanted to know what you say. I am asking you as a whiteman.'

I suggested that if he wanted their future to be in the towns, maybe he should change their Gods from forest things. 'We make our destinies by our choice of Gods.' Virgil was probably right – he'd done very well for himself in history.

'Who will look after our forest?'

'It will be like a park. You'll get food from the stores.' Surely, I am thinking, the *avookwaark* in favour of the AOGs taking over can't be Kaavon, can it? He did, after all, suggest I went on a journey to the town, to the 'Dead Magic'. But surely not. He, of all people, wouldn't get on with Nathan.

My wau's eyes are vacant. He doesn't want arguments or questions, he wants an instruction – just now, I am a whiteman. 'I shall tell the *avookwaarks* that the AOGs are safe, then?'

'I get the feeling,' I say, 'this *avookwaark* has made up his mind already.'

The next evening, I have a small meal with James, head of the Smaarks, and Alex, a *wanbanis*. They have killed a chicken, and sit me down and watch me share out my tea, which Errol has brought along for me. They sip gently, watching me do it first. Alex, a Catholic convert, has been chucking out all his traditional gear. He gives me a necklace from the centre of which hangs a shell plate; on it are holes for *tambanja*, the old pendants announcing how many heads you have taken. He jokes: all the spaces are empty. His wife cries; so does another girl I've never seen before who has fresh tattoos on her face, the tears running where the skin has been scored and rubbed with oil-lamp soot along the petal outlines.

Outside, I am run into by Nathan.

'I am praying for you, Benedict.' He says it like a warning, so I stop.

'What happens to the Niowra spirit in you if God decides to burn the spirit house down? Some people' – he meant AOGs – 'think you'll die on your journey. You'll be eaten by head-hunters.'

I think of the words, *Our incantations to you have long since begun. While we do this, your spirit can never die.* 'You are planning to burn down their spirit house? But did you know, some *avookwaarks* are encouraging their children to go to the AOG church.'

'This is the Lord's doing, not the old men.'

'None the less, they respect your firm stance, I think. They think the modern Catholics are wishy-washy, like the Anglicans.'

He says, magnanimously, 'Then maybe God will save their spirit house, and you will be safe.' He smiles, everything looking most satisfactory.

'I suppose we'll have to see, won't we?'

Wallace helps me pack my belongings. Though Korogo is usually too far away to hear, my head pounds with the faraway beat of their Man-making songs, the words they use in the Palembei style. I see the *avookwaarks* drop down from their benches onto the backs of the bandees; I see the Arvan, the punishing spirit with stricken, mask face who will damage the bandees further in a minute, when they are marching around the spirit house five times.

I hear the sobbing of broken bandees, and grit my teeth, trying to be brave myself. *Kuta, vrevook, koowook, enak, tambanak.* I see the trail of damage around their feet – loose leaves, shreds from their skirts, plastic-skinned green and red leaves. Outside the Nest, girls holding hands together in short fences, as the Arvan comes for them, straining their grace as he strikes. The crack of the *avookwaark* betelnut husks breaking between teeth, saliva still on discarded shards cast to the ground, red juice spouts. The kina shells hung up with cash to help with spiritual healing.

Wallace is saying, 'The town will not be so easy for you.'

'The forest, you mean.'

'No. It's funny, but you will find this. When you go to Wewak to start your journey, you cannot *amamas* [be happy] like a whiteman. Why not? It is magic.'

106

'Culture shock?'

'Yes, magic.'

'If you say so, Wallace. Magic.' I've learned not to argue.

Wallace says, 'You do not believe me, because you are a disobedient Brother. But it's a message from Daniel.'

'Daniel? By the way, he's still away fishing, is he – the way my wau always used to be?'

'Yes,' said Wallace, uncomfortably. 'Gone fishing.' Then, 'So, remember the town Kandengeis. They can give you much help.'

'Sounds like they're going to have to.'

He lists dozens of men among the network of relations, the 'wantok' system. A riot policeman, a local politician . . . I remember a couple of the faces – Martin Saun, a truck driver who cried very loudly, seeing us as bandees; David Tari, a luggage handler who had spotted me when I stepped off the plane on my return. A policeman had said, 'Are you Benedict Wumvunnavan?' I nodded, embarrassed by the use of the village name. 'Well, *he*' – the policeman pointed in the face of the stranger as if he was a boy – '*he* says that he's come to meet you.'

Abandoning his Talair luggage duties, this man who seemed to know me took my baggage like a servant. It was only in his shed house on the beach, seeing my crocodile marks as I changed shirts, that he held his head up to me. He took my present, a penknife, as if it was his anyway and I'd borrowed it without asking.

Wallace is red-eyed; it's to be expected from a big brother but he has been good to me, and I'm sad myself. I haven't been the easiest member of his family – frankly, I'm a problem child. 'Take Stars on the Water and go to a town, like the *avookwaarks* say.'

I tell him it's all right; I'll do it the old way.

Wallace begins to cry. I'm a blunderer in the forest; he doesn't think I'm up to the 'old way'. 'You are so peaceless to go.' He goes and sits on a stool in the posture of an *avookwaark* saying his spells; but closer, I see he is chanting from his Bible.

I tip out my possessions – what remains of them. My emergency medical kit is intact, I have a spare long-sleeved shirt and trousers, film and camera, notebooks and pens, bush knife, socks, a spare pair of underpants. Almost everything else that I want is either broken or gone; some items are just plain unrecognizable.

I put aside some spare things – some notebooks and some thin socks. I watch Priscilla pack them away neatly, 'for my return,' she says. That's the last I'll see of *them*, I think to myself.

Wallace says, 'Spencer will wake you. He will go with you to Pagwi. Then you have the town Kandengeis available, of course.'

'Heck, Wallace,' I say suddenly. 'I can't help feeling guilty about leaving those two girls, whatever you all say. Nightlight will be all right, I'm sure she's got other options up her sleeve, but Stars is the odd one out here.'

Wallace speaks as softly as he has ever spoken, and even in the firelight his eyes look glassy from crying. 'Listen to something. Stars on the Water will be joining the AOGs soon. It is a shame it is the AOGs, but it has been arranged, you see, so you can't worry.'

Even after months here, I can hardly believe I'm hearing this. 'You even think you can arrange for her to take up a church?'

'This is a suitable arrangement.'

I can see it all: Wumvunnavan leaves; Stars on the Water is free to be sent on a *Knowing the Way* Bible course; gets talking to teacher, introduces the whiteman to village and WHAM! he's trapped, a fly in coconut oil. It might even be C.K. himself.

The women look sadly at me tonight for the last time, knowing that I'll be off in the dark, even before they slip their fishing canoes into the dawn. I do not know why it has to be like this, leaving without a word in the night. Surely a proper head-hunter would have had a send-off, and I can't help feeling a little bit of a failure not having got a launch out from here.

In the night, Stars on the Water slides up beside me. She has washed with perfumed soap and smells like a white woman.

'Stars, I will see you when I come back,' I tell her.

'Let me have the bracelet from around your hand.' She brushes my yellow cotton band and then brushes my crocodile marks.

I say, 'No.' She knows by now she must be satisfied with that; I have, strangely enough, become something at least of a Man during my stay.

'See you,' she says, not leaving.

I shake her hand. She tries to bring it up to her face. I let her. But she goes away without crying and I think she knows we might not meet again like this.

Later Nightlight swims in from the dark. The village is working hard tonight.

And I can say nothing but 'I will see you when I come back.' She, however, is more talkative.

'I wanted to put a string around your wrist, for you to remember me with. But Daniel says no.'

'He's right.'

'I know that, Cousin.'

'Is Daniel well?'

'Yes. He says goodbye.'

That is all he says? She gulps for a moment, and I close my eyes, smelling the smell of her woodsmoke skin.

And, late, a hand touches me. I'm in shock in my half-sleep – this hand is pulling away my sheet. I smell the wood smoke on Nightlight, released on to me as the sheet falls away. But my mind clears.

'Brother,' a voice says rather formally, in Niowra. It is Spencer. '*Nee-armun, yagua*! Older brother, come now!'

His voice is hoarse. He must have been singing Catholic songs much of the night. The air is cool and insects quiet. This is the hour before dawn, exactly the time when we used to run naked to the water to wash, then to the Crocodile Nest – Spencer, Daniel, Johnson, Saun, Joel in our Smaark gang, one of them carrying my notebook, painting it with the grey clay from off their skins.

I take up my rucksack, hoist it down to Spencer at the bottom of the ladder. I go up to Wallace's house, wind through the mosquito net support strings. At the far end is Songbird's place. I call to her.

'Nelson. You order help?' she asks, quickly.

I wonder if there is a man in there with her, frozen with fear.

I tell her I am going, and, 'Please visit Nightlight in the morning.' Just that. She says yes; I know she understands. Then I'm down by the water's edge, toes warming in the mud. There's the dabbing of a duck out there on the water. A splash from a fish. Then the moving sheets of water, the spreading ripples from ourselves and the paddle knocking on the canoe are the only sounds in the world. And we are away from the bank, and I am looking back through the grains of mist. I feel the waters turn cold and I do not want to do this thing, not alone.

And Spencer brings me into yet colder waters; the threads of the finest tree roots are gone, and the waters are darker-seeming than the sky, and dead and silent deep down. And we are gone from the waters in which crocodiles live, and by the purple first light we enter the channel with the grass islands, and drift with the riverward, dry season flow, nudged and barged and bumped and spun, with the agitated crickets and snakes, until we are out of our territory, and into the alien.

We are in the tug of the main river, and need the outboard. We rip against the flow. The clouds are visible, neat, corrugated puffs of cream, like sago larvae in a greasy plate of gravy. Then Pagwi comes into sight. Pagwi, a metal settlement that has been trying to bud into Western life for decades. Master Ken's stores – armour plating at the end of Western outreach. I step from the crocodile-headed canoe, and ashore, feeling that this culture, this arm reaching out to me, my culture, is foreign territory.

THE NIOWRA SPIRIT NEEDS YOU AS A MAN OF TRUE MEN . . . We stand on the high bank, and I look back again, over the brown water to the marsh banks, and to the trees behind, beyond them the mountains slumbering in cloud, with their men of stronger forest, the riddle that stands between me, Australia and my return.

I'll have dealings with you later, Australia, I thought, first I need to get into the mountains. I look out at the rising banks of blue far-off trees.

PART 2

First Steps

If he lives he is stronger,
he has something from the forest.

Chapter Three

BLACK FOREST GATEAU

Spencer and I stood in the low, bright light, in front of Master Ken's store, looking at the litter-free lawn that led from the river bank, the clean sweeps of cropped grass that was the doormat of the Western world.

'So what do we do now, Brother?' Spencer asked me. 'The shops aren't even open.'

'What time do you think it is?'

'Many hours before opening.'

'Then we'll wait for Master Ken to open up.'

The women came in silently. They were gristly ladies who were tilted forward to balance the baskets of sago and tobacco hanging down their backs from their heads. They marched on by to the market where one woman would sit where once Yargee had sat, offering me tobacco.

But now the men were buzzing in to look at the stores. Boys wearing catapults around their heads gathered around a gooniangra tree and fired at the tired bats. I bought Spencer biscuits and Fanta from the store and some Benson and Hedges for Wallace, but the Korogo men came to join us and were soon sharing them among themselves. Spencer decided to inspect the trucks going to Wewak and eventually chose one that he deemed was up to standard for me. We held hands as it was loaded up with women chewing home-grown cigars.

'So, *Sambu*,' I said, speaking Niowra. 'So, Younger Brother . . .'

Spencer patted the truck, and I humped my pack in. 'And remember to stop Martin Saun's truck along the road. This truck won't take care of you.'

A boy sitting beside me in the truck shouted at me in Pidgin, '*Yumi go nau!*'

I got in. Spencer coughed. I got out again, realizing Spencer had prepared one of those Niowra speeches. He said, gravely, 'You are not ready yet, so we do not say goodbye fully. But there will be a time when you set out to taste the wind. If the wind is good, and even if it is not, then comes the spirit to guide your hand to strike.'

I said I would bear it in mind. The engine blew a blue, loose bubble of exhaust.

'Well, I'm off.' I climbed aboard. 'One thing, Spencer. I will get a welcome if – I mean, when – I come back? I mean, it was a bit low-key last time. I will get a nice welcome back?'

'Oh yes, Benedix. You will get a *sagi!*'

'I will?' I said, jumping up. A *sagi* was a dance. We'd have a good romp.

'It'll be a happy time,' Spencer said. 'You will be happy to be a *geenjumboo.*'

My truck rumbled off; I watched Spencer turn back slowly to the river, leaving his hand in the air after him. He kicked a pebble along the road with his bare feet. Then he was lost in our dust.

I wrote his little speech in my book as the truck lolloped in and out of the pot-holes, through the Sepik Plains – bristle grasses fenced with barbed wire, copses scalded by fires. After a while, I saw Martin Saun's truck by a roadside betelnut stall; he smiled at me from behind the wheel, stuck where he was into the driving seat with his sago basket belly. '*Em-nau*, Benedix.' I slipped in with Fredalin, a *wanbanis*, who hung out of the window most of the way to Wewak under his rat-nibbled straw hat until we reached the paved road and were wheeling into town. We left the truck at David Tari's beach shed and slipped through the fence surrounding the airport. We waited in the bushes, crouching like the frogs until the runway patrol truck with its sweeping spotlight had gone. Then we ran across to the thatched houses in the woods the other side.

There, among the trees, was laid a little replica of Kandengei, except that the buildings were patched with iron, had locks on the doors, and instead of the spirit house there was a shack where children listened to the secrets unravelling from the drunk men. The few town Kandengeis who had jobs shared out their wages and everyone ate a diet of tinned fish and rice, Papua New Guinea's national dish.

Daniel was right. Though I should feel at home in the town, this whiteman's creation – the street with its coffee shop, the pretty avenue of trees, the newspapers, zebra crossings, the post office – I felt an outsider. At first it was heaven – window shopping, stuffing myself with chocolate and Australian pies and fish and chips. But the novelty was over in a day or two.

I had little in common with the busy whitemen I saw running by.

Instead I walked about with the townboys. They had botched tattoos on their brows – careless spots, brow lines, eye lines, polka dots – and strafed the streets with betelnut juice, their fingers entwined, greeting each other with brotherly wrestles – lifting, falling, twisting, then the release. Together we watched the missionaries and goldminers going about their lives, staring with them as we lazed on the pavement, and idling with them as they served behind the counters in the Chinese stores or the post office, keeping their customers waiting.

I lingered in the coffee shop, getting to know Veronica, the girl serving there, feeling at home with the way she fingered the loose biscuits on sale as if she were Nightlight adjusting fish being smoked on a hearth, and she reminded me of Stars on the Water, the way she flamboyantly dabbed her armpits with the paper tissues. But the Chinese who ran the store saw her eating from the biscuit box one day, and she was given 'a final warning'.

I didn't see her again – she didn't bother turning up to work next day – but from her I'd already learnt a lot about what was going on out here. I'd heard about the gold rush.

A sample boring had gone through an 18-inch hunk of gold. Grass clumps had been pulled out of the ground with nuggets like peanuts in the roots.[1] Everyone seemed to think that Enga province, the mountains behind Kandengei, were in the heart of it. I could go elsewhere, but the Central Range was meant to be about the remotest place in Papua New Guinea – the odd little bit that could claim to be unexplored in the geographical sense. For my purposes, this was the only chance to see people still right in there with the forest – and I might be too late already. I imagined the mountain hamlets, lonely old men in doorways watching their young pack up and go for the gold – a hundred Kandengei villages dissipating their energy, the bound energy that might have helped me.

Time was running out, but I was still dawdling hopelessly with the townboys on the street, unable after nearly three months of the village to think outwards, snap into my old Western self and plan ahead.

We tried questioning nuns about routes into the Highlands. The nuns were the easiest type of missionary to spot. But each time we approached they skipped off – they'd seen the bunch of swarthy tramps moving in on them. On the third or fourth day Martin Saun, the old town hand, came to pick me up. He waved me into his truck, tucked his stomach under the wheel, and took me to a whitewoman who ran the base operations for one of the gold companies out in the forest. We found her in a securely fenced-in garden on her exercise bicycle. I went forward and shook her wet hand. She stayed on her saddle, pumping away, while she told me about her employees in the forest. 'We pay them with clothes.' The first two bales were flown in last week. 'But they were a wild gang when we first got there.'

'How long ago was that?'

'Couple of weeks back.'

She took her glasses off, looked at me, and then at the Kandengeis behind – I heard one of them scratching – then put her glasses back on. Then she stopped pedalling. 'Relax, won't you?' I looked round to Martin. 'I mean you,' she said, pointing her glasses at me. I said I'd been too long in the bush, perhaps. 'You're telling me – you look like a bush *kanaka*. Can I get you an aspirin?' The machine wound down. She went into her office, waving me in behind her, slapping a secretary's fingers as they fiddled with nail varnish, and firing her driver who was by the door. She looked at Martin's stomach suspiciously, then asked him if he wanted a job, but didn't wait for an answer, telling me instead that she was sick of this game. She was packing it all in 'like everyone else' – the *rascol* problem was out of control and they were having to bring troops into Wewak. She gave me an aspirin – for my culture shock? – then she took her glasses off again and said, 'If you want to get in to the mountains, you'd better get there in days.' She put on her glasses and went back to her exercise bicycle.

I felt better after the whiteman's medicine, the aspirin. I struck out across the road to the airport, leading the others to the MAF, that is, the Mission Aviation Fellowship, hangars. The radio operator, Steve Kadam, had the long hair of a whiteman, showing he could afford lice shampoo, but in this case not the usual moustache that shows everyone that you are a proper, shaving townboy. He locked the side door to the hangar – he'd seen the Kandengeis coming – and sat down and swung from side to side in his armchair. I asked what missionaries there were out there. 'SSEC,' he said, 'which is the same as SSEM. And there's SIL and NTM. Not so much SDA, AOG or –' He went on like this, pulling letters from the alphabet, and finally I learnt that the most knowledgeable whiteman out there was a German called Jakob Walter, from the South Seas Evangelical Church. He had a mission on April River, which was behind and west of Kandengei. There was also the New Tribes Mission at Bisorio. But none of this was of any use. Both missions were now closed to visitors.

Steve suggested we tried an alternative: go to the Windjammer Hotel, talk to the geologists who were here in Wewak, fresh from prospecting. They might have ideas. The good old Windjammer. I remembered it from my first time in Wewak – it had been a many-starred hotel of steadily lowering repute on the beach front. Perhaps in my absence it might have lowered sufficiently to allow us, the bushy men, *buskanakas*, in. Fredalin and Lawrence put on shoes and Martin parked his truck among the cars.

The cars looked extremely expensive. We looked at the shine on them. Then at the Windjammer itself. A sign said, 'Sepik International Resort Hotel'. Alongside, a garage-sized crocodile with wooden scales lay playfully. Along the Sepik International Resort Hotel itself, cowrie-shell eyes squinted from posts which were freshly carved and finished with Kiwi boot polish. The reception had Native Hut-style eyelevel thatch, and a noble crocodile-skull doorstop. Lawrence, who had only one eye, and Fredalin were stopped right there, just as they were using the crocodile skull as a shoe scraper.

I carried on, taking Martin with me. We paused, noticing another detail. The doors to the restaurant had hand-drum handles. We couldn't resist a peer through to the restaurant. The insides of the doors were carved by a tribe whose style was unlike any I knew. The figures were wood spirits with, as Martin showed me, winking, thought-provoking genitals. There were also stretched breasted females with gaping private parts.

I didn't think anyone had noticed us. A whiteman was shouting out that he had distinctly ordered prawns. 'When we order prawns in Australia we usually get, well, at least one.'

'Yes sir.'

'So. Where is it?'

The waiter showed him. There was more than one. They were there on his plate, under the garden of hibiscus foliage in a clam shell propped by a knob of tinfoil.

'Sorry, mate. Had ya wrong there.'

Boosted by the conciliatory tone, Martin and I carried on to the bar, which had crocodile scales. It was as far as we got. Martin had been looking around for an ashtray in which to spit his betelnut juice. There'd been one between two fat white women with blue hair but he tried for the ashtray right on the crocodile bar itself, depositing his spittle slowly and neatly but in front of the barman's eyes.

Martin was led away. 'Benedix, don't worry. See you *apinun* something.' I drank Martin's beer, then mine. It had been a mistake to come here among the whitemen. I wanted to leave as soon as possible. I kept my head down, fingering the crocodile scales, the head with its hobnail teeth.

'You're from what part?' a man said.

Britain, I said.

'A good place to have come from!' he said, laughing at his joke into the glass.

He turned to his drinking mates, said a word that sounded like 'pommy', then looked back to me. 'How did you get in here, anyway? Looks like you got lost in the garden.'

His friend said, looking at my jungle boots, 'Leave it, mate. He's fresh out of the bush.'

'Fair dos. What you been doing?'

I was looking for people with enough magic to launch me out and prove I was a Man of True Men – on the advice of an interesting ex-head-hunter. But I wasn't going to hand him a present of saying that. I said, 'Have you heard of Wiluna? It's in Western Australia.'

'Yeah, that does ring a bell.'

'It's a very small place . . .'

'Yeah. I must be thinking of somewhere else. The Wiluna I'm thinking of, you wouldn't be wanting to go to – bloody boongs, mate.'

'Boongs?'

'Blackfellas. Abos – ya know?'

I supposed I did.

'What's Wiluna got to do with anything, anyway?'

'Oh, that's just where I'm heading. But first I'm going to climb up into the Central Range.'

The gentler man asked if I had travelled a lot. I said yes, perking up with his interest. 'You know, Everest was almost called after my great, or was it great-great-grandfather? Sheer accident that the name fell to his successor.' This nugget of information didn't impress anybody, so I ended quickly, 'It's almost a family tradition.'

'Take my advice, mate,' his friend said, 'don't bother to pass it on.'

I wandered into the enclosed garden which had cheap statues protruding from the vegetation like disfigured roots. Peering into the rooms I saw breezeblock walls decorated with Sepik masks cracking under the air conditioning. Each room was provided with one bar of soap hacked in two.

I went out onto the beach terrace, round the back of the green, wood-shingled crocodile, and talked to women selling bilum bags, the string net bags, and the boys winkling out the cowries from the entrance post carvings. Being with them, talking Pidgin again, made me feel better. I went back to the bar and stood listening to the whitemen. That was all these two expatriates asked of you – to drink the beer they'd bought you and to pay for it by listening. And I didn't mind. I couldn't focus on these people – my people – just yet. So I did what they were asking and listened, unpressured by questions, hearing about their 'haus meris', their kitchen and cleaning girls. Sometimes, I learned now, the *haus meris* breast-fed these men's babies while they were out. 'Chocolate milk,' they said. 'We discourage it.'

'You approve of missionaries?' I asked. 'They do act as buffers to the full impact of the West.'

They began their answer. It was like placing another log on the fire – I was assured another five minutes' ease.

These geologists didn't like the missionaries, with their planes, expensive houses. 'The missionaries came over meaning to do good,' a story ended, 'and they've done very well for themselves indeed.'

I was hearing how the Summer Institute of Linguistics mission at Madang, east along the north coast, with its extensive radar, was in league with the CIA, and then about cargo cults. The sentences began, 'When I first came here' and 'In those days, of course', and they repeated the old colonial stories about the first whites here being mistaken for the ancestral spirits which one day were due to descend from the spirit world with gifts. 'It seemed that the great day of Paradise had come at last. The ghosts had come back from Heaven . . . It all made sense, you see, Ben.'

'Benedict,' I said.

'Ben, is it?' said an American, barging in to take the story up.

'Benedict.'

'See, white people must be the spirits of the dead, they thought. They didn't grow food, they brought it in in tins. So the natives built baby airstrips of their own, expecting to attract more ancestral wealth in. Neat, eh? Or they passed bits of paper across counters, playing offices, waiting for their first paycheque. Ever wonder why whites are treated with so much awe sometimes? Why they think every white man is loaded? Now you know. But the New Guineans should have been more patient. Look around Wewak, Ben. Goldminers everywhere. Prostitutes boosting the hotel trade. Here's Paradise, freshly arrived – goldminers and loggers. The whitemen, cash in hand.'[2]

I liked the twist to his tale – the ancestral stories had been right after all – but there was now a scuffle on the beach terrace. A waiter was wrestling with a little boy. At last a whiteman came up to help and the boy was thrown down the beach in the general direction of the sea.

'Claims he has a message for a Mr . . . Van Bunavan, it must be. Or Wum-unavan? That mean anything to anyone?'

'Excuse me,' I said, leaving my beer.

The boy turned out to be my *wanbanis* Fredalin – a Niowra man in a whiteman's territory had looked like a little boy. He said that David Kari, luggage handler for the Talair company, had heard it from a wife of another Niowra that Jakob Walter, the missionary we'd heard about from the MAF man, had flown in and was in the hangars. Martin Saun had come to collect me.

'Is Jakob waiting?' I asked, getting into the truck.

'We don't know,' Lawrence said, winking with his one eye.

'We're scared to ask,' said Fredalin.

Martin said, 'Jakob's a *whiteman*.'

Jakob Walter was still in the hangar. He was short and very white and he kept one hand free to splay it over his large tummy. He had a jolly face and clever blue eyes. I asked if he could help with some local information – I was going into the mountains. He put his foot up on a trolley and leaned an elbow on it. 'Sure,' he said, sounding unsure. 'Why not?' Then he noticed he was being surrounded. He said, 'Are they with me, or with you?'

'Me. They're my friends.'

'I thought they were my people from the April River. Well, the situation is not good for the forest. All the world is changing, it seems.' He sighed, lamenting. 'Most of the forests will be designated as timber, and some villages will disappear off the map when they go off to chase after the gold. Which of the maps are you using?' His accent was beginning to show as he relaxed. *Vich off . . . are you usink?* 'Obviously, one finds the aeronautical 1:1,000,000 quite unserviceable for detailed work.'

It was one I had once used in Irian Jaya, over the border. I agreed that it was quite unserviceable.

He then said, 'So.'

I nodded, 'So . . .' Then I realized it was a question. I said, 'So, what?'

'So, which maps are you using?'

Suddenly I was being threatened. I was face to face with the culture I'd been evading all week. Strategies, aims, a rationalized campaign of progress – everything I had been trying to put aside in Kandengei. Out here I suddenly felt very young, like Fredalin in the barman's arms at the Sepik International.

Jakob was a patient man – maybe it was so many years of preaching in the wilderness. He made it easier. 'Look, last year Israelis came to the mission. Backpackers. They had a big river accident. They were unprepared you see, and so they very nearly were all drowned. So I closed the mission to outsiders. It is fair enough – and now with the gold around about . . .'

I murmured, 'I wonder where they were heading?'

Jakob interjected, looking around the hangar for someone to share the joke with. 'Down to the Sepik, of course. There is nowhere else!'

I said, almost to myself, 'But I'm going the other way. Up the Central Range.'

'The mountains? No Europeans have got up there from this region yet. There are stories about a Chinese storeman escaping the Japanese in the war, but please – fifteen years ago my parishioners were hunting heads!'

I said, simply, 'I've been in a lot of forests.' But he was waiting, and getting a little frustrated, his eyes coming at me, sharpening, cutting logically through my cluttered thoughts. He needed reassurance – facts he could respond to, respectability in whiteman's terms. I thought of something and put it forward, offering it like a gift of appeasement. 'I did a degree in Environmental Science, once.'

'You don't sound very sure.'

But by now I saw I was on test. 'I've had lots of experience. I do intend to get there.'

He turned to the Kandengeis and laughed. 'He wants to go; he does not want to come back!'

The gang smiled. None of them spoke English. 'He thinks I'm a tourist,' I said to Fredalin. 'Do I look like a tourist? I suppose I must do.'

Fredalin said in Niowra, looking at his feet, 'Father, he's not a tourist. He's a number two rank Niowra.'

'What is he saying?'

Lawrence said in Pidgin, 'Father, he is Wumvunnavan.'

'That's as may be.' He looked at the sweat rings on my shirt and turned back to Lawrence, saying in Pidgin, 'By the way, you needn't call me "Father", if you don't want to. In fact I'd rather you wouldn't.'

I explained that Jakob Walter wasn't a Catholic.

'Now, you've been knocking around a bit, so I'll tell you. We have had bothersome anthropologists. You know they accuse us of harming these people. But how can this be, when we have cut the numbers of blind persons right out? The killing is down. Now people can afford to *laugh* a bit.'

He had partly missed the point. Killings, high child mortality rates, were harder for Westerners to face because they thought as individuals. But actually even head-hunting became a rather good idea if it meant the survival of the group in the harsh forest. Besides, the anthropologists were probably more worried about the upsetting of the local people's orientation with the world – their 'belief systems'. But I agreed that of course some of my friends wouldn't be alive today if it wasn't for missionary medicine.

'Talking of this, how much medicine have you got?'

'Medicine?'

'The forest is not a playground, you know.'

I thought of Errol, whacking bats out of the palm trees. Why wasn't it a playground?

But his point was a fair one, on reflection, so why did he now need to launch into a second defence? 'Before the mission the Niksek peoples were dying out. Not enough women. The little female children had been killed. You know why? Because the men were not getting a high enough price for them. Now there is still some killing from black magic, but life is tolerable. And our role is predominantly spiritual. We do not want them just to copy the whiteskins.'

I was wondering why he thought they wouldn't copy the whiteskins with all their material wealth when suddenly I noticed that Jakob was looking pleased. He knew he had drawn my interest. 'So what is your religion?'

'Religion's not my line, just now.' He wanted more. I said, 'I'm trying to learn what the forest is like – from the locals. And they believe that learning to intercede with the spirits and their Creator is something for Senior Men. For now, you obey the religious rules and go about proving yourself.' It was an answer – of sorts.

'An atheist?'

These questions were tiring. I saw how tolerant Kandengei had been with all my questioning. Sorry about that, Wallace, I must have been like this: hell.

Jakob said, 'A liberal church member? An agnostic?' I said I was none of these. 'I'm better on universal spiritual values; I'm not so hot on dogma.'

'The worst of the lot. A humanist. Lost in every way,' he said. Technically, apprentice pagan might have been nearer the mark, but luckily he hadn't dared think of that, and he was now chuckling happily. 'I bet you haven't even any maps. Isn't that so?' He stopped me, and stopped smiling. 'I don't want to know.' Then he said, 'You really are serious about going into the mountains, aren't you?' He leaned into me a little. I thought he was taking to me, despite my being 'a humanist' – which was apparently not a good thing to be.

I was in awe of him for having the certainty, the confidence, in himself not to have to listen, and though the rocksteady beat of his questions was not to my liking, it was familiar. He knew where he was in the world. He reminded me of the tiresomely rigid *avookwaarks* who, none the less, had invited me, an outsider, into their fold. After my time in the thoughtless forest, Jakob was battering me with his thoughts; I felt as vulnerable as this on the day I stood in the *geygo*, asking to go through their ceremony – and the village had done all the talking, persuading themselves to take me in. With this whiteman, Jakob, I felt the same – a foreigner. I wasn't even keeping up with this conversation; he was putting most of the effort in. I saw this, but couldn't gather myself to help my case.

'You know about the horticulture? I have started a programme that is going well. We have vegetables for the vitamins. "Sufficient unto the need," that is what we say. And the green beans are good, very good.'

I saw I was meant to contribute. But – too late! He was sighing. 'What about hydrology? You know about hydrology?'

'Very little indeed.' I must have blown my chances, but while I looked around hopelessly Jakob talked about hydrology, and I was getting another chance to redeem myself.

However, I listened instead, thinking how he must have been chosen for the mission because he could stand up and say he believed in Adam and Eve, but also because he could entertain with sermons, cut up planks, bang together a church. He was a generalist, like a forest man, but also like them a Fundamentalist, a man who was hot on dogma. Although Western culture was one that encouraged material improvement, everything else – obedience to certain religious instruction, their handicraft skills, communication skills, religious fervour – made him an *avookwaark*.

'So you know nothing about anything. Not even hydrology, which is a pity, as the village is about to be flooded at the next high water.'

He stopped, wiping his lips with a finger, wondering whether to give me a chance. Yes or no? Let zee crazy Englander in or not? I vunder. He said, 'I think . . . Yes I do. Yes, you must come to my mission. See what you want. Things are changing fast out there. Now we have no drinking, no prostitutes, no manual work on Sundays. But soon a different picture, I think. Well, you had better witness all this.'

He told me what it was like at Niksek. The fighting had stopped in about 1970. The first plane flew into the mission in 1977, and there was now a school and a nurse, Gertrude – she'd be collected by the next plane. And a Bible School teacher, whom Jakob said he'd talk to on the radio, and ask him to help me get settled. But I should ask for Tom. Tom was a fine preacher, and he was always keen to get out and about. We might go off into the forest together.

Not a-preaching, we won't, I thought.

I had passed my first test. Why, I couldn't say. Perhaps Jakob was just a good man: a friendly 'whiteskin'. Perhaps I had caught him straight from the mission and I'd seemed like just another up-and-coming tribal – a stray member of his flock. I was reminded of Kaavon taking me in. That man Kaavon, who used to kill for a living, and seemed much the same kindly but principled type as Jakob.

We walk over into the MAF office. The gang tags along. Lawrence dabs the crisp writing paper on Steve Kadam's desk, leaving a greasy trail.

On the wall there is a map. My fingers walk inland over Kandengei, then west to a Sepik tributary, the April, where Jakob's mission lies. He says I must try to walk further inland, then east, along the foothills, looking for a way up. Some way along is Bikaru, a new hamlet made by hill people who had come down into forest vacated by those drawn to the mission. Only one other whiteskin had been there. He came by helicopter and scared them away. The preacher called Tom was related to them and spoke their language.

I said I wasn't so sure about taking a preacher with me. The Bikarus might feel threatened.

'You know, Tom is loyal.' My only other choice was a man called Daniel, who had once settled an argument by burying a hatchet in someone's head. He was just back from prison. 'But Tom will die with you, if you need.'

I nodded, reassured. He'd have the loyalty of a *wanbanis*. But, looking at me, Jakob said quickly, 'Look, that was a joke, okay?'

I turn to the gang of Kandengeis, and say that Bikaru sounds like a start. The people are from the mountains. They might know a route up.

Jakob says, 'You'd better get packing – you'll need all of tomorrow. The plane goes the day after.' The Kandengeis are drifting off and I go with them, forgetting Jakob – that whiteskins need goodbyes.

I hear Jakob behind me saying, 'Er. . . See you then.'

I trotted back. 'I was forgetting my manners. Thanks, I really am grateful.'

So we go to town the next morning in the truck, and fill sacks with salt, rice, tea and sugar. We've finished – it's taken an hour. Jakob said we'd need the whole day. I wonder what I've forgotten. I add a few tins of meat, in case the hunting is not good.

Laurie Whitehead, dashing Australian pilot in immaculate white socks and black sun-glasses, weighs the baggage in. 'Okay, that's all the food. Where's the kit?'

'I've given you the pack already, haven't I?'

'The one full of tea bags? No, I mean the bag for your tent and clothing and what have you. That must be all to come.' He ticks off a form, getting on with shuffling through hand charts and maps.

'Don't worry, I'm wearing all that.'

Laurie looks up. He looks me over – my army drill trousers, olive shirt and jungle boots. 'But the tent and –?' He stops. 'Are you the bloke that Steven was talking about, with the crowd of –' He stops. Over in the shadows of the hangar, running fingers over the fastenings of tempting pieces of cargo, are Lawrence and Fredalin and David Kari and his jet-black daughter with her thumping bare feet with rubber bands around them.

'Gadday!' he says to them. They look baffled. He repeats it. 'G'day.' He says to me, 'You taking them with you?'

'No, no. They are just making sure I'm doing all right.' From Laurie's face, it doesn't seem to be enough information. So I tell him they live over on the other side of the runway, in the trees.

'Oh I get it . . . In the trees.' He is very pensive. He wants to know more – my plans, my objectives. I lose interest in his questions and start to listen to his type of voice – it comes out undirected; some breath via his nose and all the words slow, dropping, falling downbeat and wry.

He says, 'Just one other thing, you're going tomorrow, not today actually. So you needn't have dressed up.'

But it's all I've got.

Next day as he walks out to the little plane, he turns for a last look at me standing with my entourage. The oddness seems to draw his tidy mind – a local boy with his head through a straw hat, another whose blind eye looks like a dead fish's, a seedy man who has strolled over from where he should be shifting suitcases for Talair, a girl who should be at school who has feet like car brake pads, and a man bursting forth from his trousers who has just got out of a truck – now left empty with its engine idling in the middle of the road. And this Pommy bloke in the jungle gear. What's the connection?

Two other passengers are waiting, keeping their distance from us. One is a missionary who I think needs some fresh air in his lungs. He flaps his cramped shoulders and rolls his pallid eyes, conversing submissively with the other man – a socking great half New Guinean whose face is angled by his sharp sideboards. 'It's him!' says Martin Saun. At the hotel bar he'd had an arm around a Sepik woman who maintains a considerable number of *wantoks* by 'working nights' with seven different whitemen – one of them a Catholic priest. Fredalin says, 'Wumvunnavan, he is new. This man is number eight!'

Number Eight sees us smirking behind our hands. He comes up. He takes me by the elbow. He must have overheard! He clenches his fist with my arm still in it. But before Martin Saun can set the Kandengeis on him he says, 'I wanted to warn you. Keep away from those kids. They were loitering outside the Sepik International last night. Car thieves.'

Laurie calls us to the plane. He says to me, 'Benedict, I'm going to drop you off last.' He taps his clipboard with meaning. 'That way you can look at the forest from above, see if it still suits you.' He pauses and looks over at the Kandengeis. Then back to me. He is going to say something but doesn't, and starts walking me to the plane. 'You're obviously well in here with the locals, so I won't ask you if you know what you're doing. *One* thing though . . .'

'Yes?'

He raises a biro. 'Tell your friends to back off a bit once the prop is turning. They'll get the chop otherwise.'

I flag them away. I'm about to cry – I have forgotten to drop Mum and Dad a line. Or Sue, my landlady in Tooting. They must be worried sick. I realize that I can give Laurie a note to post, but it's that I hadn't thought to do it earlier myself. Their world, my world, seems so beyond reach just now, but how can they ever understand that?

The Kandengeis, my world for now, look very frail standing on the smooth tarmac in a bunch. They look like I feel in the hands of this whiteman, like mislaid cargo. Well, here goes, Daniel, wherever you are. I wave a *yimbununga* swat that Songbird made for the journey and the Kandengeis smile, seeing it flap. But Vincilla, the girl with the large but beautifully moulded feet, is crying.

Laurie straps me in. He must have been watching. He says, 'Change of mind?'

But I hardly hear him. The Kandengeis are shuffling back. They have their eyes closed, but they want to keep their faces to the plane as its wind beats them. *If he lives, he is stronger. He has something from the forest.*

Then we are sweeping up, and south over the Sepik Plains. We drop in at Samban Mission. Laurie keeps the plane idling to fend off the mosquitoes. A whiteskin with a scrub beard and straw hat runs towards us; his parishioners stand behind, dressed in brown sago-fibre skirts or cotton cloths – with the dirt, also brown. The bony missionary looks as if he'll snap, he is so weak in the jetstream. Laurie gives him a sack of mail, takes another, and then we toss up out of this swampy place and over the crags of trees, away from the Sepik, following the Yuat towards the Highlands.

Laurie shouts above the engine noise to me in one of the back seats.

'I'm taking you in a triangle. South-east to the Highlands, west along them – behind your Sepik village – then back down to April River.' I like Laurie for doing this, for not asking questions.

The forest below us is level and blotched with sago palms that from above look like stars. The land begins to swell up; further in, it rises higher, convulsing up and reaching mist and the cloud. The forest waves become tumultuous banks with white jagged spikes. Water tumbles down screes, disappears. Scratches in the forest show limestones, sandstone. We are facing the mountains, black faces leering from white clouds.

The other passengers are shouting back and forward, over the seats. 'See this was back in the sixties. Quite a different place. Early sixties and I suppose you'd have called me a nomad. Three weeks to get in there – up the Fly, up the Strickland. *Years* before the first government patrol came in. Nowadays I've lost fitness' – he patted his stomach and we bent to look at it, commiserating – 'but back then . . .'

Meanwhile Laurie gets out his lunch box, and rests it on his knee. He seems to be wondering whether to have his sandwiches this early.

'Encroachment from the West is everywhere now, you see. And encroachment is the right word – certainly not betterment.' The missionary offers no resistance. He is in his twenties, but has already been indoors too long. He's a whiteskin who needs to take up jogging; he has thin, yellow cusps of hair.

Number Eight, the other man, says he's Green. He amplifies his statement for the missionary, who, it has to be said, looks a mite stupid. 'An environmentalist – I believe in protecting the environment. Sustainable growth.'

And yet he is flying in a plane, emitting fumes, and wearing clothes made in a factory which used up non-renewable energy. I waited for him to explain how you could be Green and not live in the forest like the Niowras. *They* were Green. He doesn't say. All he says is that he's read in the *New Scientist* that there's no such thing as Virgin Forest. 'Man has been everywhere,' he says, spanning his fingers over the tree crown billows below.

I'm really lost now. A person living as part of nature doesn't molest the forest, taking its virginity. That is why he is living as part of the forest, why he has immortality with axes made from the stones of the forest. He may damage it, but temporarily, within the forest system, no more harmful than elephants as part of savannah.

Laurie works through his lunch.

It is the missionary's turn. He says, as if he's already won the argument, 'Most of my work is with the Biamis. I was the first white they'd seen. Came in from east of the Strickland. Three days' walk. But it's low altitude.' '*Altitood*', he says, kissing on the word. He's an American. 'They're still Stone Age.'

I wanted to tell him that he had got it wrong. I wanted to say there's never been such a thing as Stone Age. Not here. Ask Kaavon. In a more seasonal climate you had to learn to think of the future to get through the winter – you 'progressed' and that enabled you to live in such inhospitable places as England. But here you didn't need to store up crops. Here, before outsiders came, you were in balance: here, before the whiteman, you had no intention of moving anywhere else. You were not going anyway. You were not of any 'Age'.

But I didn't say a word. Even if it killed me – and at this rate it would – I was doing this journey by listening and learning, seeking after only the one question, how to show I was a true Man. I must not let my old questioning, empire-building spirit from the West steer me; I was allowed just the one, Junior Man's quest.

We circle down into a swathe cut from the forest, and pock-marked with taro and sweet potato gardens. There are metal roofs whose light gets into your eyes. The plane makes a noise like a canoe outboard caught in weed. Grit from the runway bites at the windscreen, making me duck. Laurie says, 'Bad strip.'

After each collection of mail, Laurie rattles the catches, tests his seat belts, signs receipts and drops in comments to temper Number Eight, who is now proclaiming his experience as a passenger in light aircraft. He talks about 'payloads' and throws some important-sounding figures around. 'And you keep the motor running after landing to clear the fuel because it's turbo charged. Isn't that right, Laurie?'

'There's the mosquitoes as well.'

Number Eight says, 'See, all planes are turbo charged here.'

We look to Laurie to see if he's going to agree. But he's making himself busy lobbing cargo out of the belly of the plane.

Now we leave Number Eight. Villagers watch from the edge of the strip, by a shed – more browned-off clothes, more single white faces smiling harder than the rest, from above them. Some women wore sheets in front of their loins that got blown aside in the blast. Leaves parted, baring thighs. The people were dumpy and small. These highlanders looked bolder than the Niowras, and smiles came to them quicker, as if they didn't know the head-hunting tradition, only head-on battles.

Over Lake Kopiago, then to Oksapmin, which has a smooth valley with knobbles of rock through the grass, scorched black like cloud shadows. The people there have a lot of money. 'Ok Tedi [gold mine] recruiting ground,' says Laurie. They look like sportsmen: they wear running shoes, and shirts with numbers and shorts with stripes – everything fresh from the shop window, and brighter than any head-dress.

The pallid missionary crawls out of the plane and shakes my hand, saying his first words to me. 'Nice getting to know ya.'

A young whiteskin sticks his head through the window, saying he's from the Peace Corps. He asks Laurie if he could 'shift some greens'. The vegetable market is going bankrupt. Everyone is buying tinned food.

Still in the Highlands, we fly north over Sisamin, the only settlement on the way to April River. I see no sign of any trail, though Jakob said two whiteskins walked down from these mountains to April River, guided by Daniel, the man who settled a neighbourhood argument with an axe.

The plane dips and banks, avoiding the swelling clouds. 'There are two types of cloud in PNG, Benedict. There are the soft ones – those without a mountain hidden in them – and there are the hard ones.'

It's his first joke, and I feel touched he's saved it until we are alone. My father was a bush pilot once, and the thought is poignant; I feel an urge to reach out and get to know this man. But suddenly my thoughts turn away.

This is the land made, the old men say, by an old woman, Babsabei.[3] She made the trees, the mountains, the rivers and the people. All the customs come from one tree, and for a long time no one knew where it was. But then a man saw some strange fruit floating down a river. He walked up river and found the tree and beside it a house belonging to Rofee, who wears a bark skirt made from the tree and looks after it. He said he wanted some fruit. He pushed her aside and he climbed and climbed, chucking fruit down. But then the tree began to grow and grow. The man became frightened, but he couldn't jump – he was too high. Finally, the tree hit the sky. His face was blackened with the impact and this, the story goes, is what we see when a blackened sky appears before a storm.

But the man still hung on to the tree. Rofee climbed up and he still wouldn't come. Then she called on the tree to fall down, and the spirit in the tree obeyed, and the fruit tumbled down and the water inside the fruits became the lakes in the mountains near Sisamin. The man fell so hard that he is still buried in the mountain, which is called Makia. The woman is underneath another mountain, the one we call Rofee.

Nowadays, if you go near these mountains, you must wear a leaf on your head. You cannot urinate or defecate near there, and no one who goes near dares anger the spirits by fighting. This is what the old men say.

'That's the lowest pass,' Laurie says, as we slip over a mossy ridge. Some of the peaks are white; they gape like teeth in a mouth waiting to be fed. I look over Laurie's shoulder at the ranks of 'Dead Magic', the dials. One I recognize as an altimeter. It says 6000 feet. I tap it, hoping it will change as I remember from somewhere a barometer does. It doesn't go down.

Now the land drops from under us. We are back in the Sepik Basin, and flying in down the April tributary – a blue snake running on white sand. 'So, there's Niksek – the mission. See it? The huts. And over there, those blue tarpaulins – that's a mining company.'

'There's gold prospecting so near the mission?'

'Well, they've agreed to ban women and booze for now.'

We bank into the airstrip, and I see metal roofs and grey shingle paths and a white windsock within a circle of painted stones. People run in, up the paths.

The engine hasn't stopped yet, but I'm excited. We're back on the Sepik Basin, not really all that far south-west from Kandengei. I know this type of forest – this is the same marsh breath of leaf oils laid on brown clear water. Wunjumboos live here.

The people are physically much like Niowras, but their chests are smaller and some women still have grass skirts and some men twin holes in the tips of their noses, cock-eyed cassowary quills bent forward from them. These people stay back, behaving like the shyer of the Kandengeis, with full smiles but a certain guile and hesitancy in their eyes. The others, the vast majority, come forward. They smooth their Western clothes, waiting for me to emerge; they are more relaxed, not cautiously sensing, just radiating. The Kandengeis will be like this second type in a few years' time.

Among the crowd wincing in the engine blast is a townboy who looks fresh from the laundry. His hair is puffed up and his shirt is dazzling. He's sitting on a little tractor, which has a trailer full of little suitcases. He must be the Bible School teacher, Andrew. A whiteskin – Gertrude, I suppose – stands in the crowd, tucking herself in around her belt. She has just changed into her town shoes. Her high heels are sinking into the grass.

Laurie unbuckles me, and then ducks under the plane to get out my baggage. The townboy, who must be the Bible teacher, comes up. 'Hello, Laurie!' Laurie, now on the wing of the plane, is inspecting fuel levels. The Bible teacher turns to me and takes my hand, almost by force, smiling. 'Brother,' he says, grinning at me.

Gertrude is telling Laurie about a recent flood, how she'd almost lost all her lemonade stock; the kitchen table is now raised on concrete blocks, she says.

'Well, I better be off now,' Laurie says. 'If you want lifting out of here on Wednesday, that will be fine. I'll bring Jakob in then.'

I say, 'When's Wednesday?' Some more traditional women are getting closer, coming in behind the men. The shine on the grass skirts as the strands swing, catches the eye.

'Wednesday? Today's Saturday, so that'll be five days away. The 30th.'

'Are we that far into June?'

'July, Benedict. And in two days, we are on to August.'

Gertrude had struck me as open and sweet-natured. Now she's staring at me. Laurie says to her, 'He's only joking.'

But I hadn't been joking.

Laurie says, 'You should have seen his friends. Die-hard Sepiks. He's been around.'

She looked a little disturbed – as if the Sepiks were a criminal caste, which certainly isn't entirely true.

Now his plane is in the sky, and my hands are being held by the little children. I feel alone. It is Gertrude, not Laurie, who got it right. Her face said it: I didn't have a clue where I was in time or space. I should be playing by Western rules, but I had accidentally left my map in Wewak and realized it on the plane. Perhaps I should have asked to have a peep at Laurie's flying chart.

Andrew is wearing a flowery shirt. He has a controlled charisma in his square face and I'm wary of him – he might be like Nathan. We talk as the children fight to carry my bags into the trailer. He asks the latest news from the outside. But though I'm newly in, I don't seem to have any news for Andrew. In the newspapers I'd only read about the gold rush. So I ask about the food here – do they eat sago? He has to ask the crowd. They tell him they don't.

He loses interest in me. He starts the tractor, and rides off ahead. 'See you soon, brother.'

The path leads through beaten-down forest and thatched houses. I'm feeling the heat after the cool of the plane's draughts. 'Sunny day now,' I say in Pidgin.

I watch the turquoise butterflies with ink peripheries, the yellow clay crickets, the bottleglass bugs in the grass, clam shell butterflies, and speckled woodchip hoppers. Would you credit it? I'm sentimental for Kandengei.

We pass some runner beans on poles. They are thriving – part of

Jakob's vitamin plan. We walk without talking, the grass skirts of the women rustling around us, the usual sago palm and also limbum for thatching. Taro gardens, broad beans on stakes over yam plots. No Kandengei in their right mind would have planted a village on the inner loop of this river. It's a foreign idea – progress. It explains the great success of Jakob's vegetable programmes. The beans are bedded down in fine alluvial soils, the silts of a rather-too-close river.

An older boy hurries up from the village. He says, in English, he's Stefanus. 'We are expecting you. Jakob talks on the radio, said you'd come and ask for ways to the mountains. Jakob is teaching people the Good News of Gods. You will want only a bush hut to live in, he said. He said you are dirty but good.'

'Did he say that?'

'He said you were English – we must offer you tea. "Even *this* crazy Englander will want tea to drink," he said.'

I thanked him. 'But tell me, should I give your old men betelnuts as a present on my arrival? That's the Sepik custom.'

'All the betelnuts and tobaccos is thrown away – we do not think the same with Catholics. We are Christians.'

I ask him where he learned English. He says, after a moment's thought, 'Good.' Then he says, 'I got a house ready for you. We go there now, and I leave your bags. My brother, he will light your fire, protect you at night. He's called Freimond.'

Philemon, the book in the Bible? Or Freimund, a German name offered by Jakob?

Stefanus says the houses we pass – much like Kandengei's, though one has a war shield leaning on its wall – aren't quite the traditional design. The 'custom houses' are in the hills. 'The old men. *They* got some customs. Like my father. He got some.' We walk further, and Stefanus is still bubbling. 'You going to sign up men for walking? I want to go for a walk because our forest is travelling.'

'Travelling?'

'There is a country on the world. It is called Happen.'

Japan?

'Happen wants our forests. The Premier, Mr Bruce Samban, says this on Radio East Sepik. And then they will take the ground from under us.'

'Gold?'

Stefanus says enthusiastically, 'So better you and I can go to Bikaru quickly, before the ground is gone, and we cannot walk. Otherwise, sorry!'

'The Bikaru are good?'

'They got five or six customs. They got many.'

'I'm looking for a way up the Highlands.'

'Looking only?'

'Looking only. For mountain people who'll take me up.'

Stefanus looks as if he is going to faint with relief.

The village opens into a lawn with country cottages around it. In the middle is a tin-capped building which sits squarely in the path, interrupting the view. It is the church.

This was the South Seas Evangelical Mission, then. A fairly traditional quarter, which we had just strolled through – garden plots, thatched houses, all out of line. And now a little shed that must be a trade store to get everyone used to a cash economy. A church, bang in the way, and then an avenue of new, orderly housing. Also by the church was Jakob's bolted-up prefabricated house with a washing line, and Gertrude's with a whiteskin child's handcrafted owl on the door. Flowerbeds were flowering, lawns spreading; it was another bit of the planet brought to heel – and the maimed, the crippled, were everywhere.

They were a product of the Health Programme. Instead of dying, everyone was hanging on. Here a man with a white mottled scar up his leg, there another with a swollen, veined limb of tight, hard tissue. Over there was a very split lip, over yonder a man with one shirtsleeve flapping, empty. There must be dozens more – these were just the most mobile, those who had got here first. They seemed to be coming forth to show themselves off; the semi-limbed, the bent-legged; they smiled with a sort of mad benediction. They were each saying *they* were someone in particular, someone who wasn't dying, who wasn't knuckling under to nature any more. They were triumphant, celebrating humanity's medicine. Their presence was a glory to Man; they were offspring of head-hunters called down to live on the river, whose banks unfortunately were liable to flood.

'Who is Tom, Stefanus? Jakob mentioned I should take him.'

Stefanus seemed to grow a little tired of life. He said that Tom was a good man. Perfect, in some ways.

I looked over just behind Jakob's house. The river was careering along on the other side of the pearl flags of the pitpit grass. Then I looked in through Jakob's window, to the framed tapestry with words on it in Gothic script, and further along the panelled walls to a photograph of pine forests. On the table were set wooden boards; on these you ate your German sausage and black bread.

I asked Stefanus where my luggage had gone.

'It has gone to your house. Freimond needed your luggage to find the tea to make you at home.'

The crowd was beginning to disperse, and I turned, catching the smell of the roses.

'PRAY before you VOTE', said a poster on the garage the other side of the flowerbed. It had peeled half away, revealing bare wood and a wasps' nest. Someone hadn't creosoted behind the poster.

I was about to sit down on the nice lawn when, standing there, I felt a threat from behind. Something was moving in on us, quick and direct. A reptilian scuttle, the whipping of a tail, the quick wipe sound of a smooth belly covering ground fast.

Stefanus said, 'Here comes Simon.'

I turned, expecting a pet, some orphaned thing from the forests – perhaps a crocodile babe. I looked around, saw nothing. But Stefanus was looking right down by my feet.

A face was looking up at me. A strong human face at the height of my knees. Physically speaking, to be blunt about it, Simon was a tripod, his two thick arms projecting forward, his torso the third part. His legs were folded beneath him, out of order. But he had succeeded, made something of his life, where a thousand or more would have failed. I smiled and said hello.

He didn't say hello. He asked in English, 'You will stay in my house please?'

'Actually, I think I'm all fixed up for accommodation.'

'It is no trouble.' He leaned his weight on one arm, and raised the other like a strut at an Alpine cottage. It was a two-storey Black Forest building with a plank like a rampart across the front. 'I am sorry you want the hut. It is good but it is not good. You can come to my house. It is up to you.'

'Stefanus has kindly offered me a place already.'

'Tea! You are an Englishman. *I* have tea.'

'Really – it's not that I do not want to.'

'I have a paraffin light. I will share it with you. It is up to you.'

Thank you, I said. I said, perhaps I could come over some time. We'd have a good natter. He said his choral chant, 'It's up to you.'

I murmured to Stefanus that I had better give in.

Stefanus said, 'Freimond is boiling your water. He will get very angry. He will cry, even.'

Just then a woman came up – her poise as she walked across the whiteskin's lawn had already told me she was a towngirl and now I saw the long hair. It was twisted into tight little lily buds. I knew she'd want to shake hands. Everyone did, and said 'God bless, brother' as well. I put out my hand. But she took my hand and put a bunch of bananas into it. 'God bless, brother.'

Underneath us, Simon's voice said, 'I have bananas to give you too.'

Stefanus said, 'I bring my presents when they are ripe, tomorrow.'

A voice from the crowd said, '*Masta* Benedict, I too have a present for you.'

They were bananas. 'And who are you?'

The answer sounded like 'Lufthansa'. Another person – his name sounded like 'Luftwaffe' – also had a present. Bananas.

I now had more bananas than I could carry. They weren't giving bunches any more; they were giving small branches. The mission had been closed to fend off outsiders and the Nikseks were starved of strangers – they had no one to display their Christian charity to. Stefanus took the offerings; he stood beside me, looking discreetly away, like a man taking the collection.

'Teatime, I think, Stefanus.'

Simon said, 'I will go home and wait for you.' He turned on the spot, leaving a swirl in the lawn, the rubber sandals worn on his hands squeaking.

'A nice gesture,' I commented as Stefanus and I staggered to my house under the bananas. Stefanus told me who the woman was: Rosa, whose husband had recently trodden on a snake nest. Seeing his mistake, he'd jumped up a tree, but the mother came up the tree, wrapped herself around his leg and bit him. He died the next day – breakfast time, Stefanus recalled.

Freimond was boiling water in a palm cooking hut in a swamp. You got up to the neighbouring little house with the help of a removable notched pole, the traditional defensive steps up.

We sat outside the house beside a ditch of malarial mosquitoes, velvet dragonflies with wings tipped with blue, and tadpoles flowing and ebbing in swirls. I shared two biscuits that Laurie had spared me from his lunch box. I was about to tell Stefanus and Freimond my plans when a black dog walked by. It wasn't like a normal Kandengei dog, ready to run from a kick but meantime savouring the air with its nose up warily; it took one look at us having a picnic, bounded over, and laid itself belly up in front of me. It had no sores, but its eyes were almost glued up; it leaned against me. It had cocker spaniel in it somewhere and he was missing its master or mistress.

'He is a whiteman's dog,' said Freimond.

'Perhaps he would like a cup of tea,' said Stefanus, and gave him one.

Then Simon came charging down the path. I saw why his approach seemed a threat – it was the intensity of activity, the sound of the inefficient walking mechanism, his black tubular arms that were bared before him like a spider's palps. 'Come if you want to come for tea; it is up to you.'

During the afternoon the air hummed not with cicadas or crickets, but with hymns and the murmurings of villagers going about their displays of charity.

After tea with Simon, I talked to Stefanus about the Bikaru. They were two days away. Tom had said he would come but not into the mountains – the head of the Salumei and Korosameri – because the men there would shoot us. We'd go along the foothills, directly east to the Bikaru, who might take me up to higher, mountain people. Bikaru were very clever. 'In the bush they can cut the neck open and put things in the *bel* [spiritual stomach] and later he can fix them, and put the head back on.'

'Just my sort of people,' I said. But in some ways I did mean it. Good or bad, they clearly knew the forest. They might even have the necessary magic to launch me out on my *geenjumboo* journey themselves. I could miss out those mountains.

In the afternoon, as I washed alone in a brook by the airstrip, Freimond waded up holding a turtle. I made no attempt to hide my crocodile marks. 'Can I have your supper with you?' he said, in Pidgin, weighing the turtle. 'Jakob says you eat wild animals and he will go well with your rice.' The turtle extended its head, and looked around. We were standing there, midstream, and Freimond saw the marks. He watched them, as if waiting for them to move. He said, 'I had a good *singsing* once at Ambunti. Now they don't allow me to go. It is very pagan.'

He must have kept what he had seen – the 'pagan' marks – to himself because they would have caused quite a stir here, among the converted. In the late afternoon we sat in the house while those villagers who had been out in their gardens all day came to shake hands. Eventually they were gone – all except two children, a boy who picked grass seeds from my trousers and a little girl in pink silk underwear, perhaps a donation from a repentant club in a Hamburg red light district, who clung to my hand, neglected and dumb. By the way the two children thrust their hands in mine and stayed with me to the dusk, they must have been two of Jakob's favourites.

The boy ran along home; Freimond and I walked with the silent girl through the last light of day to the church. We watched from the back of the building, a huge, open-sided iron shed. At the altar was an old man who looked already dead and beside him a shining-faced man with the elaborate sideburns of a townboy. He had one hand behind his back; he was holding the Bible in the other. Freimond said, looking up the aisle at him, 'Tom.'

Tom was talking in a local language, but I didn't need to be able to speak it. There were key, untranslatable words. Satan, Hell, sinners . . . Jesus, Whiteman, 'Good News'.

The old man talked excitedly from the shadows and Tom translated sentence by sentence in Pidgin – a liturgy of urgent messages. It sounded like news from a war zone; each had come red hot from a Marathon of the soul.

'Adam and Eve are mother and father of us all. We are brothers. Brothers in Christ. This is the good news. We are brothers. God is our father who is in Heaven. We do not fight. We do not fight. We are all from the same family.'

It was cheering to hear an uprooted people so certain about the world as it too was about to be uprooted around them, but I couldn't take much more just now. It wasn't even Sunday. However, it was almost dark, and they'd have to stop, I thought, watching the sun flare orange along the horizon. But pressure lamps were brought in. Now Tom the preacher and his high-pitched witness were ghastly silhouettes. Shadows of hands swept over the corrugated metal ceiling. Yellow faces, arms long, swaying like branches, fingers outstretched, raking the air.

Perhaps the small girl hadn't come to church this late before; perhaps the paraffin lamps were a new idea; whatever, she reacted violently to the manic shadows, shaking herself away from Freimond and me. I left to reassure her. Tom's voice died away behind us – *Baimbai Jisas Kraist i-kam*, Jesus will come one day.

Stefanus came out after me. I told him I was worried about taking Tom. The Bikarus might thump him, if he started preaching. They might thump all of us.

'But he must tell them. People who do not believe, *this* time when Jesus come he gathers them together and put them in a fire. It is Good News.'

'Will the Bikarus react well to the Good News? I wouldn't.'

He reassured me. I understood he'd show me a living example of the old, unconverted person – his dad. The next morning we went down a neat avenue of palms, a wide corridor of equally spaced houses, passing freshly cut swamp grass laid out on the paths, green and grey, drying for women's skirts.

A man who was the same colour as the mud stepped out from about the fifth house on the left. He wore a cape made from a hessian sack; he smiled happily. He seemed a gentleman, like Kaavon, like Jakob. Stefanus said, 'He is too afraid of Pesee-ai who can kill peoples and eat.' Stefanus described Pesee-ai, who sounded like Wunjumboo – he lived in mountains and came down to sleep with them sometimes, when they hadn't been praying enough.

However, the old man was gleaming at me, not looking very concerned about his old pagan ways. Stefanus went on: 'He isn't able to eat the pandanus fruit. If you do not eat, you do not grow. And sometimes, you can die.' But now, Stefanus said, he could eat anything. 'We have Good News.'

The old man stood there proudly with his hessian sack. I was almost sure he was suppressing a laugh. He exchanged knowing glances at a friend of his who had rattan curled around his waist and cassowary quills unashamedly in his nose.

This other man was beginning to snort. Stefanus continued, quizzically, wondering what the joke was. He scratched his hair and told me that Tom's uncle, Wanikee, was swimming at the head of the river and a water spirit took him. The body bobbed up four days later.

'Bbbbssssh!' exploded the old man.

Most of their children died,[4] Stefanus said, now turning to the gravity of day-to-day living in the old days. When they told the young men customs – this must be their version of the Crocodile Nest – the women had to eat separately, because if they accidentally picked up food the spirits meant for an initiate, they'd die. They used to live in the high houses, in fear of their neighbours the Gahuns; their doorways were as small as windows. In the past, Stefanus was, in effect, saying, the cost of living had been very high.

But the father couldn't stop himself laughing now and let out another violent eruption, spraying us both.

'He doesn't seem to think things were all that bad. Yet they were worse than Kandengei, according to you. Is he perhaps just relieved he's here, in safety? Is that it?'

Stefanus said, 'Please, let us go home.' He was leaving.

'Tenkyu tru,' I said to the old men. And to Stefanus, 'So why's he laughing?'

'I do not know, it is unlucky for me when I wanted to show him off. Instead he laughs and says the old story: "Water follows whiteskins," he says.'

'That's a saying round here, is it?'

'Yes; he thinks that water will take us all away unless we go up to the mountains.'

I said that, funnily enough, Jakob was worried about flooding as well. 'But he thinks it's all right now the dry season is here.'

'My father the pagan,' said Stefanus, 'says the water will come up in two moons' time. It will wipe away through the village to the whiteman's airstrip. It will be too disastrous.'

Which, as things turned out, was the more accurate prediction.[5]

Next morning, Freimond, helping me cook some of our stock of bananas, said, 'You really have to take Tom? I think you can just take me. You have lived a long time in the bush. So it's easy, we can run away together.'

I laughed, 'The flood won't come for a while – that's what Jakob thinks. And what else is there to run away from here?' Which just goes to show how little I knew about Niksek.

The Nikseks smiled at you without asking. Worse, they had a burning desire to serve and I was a stranger to whom they could serve up their message. But I didn't want to be done a good turn, just today. I wanted to hear about the forest – to which they no longer belonged. And they made it clear they no longer belonged: they had a Teutonic version of Western urgency and marched about Niksek as if always wanting to go somewhere.

That first day, I put it down to the climate. They'd come from the hills – their cloud-soaked forests weren't slow and steady. Up there, you had to keep moving, and down here they were too fast for the hot slow grind. But another day's worth and I'd seen more than enough evidence. I understood Freimond's remark – I wanted to run away too.

There were the church services to get you in the mood every day, and also every Wednesday and Friday afternoon, with extra sessions on Sunday. And if that didn't sustain your desire to Progress through the week, there was the Bible class and the ordinary government school.

The next day, Sunday, I knew it was daylight even before the cocks crowed – and the hymn singing hadn't even warmed up properly yet. I sat in the cooking shack on a stack of firewood, my back against a rib of limbum palm support, earth cold under my feet, trying not to listen. A black wasp ducked into its crumbly earth volcano; I took comfort in being hermit-like in my hovel – the dust crumbs of insects, the ant tunnels under construction, the sweet steam of the roasting banana skins. I was already waiting for night, when the hymn singing would stop and the frogs would mew and crack again. So far we hadn't even had the church service. Afterwards, like yesterday, there'd be a blissful afternoon lull – just the piping blast of cicadas as the leaves of the banana palms were stilled by the heat, clouds raised off the slopes – then back to singing again.

Freimond said it was church time and dutifully went his way. 'I'll be along in a minute,' I said. Freimond looked at me doubtfully. I plucked another banana. But then the little girl in the silk underwear craned around the door, took my hand and led me off.

The path seemed to be blocked with everyone going to church or going around explaining to all their neighbours why they were too busy today. We were near enough to hear the band now – one ukulele, more than enough guitars, a boy whacking bamboo pipes with a rubber sandal.

Ladies were placing hibiscus blossoms along the machined timbers of the church, and on a river boulder step up to the tree-trunk altar, with its wooden slab lectern.

A man was directing the villagers up the aisle with a rod, steering them to the plank seats, men to the left, women to the right, yanking children out to the front to sit on the ground facing us. I didn't like the *avookwaark*-like old men being marshalled like this, but the men themselves didn't object. We waited our turn. A child bent over in the aisle and a woman wiped his bottom with a taro leaf. After these two had been prodded into place, I was steered off to the men's side, the girl taken away to sit at the front, where she sobbed with the other children. No one seemed to notice them; the adults here were in a fervour, shaking hands with their neighbours as if they'd forgotten they saw them every hour of the day. Men crossed the congregation as if chancing across an old friend. They hugged each other, exchanged heady smiles, raising eyebrows in surprise, sticking out their pink tongues in delight.

We were about to begin. Three ladies came to the front, two flapping at tambourines, the third clacking her hard hands together. They looked mesmerized – concentrating on something beyond, not here, amongst all this racket. After the song, we all clapped lightly and smiled at our neighbours. I noticed I was sitting in front of Daniel, the axe murderer. I felt him breathing down my back.

There's rude applause from behind. I'm the only one who notices. I turn around to see a hornbill alighting on a cross-beam at the back. She flies over us, clacking her wings, one of which is broken and sagging. She plucks a black beetle. Tips back her head, and rolls the beetle a little way down her beak. Tosses him, knocks his head off, squeezes him twice and lobs him back.

Then the hornbill flies off, scared by something. I turn forward again and see it's Tom, who has stood up. He begins translating the three languages of those felt called to witness – the more local Nikseks, the Moroboté, and the Biamé, from where we were going. Tom tilts his head as if to hear the echo of his own voice off the metal ceiling. He presses his other ear into the blast of confession coming from the old reformed killers standing in their bare feet, their spines planted in narrow hips from which their new shorts droop.

Tom rolled his head and smiled, acting out a jive to the beat of the rhetoric, accumulating sweat under his green nylon shirt and along his fancy sideburns. There were individual contributions, but mostly the service was a series of orchestrated group efforts led by a youth with a miniature left arm. There was more hand-shaking, then the congregation brought forward gifts of yams and taro; from time to time my attention strayed to the hornbill hopping by on the lawn, flapping headlong into shrubberies or crashing into the mango tree.

The text for the day was 2 Corinthians 6. The whole of it. 'Warning against pagan influences,' said the *Good News Bible*. Verse 14 was, 'Do not try to work together as equals with unbelievers, for it cannot be done. How can right and wrong be partners? How can light and darkness live together? How can Christ and the Devil agree? What does a believer have in common with an unbeliever? How can God's temple come to terms with pagan idols?'

Here was Nathan the AOG all over again – the following of strident Paul without regard to the humility of Jesus. It was the religion of Fundamentalists, whether 'pagan' or Christian. It was the copying of a pattern, not the looking for the meaning in that pattern.

Everyone was bowing their heads – '*Yumi pre*' – and now erupting into their own prayers. It was a burbling that sounded mad and unformed, passions released not in the controlled power of ritual dance, but the many varied directions that answered lots of individuals' needs.

After all the various sermons and speeches, Andrew welcomed me to the congregation, and said how good it was to have me here as a visitor. Which was a shame in a way, because I wasn't going to be able to take much more of this – nothing personal, it was just unnatural to me. But the last guitar strummed, the last woman bobbed at the altar. Simon scuttled out, his keys jingling in his back pocket. Suddenly he was in his element, scaling the ladder to his Black Forest house with the idle swing of power of a monkey.

Today was Sunday. We could not leave today – it was the Sabbath. Nor could we gather food supplies from the gardens until tomorrow. That meant leaving on a Tuesday. I decided to wait the extra day, when Jakob would arrive. I wanted to be sure the Bikarus wouldn't mind Tom. Word might have got out about his preaching habits.

On the Wednesday, I heard Laurie's plane buzzing in. Andrew unlocked the garage – it said TAMBU, 'forbidden', across it – and started up the tractor. We set off to the airstrip, and I stood in the crowd, waving with everyone.

'You are still on your feet, Benedict?' said Jakob. But he checked to see if I smiled before he chuckled and rubbed his belly happily with his hand.

Laurie asked, 'You want to hang on in here?'

I said I hadn't begun yet, and he smiled. 'See you around, then.' He was looking kindly at me – we seemed to have something in common. I couldn't help marvelling at him and his instruments, he couldn't help marvelling at me and the Sepiks.

Jakob was pressed for time. He was leaving again tomorrow. Soon he had put on a smart baseball hat and was in dungarees, in the forest with the tractor, cutting planks with a chainsaw. He invited me to supper, and after grace we were to eat sausage and black bread – while his eyes were closed I could hardly resist reaching for it.

I looked at this whiteskin as he was carving the sausage into fair portions. This man who could cut up logs with an advanced German chainsaw believed in eternal bonfires – sulphurous landscapes where he and I would go if we didn't watch it.

He asked me a lot of questions again, but I only had the one for him: how were the Bikarus likely to react to Tom's preaching? Jakob reassured me that Tom had been near the Bikarus months ago and had told some he'd met that he'd be back with the Good News; we needn't worry. The Bikarus were waiting. 'And by the way, you must hurry up. The logging companies have got their concession rights sorted out. Also, there's a new gold mining company moving in.'

I watched him as I munched German sausage in my fingers. Jakob believes in hell, a real place of steaming yellow sulphur and molten agony, I thought, my cheeks stuffed. And after a while Jakob stopped asking questions and put down his knife and fork to watch me. Now he was wondering what *I* believed. He slotted his arms under his chin as I drank the 'blackcurrant-flavoured' liquid and lined up the rest of the sausage, Vegemite, remainder of the loaf, and all the other food left unclaimed on the table.

As I walked back in the dark, Jakob turned the generator off. At last, the people of Niksek were peaceful. I was aware of the sounds I couldn't hear during the day, the forest creeping around, a cosmos filled with the scratching of insects trying to take the land back to nature. These evenings were empty, without the company of Stars on the Water and Nightlight, and I looked up to the moon which, people say, is the very first girl in creation; and then I looked over to the second girl, the evening star, and then the others, the lights in the eyes of the other girls. I want to be able to believe in you, I thought, but if that's not possible then at least to have a sense of you – and the single eye of Yay, who will rise as the sun tomorrow.

Back in my little house, Freimond said we couldn't leave before mid-morning – an extra church service had been arranged for Jakob. We got up late instead and had a leisurely breakfast, trying not to hear the ringing in our ears.

After the service, I distributed the loads, finding Tom's pack already half full of Bibles for the Bikaru, who, needless to say, couldn't read. Jakob persuaded Tom to leave three of them behind. But after he'd prayed over us as we stood bent under our packs, he gave me one of his own, a New Testament. 'This has got everything you need in it,' he said. 'But you'd better go anyway – you look decided on it.'

I said I was. But I thanked him, and tucked it away.

It was already mid-morning. As far as I was concerned, we had lost five hours' walking time. We did a lot of hand-shaking around the village, and then walked out, led by Tom. He marched off and it was hard not to feel carried by his enthusiasm and sure objective. From the church service, he was being launched by a people who were convinced of themselves, as the Kandengeis had once been, in the times when their nests were green and not dying.

As Tom pulled us along with his head-hunter determination we passed Stefanus's father, who did a bow to me, and laughed, shaking his head. Then we walked down to the April River over grey boulders to green, tatty water and a boy waiting to ferry us across in a dug-out. I thought our journey had begun. Not quite. Tom said we had to pray before we crossed the river. We put our packs in the canoe, and crouched among the boulders. His voice wavered, fighting the roar of the water as it licked away the sands of the deforested banks. The prayer was strictly an insurance deal, a policy against acts of God; he systematically asked for cover against drowning, snake bites, bees, people.

With that done, we made the crossing, and Tom was off into the forest, eyes ahead along the trail.

However, soon, beyond the ruffled vegetation around the gardens, Tom was lagging. He wanted to pause to admire the forest. He stopped to finger the bracket fungi hanging like pink cockleshells. Aloud, he was marvelling at these simple, normal things as the work of God. Even the cassowary faeces – mushy peas in a heap. The forest was a garden, at his disposal. He rejoiced in this liberty, scarcely noticing himself beginning to sink under the weight of the Bibles and picture-book conversion kits, as they sucked up the wet air.

Tom whistled 'Amazing Grace', and sighed 'Hallelujah!' seeing a hornbill gliding overhead, dividing the air coarsely, or again at the river butterflies coming for salt from our sweat, their wings so large you felt their breeze. Up through tunnels, down through timber gullies. Tom lagged behind some more. He was not fit. On we went and his books sucked up more and more water, his pack pulled his shoulders further back.

Stefanus hummed Christian songs as we went along, foraging where he could – spearing the fish we call bigmouth, snatching an arm-length monitor lizard from its hole, whipping a snake out from under a leaf. But soon he was chanting, not singing. The words were less than the rhythm, as his mind gave space to the jetting foliage, craning trunks, fruit pods, trunk skins, insects tightly crouched among them all. Despite the years at the mission, the leaves, the birds, the fungal odours could still travel uninterrupted through his mind.

We walked on and on, Stefanus and Freimond now hunting together, back to the old times, acting again like participators in the day-to-day forest, cleaning the trail with their bush knives, foraging more and more keenly.

Tom was still admiring the forest like a tourist; he was busy loving these creatures for being works of God. He talked aloud to Jesus about the Jewish story of creation – working through the six days one by one. 'Man hadn't come yet, God was busy making the stars. And making the fish, the cassowaries, the turtles, the frogs and *olgera samting*.' When there was fruit lying across our way as if spilt from a basket, and now washed of colour, he stopped to admire them; or, as we came to a river, he would gaze at a single vermilion flower left on a rock by last night's high water.

We climbed a hill with conifers which oozed daggers of dried sap, and broke them off for firelighters, then passed a stone which had been cleaned of moss – no one came this way, so a spirit must live inside it. And near this tree with roots as tall as shields, Tom's sister had been taken by a spirit when he was a boy. She and another brother had been out in the forest, some distance apart along a trail. But Baikwaal, the stone spirit, had seen her. He pretended to be her brother and brought her home. He locked the door of his stone. She hadn't been out since.

We kept moving. Here also a girl was killed by her father. He was furious at not having received her bride price. He poured a magic egg into the river where she was washing. She drank some of the magic, and when she died they laid her body in a tree – it was the custom here instead of burying.

After half a day, the Bibles were beginning to weigh on Tom. He refused to surrender them but was having to rub his calves down in the cool of the rivers and looked like a woman who's spent too long near the fire. Now when he said 'Hallelujah!' it was as if to reassure himself he still could manage it. He sat down repeatedly in the afternoon rain – once I went back and found him just staring at the bed of white fungal caps he had collapsed among. We took it in turns to wait with him, while little grasshoppers assembled on our white sacks, waving their long antennae at each other, or a bristle brush caterpillar lurched across, looking for something to consume.

We stopped for the night at an old bush camp, a raised tent of sago leaves by a shallow gully where water cut tidily over green stones. We cut fresh leaves to plug the leaks, and laid others down as a floor, stacking the various pig skulls left lying about.

When Tom was recovered enough, he gave us a guide to his Do-It-Yourself Conversion Kit.[6] No one had asked for the explanation but he held the book in the light of the fire, blowing the embers to keep them burning bright. Stefanus stirred the snake on the fire as it burned from Tom's fanning and Freimond and I concentrated on our lizard, the rice and the frogs.

The Conversion Kit had quotes from the Bible and a cartoon of two men dying. The first was bad and you knew he was bad because he had an SP beer bottle at the side of his deathbed and in the next sequence was doing a cartwheel fall through the floorboards to Satan in the red cellar below. The second man had also left his bed. He had a Bible propped up by his pillow for his visitors to see. But this man was flying up the banisters into a bright room upstairs.

We ate the rest of our supper – the lizard, a male which turned out to be very old, his meat in dry little parcels, like unravelled string. Then the turtle. Freimond placed her upside down on the fire. As she felt the heat, her head shot out of the shell. She kicked and kicked and lay still, another cycle completed in the forest, while Tom was still droning on.

We walked another day, this one through the rain. Our packs got heavier. The forest creepers trembled in the downpour, gaps between the roots were watertroughs and across them sailed rain-plucked petals.

Tom talked louder, harder, as if to overcome the sound of the crashing rain, the runnels of mud, the forest itself. He worked through creation, through all the animals and plants, the making of Adam, the making of Eve, meanwhile battling under the weight of the books. 'No singsongs tonight,' I muttered hopefully to Freimond, as we shared out Tom's Bibles and carried on.

The mud ran from under our feet. Grabbing a branch I spiked my hand on the prickly back of a bug – its spindle feet kicked while I pulled it out of the palm of my hand. Further on the leeches were bad; one dropped into my mouth and Freimond had to pull it from my tongue. Finally, we crossed a hill that marked the beginning of Bikaru territory and walked down a river to their forest gardens. We slept the second night there, in a garden hut, and waded on down the river, the Gruvé, the next morning.

The first sign was a change in the quality of the driving mist, which unfolded a sheet of blue from its grey. We couldn't smell the woodsmoke but walked on towards it through the river shallows, slowing so that Tom could catch up and introduce us. Then, on the left bank, there was a bowl of more blue smoke rising from a break in the forest.

We stood in the river while Tom took the lead.

The settlement was half a dozen houses on high stilts, all but one of them crouching on the edge of the clearing, as if not wanting to come out into the open. The one house by the river bank had two men out on its narrow plank veranda. They hadn't seen us yet. One was slumped, black against the sky, picking his feet. The other was leaning back on the doorpost, scratching.

A high-pitched shriek cut through the rain. They'd seen us. A smaller figure sprang out through the doorway. His mouth was open. He yelled, and jabbed his arms; his face had a darting quality which, if I hadn't known better, I would have taken as aggression. 'Er, Tom?' I said. 'Tom, why are they so agitated?'

Leaves flapped up from their waists. The men seemed to be bouncing on the veranda, wondering what to do about us. Cassowary quill earrings swung out from their heads as they turned this way and that. I caught a movement over to my left, deeper in the village, but I'd missed whoever it was – probably just women scuttling to hide. A couple of dogs were also running indoors.

Tom called out quickly, but the men took no notice. I guessed then that they knew exactly who we were. They disappeared inside and came out again. They didn't know what to do with themselves. But we were near enough now to see they were grinning to each other. I had taken it as tension at first, but it was wild excitement.

Stefanus waved me on. I said, thinking of their animated faces, 'A good sign.'

We crossed to their side of the river and now five of them stood over us at the bank, watching over us, now assertive with their eyes, stroking their nipples, which were prominent on their chests. They were smiling, pleased for each other. One man had a towel as his dress, and a kina coin on a white necklace of beads, a second a bandoleer of blue nylon rope. They mostly had grass aprons that swung like thick hairy mats from around their waists, which were encircled by rings of cane.

I unlaced my boots and unfastened the leeches and followed the others indoors. It was a bachelors' house, with a fire blazing in a box of stones in the middle. We sat on our heels around the edge of the room, inspecting each other shyly as we got warm. Most of their attention was on me. They looked hard into my eyes, as if looking at the grainy blue quality of my irises. It was to be expected – I was one of their first whitemen. But, I began to see, there was more to it than that. In these cases peoples are usually a little scared of me – my novelty value. But the Bikarus, not old enough to be Junior Men yet, weren't even avoiding my eyes. From time to time, they directed their gaze at Tom, but he was still trying to revitalize himself. At last they grew a little tired of looking at us. They asked Tom a question and then tried the rest of us. We shrugged our shoulders.

'Sorry, everyone,' I said in Pidgin, 'don't speak the language.' They didn't understand that either. I went to fetch water to make some tea. Outside, the rain was picking charcoal from the ash of past fires.

Back indoors, nothing had changed. Tom was on his back and useless to everyone. The Bikarus were still looking at us. With hope, I now realized. Their eyes were directed and knowing – they were expecting something from us. With growing unease, Stefanus, Freimond and I waited for an explanation from Tom – why were the Bikarus waiting? One way or other, we were all waiting for Tom for answers, all of us looking at each other and glancing around this house, the sago-palm roof, the walls of overlapping planks that were freshly cut, still pale and scented. We looked around at the cassowary bone daggers, the arrows, bush knives, the odd spoon and sardine can, and waited for Tom.

'Freimond, what do you think Tom has gone and promised them? Break it to me gently please.'

'They think you're from the company,' Freimond said. 'They keep saying to themselves, "Company, company!"'

'Which company?'

'The whiteskin's gold company,' said Freimond.

'No, from Heaven,' said Stefanus. 'They think you have news of the Company of Heavenly Hosts.'

'Well, which is it?' I said.

'They are expecting that you are both Companies, Benedix,' Stefanus said.

'Tom,' I said, my voice wavering, 'Tom, what exactly have you been promising these people?'

The first real sign of recovery from Tom was when he began whistling a godly tune. While this went on, the Bikarus buried their heads in the teacups we passed around, and one began strumming a bamboo mouth harp. Tom then started talking to me in Pidgin, telling me the Christian message as if I hadn't heard from him today a dozen times already. It was an indirect way of broaching the subject to the Bikarus – the subject of their conversion. Tom hadn't explained himself to us yet, but at least it was something for the Bikarus to be getting on with. He sang a little tune, and every Bikaru man began copying, dimly recollecting Tom's previous visit, singing a few beats behind, diligently.

In the afternoon I took a walk around and discovered the village was empty – but for a couple of women and children and these boys. Some Senior Men would come in from their gardens in a few days' time; if I did find guides to take me into the mountains, it would have to be them.

On further investigation we learnt that a helicopter had been seen again by the Bikarus recently, reinforcing whatever fibs Tom had been telling them. They believed, and the Bikarus were right here, that the Company's arrival was imminent. This fired Tom, who said he wanted a Bible meeting. So that evening we all trooped to the only occupied family house. The young Bikarus, expecting heaven knows what, happily lit their way through the village, whirling firewood and singing Tom's hymn.

Because these people had lived in scattered hamlets in the mountains there had been no real use for a geygo, a men's clubhouse, and so the village houses weren't solely the women's domain. Inside, through the hatch entrance, I found there were two women who wore black head-nets rimmed with cowries, and they sat behind the fireplaces at both ends, restricting themselves, a new-born baby and three baby girls to the open corridors around the sides.

The men had the main, central space and into this, on that first night, came Tom, Stefanus, Freimond, myself and the Bikaru youths. The women shrank away into the dark until we couldn't see them, and Tom stood up, with the book in his hand. He ordered the Bikarus to tell him their taboos. The women might not have been here, they were so still, and the youths wanted to leave suddenly. Tom told them to speak. After some while, they obeyed. If a man slept in the women's corridor, he would get a cough and die, it was said. If this baby had not been born away from the village someone would get sick, it was said.

Tom said '*Em nau.*' Right. He flourished his Bible – it flapped like a captured bird as he waved his hand. He said that he wanted to release the Bikarus from these taboos. He gave them the good news about their being saved and read out some passages. And then he began to impose his own taboos. The Bikarus mustn't put on masks and feathers, they mustn't dance. They mustn't chew betelnut, which grew wild here, or smoke, because a spirit would make them sing.

Tom turned to us for some support – the Bikarus were looking confused, Freimond looked unenthusiastic; Stefanus didn't want to say anything himself, but prompted me with, 'If they do these things, they are spoiling the Bible.' And again, 'They are going to the fire.'

'Don't look at me,' I said. 'I'm only meant to be leading this expedition.'

Stefanus said in Pidgin, 'My father is happy to be free of the taboos. Happy in his soul.'

I said I was more interested in getting up the mountains than in religious semantics, but if he really wanted my opinion I didn't think his father was all that unhappy about the old life.

'Tom is wrong,' Freimond burst out, unexpectedly. 'We are not free of taboos at Niksek. He can't drive Jakob's car – the one with big wheels that carries the luggage and lives in a house. That is taboo. Using the chainsaw that cuts trees with a noise – that is taboo. Eating breakfast with Jakob. That is taboo.'

The Bikarus were watching us arguing among ourselves, wondering when the cash was coming.

The following night the Senior Men came in from the bush. They hadn't seen Tom before. They hadn't seen whitemen either. But they were not afraid; they walked right past Tom, trotting by with their leaf aprons rustling, the bones in their noses pert, and put their hands in mine; they looked thankful and relieved, as if all the waiting was at long last over.

Tom wasn't to be put off. He came up, hanging his tongue out, the local expression for joy. 'They have cut their hair! They've cut their hair to be clean and ready for the Good News.'

But the old men were interested in me, my white skin, not in Tom. And we all knew why.

There was a storm that night. Logs that had rotted hollow in their skins gushed like drains, and even though the thunder stayed in the mountains it made the Bikaru men crouch and shiver. It was Hatibam, a man in the sky who was beating the walls of his house with a stick. The men told the little girls to hold themselves and shout '*Sikofai-fai*,' calling him to stop it. Tom shouted that they needn't do this. But it was me the men wanted to hear from. 'The Company,' they called me.

So I had their attention, and there might be hope yet. Tom now agreed to help translate and I did a little confidence-boosting. At Kandengei we sometimes put a betelnut out on the river bank, to pay the spirits to chase the fish into the split bamboo traps, I said. Perhaps you do that too, I said. 'Yes? We're the same then!' And you tell your children to scream and bang coconuts, because this scares away the mosquitoes? Yes?

But I was leading up to a request; I wanted them to take me back to where they had come from, back up the mountains. When they heard it, one by one, two by two, they picked themselves up, and turned their attention back to Tom. Finally, the last member of my audience, a woman who had come from the shadows to hear me, picked up her breast and put it in a child's mouth; she looked to Tom as well.

The women settled the grass skirts of their girls, only occasionally looking back to me, as if wondering whether I was teasing. Otherwise they only took their eyes off Tom, the man of the Good News, when prodding the red-skinned bananas on the fire, or to kick the dog. In personal appearance they had already begun to change. One woman's skirt now had blue plastic strips bulking out the grass. The young had a comb or two each – they left them in their hair, handy for beautifying themselves. Some had badly grazed jaws from shaving over and over again with blunted razors.

And Tom's speeches, getting the Bikarus converted from old hardness to new hardness, were let fly. Outside the lightning, inside Tom. He was a shaman – he knew how to use theatre, to wield energies. He spoke as if there was no time. He used the shadow of his raking fingers on the wall, the light on his face in the dark. He praised nature for being beautiful, a garden. And then dramatically, a gesture that confuses everyone and shocks me, after all his courteous behaviour to the forest, he feeds a grasshopper to the hot glass of the paraffin lamp. We watch it flick its fat abdomen, whip its nylon antennae. 'We, not animals, are in the image of God. These things are given for us, in God's glory,' he says as the insect squirms. He tosses it aside. The dog eats it up.

*   *   *

The Gahuns, down river towards Kandengei, were my only other real hope. But there we'd be nearing the next-door evangelists, the New Tribes Mission, who had managed to gain a reputation as one of the two most rabid of the world's missionary groups.[7] The other was the Summer Institute of Linguistics, who had founded Gahun . . .

It seemed hardly worth the effort to give them a visit, especially as the Gahuns were traditional enemies and Tom's father had killed a Gahun here, in the Gruvé river, in the days before they left their land, they too drawn down to a mission. But I mustn't be put off by details – this was a man's journey, and I wasn't going to show my face in Kandengei again quite this soon. Even by my standards, it would be a disaster.

However, we didn't know the trails to get there. He said it might take two days down there by foot.

'Too long,' I said. The whole forest was shaking up. Villages were no longer villages, they were staging posts, and the momentum the missions had started was gathering daily, as the companies swooped in. Suddenly, every day seemed to count.

'But how do we get there?' Freimond said.

'We build some rafts,' I found myself saying. Never quick to grasp practical solutions in the forest, I was desperate now. Wallace, Johnson, anyone at Kandengei would have been stunned. 'Two should do, don't you think, Freimond? You're in charge of construction. Stefanus, you recruit a Bikaru to help. We'll set off down the river tomorrow.'

'You sure about this?' Freimond said.

I wasn't, but Tom agreed to leave Bikaru for another time – the Bikarus were by now getting bored waiting for cash from him – and with the Bikaru boy's help, we found the right timber near the main river, the Sitifa. We left the two rafts for tomorrow's early start.

There are no farewells. A dog, wet from the river, stands regurgitating a forest meal for its puppies as they nuzzle it. That is the only movement in the village. The men watch, the women watch. Then they go back indoors to sit and wait for the Company.

Taking the Bikaru boy to guide us through rapids, we push off into the Sitifa, steering with poles. With the Gahuns now gone down river and learning to eat from cans, the river banks were full of animals. We see sulphur crested cockatoos, white egrets, black parrots in the grassier banks, hornbills in pairs, flushes of little green parrots. We catch ten turtles and one nailfish before the sun is above the trees. And later on the left is a tree that's mottled with brown and grey lichen and has small spade leaves; it is the Rofee tree, the one in the story of Creation, which the man climbed to eat the forbidden fruit.

Our voices echo between the banks – the Bikaru sighing happily, dreaming of what might lie ahead of him as he combs his hair. Stefanus, Freimond and I whoop at the animals, and Tom yells hallelujahs. The rapids are small so far. At this rate we will be there in a few hours.

We tie the food sacks up on a frame out of the water and race on, taking more risks. I'm impatient to get to Gahun now. It seems as if even this evening will be too late. I need some people to take me to their homelands, but they're all coming the other way, their bound energy breaking. I listen to Tom's cry of hallelujah – a cry heralding a stronger one, that of the chainsaws. And as we race down river, jetting over the patches of white water, I'm aware of my smallness. One person can accomplish so little in the forest – it is a place for bands.

The sun rises. The banks of leaves glare. Our shadows on the water are black. Under the baking air the cracks in the façade of vegetation seem to widen and deepen. Soon, all the green seems to have stopped flowing through the veins of the forest. The world is waiting for dusk. Down river, the Hunstein Range comes into view, the smoky hills lying behind Kandengei, but by now my thoughts are pointing away; I must get into the mountains.

We roast the turtles in the shade of a tree that has been washed ashore onto a field of boulders, the instep of the river. Then we rejoin our rafts and Gahun is in sight.

It is worse than expected; they are not part of the West, like Niksek, nor waiting for it, like Bikaru. It has been and gone – they have mislaid it. It's a ragamuffin settlement created by an SIL missionary who's now moved on. The people look shocked, as if he has just left suddenly, slamming the door. But he left years ago.

A line of young men present themselves to me. I'm not out of my wet shirt yet but they stand in my way like a deputation of school monitors. They look anxious. They say their names in turn. 'Timothy, Philip, John, Matthew, Mark . . .'

Behind them, villagers are now running to me, throwing off their rags to show their wounds. Others are beginning to bring forward the sick, the lame. They bicker about who will be treated first. The old arrive last and ask if I can build an airstrip for them.

We are very tired from our journey. 'Not today, anyway,' I say.

Thank heavens, Freimond knows someone here. He barges through the crowds, ferrying our bags up into his thatched house. I follow; all we want to do is draw up the pole steps and hide from the Gahuns. A man stands below us and waves an ulcer on his heel. Another man presents his rotted stump of a nose. Not before time, the line of young men call people away into church. They ask if I want to preach.

Stefanus, Freimond and I sit in our house, resting and hiding, and during church children play a poor game of volleyball over a fishing net with floats. Clothes hang off the children in various disarray, all duller than the mud, the sago thatch, the wooden walls. The colour of Gahun is grey. It's a place of scaly breasts, empty nose holes and empty hearts. This is a vacuum left by the missionaries. In church I hear Tom saying that everyone must be happy with their Good News. He sounds unhappy as well.

The thighs and hips of the children are exposed as they lunge at the ball, tearing their rags; they are trying to impress me with their Western skills. I go to the old and give all our aspirins. The others I refuse – I've now heard that there's a new mission being built only a day away, and they could get free medicine from there. No one has bothered.

It rains next day. The people, the mud, the thatch darken together. As the sun comes out the thatch, the ground and skin turn brown again. These people should be out in the bush, getting food, but they prefer to wait here, to hang around in queues not really sure of what they are meant to ask me for.

We have no aspirins left, even for ourselves; we have nothing to eat but rice.

One of the young men, Philip, says tomorrow he's going through the sago swamps to Inaru, the new mission. He'll guide us; it's the New Tribes Mission reaching out this way along the foothills from Bisorio. The missionaries might have advice, if nothing else.

At night, when Freimond and I are sitting in the doorway, sheltering from Tom's singing as he dries out his Bibles over the fire, an old man with the proud face of an *avookwaark* comes up under the nearly full moon. He looks lonely, but has a brave smile for us. It is a gesture like friendship, not just church fellowship – we warm to him.

He begins telling us a story in his language. Philip translates. I am happy to listen; it's as if he is unburdening himself. When he was a boy, he says, as if reading a statement, there were planes in the air. He thought they were bees, and he hid under stones and trees. When the first whiteman came here he'd thought his soap was food. Then another whiteman came and told them to come in from the bush to hear God louder, and they came here and were happy for a while. But now they are hungry. He finishes, '*Tenkyu tru.*' Thank you very much. He turns round and leaves. It's as if I've just heard a swansong. This man has been waiting to say his history to someone who will listen. Now he has done it, and can die. That is my thought at the time, and that, indeed – as events turn out – is precisely what will happen.

We leave at dawn, without eating. Most of the village are asleep, but

the young men see us off. They stand in line, Timothy, Matthew, Mark
. . . and the rest of the apostles watching us go. A dog stands in front,
its dishmop tail slowly dropping.

Philip takes us through the swamps at a sprint. It is a matter of pure
dedication – he confronts the problem, which is the forest, and attacks
it. This way, racing, he goes as fast as a bushman moving with all his
bush skills. He just gets covered in more mud.

We vault from root to root through the black swamps after him,
sharing out Tom's Bibles and balancing on the vine strings through the
thick water. Tom is excited – he has seen the 'pagans' of Bikaru (unfortunately unavailable for conversion, just now), the Gahuns (sadly gone
temporarily astray), but now the real thing. A whiteskin's mission in
the budding; souls smoothly, systematically saved. And even I am not
all sad; like Stefanus and Freimond, I am beginning to look forward to
the stability of a settlement again. Niksek had its faults, but it was
certainty in a falling-apart world.

Trees here have a water line from recent floods. Near the River
Salumei, where Inaru Mission lies, we see the water lines turn from
the black and brown of the swamp to the grey and white of the river
itself. We know we are near, close to the floodbanks; leaves here have
been pressed to the sides of trees and gummed there with silt. They
lie packed into piles like pillows between the roots and are hardened,
sealed to each other.

Now the Salumei runs by, smooth and very grey in front of us. The
new mission is down river; we can see only the gardens from here, but
after the battling forest we can feel its air of calm, almost complacency.
I'm reminded of Niksek – perhaps it's the soil being washed from the
deforested banks. The mission has been built within easy access of flood
waters – it really does look as if they are challenging nature, wanting
it to dare.

We beat the trunks of the trees to signal that we need picking
up, and sit on the roots above the mud, picking off the leeches.
Strange. No reply. We wait some more. Finally, we hump ourselves
up a forest slope, over a hill which has mossy rock faces that are
cool on our skin, and come down through some gardens of bananas.
We are hurrying – Inaru is *too* still. We've heard dogs and chickens
but no people, and we've noticed there are no fresh tracks in the
gardens.

We cut a tree down and use it as a bridge to ford a rivulet, and
then find ourselves facing a sow. She isn't going to let us go by. Philip,
ahead on the path, runs off screaming. I'm facing her now. Tom, behind,
shouts 'Run!' I hear the sound of crashing bushes as he disappears. Not

moving, I shout, 'Idiot! You're only encouraging the poor thing. She thinks you're afraid.'

'He's right!' says Freimond, behind me. Maybe Stefanus is beside him.

'Run away!' says Stefanus.

The pig's head is locked firmly in her shoulders. She stares at me. I have never seen a pig stare so hard. But she's not panting, as a dangerous pig does, and I can't see a wound that might make her angry. So I walk forward briskly and smack her across the chops with the side of my bush knife.

'Who taught you that?' asks Tom, as the pig canters off.

'Spencer, a sort of relative of mine in Kandengei.'

'He's bushy like me,' says Freimond. 'He's a proper *buskanaka*.'

From the grasses opposite the village we can see a spread of houses on a high bank, with moored canoes swinging in the fast water. There are boys in shorts running about. We feel better, seeing life. Eventually a man paddles over, standing the way every man except me does beautifully at Kandengei, moving the canoe sideways, parallel to the current.

Tom shouts in the Bikaru language as soon as the man is in easy earshot. He doesn't tell us what they are saying for a moment. He keeps asking the man questions. Then Tom does speak to us; he says a single word: 'Plague.'

No one has died yet, and the whiteskins have medicine. Clearly, a worse danger would be if we were caught by the 'plague' deep in the forest. Everyone agrees that we might as well go over.

Before we get to the other high bank, we see the bodies along the edge in the sun – horizontal, bent, coughing, wheezing, spitting, slack. Then I notice two white people. They are standing above me on the bank. I notice they are white not because of their colour, which is almost black against the falling sun, but because of their height and weight. They are very well fed, and with their hats look like kings with crowns, men with head-dresses, men with power. They are standing defiantly, with legs wide apart and a hand-in-belt stance. The bigger man, with his arms folded, watches as the shorter man with the quieter face helps me from the canoe. He leaves the rest of my party alone.

'Jack!' the first man says, unfolding his arms to shake hands. The other man says 'Mike!' The second man has a drowsy mouse face, the moustache drooping around his mouth. When we have shaken, the first man, Jack, folds his arms again. This makes me feel uneasy; he is still acting defiantly, feeling the need to stand his ground. But what threat am I?

Because he's been aggressive, I look him over. He's an active man, fast with his hands. He would have time for practicalities, nothing else. He has a farmhand's build, but would be best left mending fences, driving piles; cows would yield their milk adequately, not well, for him.

I am judging the man like this, standing on the shore, and then I realize that they are staring even harder at me. My God, I think to myself. I've been about ten days in the bush and no one has ever come out of the forest like this before. They're acting like a remote tribe. I'm the first outsider to contact them.

A third whiteskin comes up. He is chewing something. Chewing gum? Out here? He rolls a green handkerchief over his brow.

I must already have told them my name, because Mike says, 'Charlie, he says he's called Benedict. He just came out of the forest on the far bank. With four porters. We saw the whole thing!'

'Charlie,' the third man says to me. We are out here in the forest heat, but Charlie is pacing back and forward up the bank. 'Come on over,' he says. He walks off, back down the path.

I look to Mike – his fatty, sensitive whisker face. 'Over where?'

'Charlie's got a house down the end,' the man says. 'Us two will catch you later. We've a busy skedual right now.'

I nodded. 'With the sickness everywhere . . .'

'No, we're building a new strip, and we've got twenty-two kids over, helping us.'

'You've brought whiteskin children out here?'

'Whiteskin?' Mike looks at Jack, and, I think, winks. Jack tips back his hat and smiles back at Mike. 'Brought them in by chopper.'

They have the same American accent – they're from somewhere in the south and they stretch and chew the words. I try to think of the name of an American state, but it's no good. I'd have to go back beyond Kandengei, back to England. Too far.

Jack adds, 'Summit camp. We got them here from the church. They'll be taken back soon. Anyway, we'll catch up with ya.'

As they go, they take last looks at my army clothes. I hear Jack say, 'English.' The other says, 'Yeah, and I thought Indiana Jones was an American!'

We gallop after Charlie, through the mission – the fresh lawns, immature flowerbeds. I think I smell coffee. Tom walks over to the Bible School, taking the Bikaru, up to now walking about in circles, looking at the lawn, away by the shoulder.

The rest of us catch up with Charlie near two metal-capped houses; they are swathed in insect netting and have vast, shining water tanks. It is the only clear water I've seen in over a week and we've been drinking from the swamp all day.

The whiteman says, 'You a scientist then?'

'No. I'm just passing through. Trying to get to remoter peoples in the Highlands. Perhaps someone here knows of a way. Or I could push on through to Bisorio.'

'So a botanist? Geologist? What?'

'Just nobody.' I know that won't do for a whiteman, so I say, 'You could say I'm on a personal mission.'

'Oh?' Charlie pulled to a halt. He was smiling, but he was also blocking my path. His shoulders were high, and now he was planting his knuckles on his hips. For the second time I feel threatened. And it's not just me. I hear Freimond and the others stepping back, tripping over each other.

'Well, we've got sickness. You best be off as soon as you can.'

'I was hoping to talk to people about routes to the Highlands.'

There is another whiteman on the metal roof. I stop to look at him with Freimond and Stefanus. He doesn't look real. He is beautiful; he's so vivid he's something I can even recall from England. He's holding himself like a Roman on a vase, his chin high. He might be an Asterix cartoon athlete receiving laurels from Caesar.

'That's Jeff. He's just fixing an antenna.'

Charlie walks us on in front; then we find him overtaking. 'Take my advice and go back. You don't want these people's germs. The incubation period is about ten days. How far are you from where you came from?'

'Four or five days if we take a direct route.'

'That should get you home then. Hang around though . . . and, well, this could mean trouble for you . . .'

'We could get to Bisorio tomorrow. Stay a day, come back. There might still be time.'

'Well,' Charlie says. His tone is conciliatory – but what is there to be arguing about? – 'come on in and have something.'

'Thanks,' I say. I turn and tell the others we're all going in to have something. 'Thanks,' they say, as they've learnt to do for Jakob.

Charlie is now walking right up the steps and disappearing through a netting door. I look at the plastic tub at the bottom of the steps. I say to everyone that it must be for cleaning our feet. They help yank off my boots and socks and leeches and we all dip our feet.

Freimond says, 'They've got a kitchen like Jakob's.'

Stefanus says in English, 'No. Jakob's kitchen doesn't have womens looking from it.'

I look up to see three white women and about six girls. I can smell their soap from here. It is a beautiful smell, but it makes me sad. Coming here should be like visiting England; instead I'm being treated like a vagrant.

Even through the netting, these girls have skin as pale and smooth as egret feathers. They drop back, all except one. Then a woman's voice says, 'Dear, it's rude to stare.'

Charlie comes out. He says, 'Come in, Benedict.' His eye catches the bucket full of thick fish soup water. 'I'll bring a drink out for your friends.' He glances past them. 'Okay, fellas?'

I say, 'Sorry, I think you're only getting water. I'll see what I get and try and save you some.'

Moments ago I was in the forest, I think to myself, as I walk up the smooth steps. And now I'm going through a lobby full of boots and sandals, through another net door and into a kitchen. They have a double sink, work surfaces, drawers of cutlery. One girl is opening a larder, watching me with wide eyes. I glimpse packets of herbal tea. Below, cleaning-fluid bottles, polythene bags, oven-cleaning pads. I take a deep breath, sniffing them in, smelling their cardboard packages, the print, the factory tang of fake lemon freshness.

The white girls are gathering. I'm unused to females crowding in on me. But they're asking Charlie where I have come from, and how long can I stay. There is an adolescent one with a silver brace on her teeth, but most of the girls' teeth glare; they have no betelnut stains. These girls make me want to touch them, they are so soft and delicate; they are like something from heaven – the gums pink, eyes crystal clear, the moist skin, the denim shorts without a shine of grease. They curl up on the benches and put their chins on their knees.

I stand by the sink, listening to the water run on the metal, wondering why the mothers of these girls wear make-up to look not strong, but pretty, like their daughters; all these older whiteskin females look like girls, not women.

'There you are. Have as much as you like.' They mean the water. I look at a bottle of orange squash. They do not offer it.

I have my water in a plastic beaker, drinking and drinking, sucking in the coolness. I feel a leech crawling up the inside of my leg, but stop myself unbuckling my trousers just in time – I'm not wearing underpants.

Charlie is still pushing me. 'So, what *are* you doing exactly?' He is speaking softly, so the women don't catch his tone.

I find myself telling a story about finding a crocodile. I say I'm led to believe that there may have been a third species out here.

I don't mean to tell a lie. This man is forcing me to say something. He is asking questions that don't need answering. Just as I used to make life tough by asking questions all the time – Wallace, forgive me! Charlie forces me further, driving me into a corner, defining me, catching me. I don't want to be caught. I evade capture. I say, 'It's the lack of the fossil record. According to the old men's stories, though, there was another great species.'

'Which university are you from?'

I say 'The University of East Anglia,' which is the one I graduated from.

'Kinda hard to check you out in the bush, ind it.'

But why does he need to check me out? He shows me his maps. It is still a test, but I'm too fascinated for it to work: the forest, all those webs of life, have been reduced to lines of symmetry and asymmetry. 'If you sum up the forest, you will kill it,' Kaavon said.

Outside, the Roman athlete is doing exercises. He runs with a spring, fingers out, flexing as his arms swing. Eyes pale, brows in a noble, discerning furrow. One leg forward as he sways with chest muscles as wide as Wallace's. His hips, however, are carrying a little curl of fat.

Jack charges into the kitchen and murmurs to Charlie, 'What have you found out?' For some reason he doesn't think I'll hear. He says to me, louder and slower – do I look that stupid? – 'I'm still not clear what exactly you do.' It is said gently for a man emitting such physical energy, but the way he stands deep within my circle of space, not asking to be invited in, makes us back off. He is on the offensive; no wonder so many missionaries used to get shot.

We look at the maps, all together. 'You've come from Jakob – we've gathered that much from the others. And, well, he must have invited you to his mission, and he doesn't do that without a reason. I'd say you are who you say you are.'

But why shouldn't I be?

Jack now reveals 'something of interest' to me. There is a route from Bisorio into the Highlands at the head of the Korosameri. But they have struck a lot of gold. 'The situation is uneasy.'

But there is a route . . . I tell them I've heard that people at the head of this river, the Salumei, would kill me.

Charlie says, 'Not now, they won't. They've all left for the Korosameri.'

Jack says, 'Gold at a camp called Malumata.'

'Then it sounds like this Korosameri route is the only possibility.'

'I should forget the Korosameri route. A kiap [patrol officer] came

down it in the 1970s. We put him in a canoe. He was almost dead.'
There is a pause, during which Jack bears down on me. '*That* was
coming down; and without the disease.'

I tell them I can't be put off by what was obviously only a bit
of flu.

'Kinda determined to get up there, aren't you,' says Jack.

Then Charlie says, 'Are you taking the situation in? I mean you don't
appear to know the maps, you don't have any backup, you don't know
about the gold.' He is shaking his head long and slow. 'Okay. Let me
help you to a decision. Five people died in the space of a few weeks, a
while back at Bisorio. Real good friends of George and Bob. Now just
how lucky do you feel?'

Jack leaves, Charlie following him. Two middle-aged women come into
their space and one of them says, 'You caught us at a bad moment,
Benedict.' I say I can see Charlie has a lot on his mind with all the
kids here. A young man comes up and shakes my hand. 'Scott,' he says.
'Charlie's son. You staying a few days? Show me where you've been.' I
unroll the map and show him where Charlie says I've been. While we
bend over the table, Charlie comes and goes – I look up to find him
gone, look back to find him there. Scott invites me for supper; Charlie
looks sharply at him. 'Scott . . .' Then once again, they are talking as if
I can't hear. Next thing, Charlie forces a smile. Of course I can stay for
supper, though he's not sure what the food situation is. I might have
to chip in.

I say I've got some rice. There's also some sago grubs we've been
saving from the swamp, but I'm sure I'll appreciate them more than
these kids.

His wife says, 'Sure there's enough.'

Scott has taken to me. He says, 'And we can find a space for you to
sleep.' Charlie looks at Scott, and the muscles on his jaw tighten. Scott
is saying, 'We'll get you in somewhere' and pulling on a clean T-shirt –
even indoors, it is too white for me. The logo on the shirt reads, 'You
must pain, before you gain.'

I say I'd better check on my friends before supper. Charlie says, 'Who?'
Then he follows my gaze outside through the netting – the Bikaru man
is dancing around on the lovely lawn, wearing a brand new shirt.

'Oh your friends, right.'

Charlie keeps me a little longer. He asks if he might ask me a question.
He has already just asked me three more. But he goes ahead with his
poser. 'Do you know for sure what's going to happen to you after
you die?'

'I just wanna relax with videos,' says Scott, passing by.

I say what I once said to Nathan, the AOG. 'No one can ever be sure, can they? That's the value of faith.' I hope we might leave it at that.

Charlie, though, has backed me against a sideboard. 'Well, the Bible promises "whosoever *believeth* in me *shall* not perish but *have* eternal life."'

Jack comes in again, accidentally saving me from being converted. He says to Charlie, 'Got some news on Mike's radio. Bob and George are safe and well and on their way to Sitifa river.'

I ask if that is Bob and George from Bisorio.

Jack says absently to me, 'What? Oh yeah – they're doing some outreach.' He says to Charlie, 'And they'll be visiting the settlement up there? They must be about the first white people they've seen.'

I say, 'Ah, you mean the Bikaru.'

Jack doesn't turn to me. He just drops his eyes and says, 'And how would you know?'

'I was there a few days ago.'

'That can't be correct. I know you've been in the bush, but they're right up river.'

I say they're only half a day away by raft and that they're going to have to get used to quite a stream of visitors.

Charlie says, 'So what exactly were you doing out there? Look. I'm not saying that you're being less than honest with me. But – to be frank you're not equipped like an ecologist.'

Jack says, as if rising to a challenge, 'We're not afraid of the truth.' Then he says it again, this time combing his freshly washed hair – I can smell the violet shampoo – at the same time, harrowing it straight back over his head. 'We are not afraid of the truth.'

Charlie says, 'You could be anyone.'

That's the whole point. I *am* anyone. His people are scared of people who are just anyone – outsiders, strangers. Instead of waving bows and arrows like any other remote group they wave words and their sacred book.

Behind them, a girl is eating cookies from a plastic plate. I watch the crumbs on her upper lip, the sweep of the tongue clearing them away.

The Summit team are coming in from their work on the strip, going down to the river to wash. These are all youths in their late teens. I can't tell them apart. They all have short, fair hair, browned skin. They are athletic, lean, loud. I want to be out of their way and I leave, saying I'll go and check on my friends.

Outside, the Summit team are going wild, having mud baths, and saying words like 'gory' and 'gross' and screaming as they dive in, skidding through clay that's wedding their cropped hair to their skulls, spreading their swimming trunks against their loins, dripping from their teeth. Suddenly I stop. The clay on them – I've seen it before. These figures who are so innocent and anonymous: for a second, these kids in grey paint are bandees. They are trapped in a Crocodile Nest, being trained up for the religion of their elders.

Then I am walking on down the path – aware that I have been staring once again. Now they are doing the same to me, and I feel more and more awkward, striding in army clothes, sore bare feet enjoying the lawn, the bush knife that's been in my hand for the last half-hour as casually as a pencil.

But my thoughts are gathering. These whiteskins are a powerful tribe.

The others have found a house to stay in overnight. I climb up the notched pole and indoors. We sit in a circle. I tell them that we have to get out of here as quickly as possible. The flu could be dangerous – the deaths at Bisorio. They don't object. The house is full of bodies that spit on the floor and cough in their faces. Even Tom is happy to go back now – he has severe backache from carrying too many water-logged Bibles. I suggest that it's better for me to stay up as late as possible with the whiteskins, learning all I can. They agree. It's the best thing for all of us.

I cook them some rice and some emergency tinned fish. I tell Freimond to give away all but a week's worth of rice – there are people here who have been too sick to go to their gardens. We'll be off at daybreak before the whiteskins get up.

I take off my forest clothes and put on my set of underpants, spare shirt and trousers. By now the Summit team must have finished eating, and I'll get space in the house, among all its gadgets and bits and pieces. I feel my way there through the dark, dazzled by the electric lights.

Scott lays out my lasagne and baked beans. I eat into them, and then scrape around the pans. Scott says, 'Like the book says, ask if you have need of anything.'

He's about my age and for a moment I wonder what he finds in me. Is it that he's a *geenjumboo*, a Junior Man, like me? Someone who may or may not have done his journey, but unlike me has a firm base, an absolute conviction in his inheritance, his people? Perhaps he feels sorry for me – that I haven't got a sure base for my journey yet.

Scott suggests I go over to Mike's house and ask him if he has heard anything useful on the radio. I go immediately, but find it's now as black as a cave outside. He was assuming I had a torch. I tiptoe, avoiding snakes, but after a while relax, remembering it's only clean lawn between the two houses. Nearer, I'm within Mike's blaze of lights, and watching the moths and ichneumon wasps and beetles being lured in from the forest and its pollen and sap.

Mike, the sleepy-faced man, opens the door quickly, ushering me in. 'Gotta keep the bugs out.'

He thinks I'm not used to netting, but it's the doors as well. I follow him in, my toes flexing, feeling the smooth floor. I notice he walks with fists closed and knees a little apart because of the width of his thighs.

'Boy, I hope you're moving out quickly, Benedict. These people have been just wiped out. We've never seen them like this. We're just hoping our kids don't get it – they've paid $3000 to come out here.'

To build an airstrip? They have to pay to do this?

He sees me looking at the war shield and arrows and wooden masks he has around the walls. He says they've tried to get the locals to keep their own decoration, but it is no good. They want to wear clothes now.

He doesn't see the temptation of being secure from nature. During my visit, I look over the pale wood-panelled walls, see the couch, a child curled up like a cat on it. When I visit the loo, the soap smells like bliss, I run my fingers over the toilet paper, flush twice to hear the cistern, enjoy the warm white plastic seat, read the crayoned motto, 'Give don't get, Minister, don't manipulate.'

I ask if I can possibly have a drink. Mike looks at me, startled. But I'm dehydrated from wading through swamps all day. I *have* to ask.

There is a white woman in the kitchen. She seems to be his wife – stoutish, dark curly hair that is too dry. She is domestic but not maternal to me. Her eyes are crunched up, as if she's in pain. 'Coffee – instant or ground – or tea.'

'Either.'

I get instant coffee. Mike says he grew up with Jack in Tennessee, but was on drugs and rock'n'roll while Jack was in New Guinea. Then suddenly he found somewhere different from his sleepy once-a-week church. 'Dear, when was it we were washed in the blood?'

'Washed in the *what*?' I'm intrigued by the ritual.

'Blood of the lamb.'

She says a date – the day, the month, the year. 'It's kinda like a birthday to us, now.' He's talking symbolically, like the ingesting of the body and blood at Holy Communion, but, because he is glorying in that day, the imagery comes alive. I imagine a bath of warm red in front of the altar for his bloody initiation.

'And so I'm out here, trying to bring civilization.'

He thinks he is civilized. He thinks that the locals – because he sees

163

they didn't live as long, and kill each other – are not civilized. But all they did wrong was think of the community, not the individual.

Now he further weakens his argument by extending it to other cultures. He is telling me about the Australian Aboriginals I'll meet. 'They're the most primitive people on earth.'

Primitive? Primitive art, but for the Naturally Balanced there's no value in individual expression, only in badges, symbols which kept the power of mystery. Primitive culture, but the culture is in the richness of the forest itself. Primitive religion, but they have immortality on earth, he does not.

A third of Americans go to church, most of the rest believe in ghosts, lucky mascots or in not walking under a ladder. Leonardo might have produced what is to us the most uplifting art, might have raised the individual human spirit to a level it had never attained before; Einstein might have pushed time and space into a new logical framework, but how far has it got the West? How much better are Westerners able to accept death? Whiteskins became individuals at the price of the community and, eventually, the planet. Who are the primitives?

So here he is: Mike. A missionary in New Guinea. A little over four years since he has become Born Again, and he thinks people, the primitives, can be naked and natural and replace their natural faith – belief in the forest – with one that is centred on Man. And, an acre of the world's rain forest being destroyed every second, he happily goes about converting people who, unlike him, have been sure of their religion all their lives. He is a head-hunter, like them, and by his definition of primitive – a person with an elementary belief system – he must be a primitive, like them. He smiles, thinking how wonderful the Lord is to have worked on him so fast. He chuckles again, still a little bemused by why the Lord has chosen him. So am I.

However, Mike, who, by his own yardstick, we should call a Secondary Primitive, is a kind man. As I get up and say, 'Good-night,' he has an idea. If I return to Gahun, I might catch Bob and George on their way through to here and Bisorio. They know the area better than anyone else, he says.

As I walk back to Charlie's, the generator cuts dead and I have to feel towards the light under the stars, the little eyes of a million girls.

Everyone else is in bed. Charlie has left a battery light on for me, and rigged a mosquito net. He is talking loudly with his wife. Unfortunately, forgetting the Western rules of privacy, I look through a crack in the wall. They are in bed. I go into the bathroom, steal a squirt of toothpaste to rub on my teeth, and look at the tiny black beetles covering the surfaces near the lights.

I look along the bookshelf. I can see no fiction whatsoever, just Bibles and books on the Bible. Charlie has even left books out for me, some refuting evolutionary theory, and another called *The Liberation of Planet Earth* – 'how I was rescued from my own personal alienation from God.'[8]

Going to sleep, I again find their inward-looking certainty a comfort.

At dawn, before the missionaries are up, we are getting into a canoe. Charlie comes hopping up wearing untied work boots. 'Join us for breakfast. It'll be our pleasure.' I think of cereal and milk and bread – the girl with the cookie crumbs on her lips. They might make me up a packed lunch. I saw a family-size can of beetroot in the larder.

But it's no good. Though it hurts my stomach to say it, what can we gain from people with only the flu and more questions? The Bikaru youth runs up and bounds into the canoe as well. He is like a dog scared of being left behind. We pull out, and I wave at Charlie, who has a chainsaw in one hand. He waves, not trying to hide his relief that I am off his territory.

In the forest, we travel at trotting speed. I am excited, thinking of the robust tribe with their certainty and energy, the way they worked magic.

Soon we notice that the water levels are higher than before. Maybe a foot higher in the swamp pools. Silently, leaves twist and stir on the black water. The level is still rising. We must keep moving, but we have no guide. Then the rain comes down, and the roots we walk on are greasy. After five hours, our path is a river. We retreat to a high spot and resurrect an old bush house.

We sit drinking tea, shivering and looking at the crocodile meat being stored in the roof. The skull is the length of my forearm. We'd have liked the meat, but Freimond says there's something wrong. It hasn't been stored away properly. Someone has planted the meat here for some other reason.

An early start. Streams are now rivers, and the rivers lakes. The bulging sponge growth of an ant plant flies from a tree as we tear by. Orange ants with spindle legs run trapped under the water skin, white-trunked trees disappear, turning green in the rain.

We wade in to Gahun. The young Christian team – Matthew, Mark, Luke, John or whoever – are nowhere to be seen. Instead of hordes of worshipful beggars, the village is filled with dull resentment. I forgot about their airstrip!

Within hours a delegation comes to us led by a man with an adjustable metal clip bracelet. He says he left some meat in the bush house. He demands compensation. The party shouts a bit then goes away. We know they will be back.

Stefanus begins to get scared. He tries to keep his mind on other things, sitting with a limbum tray between his legs and backcombing his hair for lice, which the Bikaru kills, one or two at a time. I ask Tom if he's prepared to leave in the early dawn of tomorrow, which is a Sunday. He takes another look at the Gahuns and perhaps he remembers his father killed one of them. He says yes. But he will pray not to have to.

Even I am praying we don't have to. The Gahuns' party comes back. They ask for 10,000 kina in compensation. I could buy 50,000 tins of meat for that. I only have 200 kina on me. I don't say we can't pay, but they know we can't and come back with their knives.

Then two things happen to change everything. The first is my casual mention that George and Bob are coming through. The Gahuns start pacing out the volleyball pitch in the middle of the village. Are they wondering whether they can fit an airstrip in? Next, a party from Niksek arrives unexpectedly – seven of them, one of them Daniel, who, everyone knows, once deftly split a man's head open. With him is his friend – the man who held the victim's shoulders at the time.

There is no trouble from the Gahuns from now on. By Sunday we are being showered with presents – a block of sago, pumpkin leaves, and some porky crocodile meat.

Tom conducts a long, well-attended church service, handing around his coffee mug for a collection. It comes back still empty. He looks at it disbelievingly, and looks at it again as he conducts Psalm 100, the one that's always chosen when the congregation is asked for suggestions. Then, before the service is over, the congregation clears off. Outside, children are screaming. Bob and George are arriving.

'But it is Sunday,' says Tom, dropping his own coins into the mug from the top pocket of his T-shirt, 'Drain and Madden Plumbing and draining contractors'.

Bob and George do not travel simply. They prefer a cavalcade. The vanguard breaks through the forest fifteen minutes ahead of the main body of the army – men carrying radio batteries, men carrying noodles, men with tin cans, all of them with necks strung tight as they bear the weight of the bags on their foreheads. They swarm through the forest, flattening the flora, widening paths, blazing trails.

Then George and Bob themselves. They step into the shallow river as if it is cold. They tread across it, as if on a tightrope. They wear identical red baseball hats and wristwatches that look heavy. Water runs the mud off their white knees.

The villagers surround the thinner whiteman, who seems to be loving the mob atmosphere – as if the Gahuns are happy children, not grabbing, imploring men. He comes right through the crowd to me and touches my arm. He lets out a toothy grin. 'Hi! Bob!' He leans into my face and waits, tight. 'Benedict!' I say.

The response loosens him again. 'Good to meet you, Benedict!'

George is quieter, more level-headed but also friendly. 'And what brings you out here?' He wears glasses, but they don't show on his face. It's not the thin glass, or discreet frames, but because for the present there is little expression in his eyes to block. He is very controlled.

I say I'm looking for a route into the mountains to another remote village. I've just come from Inaru.

'They gave you a welcome?' George's tongue runs along a chipped tooth at the front.

'Well, I think I gave them a shock.'

Bob says, 'Hey, Benedict, you sure gave us one.'

We agree to talk later. I give them time to move into the other, walled-off side of the house. I hear something sizzling in a pan, and then smell bacon. One voice says, 'Do you think we can drop a few men next time we go on a hike? He's got a neat operation going there.'

Listening to them I feel we have a common understanding – it's of a mission to accomplish. It's the camaraderie of old soldiers. I feel that with them I have a chance.

Tom starts another church service in the evening, preaching to a more-or-less empty church. The Gahuns are waiting to petition Bob and George.

But the missionaries have put me ahead in the queue. We sit and talk. Senior Gahuns are seated around and between us, waiting like dogs for a hunting trip. Others are pressing through the walls so hard they have to breathe from our air through the cracks.

Bob says, 'Sorry if the guys were over-sensitive in Inaru. As you said, people don't walk in from the jungle like that, you know.'

'Man,' George says, 'some of the stories that get told about us are bizarre – giving them poison, dropping sticks and bricks out of the sky at them.'[9]

'You've spent time in the bush. You know what it's like. These people don't want to stay like this. The outsiders – Survival International, anthropologists, journalists – have not got the minds of the people right. I've been years in the field, and I can tell you that for a fact.'

He was right. This was not the Eden that travel writers still talked of;

there never had been innocence, except of us. And now we were here the young didn't want the forest. They wanted certainty and security. And Christianity and town lore were winning religions; they'd do fine for them.

So far Bob or George had only commented, not defended themselves, just as the New Tribes Mission made it a policy not to answer the colourful exposés that journalists wrote from time to time. They, the NTM, were totally uncompromising. They were absolutely confident. An intact tribe. These two warriors of the NTM were, after an urban, Dead Magic fashion, Men of True Men.

I tested them, as Jakob Walters had once tested me. 'But you've got to face it that, even if your message is correct, they might only be taking Christianity because they want the goodies.'

'In our training we addressed this time and time again. It's especially crucial here in PNG with the cargo cults. So we tell them time and time again – by being a Christian you will not get clothes, or be able to stop making sak-sak [sago]. Life will be as hard in that way. We tell it and we tell it – until we are convinced that it's a fact to them. I also tell them that in our terms this isn't wealthy. That I've given up a lot.'

I think to myself, 'Yes, I can do business with these two men. I really can – because they are talking nonsense.' (Now they're rolling down their socks so we can compare leech bites.) 'They see the world as they want to see it. They are bright, I'm afraid more so than Mike back at the mission, but they follow their lines of logic without looking to either side. They are correct at times, incorrect at others, yet are not deflected. They *are* warriors.'

The missionaries are a conquering tribe; their men are head-hunters, their women hidden according to St Paul, their minds bent according to their own world. They are going in a different direction from me. I'm looking towards balance, they are looking away from it. They use Dead Magic; but they will do. I can use their power.

I press on. *I* am asking the questions – is it the whiteman rising in me, or is it the Junior Man's honest striving after his quest? Whichever it is, I ask, excitedly, about routes to the mountain from their mission at Bisorio.

The news couldn't be worse. Helicopters are coming in and out, ferrying stores from the airstrip up to the mountains. They have themselves tried to make it up the head of the Korosameri, now the centre of the gold mining, at Malumata. They had to come back because of another plague. Now, with the gold fever, it was *more* dangerous. 'You can pay people as much as you like, but with gold on their minds they'll drop you, if they think they are going to miss out.'

Besides, most of the Highlands were deserted now. Those who hadn't come down to missions years ago had got up and left this year.

'The Yaifos!' said George, suddenly – all the Gahuns eavesdropping through the wall planks went quiet.

'What about the Yaifos?'

'Yes *sir*,' Bob said, striking me with an unshakeable smile. 'There's an idea. The Yaifos might be up there still.'

'Who are the Yaifos?'

'Are they our guys, or SIL?' Bob said, passing his hand through his hair. The Gahun children watched it go, the fingers parting the smooth, even strands.

George said that the Yaifos were mainly their guys. They were at the head of the river beside Inaru, the Salumei. Whether it was too late or not for me to get in there depended on whether they'd followed the helicopters going east to Malumata.

Bob says, 'We'd have liked to do some outreach there, but with the gold – well, time's up.'

George says, 'They'll be one of the last – maybe *the* last – village to be reached in New Guinea. Can't be far off it.' Some Yaifos had been down to Bisorio mission. 'No outsiders have made it up there though.'

Bob says, 'And we've had a strip in at Bisorio for *twelve years* now.'

He tells me to give him two weeks. Then he'll be at their HQ in Goroka and he'll try and get me on a flight to his mission, if I still want that.

George says, touching the glasses that sit discreetly on his face, 'You ask who the Yaifos are. The straight answer is that as far as you're concerned the Yaifos are one thing, and one thing only: the Yaifos are your hope.'

The Yaifos and you two other warriors, I thought.

Chapter Four

WHITESKIN WARRIORS

If he lives, he is stronger . . . The caravan is getting under way. It's a military operation conducted with discipline: radio antennae dismantled, packs fastened, scouts dispatched ahead to begin blazing the trail.

The Gahuns throng around the whiteskins, taking it in turn to give their final requests for medicines and runways. George and Bob, pulling up their socks, adjusting their caps, say what they've been saying all night, that the Lord has sent them to help the Biamé-speaking peoples, the Inaru, Bisorio, Bikaru. They offer them prayers instead – it sounds like a consolation. The Gahuns bow their heads.

Moments later – some Gahuns still haven't reopened their eyes – the patrol has begun to leave. The lines of converts recede into the trees, an army of leaf-cutting ants munching through the vegetation. The Gahuns listen as the sound of devouring fades. Then they turn round, empty-handed. They wander back to the houses where they've left their elders alone and confused.

There is a sharp howl, the noise of a stamped-on dog. No one takes much notice at first – dogs often howl in Gahun. But our house is close to the sound and I get to my feet; I've heard the sound before – a ghostly shriek into the night once at Kandengei. It was the moment of Yargee's death. And I see that the same sound comes from the house of the old man who once told me his life story, declaiming it like his epitaph. A woman comes out of the house and throws herself down the steps. Then the other Gahuns erupt, running to their houses and back again, screaming and convulsing at the sky.

Tom says prayers over the body, which reflects the early light, skin glistening and loose, that of a lizard's crinkled throat. But the village is angry – at the death, and at life, the ambitions whiteskins have equipped them with. We leave quickly, relying on a church leader to punt us over the swollen Sitifa river to a path.

We walk quickly. It's not just a question of getting away from the mob, it's because Bob and George have jolted us. We have all seen the imminence of the end. The gold is coming and time is running out. Timelessness, the forest, is ending.

Trotting back to Niksek we forget the forest that is baring its leaves at us; we break the ageless forest cycles by thinking to the future. Tom looks forward to a good lie-down, Stefanus is saying he is going to buy a watch 'with hands that are sticks' and Freimond wants one too. We can all see that there is soon going to be no past to cling to; times are changing.

For my part, I'm on a quest. I must pursue power wherever it offers itself, and I'm intent on using the church army. Back at the village, Wallace once said that Kaavon could walk through the forest with a magic stick that peeled the vegetation away ahead of him, allowing him a path. I can see that Bob and George have the same magic; the only difference is that they feel they can use it without restriction, slicing through the trees, ants with an appetite that the forest can't meet.

Two days later we arrive at Niksek; the river lies ahead of us, and it is brown, not grey. It has doubled in width, and carries itself with little regard to the village. It is plucking away the fruit, the vegetables, the gardens themselves. Another flood like this, and Niksek itself will be plucked as well.

Half-way across the river in a canoe, we see Laurie's plane in the sky; it is like a bird from Australia, circling as a good omen. I race to catch him. My goodbyes are brief. Stefanus and Tom wave from the side of the strip and Freimond helps my rucksack in. It is only Freimond who shows regret that his part in my expedition is over, that changing times have denied him the chance of a young man's quest.

As we fly, Laurie says, 'Have a good time?'

A moment ago I was running through the jungle, now I've been stuffed into a co-pilot's seat. But I do my best to talk. Looking out at the forest, I say, 'Good exercise, anyway.'

'I thought you'd enjoy it. You were different.'

I say, 'It's just about had it, this forest.'

'Have a sandwich, mate. So it's back to England, is it?'

I took the sandwich, swallowed it in one go. 'Well, not exactly.'

While I'm at it, I stick with whiteskins, taking a boat along the coast to Madang to wait the two weeks with friends who'll be sensitive enough not to quiz me – Matthew and Serena Jebb at the Christensen Research Institute. I inspect Matthew's collection of handsome ant plants, his tanks of argumentative starfish and a black kite that had been rescued in the road. Every morning, more and more impatient for the off, I run the white coral drive, stopping to look at the red crabs traversing it, the dead centipedes curled like broken watch chains, dried frogs and toads like townboys' pudgy hands. To further help pass this waiting time, I go to the Goroka Highland Show. It's meant as a dance display but is also an excuse for tribal get-togethers: as well as the locals, there are the New Tribes Mission, the Summer Institute of Linguistics – all the strongest tribes in PNG are represented. There are more missionaries per head than in any other country, more missionaries than doctors per head in Britain, and most of them seem to be there at the dance show. My favourite is wearing a shirt and tie – in that heat! – and he carries his Bible in a cardboard presentation box. He's a convert fresh in from the bush and he's starving because he's forbidden to eat most of the things I've been eating over the last weeks – pigs, cuscus, snakes and more besides are taboo. He's a Seventh Day Adventist, the most hardline mission, the fastest-growing in the country.

But it's the people with feather head-dresses that I enjoy more than the Westernized ones. Call me an old softie if you like, but the spectacle of men still prepared to get out of their shorts and into bark cloth, the women prepared to throw off their T-shirts and rub on axle grease to make their breasts shine, all this old-fashioned glamour warms the cockles of my heart.

At last, two weeks are up. I call Bob on the phone.

'Hi. And what can I do for you, sir?'

'It's about that plane into Bisorio.'

'Oh,' he says slowly. After a silence, he asks, 'Are you sure you want this?'

I do.

'Okay.' He puts his hand over the receiver, then comes back to me. 'That'll be fine, I think. We're a bit shy of outsiders, as you know, but I'll work on it.'

A day or two later, Bob rings back. 'Well, sir, you're on.'

With two sacks of supplies, I catch a bus back up to Goroka. I weigh in my luggage at the Mission hangar: powdered milk, tea and sugar, a few cans of fish and six weeks' rice and oats for myself and four guides. Fresh aspirins, anti-malarials, one course of antibiotics – that'll do for medicine. Bush knives, plates and spoons and cups. I need blankets for the mountains, mirrors and more knives as gifts for the Yaifos. I go to the bank, and send instructions to England to have my remaining expedition funds sent to Alice Springs, Australia – the centre of the island seems a reasonable target for the moment. The remainder of the money I cash into small value notes.

The flight will be the next day. I drop in at the Aero Club, which is almost next door to the hangar. A man at the bar stands with the upper part of his body rotating slowly from his fixed feet. 'Must be just about the only aero club in the world without an aeroplane, mate,' he says as I walk gingerly in. He's Australian. 'Your shout, is it?' I buy him a drink – I've heard of the custom of 'shouting' before, it was in a Thomas Hardy novel.

Here they have a Happy Hour, they have dartboards, a snooker table, a propeller on the wall, and stories of *buskanakas* who'd struck gold, hiring helicopters to take them out of the bush and on a spending spree. They ruined hotel bathroom ceramics by punching nails into the walls for their children to use instead of saplings to wipe their bottoms.

We are a stone's throw from the runway and plane fumes come in with the breeze, as the stories go on – their plans to lynch Christina Dodwell, the last person to have written them up.

They prop up their bars and moan, aggressive to the outside world, telling me their housemaids are beaten by their husbands invariably on the way back from devotion at *lotu*, church. 'They just don't connect. There's no causal connection.' They sigh at me. 'Stay here ten years, and you'll have something to say. Me? I'm leaving. Last one out turn off the lights.'

The old school of expat is a threatened group, like the *avookwaarks*, but there's a difference; they know I haven't come here to sympathize with them.

Mal sways in. He's part-owner of Pacific Helicopters: large, rough around the edges, flat-footed, shaven-headed. He has a bleached-haired wife – French, fussy, hyperactive. She has a red sports car that sweeps around the grass seed-scattered roads, mixing Goroka's bed of trapped-pollen air.

I admire Mal for his boldness and simplicity – 'No one gets work from me unless I get my money from them.' He's a Senior Man, an experienced warrior, the type I'm one day meant to be. He's been around since the 'old days', he tells me. 'I was initiated into a tribe once. Had mud all over my face and all that bullshit. Nettles put up my nose to get rid of my female blood and all that. I can tell you, you've got to be around here for years before you *begin* to understand.' I looked at the time. An altimeter served as a clock and it said 5000 feet: five o'clock. 'Few years back a man from the tribe said, "Can you get me 26 kina of meat, *wantok*?" Bought it, gave it to him. I said, "Right. That'll be 26 kina." He paid. Years on, asked him why he hadn't refused to pay – he was my relative. Know what he said? He said, "I paid because I knew you'd died. Only the dead are mean."'

The Dead Magic of towns, I thought. He must be talking about Kaavon's dead magic – whiteskin magic that does not rely on the living forest.

'That's what he told me only a few years back. "Only the dead are mean," he said. Yeah, *I* can tell you some stories.'

He can too. Most of them are true, and it's not so important if they're not. Westerners will say that lying is an accepted creative form out here. But that's missing the point. It's like tabloid journalism: a thread of truth is sufficient; what counts is entertainment. I nod at Mal, understanding. I'm sympathetic; the value of the story is in illustrating truths, not recounting detail, in these isolated communities, those of the Niowra, the Expatriate.

'You!' Mal says to me. 'Stop giving me those strange eyes.'

At the New Tribes Mission, as at Kandengei, they are unused to strangers. The hangar crew give me all the greeting – 'Hi!' – and are intrigued but not pleased; they seem to be putting a brave face on it. As I don my boots, one says to another, 'What the heck . . .?' 'Him? Oh, he's just trekking into the bush.' 'From *Bisorio*?' 'I know, I know. It beats me too. But Bob says we can give him a ride in, so I guess it's all right.'

There are two other passengers, both of them pilots being 'familiarized' with the region. They have nothing to say to me apart from 'Time to saddle up,' when it's time to put on our safety harnesses. We sail into the sky and swing out of the mountain-pocketed valley through air bluish from grass fires, on through the Wahgi – Sepik Divide. Tim, who has sandy hair and a straight, rounded-off body, shapes the mountains ahead with his hands, guiding the man with the controls through them. The pilots look at their charts, checking the obstacles along the route – 'That looks like a mean mountain.' We fly west towards Enga Province, the land paved with gold.

Then the instrument panel fails. The altimeter has packed up and the batteries aren't getting charged. Quickly we bank and turn back, keeping from the swelling clouds, working with a stopwatch and compass. They're all trained pilots but their lips are moving; they're praying.

We touch down. Before the engine has stopped the pilot says, 'A prayer for our deliverance: Lord, we just wanna thank you . . .'

We try again, praying before take-off this time. West again, then north, towards the Sepik, and dropping, curling in from the clouds down to Bisorio, a village perched by the Korosameri just where it spreads out from the mountains in lines of grey mud and large pebbles.

Little naked children with huge, flaky bellies ran to their mothers. The women were running too. Their cotton dresses and sago skirts flapped around their knees as they skipped in the draught of the plane.

Men, either in mission shorts or still in forest leaves, either with empty holes in their noses or shiny bone nose plugs, came right up to the plane, trying to look in. The fine quills in the men's noses seemed to be bristling in anticipation. A reception committee, I thought. George shouldn't have bothered.

With the door open I could hear the chattering voices. Kina coins and shells chimed from the loins of the toddlers as they ran and jumped.

George came up and shook my hand. 'They think you're the gold company,' he said. He turned to the crowd. 'Not today,' seemed to be the gist of it.

I was the only person getting out of the plane. Otherwise, there was only my stores, and a golf bag for George. He took me to a nearby house of the Sepik variety. The village followed – all of them. Whatever George had said, I was dressed for outdoors, like a gold prospector, not for indoors, like a missionary.

I was already getting the picture. There were two populations in the village: the Bisorios, who had been recently converted and were thinking about abandoning the mission for gold; and everyone else, who'd abandoned their own villages only in the last months and were freshly arrived for the gold.

They listened as George introduced me in Biamé, saying I was heading into the mountains to find the Yaifos. Most of the crowds left to stand outside – I could hear them out there, discussing me, while the remainder, perhaps twenty, settled down here. This lot must be only recently down from the mountains; they crouched at my feet, smoking, chewing *buai*, some in shorts, some with bundles of leaves front and back, wanting to serve me for Mammon, in the way the Nikseks had wanted to serve me for God. George said, 'Well, I'll leave you for the moment. I'd say you've got precisely two weeks.'

The company at Malumata, at the head of the Korosameri, recruited from here, but everyone was actually waiting for a second company due to work the alluvials right here, around the mission. 'Two weeks. Have your guides clear of here by then, I should.'

He left me to it. More men left with him. Three others stood fencing me in, chewing wild betelnuts. One of them took a loose plastic strap from my sacks and bound it around his head, strapping down his brown and white cuscus fur cap. All the time he was doing this, tying the knot, adjusting himself, his eyes never left me.

'Outside, they're asking how much you'll pay,' George said, coming back in.

'The government rate, 3.75 kina. It's all I can afford.'

The men collected themselves together and drifted off.

'One or two hurdles to clear before I go anywhere,' I said to George. 'But it's important that they don't come just for the money or they might drop me in favour of the gold. That happened in the Amazon and I might not get away with it a second time. I need friends.'

'Another hurdle you ought to know about: they're chasing a man through the Highlands, and it might mean they're touchy about going up there. He killed a Bisorio woman – stabbed her in the chest – and he's a Walialife, allied to the Yaifos.' He was leaving again, this time leaving me with an empty house. 'I'll come back to you on that one.'

I walked about the mission – lawns, garden sheds, a thatched church, clothes lines, houses in lines, paths in lines . . .

There was George and Harriet, his wife, and another whiteskin called Bob Parry. He was a handyman here and he had a weakness for orchids; he had brown discs up his calves which were scars from old tropical ulcers. He plodded about the mission thoughtfully, like a gardener, his hat soaked daily with perspiration. When at last we got talking by a flowerbed he spoke slowly, through almost closed lips, and in a quiet monotone as if he was sapped of energy. He told me that while he spent a year back home in Australia recovering from hepatitis, all his orchid collection had perished. He had been brought up on a farm, and always counted himself as a basic sort of man. I left him to go on with his duties and as he rode his tractor up and down the airstrip I could see him simply wondering, *thanking*.

One of the things he was thanking God for was the recent washing-away of the river swamps. 'The Lord had seen fit to help us by directing the water right on through.' Unfortunately, from what I knew of hydrology, someone or other would soon see fit to direct the water back the other way. The whiteskins had done it again – built on a floodbank.

George and I met on a path by his Bible classroom. 'How are you making out?'

I said everything was fine, I just needed time.

'Which is what you haven't got,' George said. 'Word of advice, Benedict. Things are erupting here – I couldn't really speak earlier. Careful over those guides. You're going to depend on them and there are all sorts of reasons why they might or might not want to go with you. If you like, I'll give them a look over.'

Days went by. I did recruit guides, but George dismissed them, every one. They were either lazy or stupid or killers or just plain untrustworthy – like Benny, for instance, an oily-skinned man with large, awkward lips which flexed and rolled as he spoke. His left eye was half-closed, and seen from that side he looked dopey.

He was not dopey, however. 'Let me tell you about Mr B,' George said, not using Benny's name because the kitchen boy, Namoleeyo, was standing by the sink in Bob's old wellingtons, guzzling the missionaries' leftovers. 'Mr B's the most powerful man here. Maybe he thinks he can use your trip to hunt down that killer up there. Certainly he'll want to be back to negotiate with the goldminers. That man is an orator like I've never seen before. He can swing whole crowds. The Bisorios are kind of in awe of him. He could talk water onto a duck's back, isn't that right, Bob?'

Bob Parry said, 'He could persuade a jury to hang with him. He'd have the judge weeping right beside him, behind bars. If you're unlucky enough to be still here when the goldminers come you'll see exactly what we're talking about. But let's hope you're well clear.'

The house where I lived was a depository for young hopefuls, Lost Boys in search of a Never-Never Land of gold. They looked like strays and drop-outs, and their shirts were like dusty cobwebs, they were so full of holes. Only one of them wanted to come: Tsogamoi, the owner of the house. He was a very dark-skinned boy who had a secretive, mischievous way with his eyes. He had a large oval hole through his nose and wore a yellow workman's helmet, looted from Malumata. He got pocket money by working sago-palm thatch for missionary roofing, and normally was to be seen with his back to the world, humming, tucked deep into the shade, stitching the leaves together, his glassy black eyes scheming. At night he flew down from the house and out across the lawns to the river, like a bat, his towel knotted around his shoulder and flapping behind him. I agreed to sign him up. What choice did I have? There were only ten days to go now and I was nowhere near finding my full complement of four men.

Between recruiting drives, I watched from the ragged veranda as Tsogamoi took delivery of the bales of leaves from the canoes, and plaited the thatch for Bob, taking two leaves at a time and binding them in the Sepik style. For variation, at other times he did it the local way, stitching the leaves alternately in and out as they browned in the sun.

Once he came out from under his breadfruit tree to tell me what the journey would be like. 'When you drink water, you will feel pain inside. It is so cold, that is why.' The paths were tricky as well. 'Your eyes will turn and you will want to fall off the mountain.'

Many sounds here were from summers back in England – lawn mowers working around the two mission houses, white children running with guns in and out of doors, a girl saying, 'Is that enough, Mom?' as Sue, Bob's wife, hooked lemons down from a tree. Other sounds were more local – the screech and clap of forest birds, the naked boys with shells hung between their legs, astride logs in the river, Bob in the workshop sharpening knives on a grinding wheel for the converts. I could hear him appealing slowly, emphatically in Pidgin about their friends, the Yaifos. 'It's no good they stay in the bush. They must come close to the mission, and so hear about the Lord.' He put out the words, laying his simple, honest traps for them.

Later in the day, I noticed Bob in the flowerbeds, perhaps plucking deadheads. I knew he wanted me to stop and talk because he was removing his hat the way he always did. The sparse hair on his neck was wet, in tongues, and he was raked with mud. Two white children with guns were about to ambush him but Sue called the novice warriors in. 'They're crazy about G.I. Joe, just now,' she explained.

Bob stood with me by the breadfruit tree. I watched them go, zapping each other from behind the shrubbery, not at all how Jesus would have brought up a child, while he began to inspect the orchids on the branches as if they might fall off. But he said, somewhat unexpectedly, 'Benedict, the problem of this age is that we are all taught relativism. There's no absolute good, no absolute bad, you know? It's so hard for us to accept we're sinners – ever since our fall from Eden. Nowadays, people can't conceive this.'

He was right; I couldn't conceive this at all. But his message was reassuring. I had come to the right place, a tribe of great faith in their values. He might ponder a lot about the world as he clipped hedges and lawns, but his views were safely fixed.

Behind the netting in Bob's house, the clicking of a computer keyboard under the young girl's fingers, and a whiteskin's heavy, townboy feet on the smooth, lino floor . . .

Outside, a baptism. 'Boy, what a testimony,' George said, slowly wading out into the river, his orange T-shirt ballooning. A church leader guided a frail old woman out behind him into the cold. She stood in the grey current, her skirt taking up the water, waiting for the plunge and wearing George's hand on her head like a hat. She looked scared. Harriet, on the river bank, with brown rings round her eyes, smiled reassurance, but became distracted by a fly on her neck; then the fly was on her straight hair, mousy strands of which waved down to her clean white collar.

George said, 'Honey, I sure wish we had a coat to give her.'

And then, in case it wasn't just the cold that was the worry, he explained that this wasn't some magic ritual; this wasn't a ceremony to wash away sins, just a sign that a decision had been made – that now all her sins would be carried for her.

But it *was* magic. And sometimes, preaching in the church with its thatched conical tower, its strip light that stayed on day and night, he seemed to know it himself. Seemed to know he was a shaman, as he sat barefoot, cross-legged on a table, having done away with altar, pews, Bibles, just his preaching to the Bisorios on the floor, welding their energy into one force.

We heard the whine of an uninvited plane coming in. Soon, while George and I stood staring, men were ordering the marvelling crowds into lines. Before we'd even established the name of the company, they'd organized everyone to pass brown boxes of provisions down a line to a mission shed, which they seemed to have commandeered. It was only a supply drop, but Bob watched the eager faces of his converts as they happily lobbed the boxes; he looked helpless.

George murmured to Bob as they watched their converts squabble over boxes, 'They could ruin us.'

Five days went by. In the early morning of each, I ran up and down the airstrip to keep fit; then I sat on our veranda, boiling a pot of water for tea as Susan put out the washing, pinning out her white sheets with wooden pegs.

Each morning, my training run. The mists licking the heat off the rays, the shelves of forest rising out of them with the day. As I got my breath back, Tsogamoi and I sat together under the old thatch, looking out at the whiteskins in their neatly sealed-up homes across the lawn. Whenever I offered Tsogamoi tea, he said, '*Thaaank* you!' extravagantly in English picked up from Bob. But he said little else and it was hard to see what he meant by the expressions in his eyes. Nor did I want to push him to talk; sometimes his eyes were daring me; I was sure he would flare up and sulk if I pushed him into conversation – as he did once when he saw Sue take a tray of steaming lunch to George and Harriet. 'Just going along to the Walkers, now,' she called to Bob, as if there were other neighbours they were likely to have lunch with.

Tsogamoi's black eyes seemed to redden. He burst out, 'They do not "share and share alike"!' He didn't like the whitemen's nut roasts but I knew he liked the look of their kitchen knives. When we ran out of firewood he said I should get some from Bob. I noticed that peculiar darkness in his eyes, a moody intensity that looked like trouble.

I said, 'But whitemen use gas.'

I went along anyway, taking my cooking pot for some hot water. It wouldn't be much to ask.

Bob was standing on his own veranda, getting a view of his orchids. As I got near, a freckled white girl came out to stare at me. I asked Bob if I could possibly have some hot water because I was out of firewood. He looked at me with utter shock, as the missionary called Mike had once when I'd asked for a drink; it was virtually as if I had asked him to sleep with me.

From inside, Sue called to the girl, 'Dear, have you washed yet?'

Bob was still thinking hard about my request. 'Okey-doke,' he said, finally.

I went in and filled my pot. The girl rested her chin on the work surface. 'Mom? Where does he come from?'

Mum called back. 'From behind Mailé's house.'

'Egh! Mom!' She points at the black smear I've left – carbon from the bottom of my pot.

Bob led me out, saying he'd give me a 'holla' when it was boiled. He shut the net door.

In a while, I heard people settling down around the table. I smelled gravy. I waited in the house. Sue called out and when I sniffed the meat again my heart rose. I said to Tsogamoi, 'Don't worry, I'll halve it with you.' I rubbed my teeth with my fingers, and combed my hair with my hands. I went over. I knocked before entering and apologized for disturbing the seated guests – surprise! It was 'the Walkers', George and Harriet. They had dressed up and travelled all the way from next door.

'That's quite all right,' Bob said, and handed me the kettle. They did not weaken. As a tribe, how could you beat them? I forgot about the food, and skipped happily across the lawn. They were marvellous.

The answer was, of course, gold. That was how you beat them. Now, four days to go, and only two guides signed up, the Bisorios and newcomers were hanging around all day, not settling to their Bible classes, just counting the hours.

I wore my boots around the mission, getting my feet used to them again, strutting about, squeaking on the wet blades of grass, squirting warm water out from the treads, trying not to mark the lawns. As far as languages went, Yaifo and Bisorio were 'very much in the same ball park', George had said, so I got together a word list with Tsogamoi, occasionally looking up from the veranda, smelling the soap or hearing the click of the pegs, as Susan's bare white arms spread to the laundry line.

Three days before the Company came. I at last had four guides, all of them, like Tsogamoi, distant relatives of the Yaifo. We'd leave at dawn.

George asked me for a farewell supper over at Bob's house. 'Don't know what it will be,' he said.

'Nut loaf again,' I said to myself. I'd already smelt it.

I left Tsogamoi some sweet potatoes to eat with the soft-shelled turtle he had caught. It was as floppy as Bob's hat, its head lost in its skin, its nose a slender beak. Just my luck for him to have caught some decent meat tonight. It smelt considerably better than the nut roast.

'Would you say grace, honey?'

'Sure . . . Lord, we just wanna thang you . . .' We ate, and I left some for Namoleeyo, the kitchen boy, who was waiting by the sink, begging at me with his eyes.

While Namoleeyo finished the apple crisp, his shiny brown stomach expanding out from under his T-shirt, George said he'd call in the guides, sound them out about the journey. Harriet took the girl away.

Two youths came in, both with large, smiling faces, dark red teeth and old side-burns showing through new stubble. They sat on the floor, out of the way. Then, beaming all over, Tsogamoi, chief guide, noisily, importantly, took a seat at the table. He had been rubbing his teeth with betelnut husks, creating a white, flat, gapless wall. He was wearing his yellow workman's hat, and had a woman's handbag on his arm. 'Good even-ing,' he said, his only other English phrase.

The other guides look up at the plastic sheeting under the thatch; they twitch, hearing the whistlings of the radio. George said, 'Hey, on the walk you get to go across a *kanda* [cane] bridge. And they're saying it reaches from here to the benzine shed. They're saying you'll see the bridge, let out a cry and come running back. It's so long you have to cross it five at a time. One at a time and it flips over and throws you in the water.'

Someone called Tsogamoi from outside on the veranda. He didn't get up but shouted out through the netting.

'News from the Highlands,' George said, pulling his string vest away from his chest, where it was evidently sticking. We waited while the boy shouted out above the sound of the generator.

I watched Tsogamoi's face as it lowered. I said, 'What's up?' George said that five young Yaifos had been seen passing through a village. They were on the way up to the gold site at Malumata. 'Flies to honey,' George said.

I asked how many men were up there now, still at Yaifo. No one knew

– there *had* been twelve young men, a total population of fifty-five or so in the district.

'Nothing you can do but go,' George said. 'Before it's too late. The miners will be here in two days – unless they're held up somewhere along the line, which is possible.'

'That's the lifeblood gone,' I said. As we were leaving, Namoleeyo mumbled that he wanted to resign in two days. George hugged him. 'Boy, these boys so want that gold.'

I went to the house, checked the supplies for tomorrow's start and wrote with the firelight. 'I am a week too late. Bang! The heart of them goes. Their youth blood.' How were they going to launch me now?

There was worse. In the morning Tsogamoi stayed stubbornly in bed. It must be the turtle, I thought. But when he got up, he kept his eyes low and while I tied my boots he swung idly from a crossbeam. He would hardly talk at all. When I asked him what was wrong, he moved back, to another crossbeam.

'Benedict?' George's voice. He stood below the hut veranda, a face peering up towards our little doorway. 'A guy has come to my house to ask me to tell you that you can't go.'

'Oh?'

'They've caught the man who killed the Bisorio woman. He's, like I say, a half relative of the Yaifos.' He let me chew on that. 'That's all I'm saying. I'm not saying what you should do, or anything, but that's the situation.' I asked him to expand, and I was soon wishing I hadn't. 'See, this is a once in a lifetime chance for them. This man fears nothing. I do mean nothing. He'd stick a knife in you as soon as smile at you. They say he can disappear just like that – disappear into the bush. But they've got him!' They were having a kind of court case. 'We're lucky there isn't going to be a fight . . .'

The Bisorios needed every man they could get to support their side in the meeting to be held at Malumata, that was what they'd told George. But when he was gone, Tsogamoi took off his plastic hat and looked into it, and looked outside. He told me everyone was also saying the Yaifos might attack our party.

The expedition was in tatters. We would have to wait until the court case ended and the gold was bound to be here sooner. I now expected Tsogamoi to wander off outside, leave me to dwell on what he'd said. He didn't. He sat down close to me on the food sacks. I wanted to hug him.

It would be a week perhaps, Tsogamoi said. Two days' walk for the Bisorios through the bush up to Malumata, two days there, two back.

'And you'll stick with me?' I wondered. 'When the gold comes, you'll stick with me?'

Men assembled on the river bank, beginning to leave for Malumata. George took Benny aside under the breadfruit tree to ask him to warn everyone about a drink called alcohol – how it would lead to wife-beating, fighting. It had made a first appearance here last night – one man had become unconscious and Tsogamoi had bitten his ear to bring him round. But Benny, usually a man with a greasy smile, wasn't playing his old game any more. Before George had finished the warning, Benny got up, gave a smile that was like a sneer, and walked away.

George watched him go. Bob said, 'He thinks he's going to be a millionaire next week.'

'It'll come,' George said to no one in particular, getting up. 'The booze will come – but what can we do?'

The first men charged off into the forest, up to Malumata. I asked George to talk to Tsogamoi. 'I just want him to say how he feels.' He held Tsogamoi's shoulder. Tsogamoi grinned, but talked so quietly George couldn't hear. 'Now he's got all embarrassed,' George said. 'He's feeling bad – he's made a commitment to you.'

Later in the day, there was buzzing coming at us from the sky. Everyone started running, a tide of half-crazed faces bobbing along to the airstrip. It was a chopper.

Bob had come from his tractor; he was still in his wellingtons. I said to him, 'Is this it?'

'Must be the goldminers, all right. No one else comes here.'

I was thinking aloud, 'I'm finished then.'

'You're not the only one.'

But the people in the chopper were New Guineans. Five of them – in suits. They were wearing suits in the jungle! And they were wearing ties – they must be politicians.

The first man out apologized – the Premier himself was meant to come. Bob said, 'Er, Benedict, can you get George?'

George was already on his way. He took the men in suits to his house. From the pilot we learned it was a border dispute – there was gold on the local border and the East Sepik and Enga provincial governments were fighting it out. Bob offered him a glass of lemonade. 'You can come in as well, if you like, Benedict.' The pilot was a gaunt man from Quebec who said the word 'Jesus' a lot, making Bob wince every time. 'Jesus wept!' 'Jesus Christ!' Soon, Bob and I realized this man could reveal the day of the forthcoming catastrophe. With a quick flick through his flight schedules, the pilot told us Equatorial Gold were coming tomorrow. A timber company was also booked for later in the month.

'The day after tomorrow, then . . .' I said.

'On a Sunday?' Bob said.

Namoleeyo ran out of the house, bursting with the news.

I tapped my fingers, waiting, thinking of the Yaifos up there at Malumata, putting on Western clothes, bewildered by the helicopters and spade-digging, feeling the weakening of their bonds, feeling how easily they were sucked to the gold.

And the missionaries too were weakening. The missionaries, the 'Secondary Primitives', had come all the way round the world looking for tribal people. They had left the West in search of people who were their own sort, people with whom they were compatible. But now, far from living happily united together as tribals, they were suffering as the gold fever sapped their energy away.

We were in it together, the missionaries and I. Bob invited me in for lunch – lemonade, bread and margarine, tinned beetroot. He showed me a vegetable patch which contained a plant for rubbing on skin to get rid of fungus – 'the Bisorios only want the whiteman's stuff now.' And he stopped his lawn mower to point out a turquoise, flinty-shelled fly. 'Now isn't that beautiful?' he says, looking down his ruddy cheeks, between his close-drawn lips, 'To me that is glorious. Why should God make that if not for the glory of man?'

There were several different answers to that, but it didn't matter to Bob. He left me to go round the mission, locking up, bolting, padlocking. No more Pidgin classes, no more maintenance shop, a cutback on Bible School. For my part I went to the village shop and bought up more supplies to withstand the siege. 'Yes,' Bob said, stooping to nip another weed in the bud, 'the world is closing in here, fast.'

The next day at dawn, I was doing my usual six-mile run. Everyone was up, but slow, standing about, drifting in the mist. The paths were full, there were so many people in the mission nowadays. Many of these people were strangers with trophies from other mining exploits – pieces of map decorating their hair, biros through their earlobes.

Bob stopped me to say that the Company had radioed. They wanted fifty men. It'll strip the mission bare, he said. They'd even have to ferry more men in from Meska, down river.

Sue called out, 'Hurry, they're coming.' She had dressed up. She was wearing a terribly pink plain dress, and trotted out to search the sky, still holding her lipstick as she shaded her eyes.

But it was a helicopter for Indaba, the company at Malumata. The blades whirled above the greedy faces while a whiteskin struggled to get out of his safety harness. 'Exploration PNG been here yet?' were

Right: Hmong Shaman and his wife divining the progress of the journey from chicken bones

Below: A senior Kandengei man and his boy protégé. The man is wearing a cuscus fur hat, the child a cassowary feather headdress

'Tribal' display at the
Goroka Highland Show:

Above: Huli dancers

Left: A Wahgi Valley man
wearing pearlshell and bird
of paradise streamer feather
nose decorations

Right: Paint, seed jewellery,
leaf wands and feather
crowns combine to exagger-
ate the movements of the
dancers

Opposite left: Men with bark-skin dress and dance banners at Goroka

Below: Men marching out of the Crocodile Nest act with the spirit of the Crocodile Ancestor

Above: Women offer themselves up to be beaten by the malevolent 'spirit', who is on his way to the Korogo village *Waarkdumba* (Crocodile Nest) in the far distance to do the same to initiates. While one woman is thrashed, a girl stands ready to provide a stick and open her dress for her turn

Left: A Kandengei fellow initiate, Nicholas, hunting for birds' eggs

Below: Scratching out a possible route on a path at Niksek Mission, with guides (left to right) Stefanus, Freimond and Tom

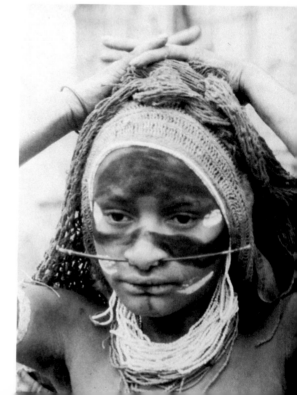

Above: The watchful Grandmother in her camp, with a mosquito swat on her lap

Above right: A camp along the trail to Pikaru. Tom contemplates his *Good News* Bible and one possible source of evil, that night's supper, a snake

Right: A Yaifo woman with cassowary quill nose-piece

Above: *Bandees* (initiates) in the
Crocodile Nest

Left: A Pikaru girl and friend

Below: A Yaifo boy, soon after our arrival

Above: Yaifos

Right: Yaifo men on a hunting excursion

Below: With the remote Yaifos, in the Central Highlands of Papua New Guinea

Left: Remote New Guinea Highlands

Inset: Heroic Tsogamoi being groomed at Hagi, *en route* to Yaifo

Right: Fee-fee and a Yaifo man indoors

Below: Fee-fee, another child and Ashkai playing ball with a pig bladder in the mists of Yaifo

Left: Over the Central Range, a Hewa woman wearing clay paint, a long grass skirt and Job's tear seed necklaces for mourning

Below: On the run towards the ridge: Yado crossing an early Yaifo river tributary

Bret and an Aboriginal boy in
the Dingo Man's garden, a camel
wagon wheel behind

Above: A visitor to the Sandalwood Mob on her tyre-less bicycle. A 'humpy' shelter is in the background

Left: Stewy firing his ging (a form of catapult): Blue Hill

Above: Some of the Sandalwood
Mob in action. Malala is in the rear

Right: Dusty at an ancestral
rockhole, Ululong, near Mungale

Below: Micky working a *womera*
(spear thrower) at Mungale

On the outskirts of Bondini Reserve, Wiluna

his first words. He was relieved when we shook our heads. He had a pimple on his nose and was wearing a boiler suit. He was weak-legged – one work boot trailed to the side as he directed matters, elbows back, hands by his baggy, loose chest. 'I need some labour – twenty or so.' He counted the first few off.

Tsogamoi was watching the men go forward. He did not move.

'Stay with me,' I thought. Please.

The chopper could take five people at a go. They'd be back down in a minute for some more.

George said to me, 'Kind've a shame you can't kidnap your Yaifos and bring them down.'

We heard the chopper beat through the clouds, back down to us. Bob said, 'Or even write a note. There's no one who can read.'

George said, 'No, wait – Mailé. Mailé's up there – our Bible teacher. He went for the court case.'

Bob said, 'It's a long shot, isn't it, George? The court case isn't all that near the miners' camp.'

I was already running to my house. I bounded onto the veranda and through the little doorway. 'My notebook, where is it?' I said aloud. I rip out a sheet. Now the chopper is outside, filling up with men. But I can't remember any Pidgin! Running outside, I scribble something and dive into the wash of the blades. I hand the note to the pilot in his seat. He can't hear me with the noise, but glances at the paper and puts his thumb up. He hoists up into the air.

Bob said, 'I'm intrigued. What did you write that is going to get the Yaifos down here, two days' walk away? They don't know what money is, even.'

I couldn't give an answer. I didn't know. Had I even written Mailé's name on the note? How did you spell his name anyway?

The chopper came back, with 'polybagged' rock samples. I ran to the Canadian pilot; he put headphones on me so we could talk. He had given the note to 'a local guy', he said. He thought the man could speak Pidgin, 'but, well, I'm not hot on it myself. Hope it wasn't anything too important.'

George told the crowd waiting in the wake of the helicopter that they might as well have a church service tonight. Tomorrow wasn't going to be a 'regular Sunday'.

They sat in the church, and George told them about the potential evils of beer and money. He said it was a test, these things being offered them. But the mood as the church floor cleared was excitement. These were end-of-school pupils.

I walked out of the service with Tsogamoi. George hugged him. 'Stay with it,' he said. Tsogamoi grinned, letting some of his sharp wall of teeth out from behind his tight lips.

'Don't know why he's stuck with me so long,' I said to George. 'The other three guides certainly won't last when the gold comes. It's the Yaifos I'm relying on.'

In the dusk, Bob came to our house. He had never come over like this before and he came to say one thing. 'You all set? No need to panic until tomorrow.'

I spent the evening specially cooking up sweet potatoes and tinned fish for Tsogamoi.

'Benedix, aaaaaah! Thank you!' Tsogamoi especially liked tinned fish. 'Still coming with me?'

He showed his blunt white teeth, but it wasn't an open smile. He said, back in his bad Pidgin, 'If the Yaifo comes, yes, I please to go.'

I went and bought extra tinned fish for him to take on the journey.

The next morning, as the boys were running through the village, sailing giant breadfruit leaves behind them, we heard the sound. It was a sound new to the forest, a huge engine-grinding roar that startled all the hornbills from the far bank.

The damp morning air was ripped by blades, metal parts smashed against metal parts, ball bearings ground in hot oil, and in came the Twin Otter with Equatorial Gold. For the locals, open-eyed and singing, it was like Palm Sunday.

A whiteskin opened the door. He had stiff shoulders and silver side whiskers, a sticky tobacco stain on the right-hand corner of his mouth. The crowd waved their hands and feathers, receiving him with adoration: Jesus on a modern donkey.

He wasn't expecting it. He blinked the small, dark eyes that clung close to his nose and turned away, back to the pilot. He talked quickly and incisively; he didn't seem to want to come out again.

Then five New Guinean men jumped from the plane, and cleared a space with their shouting. While the whiteskin sat, still in his seat, they began lobbing out boxes to the crowd. Benny remembered what the whiteskins had done last time and got the boxes moving along in something like a line to an imprecise destination on the mission lawn.

Box after box spilled out – a fridge, a shower unit, a table, and more boxes, each slapped from hand to hand, bounced along the ground until they got to the end of the line and hit the grass with a sickening thud. All were labelled 'Exploration PNG' in fluorescent orange, and some had extra, neater labels in plastic tape: J.M. Wolfe.

I retreated, not wanting to see Tsogamoi taken.

But the mining gang, who were short and pale brown and probably Highlanders, were flooding after me. They had seen how conveniently near the airstrip this house was, and they wanted it. Now they were heading straight this way, manhandling boxes. Inside, they piled their boxes over my supply stacks and then started biffing the doorframe with the fridge, ramming it to enlarge the entrance. Locals, seeing this obstacle was apparently in the way of their gold fortune, helped out with bush knives. Tsogamoi, indoors with me, began protesting. It was his house. 'Shut up!' the team said. And when he started pushing the invading fridge out again from this side, 'You are just bushies!' But Tsogamoi's eyes were sharpening and in a moment blood was going to be spilt. I suggested putting the fridge under the house – which is what they did, dropping it the four feet down.

Outside, things were simmering down. Benny was building his power base, taking time to put down names of people for work and using the fear of not getting on his blank list to steer them.

The plane shuttled back and forth all morning. I did not want to see what Tsogamoi chose to do. I stayed well away, going off to rub the anti-fungus leaf on my suspect pink blotches. By the afternoon, Benny had his list full. Fifty names; I went to look. Tsogamoi's name was not on the list.

The whiteskin was an Australian, Kevin. He lay on his back all evening calculating dimensions in his head, measuring invisible somethings between his fingers. He said this village put him in mind of another 'construction site'. The labour there worshipped President Johnson, because missionaries could still get Johnson outboard motors despite his being dead. They were cannibals, of course. 'They ate a white man once – including his shoes. Thought they were part of him.' When a plane came the next morning Kevin walked to it with a splayed hand, still measuring the imaginary. 'See yas.'

'You're going?'

'I'm only here to bring in equipment. The boss comes tomorrow.'

We all watched him go, the children among us putting the brown parcel tape on their cheeks. A mild, moon-faced old Bisorio man wearing a kitchen apron as a loincloth told George he remembered the last time men came to find gold here. It was before the mission. He had seen them in the bushes, at the time being part of a war party heading for Inaru – the raid, he reflected, when the father of Odea, the boy who ran the store, lost his head. 'Ate it as well,' Bob said as the plane left us.

I slept for a second night with cigarette stubs and onion peelings, the five work gang members and 'Cookie', a fatherly little man who had travelled the length of the country and had four wives, who, we were all hoping, weren't going to turn up here. The shed was crowded enough already.

The boss, J.M. Wolfe, another whiteskin, was large. His shorts were hardly to be seen from under his belly. His beard was greying, his moustache dark, creeping over his lips. He didn't see me in the shadows but introduced himself to George, who had packed in his Bible teaching sessions 'for the duration'. I heard George explain how things worked here – or had worked up to now.

'They might not know what to do with money, but at least they know what money is.' When he first came they were 'real bushy'. He had had to put a tin on display – coins went out to pay them, went back in in exchange for clothing. He didn't make the clothes himself, he'd told them. However for two years he'd heard the men discussing pounding him to get the truth out – where did his money come from? 'Yeah, it was *that* kinda deal.'

This new whiteskin, Jo, was filled in. 'Okay, it's a deal where . . .' or 'Problems with the airstrip? Funnel that one through Bob Parry,' or, 'Yeah. They catch on real quick if . . .'

Jo thanked George, and turned to the assembly. But he didn't address the multitudes, he looked through them. He asked who the head man was, and got Benny instead. He talked in English, though there were only Pidgin speakers here. His voice was high and strangled. He kept on the move, coming in and out of Tsogamoi's house, laying down guidelines for the double bed that was being constructed over Tsogamoi's sleeping place. Corrie, a deaf boy, had already been evicted with the others. I hung on. Jo used English, the language only spoken by his gang, as a tool to dominate. He also cracked jokes delivered with oversized, imperious gesticulations. He passed the dazzled locals saying, 'Got a double adapter in your pocket?' Or, 'Why don't you fetch a glass of water to put in the freezer? That way when I next bash my head on the door I'll be able to control myself.'

Then, taking his time, he went to speak to the masses properly, in Pidgin. 'First rule. No chewing of betelnuts. You can rot your mouth and teeth in your own time, not mine.'

Benny walked about behind, with lists. I was standing with George and Tsogamoi, waiting – it was time to fix labour rates. The mission could be ruined, I could be ruined. But whatever rate they decided, I knew that they must decide before the Yaifos arrived here – assuming they did come. The Yaifos might have been sucked in at Malumata; they might also be sucked in here. The goldminers must seal up their tribe.

Jo came over for a quick word with George. He still hadn't noticed me, blending with crowds. 'I'm going for the government rate, with no employment at weekends – that's where they'd win with the time and a half and double time. They'll get their *kaikai* [food] though.'

He walked back into the crowd, and casually mentioned the pay rates, moving on quickly to inspect the meat, which no one had put in the freezer. We all knew the money matter wasn't going to end there.

Cookie made me some tea, and I shared it with Tsogamoi. 'Benedix, Thannnk you!'

The whiteskin came to the door, and hung wedged in the frame just as the fridge had done, though with legs dangling from him. He said, 'Sorry there, don't think we've been introduced.'

I had been with him all day. He invited me for a meal. 'What's cooking, arse of horse?'

The evening came on. Cookie sizzled meat in the frying pan. Outside, men milled in the dark, wondering what to do about extracting more money from the whiteman. I was only thinking to myself, 'If you are coming, then don't come yet, Yaifos.' If the company could settle their business tonight, then all would be perfect. The mission was in disarray; their loosed energy was everywhere – you could hear it, the mob outside. It seemed to hang from the humid night air, waiting to be formed into the new-born gold tribe. If ever there was a moment *not* to launch out from here, it was now. If ever there was a moment to spring from here, it would be a day or so away, when the goldminers had made their own people. Stay away, Yaifos, for now.

The whiteskin and I sat at the table. He could trace his ancestry back to General Wolfe of Quebec, he said. He leaned back in his chair, legs crossed, straight. Hands behind his head, his mountainous stomach separating us. He mocked the human storm brewing outside. 'Can't the ladies discuss anything without crying and yelling?' The imported work crew said nothing. 'Where's Uncle Benny? Out there somewhere, I suppose?'

'He's there all right,' I said.

Jo was a veteran of these campaigns, I learned. 'There's really that much gold around?' I asked. 'Or is it just the usual gold fever stories?'

'Is there gold around?' He said he'd illustrate how much gold there was around. At Ok Tedi some men came and asked him if they could buy some batteries. He said no, but there was a store just down the road. He saw the men coming by later, holding a cassette recorder. The store hadn't had any batteries, but the recorder came with them ready supplied. So they'd bought it. 'Bought a cassette recorder to wrap the batteries in!' That was how much money there was around.

For the first time he asked me what I was doing out here. I told him a bit and he asked what I would do if I got appendicitis. I said I supposed I would try to get someone to carry me out, and if it got unbearable I'd try to cut it out myself.

He nodded jovially, thinking I was gamely attempting to match his pioneer spirit. He stirred his meat, on the plate, happy to oblige by taking me on. 'Yeah, lick ya knife clean, open yourself, look around your guts for something that's aching and pull it off. Otherwise you can curl up and kiss ya arse goodbye!'

While we finished the meal, Paul, the Meska village Kansol, elected representative, came in to start negotiations. He didn't stand a chance. The whiteskin had made this his territory and Paul was coming right into the middle of it, right to his adversary's table. Had he been taught in a Crocodile Nest, he would not have done this.

Jo leaned back, leisurely finishing pudding, his team taking up all the best vantage points. While Paul was setting himself up as victim, Benny was waiting in the doorway holding the seams of his long trousers like the old school of Papuan, those fostered by the Australians. He stood showing his boyish, watery-eyed, harmless look of the Kanaka for a second, then left to carry on spreading discontent outside.

I gave up my seat at the desk. Jo offered it to Paul, making the gesture work as a magnanimous act, further emphasizing the difference in status. Paul tapped his pen on a school exercise book, placing his bare foot across his knee, vainly trying to look like an office man. Jo talked fast in English about government pay schemes. Paul said, airily, that he knew about this. '*Mi got save long dispela*'. But he was pulling his trouser flares, already looking lost.

Waving his hands in what must have been meant as an authoritative gesture, fingers up, he told Jo to find out the true government rates. Jo said, 'You are Kansol. It's your job to know what they are.'

'What's the address?' the Kansol said, again trying the hand gesture. His eyes were searching for a more sympathetic face, and only finding the work gang, who were tapping biros on their bucket seats, spitting, coughing.

Outside, everyone was waiting, but with less patience now. They were angry with the Kansol as much as the whiteskin. The planks of the veranda creaked as men paced. Some men, wiser men, were saying that Paul should leave it. Others said, No. Fight him now.

Then I heard the sound of a sharp whip of cane. A bow being fired. The whiteskin hadn't heard it. I got up, and slowly bent my head outside. I saw a lot of faces, teeth and eyes and cowrie-shell necklaces stirring amongst each other, and several canes that might be arrows. But the faces smiled up at me. It had only been showmanship.

Suddenly, as I stood there up on the veranda, somebody was rubbing my legs intimately. Tsogamoi, his hard jaw on my shin and his hard teeth grinning up at me. He shone his newly acquired Exploration PNG torch in my face and said, '*Tupela* Yaifo!' Two Yaifos! 'They come, Benedix – Mailé is come and the court case is over and done!'

I gave Tsogamoi a friendly biff on the shoulder. 'We might get up those mountains yet!' It looked hopeful; but the Yaifos mustn't come yet.

George was coming. He asked how things were going indoors. I shrugged. He said he had decided to leave tomorrow. There wasn't much to do for a while, and he wanted to parachute a drawing of a church hut and some hammers and nails into Bikaru. 'It's a kinda hint.'

Last month the Bikaru hadn't seen a white face close up; now they had a postal service.

George said he wouldn't be able to help me any longer. 'But it's up to the Yaifos anyway, I guess.'

He went back through the crowds. After he was gone from view, I heard Benny say that the missionaries might like to double their wage rates if they wanted to stay.

I went back indoors, still thinking to myself, 'Not yet, Yaifos. Not yet,' squeezing by Cookie, who had witnessed a hundred such power struggles. He sat calmly on a black painted drum of Shell Sport 2 engine oil.

Paul was looking in a sorry state. His skin appeared darker than ten minutes ago and he needed a rest. The whiteskin said to me across the house, 'Same everywhere here. Offer them some money and they reckon they're worth five times as much.'

But Benny was now in the doorway. He spoke in Pidgin, not English. '*Masta*, the Meskas are going down river. They cannot wait for you.'

Jo looked up a little fast. But he was still twiddling his thumbs. 'How many men is that?'

'Twenty men.' He stopped twiddling his thumbs. Benny said, 'Shall I tell the men to wait?'

Jo started his thumbs up again. 'You do that.'

Benny went away. I followed him outside; he waited at the bottom of the veranda. Then he came back up and stayed by the door. 'I think they do not want to stay, *Masta*.'

Everyone was watching Benny. Jo had lost the focus of power. He was motionless, apart from the regular, now stiff beat of his thumbs.

Benny was waiting in the doorway, not coming in. 'They want to wait down in Meska. For a week . . . or two.'

After a long while of silence, Jo shouted, 'All right!' He sat up. 'All right, I'll give you your four kina.' He roars it. 'Satisfied?' He looks to me – the only outside reference point. But I'm wondering what's so good about four kina, only a quarter of a kina increase, not enough for a packet of biscuits.

Benny comes in properly. He is grinning, shaking hands, making it his victory. Paul leaves quietly.

Jo gets up and says to me, 'Always a few shit stirrers.'

Next morning, he reports back to base on his radio, 'Everything according to schedule.' Over breakfast, he tells me he was expecting to concede four times that. Then he goes out, saying he wants everyone lined up. 'Where's the line? I can't see the line – and I figure it's my turn to grizzle at you as you grizzled at me all yesterday.'

Some men have used different names on Benny's list, signing on several times over without knowing it. While that's sorted out, Jo hands around extra treats to his team. 'Hold the bus, hold the bus,' he says, searching for cigarettes. 'Could have anything here – a blow-up rubber doll . . .'

He sits down and chews through his breakfast apple juice – it has ice in it because the fridge thermostat was broken in transport – then arranges a boat up river to a probable construction site.

Now the village is empty; the women are off hunting for vegetables to sell to the goldminers and the men are all off with Jo. The afternoon ticks and fizzes by. As I sort my stores, Tsogamoi draws up and bends down to press fresh news into my ear, as if it's our secret. He's solved a problem that's been niggling me – how to get him off the mountain if I manage to carry on up it from the Yaifo village. Tsogamoi's brother, the one who has wooden chips in his nose, has found himself not on the list of fifty workers and will come with us, even at my measly rates – less even than the government rate, if you take into account the unpaid walk home.

'Benedix,' Tsogamoi adds, 'the Yaifos is nearby.' They are hanging back along the path; they've been scared by the sight of Malumata and must be wondering whether it's as bad here.

'Come on, come on,' I keep saying during the day. 'Now's the time.' But there is nothing to do but wait.

Bob says, 'Well, off tomorrow . . . Somehow, you've pulled it off.'

Susan offers to wash my clothes but they've got grease on them now and I want them like that to keep the rain off. I sit at Jo's table, writing my notes, tapping my pencil. A man with smooth, stretched, worried eyes comes to me. He says I'm taking two sons of his. I notice his feet – heavy, like rounded buttresses. He is a forest man; I think he's telling me the truth, that he isn't after money. He says, if my sons want to go with you, that's fine – something between us. '*Samting bilong yupela.*' But he wants me to be warned. Once up in the mountains, the Yaifo are warring people – *man bilong pait.*

I go to the end of the village and the vegetable patch containing the anti-skin-fungus plant. But the course of treatment must end. The plant has been demolished by the feet of the goldminers.

Jo comes back from his camp, and says to Cookie, 'Hello missis.' He tells him to get cooking. 'Put in a bit of everything. Tomato, chilli, pet dog . . .' He puts his feet up. 'Here's all the girls!' he says as his team troops in. One of the men dabs at a cut toe. 'Seen funny treatment in my time,' Jo says, 'baby powder's a new one. Haven't you used a Band-aid before? And if that doesn't work, we'll get an axe and chop it off. Sew a button on it.'

He turns to me. 'Life wasn't meant to be easy.' Then, 'I'd better go out and pay. Make the little buttercups shine.'

He takes the desk with him, and the men queue to have their names checked off. 'Jo-sshooah,' one of them says, testing out the sound of his new Western name. Then he says the name of the river where his hamlet used to be. 'Wilifa.'

'Joshua Wheelbarrow. Right. Next!'

They come at dusk, running in shyly. I see only their shadows – the feathers.

That is all anyone sees, at first. I try and remember more details afterwards, but only have an impression of their giant running strides, and the Bisorios watching them go past in the dim light, everyone stopping exactly where they are, and seeming to stiffen a little.

I decide not to go to introduce myself – they are under enough pressure from outsiders already. They stay in Mailé's house, as if sheltering. I tell Tsogamoi to keep an eye on them. He takes them some sweet potatoes and comes back grinning. 'Aaaaah, Benedix, they is too good!'

'Preparing for the rigours of another day in the wilderness. Where's that toilet paper – you dug it out yet? Thinking back to your work performance out there today, I could *well* have an accident in my trousers.' While his team prepares for a day on the construction site, Jo convenes a vegetable market, his thighs fattening as he squats to inspect pumpkin, greens, papaya, bananas, the start of a consumer economy.

Tsogamoi nudges me. Looking up, I see the Yaifos. They are taking advantage of the distraction to visit the store. They have strong bodies that look even stronger under cowrie-shell headbands, the black quill earrings hanging to their shoulders, the quiffs of white pandanus fibre in armbands and cassowary skin sheaths down their backs. I walk over, taking Tsogamoi, as they peer at the shelves behind the counter, smelling them.

They do not see me coming, they are staring so hard at the stores. As I squeeze past, their feathers tickle me. They have a plumage like a cockatoo, red parrot and banded hawk feathers shooting from grease-clogged hair and stacked up and held with a leaf band and bamboo peg; white feathers, golden bird of paradise feathers cut lengthways to spiral from ear strings. From the nose sides spring white feathers pared away except at the tip, which forms a brush. They grin as Tsogamoi asks their names for me. They don't look my way, but play with their hair or the bone bars through their noses. Then they look back at the shelves.

Bisorios walk over from the market with money from selling vege-tables. While they do their buying of T-shirts the Bisorios give the Yaifos coins at arm's length. The Yaifos themselves are aware of their warrior status; their heavy limbs are lightly poised and swinging grandly. Through the afternoon, the donations come in, the Yaifos running back and forward to the store, not buying anything. In the evening they are still there, playing with their coins in tin boxes. They still haven't spent their money; staring is enough. Tsogamoi asks them what they want. They point at the wicks and mirrors, then move on down the rows – torches, bulbs, soap, rice . . . They frown when he takes a coin from their tins. He buys them just a few wicks for cigarette lighters and a plastic sleeping mat each. They come away, very quiet, grinning. Seeing me, they stop, look at each other, then repeat their names slowly again, and run on.

The bags are all set, but Tsogamoi's brother, the fourth guide, has a cough. Bob invites me for what is meant to be another of his last suppers. I turn up late, having scratched around hopelessly for a replacement guide.

I sit at Bob's supper table, knowing I should eat for tomorrow's march, but not interested. Outside, I see the Yaifos running and jumping under cover of dark, their cassowary feathers rising off their backs, their leaf bustles like the bird's rump, fibrous and fine, like worn quills.

They are excited at going home; they are bolting. They are feeling weak out here, away from their own nest and with the gold company so strong. I know they won't wait another day. I watch them through the netting, bathed in the moth-battered neon light, the feathers waving. Namoleeyo comes, fresh from George's kitchen. He leaves his wellingtons by the door. He eats the mince, the leftover potato, the tomato sauce, apple pie and fruit salad.

'What about him?' Bob says, winking towards Namoleeyo, who didn't get on the payroll. 'Michael? Want some exercise to work off your tummy?'

'That's not Michael, that's Namoleeyo.'

'Not now. Not since last week.'

Michael leans on the sink, his jeans sucking up the dish water. I see he has written 'Michael' in biro on his trousers. He goes outside to wash, and Bob gives me a tip. 'The sure way to his heart is food.'

I follow Namoleeyo to the beach, where he's writing a word in the sand: 'Michael'. I promise him extra rations, and a diving mask so he can catch extra food on the way. He comes running out of the water.

Namoleeyo speaks better Pidgin than Tsogamoi and takes me to meet the Yaifos properly. They are alone, curled on the ground. They peep from their feathers, curious at me. Everyone else in the village is wide awake, talking about wages; they look as if they are at roost.

With Namoleeyo's help, in the Bisorio language I say 'Goodbye,' meaning until tomorrow. 'Beealé.' They look at each other, their eyes dipping, sleepily.

Namoleeyo says, 'These two find no fun. They must be off tomorrow.' Sooner the better, I say. After three weeks' wait, the timing is perfect.

I go to see Harriet to say goodbye and thank her for the support. She says Namoleeyo will be 'good for Tsogamoi's melancholia' – those are her last words to me. She has explained that Namoleeyo has relatives left in the mountains, like Tsogamoi. 'That probably swung it for you.'

I check my stores: rice, sugar, tea, more rice and yet more rice. Cookie sits letting his round, smiley face go, telling stories of when he was an assistant cook to the Japanese, in the war. He checks *his* stores. Tinned fruit, Worcester sauce, tuna fish, Vegemite . . .

The Yaifos test the weight of their food sacks, put them in their string bags, pummelling any protruding corners. Tsogamoi straps me into my rucksack. I take the Yaifos' spare arrows as Jo, the whiteskin, walks by in a towel, smelling of talc. He looks at the arrows, some of which are multi-pronged, for fish, some with long smooth blades, for pigs and people, some heavily barbed, for birds, pigs and people. He gives me an odd look.

Bob tips his hat, and swings up onto his tractor; Harriet and Sue wave from behind their netting. And we leave through the village, the Yaifos ahead, running to get out of here. But first we have to go right through the miners' camp, which is up river.

The day before yesterday, this was forest. Now it's fifty men with thirty shovels looking at the holes they've just dug in the red clay. Branches that were once overhead are now being thumped into the ground as posts. We pass through the site without stopping, Jo standing on a stump under his hat, the gang clearing soil into the river, wondering what gold is and whether they're knee deep in it. But, seeing the construction site, I realize something, and I pause and shake my head. No one has told the workers either: Exploration PNG is just here to set up the site. The mining company hasn't even arrived yet.

Many workers stop to watch us go, the sweat on them running black with the dirt. I recognize 'Joshua Wheelbarrow'; he's letting his loin leaves wither and shrink; he has a pair of red shorts underneath. He stops to look as we go by, at the same time scraping the sweaty earth off his belly with a bush knife blade; then he gets on with digging, his eyes glued for the gold. We cross the Salumei, borrowing Jo's canoe, and spring out and into the forest – right in, running through the lowlands, following the river course as it turns to come in from the foothills of the south.

We are still going fast. The Yaifos are, for the moment, still intent on escape but I want to put distance behind us before the afternoon rains come; I'll feel better when the lowland waters have cut us off from the Company. Birds do not hear us coming – brown ducks, white cockatoos, lunging kingfishers, naughtily stalking herons, two sleek black and white birds side by side, flapping their tails, one the negative of the other.

Each time we stop for a rest, the Yaifos tuck their leaf tails between their legs, and, using them as a cushion, sit on the damp ground. The larger man, Kaibayoo, who has a body that is somehow cosy, something to hug, squeezes river water off the more angular, younger man with foam rubber. Then he puts the foam away between his spine and his string bag, and we walk again. Good; we are making progress. We'll get beyond this marsh before the rain.

As we go, the Yaifos snatch leaves to use as drinking cups; their packs prevent them bending to take their lips directly to the water. Namoleeyo carries water in his wellies, dousing himself from time to time. When I fall, Kaibayoo, the large Yaifo, laughs, then disarms the laugh by showing his tongue – it wags, looking pink and silly, from his dark face. He waits for me to haul myself out of the mud.

The rain. Leaves are knocked down from the tree canopy as it roars through the forest. I imagine the streams rising behind us; it would be hard to retreat now.

We stop for the night at an old camp. While I fetch water for the cooking pot, the Yaifos dig into their knotted hair, raking it through with their new combs. They give up after a while. But the younger Yaifo puts on a shirt, taking a very long time with the buttons and hanging it all askew. The older plays with his new things in his tin box, and blows his battery torch to try to make it glow.

We cook rice. But the Yaifos like only the crusts around the outside of the pot and from now on we have to cook in two stages; once, for us, and then again for the Yaifos, putting the rice back in the fire to burn.

We are still walking through flat land, along the Salumei. There's no sign of a change of heart, though the Yaifos have not come away from the Company unmarked; they continue to chop at their hair and take it in turns to wear their shirt, or tear up the plastic rice wrappers with their teeth, and use their bone needles to pin them on themselves.

We camp the next night in a swamp, making a shelter from the sago leaves, splitting them lengthways and laying them on a lean-to. I take off my shirt as I work, trying to do my bit, forgetting that everyone will see my crocodile marks. They reach out and touch. For all of them, even Tsogamoi, they are a curiosity. No more than that – a sailor's tattoo. But I notice the Yaifos' large fingers are unexpectedly soft and tender; their touch is as gentle as a lick.

In the morning, while I fasten my boots, the Yaifos sit on their beds of leaves giggling, having their nails cut by Tsogamoi for the first time. They keep their claw-like thumb nails – they're useful for opening tins.

At last we are leaving the laulau trees, rain trees, sago palms of the lowlands, of Kandengei. Soon there will be no monitor lizards, no turtles, no lake fish, no crocodiles grunting and quacking at night. The forests begin to buckle around us. Good; in a matter of a day or two the Yaifos will smell home.

I am with Kaibayoo, the larger Yaifo, walking behind him. When we sit and rest, he watches me from behind the sweet potato he's eating. I watch him when he's plunging down into a pool for the cool of it, among the little blue butterflies. Or shooting a pair of lesser birds of paradise, parcelling away their golden plumage for a head-dress and adjusting the pair of red spindle feathers for his nose holes.

They are all going home – the Yaifos, Tsogamoi and Namoleeyo – going back to where they were reared. I am going further and further from Kandengei. They know they are nearing the source of their power, and I feel I'm weakening. Like the others, of course, my thighs feel torn, my back aches from the eighty-pound pack, but I feel it more. I do not know where I'm going to end up. But Kaavon said, 'He is stronger, he has something from the forest', so I try to concentrate again on the forest around me. We are climbing the east bank of the Salumei, but I try to take no interest in the geography, only in the immediate – the wet cobwebs, the slap and tickle of the thick leaves, the power in Kaibayoo as he yelps or takes a sharp breath when I slip.

We are not committed yet. Until we are over to the west side of the Salumei, over the long cane bridge, we might yet turn back. I walk closer to Kaibayoo. I notice he's getting happier. He curls a tendril of bracken around his hair. He points to a cockatoo side-stepping on a close tree branch; he sits with me, heating tobacco leaves with blocks of tree resin, and he plays his mouth harp in the mornings while I am battling to relace my boots. The nearer and nearer he is to home, the happier and stronger he is.

Sometimes Tsogamoi comes up from the back of the party and badgers me about what I will do once I get to the Yaifos. 'Benedix, I can go home and leave you with the Yaifo? It is not fair.' He asks me again and again what's going to happen. It's a good question. The answer is that if the Yaifos can give me a decent send-off, the sort that Kandengei could not do, then I'll be strong enough to get over the mountain into Enga Province, where the gold rush is.

The hills are now steep, like barriers. We clamber up and over them, Kaibayoo leading me with gentle whistles, appearing pained when I fall. We come through old gardens, tart pineapples standing like cacti in hostile grasses, and pass a third night in another old garden, bedding down bracken in an old leaf shelter, smoking tobacco from the trays put up in the trees, away from pigs. We have the soft brown bird of paradise meat with our rice and the next morning start early to avoid the blood-sucking flies and sweat bees. We can soon hear the Salumei.

It cuts across us in a deep ravine, thirty feet below. A recent flood has taken an old cane bridge with it, pulling a comb through the forest. Even the new bridge is looking dangerous, but Kaibayoo steps out into the spray clouds and reinforces it with fresh cane strands, flicking them around the base poles with a foot. We cross one at a time, without baggage, and then the lighter Yaifo makes painstakingly slow trips back and forward, bringing over a small package each time.

On up the right side of the deepening valley, through into a fresh breeze, a hamlet abandoned for the mission. We grub for food – pandanus, breadfruit, betelnut, taro – and search the clouds for the mountain ridge.

Smelling rain we make for an abandoned house, and fall asleep using the old pillows, poles which are black from hair grease. A puny bitch dog limps in from out of the trees; she is shaking with excitement but is cowering, wondering what she has done to have been abandoned like this.

It rains through the night and next day, making the logs slippery. I'm as helpless as the dog; we both tag behind Kaibayoo, looking up at him hopefully, ducking together, wincing together as a heavy object, a giant frog, curves through the air before our eyes.

Another garden, this one with a new house. We climb the notched pole to the narrow entrance and work around the passage to enter the room through doorways like windows. We wait for the rains to lessen; then move on.

From now Kaibayoo will walk ahead of us, singing out for the Yaifos. 'They is not good at strangers,' Tsogamoi says.

'WHUP!'

'Whap!'

'WHUP!'

They yelp alternately, whipping the air, reaching up through the first mists, scooping out the valley bowls. The Yaifos are bouncing along now; I feel carried. I get a warm feeling around my navel. Namoleeyo is unimpressed with my newfound speed. He calls me from behind. 'Benedix, you think you can get over the mountains with the Yaifos? No, Benedix. They are still fighting people.'

'Well, I take your point. But it's just a feeling. These people really have it – what I'm looking for.' But Namoleeyo looks past me, up the trail, wanting to get on. He wipes his forehead with his new yellow cap; more sweat springs out.

So I address Tsogamoi instead. 'A few more of them, and I'll be launched up and over the mountains with no trouble at all.'

'Aaaaah, Benedix, not so easy,' he says. And then, firmly, 'I walk before you now,' and he overtakes.

We walk over the Coderee river, near its junction with the Salumei, which up here is called the Wilifa. I eat the fern tips growing along the path that cranes up and around giant limestone boulders. The mangy dog follows, howling. It walks slowly, with a bewildered face, the balding skin moving side to side over its shoulders, none to spare.

I feel I ought to carry the dog, but know this is an impulse from somewhere like the mission, which is outside the forest. The forest itself has tougher living standards.

Now we are at a hamlet called Hagi, where Namoleeyo was brought up. We stop and let him go ahead while we wait. Black bees pour in and out of a pine tree, smoky trails that veer off through the slopes, licking the forest and swinging home.

There is only a little house, and sitting in front of it two young girls, a woman wearing a black head-net and also a baby on her back, and a boy holding her skirt hem. When Namoleeyo calls, they say nothing; they look up, and straighten. Two boys of about ten, wearing only a cockle-shell each, are behind, holding a pig by a rope to its foot. Seeing me, they leave the pig. They walk backwards, getting themselves tucked away indoors; then I hear them bolt into the inner room. The rest of our party follows them in and when I try and go indoors, the females scuffle and squeak to get out. I retreat, wondering what reaction I'll get from the Yaifos, 'man bilong pait.'

We make our own shelter outside. The mother, who has a black cas-sowary quill through her nose, comes out to watch, rolling a smooth yellow bamboo tube on a wooden needle placed in her hair, a portable lice-killing kit.

Because we don't sleep – Namoleeyo is bitten by a centipede which we never find, and the pig sucks and munches all night – we have a rest day. The Yaifos bake a pandanus fruit and the Hagis run out with tree kangaroo shoulder-blade spoons and scoop up the salty juice.

'WHUP!'

'Whap!'

'WHUP!'

We push on to Yaifo country, zigzagging the slopes. Another night with an older couple who have to hold their young son down when I enter the house, and on up a dry river, a shaft of sharp boulders. Namoleeyo and Tsogamoi now sing out with the other two across Yaifo valley, a westerly fork of the Wilifa; the dog howls along as well, wagging. We wait for an answer. None. The dog sits, waiting for more howling, watching for us to begin, but we carry on, working around the valley bowl, on shales and mudstones that my boots cannot grip. The men have to form a fence; I squeeze along the inside, my face in their hair, which now has a mossy dampness from the mist.

'WHUP!' 'Whap!' 'WHUP!' The calls become continuous. We are getting near. The sounds swing out around the valley bowl, being shaped by it, and coming back with its impression.

We know we are almost there when the two Yaifos pluck leaves to tie their hair up in fresher looking bunches. Tsogamoi grabs my hand. 'Yai-fo!' There are five or six men down there by a house on a spur of the valley. They seem to be hopping in a circle, flashing whites and reds at us – these might be paint or feathers. Then they disappear indoors. I realize that for the past five minutes it hasn't been our echo I've been hearing, it was the men down there, the ones doing ring-a-ring-a-roses.

I keep at Kaibayoo's heels all the way up through the gardens and the tumbling soil gashes in the mountainside. We watch the house as we come closer, and closer still. Namoleeyo tells me, orders me, to go to the back of our group. We reach the dance area, see a duck feather, the red and yellow dance leaves. Perhaps they'll spring from the house. Nearer and nearer. But they don't. The Yaifos aren't inside.

The next morning, hunks of mist are lying in the sharp divots and gentle scoops of the Wilifa valley. We continue up; but hear nothing. We come to one house. It is empty. Kaibayoo keeps calling. 'WHUP! WHUP! WHUP!' Just him calling now. We make our way up to the second house.

Kaibayoo is well ahead, working up through the gardens. Finally, he drops his pack at the top.

'This is it, then,' I say to Tsogamoi, gesturing at the two houses. 'Yaifo – the village. But where are the villagers?'

Tsogamoi keeps going, his head up.

Up through the garden furrows we go, until we are at the back of the house. It is large and new – a good sign. They've invested in this place.

This is it; we can smell the woodsmoke. But no one is here except the two Yaifos, who are walking about, calling. I lay down my pack and we stand with them in the middle of a level circle of clay, a shelf behind the house. The forest steaming behind, dark and sullen.

'They've gone,' I say.

Tsogamoi puts down his pack, and says nothing. His eyes are not tired from the walk, they are restless; he is expecting something. The two Yaifos, on the other hand, are more relaxed.

'Namoleeyo?' I say.

Namoleeyo behaves exactly like Tsogamoi; he's alert, though smiling briefly as he waits. I don't think he's frightened.

I jump. Kaibayoo, just a few yards off, has started a call, whooping at the forest again. We wait. Then, half a minute late, the echo comes back. It is as if the forest had kept it to itself all that time. Now it is letting the sound go. I stand still, knowing very well that in fact the moss on the trees and the valley mist swallowed Kaibayoo's call completely. They gave us nothing back; the answering sound was from the forest.

'Tsogamoi, I don't like Hide and Seek,' I said. He isn't in a mind to talk just now so I explain my predicament to Namoleeyo. 'I just don't like party games. Never have done.'

The call rises and rises. It spreads down and around us, circling in through the gardens.

We see the feathers first, the flapping whites and reds; and then red paint, and then the bows, each drawn, with an arrow in place. But, strangely, I'm relieved. We can see what it is that's putting us on edge.

'WHAH! WHAH! WHAH!'

However, it's at this point that I remember the court case. Who *did* win in the end? The Bisorios, which might make the Yaifos angry? Or was it the friend of the Yaifos – the one that was a cold-blooded murderer?

'Well armed,' I comment. 'Is that all right, Tsogamoi, that they are well armed? Hello? Tsogamoi, Namoleeyo? Anyone?'

I stand there among them, trying to smile.

'WHAH! WHAH! WHAH!'

They would have done something nasty to us with their arrows by now if they had wanted to, and they are too busy to notice if I take a few pictures, so I juggle with my shoulder bag and jiggle the focusing and snap away, disliking photography, the capturing in it, but knowing this particular scene anyway will never be repeated. Several men are coming up through the gardens, joining in the party, slapping their bow strings, encasing us in a whirling smell of musk.

'This is a welcome, Tsogamoi? Only I'm not used to this sort.'

He answers at last. 'Aaaaaah, yes. This is Yaifo style welcome.'

'I don't know if I'm getting the full appreciation of it.'

The feet are silent on the clay, the sounds we hear are their calls, the feathers and leaves and the cane bow strings. The ground moves to their pounding, silent feet. The air swings to the batting feathers – the chimney-sweep-brush hats, the cascading plumes, head-dresses with feathers jumping like flames, igniting the air. They spring around us, encircling, putting us in their power. As if it was necessary, two more armed men bound from out of the house.

Everyone stops. I notice that our two Yaifo guides have gone indoors, leaving us here with their family, who are now leaning on their bows or still clattering to a halt. One older man takes a step forward. He's wearing the closest I've ever seen to a whiteman's idea of 'warpaint'. Many an evangelist has probably woken in the night screaming from a nightmare that looked just like this.

'Tsogamoi, who are your distant relatives? Are they here?'

But the Senior Man begins speaking to Namoleeyo.

I say, 'You know him, Namoleeyo? Why didn't you say? I've been getting myself all worked up.'

'I think you'd better introduce yourself,' Namoleeyo says, stiffly.

I think they ought to work off some more of their energy first, but I give Tsogamoi the camera. 'I suppose I better have a record of this – no one ever believes these moments.' I hear Tsogamoi struggling with the camera behind. 'Just keep clicking, like I showed you.' I've already wasted the best part of a good film teaching him to shoot the camera – and he does just that, shoot. Like a bow, it doesn't matter to him if the camera is pointing at a slant – just as long as the subject is lined up and shot.

They stand in a row, with their arms folded. Their shoulders are high – great mounds of tension. Many men are glaring, but in a frank way. I understand I'm not to take it personally. And the closer I am to the Senior Man, the better I feel. On close inspection he looks bleary and light-headed from the dance, as if he's been at the bottle. He's highly regarded here; he may be a type of *avookwaark*.

I smile to the crowd, trying to put across my innocence in sign language – walking with my fingers and sighing and wiping my brow and directing special attention at the older man. His hair is bound up in spotted cuscus pelts. Slowly, the Yaifos begin to show their appreciation, letting their arms fall. In pairs they tip forward towards me and feel my hand. I offer it along the line.

Soon even the boys among the Yaifos relax with their weight on one leg, and play with their feathers. I see that it's all right now for me to sit down. I sit on the pole to the house and tug at my laces. My feet are killing me.

As I peel back the canvas, the audience stirs. Some Junior Men grimace; the boys moan – I think they are about to cry.

'What's up?'

Tsogamoi is smiling, so it's all right. He says, 'They not seen shoes before!'

'They're canvas. American jungle boots – Vietnam issue,' I say. 'Useless.' But they think these are my feet? If so, perhaps the yarn about the cannibals eating the shoes was true after all.

'They not seen shoes at all. They can be happy if you show them your real toes.'

So I showed the Yaifos my real toes – white, and puckered, and shrivelled from the long bathe in perspiration. Lying as they were, strung out on the end of a foot held on by ankle support bandage, they were horrible; but the Yaifos seemed glad to see them. The *avookwaark* with the bleary red eyes came to touch, followed by the children, who tapped the soft white nails. I suppose my pathetic feet were as good proof as you could get that I was harmless.

'They are happy to shake your foot,' said Tsogamoi.

Yes, I agreed. We were going to get on absolutely fine.

Chapter Five

SOMETHING FROM THE TREES

The women were waiting indoors; they were like a different race – shy, small. They came and went using the narrow open corridors around the sides, lugging root crops or bamboo water containers without any comment, using the cover of the shadows, just occasionally throwing rounded silhouettes of low heads, breasts, babies with grappling gums. We settled ourselves in the central space with the other men, and Tsogamoi got them to boil up water in my pot suspended from a cane from one of the women's corridor fires. We shared our tea around – the Yaifos sniffing it, we drinking it – while Kaibayoo told them about Bisorio, 'Bssssss,' guiding his hands down like a plane. Some younger men had already been there. They joined in, showing how the planes that all the Yaifos had seen passing overhead did their landing approach. 'Bsssss!'

I thought I'd better do something about my torn-up feet. I stood up, trying to keep below the level of the acid smoke.

'*Eeba?*' I said, in the general direction of the men. Water? I pointed at my feet, which, in anyone's language, only too obviously needed a long cool soak. Two older men, one of them Ma-ee, the *avookwaark* with the hung-over eyes, led me off by my hands. 'See you in a bit,' I said to Tsogamoi.

I was being conducted off for a wash – at least I hoped I was – by elder statesmen and I felt honoured it wasn't a job left to boys. My wash-bag dangling around my neck, they took me out across the clay dance area and over a pig fence, over logs and into the forest, down to a brook. At last they let go of me. Ma-ee flung an old eel trap down to block the flow and give us a pool. The water rose; my toes sank gratefully into cold silt and water.

They stood aside while I took off my clothes and lathered the soap. Then they came in closer – it must be the crocodile marks. Their eyes chased up and down my front and back, down my arms and thighs to

205

where the hundreds of ripples ended in wings. I handed over the soap for the two men to have a go; they copied the wiping motion, laughing at the soap's movement in their hands. Then they dropped the soap and rubbed themselves with sprigs of leaves instead. When they'd finished, they took the soap and started rubbing my back thoroughly with it, as if polishing a shell breast plate. They buffed and polished; perhaps they thought the marks would come off. Whatever the case, they were trusting me, and I them, and the moment meant a lot, so soon after my arrival out of the mists.

I was in a generous mood; these people showed every sign of being capable and willing to get me over the mountain. I opened the sacks and dug out some oats. Fee-fee, a boy with remarkably dazzling eyes, ran to fill my pot with water again.

We all sat in quietness and watched the pot boiling over onto one of the two fires. A woman with a flat forehead and innocently offering face peered into it every so often. I passed the porridge round on plates; the Yaifos prodded it and poked it and waited for it to dry out. Before it was ready, though, most accidentally spilt it. The Yaifos could tight-rope along branches, but they couldn't keep liquid on a plate.

I laid out some gifts. The Yaifos gathered around in a circle, squatting on the floor as I put out mirrors, blankets, safety pins, razor blades and needles and thread. A boy who was blind in one eye, his face bent up in a permanent wink, passed them round. All afternoon the Yaifos played with them; to a Westerner it would be horrifying – the spoiling of them. The sight of the safety pins in their ears, wrappings from biscuits across the forehead; display cards replaced the leaves drying in their hair. But the gold was a week's walk away now, and their cultural bonds breaking. Had I come direct here from England I might have been more sentimental, but certainly the Yaifos wouldn't have understood it, the innocence that outsiders saw in their forest habits.

Anyway, now was a good time, surely, to introduce the idea of my triumphant launch out from here over the mountains. But when Namoleeyo asked the Yaifos on my behalf, they just carried on playing. He asked again, tackling Ma-ee directly. He said, in the Yaifos' falling strain, 'O-ooh.' Yes.

'Yes?' I said to Namoleeyo. 'Yes, they'll take me?'

'Yes, they heard the question.'

It didn't worry me that the Yaifos hadn't asked for anything and I'd just given away all my bargaining counters. Not yet; this was the country of 'payback'. I'd get something, at least, back. And these people were solid. They had their pact with the forest and could without too much effort get me over the ridge, get me on my way to Australia. So far it was a mere detail that the Yaifos were caressing the bush knives, grabbing the mirrors and grinning at themselves. These were gimmicks. They expected no less from me – I had come from Bisorio, land of helicopters and kitchens. After an hour or two the men folded up their nose antennae so they didn't protrude, and slept.

I lay down as well. Sometimes I woke and looked at the women – not sleeping, but all the time tapping, weaving, stirring. I'd see a woman with a baby at her breast, feeding discreetly behind a pandanus leaf screen, her eyes like marbles, as clear as a child's, though the veins on her breasts were thick blue worms. Or on the other side I'd see Kow-kam, an unmarried woman with a square, muscular face and neat, upturned chin, her hair in a high topknot, heavy bunches of fine, white Job's tear seed-pod beads around her neck. They made me lonely for the calm of a place I could call my own home. I thought of Nightlight down there in the valley, underneath those scudding mists, deep down in the warm forests of the lake.

I went on dozing until I was woken by the sound of men felling trees. It was still daylight. I went outside to look at the men working on the garden, and sat on a log with my notebook in the mist. Ma-ee followed shyly, and then ogled at my book. Fee-fee, Ashkai and another little boy came up behind him, using Ma-ee as a shield while he ran the back of his finger on the new page, letting his nail run on the smoothness, feeling for the clean, even sound. Then he ran it on the pages I'd already used, listening to the indentations, using his finger like a gramophone needle, converting my writing to sound, a medium he was more familiar with. Then he went away; chuckling, as if he had answered a question.

Tsogamoi joined me and asked when we were leaving for Bisorio. 'Benedict, it is cold here.' I told him I was still resolved. I was crossing the mountains. His teeth seemed to flash. I told him not to take it too hard. He could carry on down with Namoleeyo. Just give me a few days to work on the Yaifos.

'You have not a few days.' He shook his teeth at me. 'Time is run out for this village.'

I said that couldn't be right. They were building a new garden; they were planning to be here for quite a while.

'Benedix, no, no.'

'No? What then?'

'Benedix, they seen the chopper flying over for the Malumata gold.'

Chop, squeak, chop, squeak, of the axe as the men laid into the trees, cutting through them at about four feet high, to avoid the root buttresses.

'But this is a new garden. You can't fool me, you know. Not often anyway. Though you wouldn't think it, Tsogamoi, I'm really quite an old hand in the forest.'

'Benedix, this is not a garden. No. This is a special nest. A special nest to call a chopper to lie here.'

I stayed out to watch the nest being built. The air grew chilly, and I went indoors, but now I couldn't get the sound out of my head – the chop, squeak, chop, squeak, then finally the crack and boom and echoing boom shudder as the trees came down. I had come looking for a type of replacement Crocodile Nest, and they were building a helicopter nest.

The men came in, hurling down fresh firewood off their backs. The upper air of the hut became acrid as the fresh wood steamed and blistered. I lay in a lacklustre way among my bags. Tsogamoi looked at me from time to time. I said, 'They don't really feel like going up the mountain, do they?'

He showed his teeth. 'Not so much.'

'Can you stay a bit, though?' I showed my feet – where flecks of skin were missing, as if removed by a choosy insect.

'Benedix, Namoleeyo wants to leave in three days. I can stay but, sorry, it is hard.'

That was my position then. I had those three days in which to get the Yaifos on my side.

In the night I got up twice to walk around. I strolled to the edge of the forest, and scratched at the luminous fungi glowing from the trees. I tried to sleep again, couldn't, went out a second time and now it was the early dawn and the sun was on the peaks around and about, black crags that only whitemen would want to conquer.

The sky was blue and purple, with cream splashes behind the black foothills. I looked back, down the Salumei to the rug of cloud over the Sepik plains. What now, top man, Mr Kaavon? Mr Crayfish? I saw I needed to gather these people, and do whatever I'd done to the Kandengeis to make them hold the ceremony, but where were my persuasive qualities now?

Ma-ee comes out, stretching, his sleepy eyes with their turtle-slow lids still ringed with black paint from yesterday's welcome. He wags his hand, calling me over. He points to the east, where the cream light is spreading quickly as the sun struggles to rise over the peaks. 'Yargé,' he says. He wipes his finger overhead to the west, showing the course of the sun. Then he points back to the direction of Malumata, the gold camp where Yargé comes up. This time he makes a noise. 'Brr. Brr.' It is engine noise. 'Balus, balus,' he says – the Pidgin for plane.

His own language hasn't a word for it. Nor helicopter, which he is now indicating with a jigging, slow finger. His finger marks out the pattern of air traffic against the morning sky – the rippled mauve, the splintered red, the wash of yellow.

Indoors, I pulled sweet potatoes from the ashes and patted the blackness off them. A child ran about, blocking the first golden beams coming through the wall. Another man told Ashkai to sit behind him, legs either side, and pick through his hair.

I said to Tsogamoi, 'I've been looking for something from the forest. These people have got it. Strength, you could call it. If only . . .'

'Benedix, we are too far from strength.'

'But nearer than ever, Tsogamoi.'

'Yes but days are going, and you need some Yaifos.'

'It's not far. Ten days maximum. There's all those goldminers on the other side. The Yaifos need just get me over the ridge. Then all I have to do is keep walking.'

He said, 'Benedix, sorry you want to do this.'

I said aloud, 'If only I could have stayed for a year or two. If only *they* could. They are about as far from knowing about the West as anyone on the planet.'

Tsogamoi brought me back to my present predicament. 'But today, tomorrow day, the next one, the Yaifo, Benedix, will leave the mountain.'

I went to wander in the forest, growling resentfully at my weakness in it. Coming back, I found myself alone in the dance area with one of the young married women called Samalla. She was heavy-boned and kept her chin high; on our arrival she had pulled on a red dress that had the outmoded, jumble-sale quality of a missionary hand-out, but now her body had been let out. Her breasts were high, rather loose and small, and raised because she was holding a grey towel around her shoulders. Her thighs were heavy, I saw, as one or other slanted out from her grass skirt as she walked in a semi-circle, swerving away and then round to me. The sun glowed off her shoulders, where they rolled out smoothly from the towel. I sat down on a tree stump right by the front door so that no one would misunderstand the situation. It was drizzling but I was captivated. What on earth did she think she was doing out here, half-way up a mountain, this married woman walking back and forth before me, ankles very slender, feet large, showing off cassowary quill earrings and a topknot, and her matt skin so clear and smooth it was troubling to me, a young man?

These were mountain people, '*man bilong pait*', used to wandering, living in small groups. Was she just being her semi-nomadic self? Or was this a test to see if I was after the Yaifo women? I looked around, and spotted a second woman, called Baria, hovering in the doorway. I'd met her down at Hagi; she was the lady with a thick cassowary quill through the nose and with no lower teeth. She was guarding or administrating, I couldn't see which, while Samalla looked at me, asking for something right into my freckled blue eyes. Perhaps she wanted a present for herself – men had taken all the other presents, as normal. I raised my eyebrows, expectant. She did the same. I asked if she spoke Pidgin. She pouted a little, letting out her lower lip slowly and carefully. But she was not abashed. She raised her chin, strutted a little further from me and went off into the forest.

Was she trying to lead me astray? I played with a beetle with the green burnished metallic look of ancient glass. Further off, the wind parted the foot-long antennae of grasshoppers as they fished the air, flinching when I sneezed.

Later Samalla returned, going straight indoors. Baria laughed in the corridor, and I was left outside wondering, as usual, what was going on. Had I passed a test, or failed one?

The clear-eyed, bright-faced boy called Fee-fee came dancing out of the house with Yaluma, another boy, and Askai, the mad-eyed one. They started patting a balloon made from a pig belly, knocking it through the mist, the feathers which were tied in their topknots flitting over their shaven heads. Indoors, the men were giggling – probably having their hair chewed through by dogs, who seemed to adore lice-hunting. Namoleeyo came to see me. He said he was sorry. Tomorrow they were going.

I said, 'But you said three days!'

He counted off the days with his fingers. The day of arrival, yesterday, and today.

I found Tsogamoi lying in ecstasy indoors, a dog's muzzle working backwards and forwards in his hair. I understood why he was leaving, I said. But I wasn't going to leave with them.

He pushed the dog off. 'This is a cold place, you will last badly.'

'I don't do so badly in Tooting.'

In the evening Ma-ee started the fire to cook some meat – a cuscus, and two birds that Fee-fee had shot. Called 'lubowee', they were black, with thin, short, downward-curved beaks, a single whiskery feather extending back from behind the rusty splashed eye. I watched as Ma-ee worked to get a flame, standing over a split stick, sawing it with a cane and letting the hot crumbs fall on bark cloth.

I felt like a witness, a material witness. These people – their black palm arrow tips chiselled with a rat's incisor, their women's head-nets with bands of small nassa shells – would fade any day. They were unable to hold plates and cups level but every act they did was within the bounds of the forest, live magic. I said aloud, but to myself, 'I can't give in now.'

Tsogamoi said, 'Benedix. No, no. So steep.'

'I can't go back now. I'll stay, hope for the best.'

'You'll be fallen off the mountain. The gold can pull you off, Benedix, with the Yaifo.'

I didn't want to listen. I got up and took their long hand-drum from the wall, and tapped on the yellow tree kangaroo skin, listening to the sound of a mere press of a finger, the spirit of the drum building it, holding it, letting it go four feet away, where the drum end was carved in a ring of red and white clay-painted blocks.

Seeing my interest, Ma-ee went to get something from the rafters over the fireplace. As he reached, I saw he now had a one-inch nail through his nose in place of a bone stub. He brought a roll of bark cloth down and laid out some feathers. They were weighted with beeswax: quiffs and plumage swirls, red seeds like abacus counters up the stem, designed to swing as you danced. He spent a long time looking for the best ones – some with tabs of cuscus fur, some with cowrie shells that must have been exchanged by a hundred hands, all the way here from the sea. He chose the best, and presented them to me like flowers, as if courting.

'Is this my present, Tsogamoi? In exchange for all mine?' I said it was a lovely present. I was touched, and there were five of them – *tambanak*, the Niowra sacred number. 'However, given the choice, I'd prefer the mountain trip.'

'That's your goodbye present,' Namoleeyo said, a little unkindly, I thought.

Ma-ee was talking. I realized he was talking to me. He went on and on, happily, not waiting for anyone to try and translate. Namoleeyo said, 'He thinks you know the story about how the world was formed by a man called Asmano. How would you know him?'

'I don't know him by that name. But was he the one who made everything except the sun and his sister, the moon? Why's he telling me a story anyway?' The last time an old man did this it was at Gahun and he'd ended up dead.

Namoleeyo said, 'They think you're from the Sepik.'

'Well I am, after a fashion.'

Now he was telling the story of why the Yaifos lived up here. The world had flooded, as I already knew from Kandengei, and, something I didn't know, there were two other survivors: a man and woman had turned into mosquitoes, and come up here hidden in the hair of a rat.

Ma-ee told me his history like this. I said to Tsogamoi, 'The man must have a soft spot for me. He washed me in the stream, and now this.' Again, there was room for optimism. 'I'm going to be fine here,' I said to Tsogamoi. 'I think you're exaggerating the difficulty. These people like me.'

'Benedix, no use.'

I said that I even suspected one of the women liked me – Samalla.

'Benedix, they can trick you, the Yaifo.'

I said my feet were better now, and I still had plenty of supplies. 'They will take me, Tsogamoi. I know it.' In preparation for tomorrow's journey downhill, he was dabbing a sore on his foot with the paraffin wick of our home-made jam-jar lamp.

He wagged his head. 'No use going upwards.'

But in the morning he didn't leave me; I shook hands only with Namoleeyo. He got into his wellingtons and plodded down the mountain with another Yaifo, who, I thought I saw, had a bright new light in his eye – that brightness that has an affinity with gold. He'd never be back.

Why was Tsogamoi prepared to do this for me? I couldn't see the sense in it. And there became more reasons for Tsogamoi to leave, because the atmosphere changed somewhat, with the loss of the Yaifo to the gold. It brought out the nomadic in these mountain people. They got up; they sat down again. They were marking time. They were going to move. I could hold only the slimmest of hopes that it was to take me up the mountain.

But they kept their thoughts inaccessible. They wouldn't answer Tsogamoi and I couldn't push Tsogamoi any further because of his temperament – the quirky melancholia in him. However, we both agreed that the Yaifos were going to move, and most likely it was a downhill move. I must just hope against hope that I could swing it the other way.

Think positively, Benedix, I thought. Assume we are going up. In that case we would have to make a dash for it – the Yaifos didn't have clothes for warmth. We'd allow ten days for the walk over the mountains, and take two men. I separated the food out for this, sewed loose stitching, mopped my foot sores, and then did all these tasks once again, this time drawing the Yaifos in to help me, trying to magic them into coming along.

The next morning we woke to find Samalla had gone, with her

husband and three men. Their two dogs had been tied by the feet, to stop them following. They howled in a chorus.

Tsogamoi made an approach to Kaibayoo, asking him to come with us; he shook his head, unwilling to be interrupted. He continued unpicking the stitching from the sleeping mats, working the strands with a flying-fox-bone needle into an armband; the others, those not content with playing with glittery objects, paced about in their new, restless mood.

A boy of Ma-ee's, who was about seven, cried, and bawled, scratching around the little tuft of hair left on his head. '*Nago, nago!*'

'What does "nago" mean?'

Tsogamoi said, 'He is saying, "*I* want to go, *I* want to go!"'

'Go where?'

'Downwards. Or upwards.' Tsogamoi clamped himself up. I could tell he would start fuming deep inside if I kept nagging. I risked one more question. 'Can't you ask?'

Smoulder, smoulder. 'No.'

'Come on, I'll make some tea.' Fee-fee and I went to fetch some water.

I tried again later, when I caught Tsogamoi humming to himself. 'Tsogamoi, tell me more about the journey.'

From all he had gathered, there would be many cold days. However, there were caves we could sleep in. It would be so cold in the day that our feet would be dead. However, that would help the pain, maybe.

Samalla came back the next day. Her right breast was spotted with white paint. Up her thighs rose parallel bands, which flashed as she walked where her skirt opened and closed.

'What's the woman playing at, Tsogamoi? I've told you before, it looks like she wants her way with me.'

'Benedix, they are all cunning. You sit still.'

I reminded Tsogamoi that the Yaifos were, if distantly, his kith and kin. He must talk to them. But he turned from me, silent, pulling away.

Come on, Tsogamoi, don't fail me now.

The air was hot with these Yaifos stirring up the fire smoke around us, fidgeting, buzzing here and there, making the atmosphere charged and close. 'Too much energy,' I scribbled in my book. 'It's up-ended. Directed, expectant.' *They* knew where they were going.

I noticed that some men now had wicker armbands on; others had gone further: they'd fastened in pale hanks of pandanus prop root fibre.

I had a nasty feeling I had seen this before – they were going to indulge in one of their dances again. Feathers were tweaked and straightened, cassowary-skin capes were dusted, bone needles jabbed through cuscus headbands, strings made – rolled out on the men's thighs, which were bare from string-making since childhood. Sorties were made for fresh leaves; legbands were eased on with the help of my spoons. Boys went out and found fresh hawk and owl feathers, and those with parrot and hornbill primary colours. Skulls were freshly shaven to leave little topknot brushes; feathers tied in like seaweed wracks. The fireplaces were raided for Namoleeyo's waste silver foil soup packets, these tied in place instead of leaves.

'Is it time to ask them what they are doing, once again?'

Tsogamoi glowered, and his dark eyes became inflamed the way they did.

I answered myself. 'I suppose it isn't.'

Shell discs were hung from noses, bone bars placed through. Often they had trouble with their nose holes; the Yaifos had to lick the bones or shave bits off to reinsert them. Time was visibly running out for these dances. This was an effort. But they could still make that effort. And they took up their old feathers, wiped them on their thighs, and made ready.

A black feather now lay speared through Fee-fee's topknot, and a white one on a thinned quill hung from Ashkai.

I wrote in my notebook, 'I'm in their power. These people are on the brink of extinction, my kind has won and is destroying you. We can destroy the world, and yet for now I'm in your power . . .'

Two men, one of them the more slender guide who'd helped me here, sat on the floor, having their heads layered with banana leaves, which were gradually pegged into a helmet. This was stabbed with feather wands, hundreds of feather darts, mostly weighted, many encrusted with cowries or cuscus hair, and cut into a jagged shape or into a twist.

'Any ideas?'

'Benedix, they make goodbye festivity.' I checked the last word to myself. Yes, he did say *amamas*. Festive dance. Festivity was good, wasn't it?

When the two men stood up they could not see much; they were given leaf skirts and the long drums, which they tuned over the fire. They dilly-dallied, brewing up their energy, their magic, pacing anti-clockwise around the central house-pole. There was no synchronization, but their legs were loosening; they beat the drums, becoming louder, and a march rhythm. The beat came together, and then apart as the two men span slowly, with quick knee bends. The other Yaifos were still preening, pacing needlessly. But they began to be drawn to the two men's music. They picked up their bows and arrows, and harmonized, padding in the circle to the march beat.

They began to sing softly – not modern words, according to Tsogamoi, who sat where he was beside me amid the rising dust, the sweetening smell of crushed leaf ornamentation. They were chant sounds, a single yodel line which jogged along to a falsetto exclamation as the beat gathered, the two drummers coming to a unison. Then dying. Then again, and again, each dance the same, the drums only together by the end of each line, the dance troupe joining and falling apart. The dance went on like that, a series of low building blocks that were never being stacked. This was no crocodile dance, stepping in the steps of ancestors. This was the general recycling of magic, not the building of it to create something, a new crocodile man or protective Crocodile Nest. They were taking every small energy they made, and putting it aside, offering it to the cooking pot. This thumping of feet and drums, this whacking of feathers and plucking of voices round and around the pole was spirituality, not religion. It was unbridled heart beating and soul expression – the boys with their treble yelling, men with stomachs out, hopping with bows and arrows, and shedding their human loads – just being in the forest cycle.

They sweated and clattered and built and released. There was no climax. I waited for it, watching Tsogamoi taken by it – clapping, then standing then striding with them. But there was no pointing of the energy, no crescendo, just the laying of this foundation. This was a foreword to another more energetic dance.

And the women sat working bilum bags, stitching, stitching across their knees while the men danced. They only broke to rearrange the material across their shiny knees. On and on the men chanted and marched and still the women sat there with never a chorus, never a word. It was a male ceremony this, male duty. I felt picked up myself, and stamped about a bit, held by the vitality here.

But later I went outside, suddenly wanting to be alone. Though I felt uplifted by the partying, this wasn't a dance I could be part of, and I felt that painfully. At Kandengei I took my place as a Junior Man, but here I had no place, I could just feel the energy coursing around me, not raising my spirits directly, as it had theirs.

It was dark and cold and the bleak mountains stared me in the face. To the east the hill ranges were slate grey, trees finely etched in silhouette. There was a marbled wedge of purple to the north, conical limestone teeth up the western flank. The sky was dusted with the early dawn ochre. The forest was the darkest green.

I let my thoughts drop down through the sky to Kandengei. Well into the dry season. Long ago, the laulau fruit would have been over, and the cuscus plodded back, deep into the forest – the skins of the unluckier ones would have been tied out in the sun, salted and powdered with fire ash, left for the ants to pick clean.

How different would things have turned out if I'd brought Stars on the Water along with me? I might not have got this far – she would have slowed me on the road, but with her perhaps I might not have needed the Yaifos. So I thought of her, her neck a smooth black root growing from the stone, her head pitched, listening for a spy outside. Her perspiration again rises over me; mine over her. The air is thick from the dew of our skin. And I thought over what the other men said – that she was dangerous. They called her a girl, because they saw how she played with men, did it for fun, she didn't manipulate like a woman yet. In the town she laid herself down for anyone and they feared her disregard for taboos, and because she belonged in a whiteman's office her nickname was 'typist'. But even if we had stuck to Wewak, together we might still have got on better than I'm doing now. Stupid Benedix, she'd have said. You and your stupid old-fashioned walk through the forest. But we would see. Up or down the mountain, Yaifos?

I looked back at the house, the slits of light from the fires. The ritual was dying with the daylight; I heard men sitting down heavily, casting off their masks. *You are not ready yet, so we do not say goodbye fully. But there will be a time when you set out to taste the wind . . .* Were *they* ready? If not now, then they'd never launch me.

The ground was cool, mosses fat, trees dripping last night's mist. I turned towards the house, and suddenly realized I had been watched all the time I'd been out here. One of the women – one of this sex that never seemed to sleep – was pitched like an extra post by the poles sloping up to the doorway. She was hunched under her string bag, stoic, waiting for me to pass. I was conscious of her still attention even as I climbed the pole to get indoors again. The women and their sacrificial males. THE NIOWRA SPIRIT FINDS NO USE IN HATCHING

HOUSE-BOUND MEN . . . I turned back to look again; but she was only a mossy tree stump.

Indoors, bodies lie across the palm-leaf-strewn floor. Their feathers are bent, their bunches of armband leaves are dry and twisted. They are coughing – it's the bitter dust raised during the dance. Feathers get in my eye as I lie with the others, not able to sleep, again, like the others. Only the women are awake – I can hear the pat, pat of women slapping baked sweet potatoes. The dog goes up to a sleeping youth and chews at his topknot, playfully, but gets no attention.

I get up, and then lie down again, feeling happier now I'm back with the contented Yaifos; I'll let this energy go whichever way the Yaifos want it. I am in their hands. All day it is the same; we do not even eat. But this is not the loss of energy after a party in London, ashtrays and empty bottles and depression. The party is still going on; the men lie around full of spirit, not empty but humming. It's infectious. I'm tempted to do it myself. I'm not surprised when Tsogamoi says, 'Tomorrow, I think, Benedix, we go up.'

We rise from the ashes. There is no 'goodbye', no clear point of farewell. It is a continuation of the dance. We jig down the slope to the main river, led by a man called Gorsai who has a beard rimming his jaw, bird of paradise red streamer feathers from his nose. A strong, talkative boy called Yado is coming along as well, and other Yaifos run with us for a while, carrying packs, shaking their hands in the sky as they drop back, Samalla with them, offering nothing in the end but the endorsement of the male energy.

Fee-fee and Ashkai come further, both clutching little eggs in leaf packages, stopping only to pick foliage for their cane belts, beating the leaves to soften them to cotton.

We run on; leeches swing out at us; a leaf rolls down the slope like a plate; Fee-fee springs on a grey-backed rat and tells me its name, 'gonaiya', presenting the word quietly as a song.

We bridge a stream with poles, then another, and a river, and lie down at a garden called Sadaré, where lesser birds of paradise rock in branches, flicking heavy quiffs of gold and white in a bower around them.

The boys wave us off, calling their goodbyes after us, '*Beealé, beealé-o, beealé.*' Now we are on our own, there are no freshly cut branches on the trail. Pressed to a cliff, the screes of the severe west side of the Yaifo, I watch little purple flowers puff into the sky, petals exploding open. We cut the tributaries – the Gula, then Pagka, and others. Any one of these might stop us – we haven't enough food to wait to build bridges. But we use the islands, straddle fallen trees, hang from branches. We feel the wind from the waves, and then the thunderous sound of the foam is blotted out as our path dips deep behind moss banks, and the hollow tubes of pitcher plants crack under us. '*Beealé!*' Goodbye! Gorsai says as I go down. Juices gush from a liana he hands me as a rope.

'*Tdalee! Tdalee!*' Yado calls, his war cry. 'Onward!'

Gorsai's party paint is washed away; it runs greasily down him. We see the mirror of our blind progress on the opposite Yaifo valley face; moss in our ears, filmy ferns licking us, bracken carving into our fingers, the draught from a falling leaf. Hobbling stick insects, caterpillars with thorny twig backs; under crumpling roots, over sinks of sphagnum. Tsogamoi's calves shake from cold in the ripping water; bees sting my face; sky comes through insect-blasted leaves.

Our progress is too slow. 'I'm cutting rations by a quarter,' I write. 'Feeling nervous. Two days extra in hand not a lot.'

A taipan slips away through bark – a nylon cord of a bluish brown that doesn't disturb a leaf, but of a type that once killed Tsogamoi's uncle in a day – slow for one of the deadliest snakes around.

Still hacking along the west face of the Yaifo valley. Safely over the Olo, the Eelee. I'm clambered over by a peculiarly large leech. It is longer than any of my fingers and a very bright pale green with a sleek black stripe. I can feel the weight as it puts down its huge circular foot – its cold tread.

We pitch a frame under the instep of a cliff, flooring it with wild banana leaves. The ceiling is black with old fire smoke; beneath us are chipped stones from old fire beds.

'We are getting there. No slowing yet,' I write.

Off again; Gorsai working ahead, his feet rasping holes in the shale, his eyes bloodshot from the weight of the pack. We're relying on this one man, who last did this route as a child – his calves are still like a nine-year-old's.

Wild banana palms as tall as orchard trees; another cave house, this with a backward sloping face of twenty-five feet, a plume of smoke stains rising to the top, a tobacco patch thriving down below. We sleep soundly – so soundly that even before I open my eyes I know that we have overslept. The forest is already light, the air is ringing with insects, and the party is finally over.

We lay around the fire, physically shattered and so still that lizards began to run over us.

None of the others was good at keeping warm. Yado waited until the afternoon to put on his dry shirt, Gorsai used his blanket only as a pillow. Tsogamoi said all his limbs were dead, but wouldn't sit over the fire.

We discussed it sensibly. We'd wait another day here, feed ourselves up, dashing for the ridge that was still two days away. The next morning, we gathered ourselves together. Tsogamoi chipped at a carbuncle with an axe. Gorsai scraped a twig into a wooden hairpin. We made a hose of leaves and drank from the rain drips running down the cave wall, tasting of woodsmoke, and ate two cassowary eggs, and a cuscus that Gorsai found in a tree hole; there was a baby in her pouch, growing cold and frightened and making rapid bird-chuckle sounds that echoed off the cave wall. We shared that around as well.

The following dawn, Gorsai put away his decorations, replacing the quills in his nose with bracken, and I put my hands in my boots to draw out leeches. We stepped out through the curtain of water dripping from the overhanging ferns.

The Yaifo was running with less certainty, leaping and lurching down steep boulders. Gorsai led me up, shuffling a foot along the underside of boulders, fishing out eels.

Over the Fe-é; on through moss vaults and rot-shattered trees; an insect alights on a leaf and water droplets cascade through the low sunbeams. We follow Gorsai's prints – dry where he's compressed the moss, wet on rocks – and whistle for him as if he's a dog.

A cloud dropped down on us. We emerged dripping. We were all tiring, but we were going faster now than ever. These were last efforts. Moss shears under me and I fall into a peaty, black crevasse. My knees are now like rusty hinges, but I've been lucky.

Mists blowing through spindly conifers that looked in pain, as if they had cramp. Shields of orange lichen, trees under moss burdens, plants sitting tight, hanging on grimly, but still sliding downslope in sludges. Tsogamoi was also limping now, Yado trailing badly. We must rest the night here – a beach under a gurgling, dripping overhang, the martins whistling in and out of caves. We could see the mountain wall from here – purple sheets of rock and yet more trees that were collapsing and dying. There was no visible way up.

I washed; the anaesthetic of the cool water made me want to cry with relief. I had forgotten how tiring pain could be.

Four days' food supply left. 'I am conscious of the guides accelerating,' I wrote. 'Lighter loads – or desperation.'

We looked for bats, or for martins' nests. No luck. But something unexpected: the pleasure of walking on the shingle, the smooth open ground. I wasn't used to sure, untreacherous surfaces. This barren shore was freedom, a space away from the forest. I felt a flush of excitement – as if I were near an answer. Australia, a wider space, was going to be the right place.

In the night, thunder cracked against our cave shelter, rebounding on the neighbouring rock walls.

The final push. We hopped from stone to stone up the Yaifo; for a while I could dip my knee in the river, replacing the warming water of my knee-bandage, then we climbed away, through wild taro.

The moss here came away in pelts as we brushed by. Very little could grip; the rocks were bare and coated with a black cream. The bird sounds grew quieter. We'd already lost the insect buzz and now the river noises were absorbed too. Tsogamoi pointed to his bare feet as they soaked up the cold. 'Heavy.'

We lost sight of Yado. Gorsai dug at the cold moss and grunted like an angry pig. He wanted to keep his feet moving. Finally, he couldn't hold back any more; he charged on up, swinging his legs one over the other, partially paralysed by the cold. I plodded after him, step by step, counting each one. One, two, three, four, five. *Tambanak*. Up and up; I looked back at the wells of mist, the deep blue and black mountain caps, bushes like ricks. I am alone. Gorsai is somewhere ahead, Tsogamoi behind.

In the Crocodile Nest, I find myself saying, we learned that splashing water five times over yourself in a certain, secret way makes you invisible. You will be so still, so in tune through doing what the crocodile ancestors did, that you are part of the forest – no bird can see you're a human. They will land on your head and even make a nest.

One, two, three, four . . . *Tambanak*.

I now find I'm absorbing some of the forest. It is colouring my counting rhythm, making it a chant.

> Small fry,
> snapped by frog,
> in orchid bowl on upper log.

I stop in this utter silence. I cannot hear birds, or even the water drips. And walk on. The trees looking as if they are appealing, and as I tread, the moss spitting.

> Tasting tears from a dead tree's eye,
> snakes unwind
> and they don't know why
> I'm here.

Moss turrets, hollow gutter trees. I'm shivering. No leaf litter, only

unrolled chlorophyll carpets and the sweat of clouds and knowing all
the time that where trees have at last fallen they have fallen right off
the mountain.

> Tightrope trees with a belly full of sap,
> roots of claws too old to tap
> your mind.

The danger of my falling through the moss, dropping for a thousand
feet, seizes me. It's because I suddenly doubt what I'm doing here.
All this just to prove I'm a Man of True Men. It suddenly sounds
no better than a *Boy's Own* adventure, that I'm doing this for sport,
finding another Western way of belittling nature. But I carry on. I
must ritualize this thought away. I march up the mountain, singing
my chant, and the numbers one to five. I remind myself I am allowed
to be a warrior for now. The head-hunting journey was always part
of living with the forest. So now I encourage the competitive in me,
chanting and dancing. I have to believe I am at least as strong as anyone
else. Stronger than any outsider I might invent, any old John Clematis,
Ph.D., for instance, losing his grip.

> He fingers branches, his boots array,
> hardly blanches – he'll find a way.
> But boots find nothing, he goes to pieces,
> smelling death in the fungal greases – and falls . . .

I pause. Take five steps.

> Catches spine, spins again,
> faster now,
> elongated
> kisses bark
> describes an arc
> hooks an orchid,
> limbs distorted, finds the clay.
> Which does not yield.

'Poor Clematis,' I thought, looking at the sparse sun, diluted by the
mist, 'explorer *in extremis*.'

One, two . . .

I am on the ridge. The trees around me have their broken, disjointed
arms outstretched. They are looking dehydrated and burnt, though they
are wringing wet. As for me, I feel washed, purified.

'You are here,' a voice said. Tsogamoi had found me.

'Isn't it great?'

'Benedix, it is great and too cold,' he said.

I looked back, over my shoulder, down to Kandengei in the sun. He is stronger . . . I thought. He has something from the forest. I was still a Westerner. I still felt bad, seeing a baby cuscus crying for its mother that we had just killed. Deep underneath, too, there'd always be my cultural heritage, its medieval metaphysics – God in the sky, a father, and the earth as mother, Mother Nature. But I knew also what Kandengei expected of me and I looked forward, out in the general direction of Australia and its desert – no tangles of forest, no shadows to trick you; instead an openness, an expression of honesty. A land that lay open like an invitation.

We dropped down; again we were shuffling leaves underfoot, slapping them away from our faces. We regroup in a small shelter roofed with bark – there are no palm leaves for thatch – and we have to make a fire from the dry insides of dead trees. Gorsai wears a pandanus-leaf cape to keep the rain off, and it is the next afternoon before we are in sunshine; we traverse twenty feet above a white river on a tree that rolls and pivots in the spray plumes, and come down through gardens. From one house, the first I've seen without stilts, a whiff of smoke – but the fire is almost dead. Footprints – a child, man and pig. We are going silently. Our group has tightened up. The Yaifos signal me to stay back. The voice of a child crying. Fresh smoke; over a pig fence. Another garden. But before we can call out a warning, we stumble over a man bent into the soil, his back a hairy black coconut mat. He jumps into the air with shock. He is a blinking mole-eyed man. 'Like Adam himself,' Bob Parry, the missionary, would have said.

He's pleased to talk to Tsogamoi – something to do with his family connection. A lone adolescent cassowary trots after us as we come into the hamlet, almost tripping over a second Hewa – a woman painted over in mourning clay. Apart from being like a yellow mud pack she wears a special, long, floor-length grass dress and copious Job's tears beads encasing her neck.

The man paints pictures of planes all over the sky. 'His children is gone, Benedix,' Tsogamoi says. 'The gold is taken them off.' There are no men left to guide me on from here.

We stay, eating his corn all night, then walk on, stopping only once, thinking we hear the drone of a plane. Further down through the forests, we arrive at a fly-blown settlement which the inhabitants – the few that are left – don't seem to care about very much.

All their men have gone to find gold as well. A woman with a slack-skinned belly comes out to look at us – we've come from the other side of the mountains. She squats, flapping her grass skirt down between her legs, making herself comfortable. The dribbling-nosed children who are left – wool is on the run from their jerseys, and they have cotton aprons instead of leaves – come for a look too.

We do, however, find two guides. They have just left home, a remote Hewa settlement, and are on the way to the gold themselves. They haven't seen a whiteman before and are scared of me – my height or my skin. They take up the packs and run.

'So, Tsogamoi, this is it.'

He looks at my boots, built with Vietnam in mind, a metal plate along the instep for booby traps. Barely more than a month's use and now there's hardly a day's walk left in them.

He takes his pay without counting it. He doesn't watch me, as I shake his hand, but only the bag he has been carrying, as it is taken off down the hill by the two Hewas. I pay the Yaifos. They say 'Beealé' gently, shaking hands with care.

Now my two Hewa guides have gone, and Tsogamoi and I are still standing together in silence, each looking away from the other. The Yaifos are ready to start back and stand facing the way we've just come, back to home. The flies gather over us among the sugar-cane chewings and thrown-out corn leaves. I feel them trying to get through the holes in my boots and snuggle into my sores.

'Messy village,' says Tsogamoi.

I am going to miss his strange, dark, loyal ways very much.

'No heart to it, now,' I say. The flies tap at us. 'I'd be able to get there even with a broken leg, now.'

'Two, three days something, Benedix, to Korumbé. That's all.'

I say goodbye. 'Beealé.'

'Beealé,' he says – responding to the word, not responding to me. I walk off and stop. He waits, as if expecting me to call him back for further duties.

He sits down on a log as I drop down the slope. When I next look there's a change in his face – relief? Suddenly he is soaring. He claps the Yaifos on the back, encouraging them to hurry up. He is skipping up the mountain on his swollen leg, striking out for home.

I stop a night at Korapé, on its hill of yellow and red clay. I pay the guides off, and they stare at the money, never having seen it before. They can smell the gold here, though. Under their head-dresses and leaves, the locals have better clothes than we do. They gape at me, and ask each other where I came from. They are Highlanders – fair, small and square people, with tattoos on their faces and their breasts.

The next day my guides say they want to come on with me to see the gold at Korumbé. As we walk in the forest they put away their cuscus-fur collars and metallic beetle headbands; their Hewa names turn into Luke and 'Hark' – Mark?

We come to a cane bridge which is decrepit. It's going to break any day. But there's no turning back now. I have to coax the Hewas over, going first myself, bouncing on it. Safely on the other side, I find I'm sweating. I don't think anyone ought to try the bridge again.

Another day and we are skating down the scree to the substantial Uku river as it explodes its way past boulders. Planes come right overhead; we are near the end now. While the Hewas dither, seeing the water, hearing it, I charge right through, grabbing a staff of driftwood on the way.

Then, back in the forest, we join a road worked by feet. Along it are strewn Peanut Crunch and Woppa wrappers, uneaten Cuptea biscuits, cherry cream biscuit wrappers . . . On, over an iron version of a cane footbridge. We climb the last hill, a thousand or so feet. I'm sure my feet are bleeding and I hear the boots squelch but don't dare look down. At the top, women are gardening under golfing umbrellas, and wearing shirts which are clean and bright – town clothes on forest people; in a ditch I see more litter – a flung-away shirt that's better than mine.

Children tag on; they whistle and duck, teasing me – this mad, stumbling figure. They get bored with me not responding and walk beside me – bare feet, but new caps.

I hear planes and choppers close at hand, but still haven't seen them. I am keeping my head down, trying to concentrate on walking. The tracks coming towards me are mainly of shoes, those going with me are mainly of bare feet – can this be how fast this world is changing? Some men are coming along now, carrying Pepsi cans which are moist with condensation – they must have been cooled in a fridge. The youths toss the children crisp packets, and all but one child goes off to follow them, screaming for more.

The one remaining child runs alongside me. I realize by his efforts to keep up that I must actually be going at a trot. He tells me he isn't at school today. The two Junior Schools have closed – first the pupils went off to dig for gold, then the teachers.

I'm still taking in what the boy said, when he drops something. And what I see on the ground makes me stop. The momentum of two weeks' walking – or however long it is – has been stopped by what I see lying there. It is a bundle of banknotes. He tells me how much. Four thousand kina. I flick through them, checking. He says there's another five thousand in the other pocket. I ask to see. I want to be able to tell people about this. There they are, the notes hanging half out of the second pocket, and there's enough in one pocket alone to buy a brand new family car.

Twisties, Peanut Cookies, Milo tins. The first tin roof. I hear a wireless. Graffiti on plank walls. Hammer on metal – another store going up. A pig fence is being erected, I think. Then I see a man putting on a padlock.

I've got to the edge of the ridge. Below me, I see the whole scene. No men digging, as I expected, but people ambling on a flat stretch of land, which must be an airstrip. They are gathered in clutches, sitting on rice sacks, drinking Fanta, waving playing cards. Some are fighting, most are laughing. But what strikes me most about the view is not this, or the little wooden Lutheran house with a cross on top of it, or the smell of the sheets out to dry, bedspread embroidered with rolling European chalk downland and the very same church, though not with the large bolt across the door; and not the churchman's offer of a frozen chicken or his Motor Racing Grand Prix posters, not the fact that this morning on the airstrip he'd picked up a gold nugget thrown away by a man climbing aboard a flight because he couldn't fit it into his jar. None of this, nor the helicopters flying in and out, nor that the churchman can't buy me any coffee – people have bought the jars to empty out and put gold in. But that the people below me gambling alongside the airstrip, waiting for flights out of here, are children.

Here there is no discipline of any sort – no Crocodile Nests, no Bible Schools, no Junior Schools. Here the young rule over the old and the natural order is inverted. And at last I'm beginning to see that Kaavon knows only too well that he needs the AOGs. He's seen what lies behind this, the dissolving action of the West. It's threatening the village's strength and he knows they'll need all the help they can get to keep power – certainly if they're going to do a better job than Jakob at Niksek and Bob and George at Bisorio.

The next day I'm flying out, rising over the grasses and mountains. The boy seated next to me has a digital watch that he checks every ten minutes. He says it's Wednesday the 5th.

'Of what?'

October, he says.

'That late?'

I look out and see the people grubbing in the clay at Mount Kare – teachers, children, German overseas volunteers. As we fly over this hell of a place, I marvel at my deliverance, and look out south through the skies, at last flying free, off to prove I'm a Junior grade of adult.

PART 3

Men of True Men

*'There will be a time when you set out to taste the wind.
If the wind is good, and even if it is not, then comes the
spirit to guide your hand to strike.'*

Chapter Six

THE DIRE STRAIT

Australia – where, to quote Wallace, I might see the trees from the wood – is an island; that is, you have to cross water to get to it.

Under normal circumstances, I heard, you took a plane from Port Moresby. But circumstances were not normal. I felt more like a bush bunny than ever, here in the capital. Town life was a shock, worse than Wewak had been. The petrol fumes, the car horns. And I wasn't the only one who found it more hostile than the forest. Now that the missionaries had rendered the forest safe, emptied it of old-style head-hunters and transformed it into leafy suburbia, the town was full of other Junior Men violently seeking to prove their Junior Manhood. No; better all round if I adjusted slowly, getting to Australia under my own steam. It couldn't be all that far.

The man in charge of the Salvation Army hostel in Moresby was a softly-spoken Australian who wore a white uniform, like a sailor's. It must have been Salvation Army tropical issue. 'Looks like you need a hand,' he said, taking me by the elbow.

He was just like Jakob, Laurie, Kaavon and all the others before him. Why did strangers always do this, take me in? The phenomenon had always served me well, but I was beginning to feel like one of life's victims, someone who must be helped. Be that as it may, I was grateful. And though the Salvation Army officer said he hadn't heard of anyone crossing by canoe he remembered that as a boy there'd been Japanese pearl fishing boats out there. In danger of creasing his starched sleeves, he leaned past the portrait photograph of General Booth to a wall map. Together, we measured the shortest gap, which was between Daru, the central south of New Guinea, and the tip of Australia. The Torres Strait, the map said. The name looked like an exaggeration for such a narrow channel. Men, those not afraid of cutting themselves on coral and attracting sharks, probably swam across in fine weather. I measured my thumb off against the scale. It couldn't be more than . . . Oh dear. Two hundred kilometres.

Outside there was a sickening grating of metal against metal, the sound of two vehicles meeting full face, chewing into each other in the middle of the road. 'The band,' the Salvation Army man said. 'They're warming up.' He reached for his ship's captain's hat. I went out behind him to watch from the veranda. Further off, through the security fence, there was a view of burnt, hilly savannah, men loafing around the pie and chip shops, women sitting in the dust. Near at hand, within the compound, three or four boys in white suits and shiny buttons were experimenting with cymbals and tambourines. Men were polishing cornets on their cuffs, women bouncing their babies on the big bass drum.

The security fence was being unpadlocked. The captain shuffled his platoon into order, inspected them stiffly, and turned forward, preparing to march. He smiled grimly. Then they stamped out through the gates. And now the Salvation Army was at large on the streets. Boom! Boom! Squawk, squawk, boom! They boldly set out to the betelnut market some two hundred yards away. Out there, among the men filling out their gambling cards and between the betelnut-crunching women, the piles of betelnut and the meagre offerings of the market – buai, a couple of pawpaw, a few ropes of peanuts, plastic string – they sang a hymn and returned. 'Boom! Squawk! BOOM!'

Then the main gates were padlocked again.

Back in my dormitory, praying to be back in the middle of nowhere again, I knew I had to go by water. The very thought of a dug-out, all my unfortunate accidents at Kandengei, was enough to make me sea-sick, but I was, after all, meant to be Wumvunnavan. A geenjumboo, a potential killer!

At Daru, the air was sticky and warm – probably the effect of the swamps the airstrip seemed to be surrounded by. I walked across the tarmac to collect my belongings from a shed which was meant to be the baggage handling building. There I had to step aside to avoid people who were rushing on to the plane I'd just left. They seemed to be suffering from nervous exhaustion. Others ran past with the fixed eyes of people intent on escape.

Welcome to Daru, a keeling sign said. It didn't look as if it meant it.

Those were my first impressions – those of a destitute place. I had prayed to be back in the middle of nowhere and it served me right. My prayer had been answered only too accurately. Yet on the map Daru had been shown as a provincial capital. It sat near the mouth of the

Fly, a river the size of the Sepik. I felt cheated, standing with my bag, facing nowhere. A fat whiteskin wearing a bush hat called me over. He said, 'Bedder give you a lift into town, mate.'

So there *was* a town, at least. And, having raised my hopes so cruelly, he drove me off down the track.

He was the manager of a hotel, he explained. But I wouldn't want to stay there, he said – 'not at 65 kina a night!' The only guests he had were on government expense accounts. 'So where *will* you stay?'

'At one of the other hotels, I suppose.'

He had news for me, he said. The other hotel had closed – fell to bits. 'Shake-up, mate. You don't think we could charge that much if there was an alternative, do ya?'

I said, 'I don't suppose you could, no.'

'Too right, mate. That's sixty-five beers.'

Daru had done pretty badly for itself. Though there were worse places in the world – and within Australia I was destined to end up in one of them – there couldn't be many. Maybe three or four.

Back in Kandengei, after the journey was done, how would I describe this provincial capital to the *avookwaarks*? 'It wouldn't be true to say Daru was ugly – not all over. But the pretty bits, a residential district of wooden housing on stilts above lawns and flowerbeds, looked as if they were subsidized by outsiders – missionaries, governments, people who wanted to raise morale to stop the Daruvians coming near them. Most people lived in the shanty area where, at night, you'd only be seen dead. The residents of the nice corner, with the church and the police station, must have given daily thanks for the distance the rugby pitch and airport road gave them from the other area. Every inch counted.'

'It was as if the people were running on to the plane to get out of here,' I said to the hotel manager, searching his eyes.

'Refugees.'

He wasn't joking, either. But they were from Irian Jaya, over the border, the half of the island that was in the hands of Indonesia. I felt better for a while.

I said I was heading over to Australia. The man said, 'Well, it's physically possible, I suppose. If you've a stomach for it.' However, no one ever did have a stomach for it. 'Not to go all the way. It must be two days even with sixty-horse outboards.'

I didn't want to think any more about the journey, so I told him about what I'd do after – go to Wiluna, which was in the Western Desert.

'Wiluna . . . Does that ring a bell? There's something about it.'

But together we decided it couldn't be Wiluna. Wiluna was, after all, on the edge of nowhere and really only an old goldmining town, now almost abandoned, wasn't it?

At the end of the long straight road, which had only people, not cars on it, was a short line of stores – a half-hearted supermarket with five bouncers at the exit, a chip shop, a 'general store' selling biscuits, cold drinks and fishing tackle, and the bank, which looked like a village post office. This line swung into the waterfront, a low-calibre harbour of little fishing boats, most of them holed. Then we were at some army camp fencing – the hotel entrance.

The manager kindly agreed to look after my bags for me; he left them with the German shepherd dog guarding the reception.

The harbour was just past the market, where now, mid-morning, there were only dogs ferreting around among the fish smells, raising a dazzling array of flies. Further along, the men by the waterside seemed to be posing in the manner of pirates. They sat on upturned hulls, picking at fishing lines and ropes. They had earrings, Van Dyke beards and tattoos on their hands. The patterns were not the whimsical squiggles of bush people; one man had a bulbous woman lying back on his arm, showing off her attributes, another a deadly-looking spider. The men spoke no Pidgin, only their *tok ples*, their local language, and some English – usually Australian swear-words. They seemed to expect me to run away from them.

But I didn't run away. They didn't look as bad as the Yaifos dancing and were certainly no worse than the Kandengeis. I asked if anyone was going in the direction of Australia. They laughed, and got on with splicing ropes, scraping barnacles. But after an hour of my nagging, the heat of the sun seemed to get to them. They didn't laugh so much. They waved their knives and said, 'Get the fak out of here.'

However, one man wasn't shouting, he was laughing, and he said, 'Find Anton – *he'll* sort you out!' He pointed to this Anton, who was snoozing on his hull, reeking of beer. I tapped his arm. He keeled over. His hat rolled off. It was going to be off the harbourside in a minute, so I stamped on it. I returned, beating it roughly back into its original shape. I didn't think anyone had seen.

As I put the hat back on top of Anton, a skinny youth who was probably a student came up and politely introduced himself. I noticed he was walking me away from the harbour. Soon I had told him my problem – wanting to go to Australia. He said he'd take me along to meet another Englishman. A teacher, Woodlocke. He ran Daru's best rugby team.

We set off down the long airport road, with the rugby pitch and polite houses on the left and the shanty houses on the right, and met the other

Englishman coming our way. Woodlocke had a sportsman's glow about him and friendly but assertive blue eyes.

Peter said, 'I found him down by the harbour.' He made 'harbour' sound an evil word. Hearing it, Woodlocke looked in agony.

'Remember what they looked like?' He was still grimacing.

I said I could only remember the details of their tattoos. And that one of them had a hat that I'd unfortunately squashed and he was called Anton.

'Big guy? Scar by one eye?'

'That's the one.'

Woodlocke shook his head at me. 'Murdered two men.'

Fortunately, in Daru, it seemed, having murdered someone was quite normal. 'Most of the *rascols* are on my team,' Woodlocke said. 'Best people to have as your friends.'

He gave me a few tips. Saturday night was fighting night in Daru. Men came in from fishing on the Friday – Fridays could also be bad. And Sundays. Many of the injuries were from bottles to the head and he always had a bit of trouble making up a team for Monday practice.

Today was a Monday, as it happened, and he was missing his best forward, who'd been gaoled. I got the information slowly, in instalments, as he thought through the dreadful loss to the team. 'Killed a man . . . With an axe, actually . . . His father.' And turning to Peter, 'By the way, he's busted out of gaol. We're hoping he'll turn up for the final on Saturday.'

I was invited back to Woodlocke's house, around the legs of which he was encouraging jungle to grow like ivy. He gave me coffee and said going to Australia wasn't something people did. The local people did manage it from time to time but the government took a hard line with outsiders out there – the drugs, quarantine, refugees, 'and so on'. What's more, it was a bad time of year – all boats and crews were needed for the crayfish. In addition, the rugby grand final was coming up. 'It's more than a rugger match, it's tribal.'

He asked why didn't I go to Port Moresby, and fly.

I thought aloud, 'But anyone can do that.'

'That's what I mean.'

But by now I had to do this journey by sea. I couldn't back down every time things got a bit awkward. I needed to stick my teeth into something while I adjusted myself to life out of the forest. And anyway, what sort of quest would this make if I went tourist class in an airliner? I could count myself lucky that I didn't need to go home to Kandengei with a brace of enemy heads under my arm.

'My mind's made up,' I said.

Woodlocke said to Peter, 'Who's ever heard of crossing from here to Australia! The emigration man will have a fit.'

I said, 'Emigration man?'

'In the Department of Foreign Affairs. And the Aussies. They have spotter planes out looking for illegal immigrants and drugs. They don't like whites out there – and as for the quarantine. . . You'll be passing through the Torres Strait even before you get near T.I. to register. They won't want that.'

I discovered that T.I. was Thursday Island, the first Australian territory with any large habitation.

That night I slept on Woodlocke's floor and in the morning met Peter on the long road into town. It was where most people met. Peter introduced me to Max, who, like Peter, wasn't doing anything definite with his life. Max was plump and small, and enjoyed life so much that he didn't even have a bad word to say about Daru. He said I had come to just the right person. 'I can fix it for you.'

Peter disagreed. 'No you can't, Max. Don't bullshit him – he's got a degree, like me.'

'You failed yours.' They disputed this point for a while and then Max explained that his uncle Ralf was trying to go to a family wedding at Yam Island, about half-way across the Torres Strait. Max had relatives at T.I. and he'd grab any chance he could to visit them because there was a girl there he wanted to marry.

'What do they look like, Torres Strait people? I suppose, a cross between the New Guinean Melanesians and Papuans and the mainland Aboriginals?'

'They are fat.'

'Fat? What else?'

'Nothing else. Oh yes. And they have the highest diabetes in the world, nearly.'

It was their wealth. There was lots of sunshine and food on their islands, but better than that they were part of Australia and as such entitled to the welfare benefits. Unemployment benefits, pensions, community grants – they shared them round generously.

Whether really overweight or not, that more than explained why Max was marrying one of them. As for the emigration man, he was a drinking mate of Max's. I warned that he wouldn't want to be seen to bend the rules for a foreigner; Max said I wasn't to worry – he'd fix it. First we must find a craft.

Still reeling from the forest, I sank into the task. I hated all the new faces, the occasional car I saw scared me and I could never remember to shop for food during opening hours; when I did I pigged myself in the road. Max and I toured the ins and outs of Daru, trying to find a canoe. Drunk policemen, the harbourside men, men walking red-eyed over the broken-bottle beach, heedless of the glass picked up by their feet. We tried a sailor whose hut backed on to the tomb of a late 19th-century missionary, Reverend Chalmers, a previous Briton killed by the locals.[1] We tried them all.

Nothing. Recent rough weather had held up the crayfishing, and there was a greater urgency than ever to get on with it now. We bumped into the Foreign Affairs Officer himself, walking the long road in a white shirt and belted black trousers. Though I had now invested in a new shirt, he eyed me suspiciously – a new white face.

'Wotcha, Jonny!' Max said.

The official glared at Max, and looked over his shoulder to see if anyone had heard. Then he tried to duck away, off the grassy track leading to the nice side of Daru. Max caught up with him. 'What's up, Jonny?'

I went up hurriedly to show a little due respect. The official was dusting himself down, as if Max had soiled his jacket. He was stepping back as Max talked and was now perilously near a small drainage ditch. 'Not in public, Max!'

Max introduced me, not mentioning our journey. The official said, 'Have a pleasant stay in Daru, Mr Allen. Any problems – muggings, rapes, and other phenomena – please do not hesitate to contact me. You will see my office perching above the police station.'

'There's no need to worry yet,' Max said, as the search for a transport continued. Now we were scraping the bottom of the barrel – the shanty district within which Ralf lived. The shacks propped themselves up between sugar-cane bunches and cassava plots, the splashes of banana foliage and mud yards which served as kitchens. The fires in petrol drum troughs were cookers, and the poisonous puddles were the drainage from washing up and toilets. Among all this, boys walking home with exercise books, coughing toddlers, other children running after hens with knives, frogs squatting in ditches and making elastic clicking sounds, old men tramping along with strings of fish like minnows.

Ralf was about forty-five and had hard, poky eyes. He had just found an ancient modest twenty-five horsepower motor on a rubbish tip. It had barnacles – obviously no use to anyone. We had a good laugh. 'Let's hope we don't have to go using this one!'

While we searched for our canoe, for want of anything better to do, Ralf tried to crack the outboard open for spare parts.

That same day, we found someone who was going to the same wedding on Yam Island, half-way. They had a fifteen-foot canoe with a good sail, and a little outboard motor for the worst of the currents.

Readying the vessel for tomorrow's outward tide, we shifted it from the storm beach with a dozen drunk men and women, stomping over the glass, taking the canoe out through the floating bottles of the shallows.

We'd ride over the reefs as the water rose, Ralf explained as we walked shoreward again. There were four major reefs out there, he said, and getting caught by any of them might mean skirting round for twenty or more miles, involving more risks with treacherous cross-rips.

We had now reached the storm beach. We stopped. We had left a substantial part of the canoe hull and some of the outrigger behind.

As we came back past the rugby pitch – Woodlocke running on the spot with a crowd of bandaged men – we were overtaken by a man who said, 'Never mind the canoe, the crew shouldn't leave the harbour.'

'He's jealous,' Max said. 'And don't worry about the canoe. We'll fix it.'

We did, in a way. We took off planks from Ralf's house, using them to reinforce the hull or bartering them for outrigger wood. Gradually, over three days, the vessel was reassembled. Chickens and children fought and scratched around the yard. Further off came the war cries from the rugby semi-final battle.

At last the canoe was in one piece. We went along to 'Foreign Affairs', behind the Catholic church, up some outside steps at the back of the police station. 'An old drinking mate,' Max repeated. 'I will fix it.'

We were kept at the door for an hour. From the office came the sounds of frantic tidying. Then a voice ordered us in. The officer sat in a frosted glass chamber, behind a desk weighed down with orderly towers of paperwork. He told me to sit down and begin filling out forms. 'Duplicate, if you please. All your particulars. Date and time of incident, circumstances, witnesses.'

Max told the official that we wanted to go to Australia by canoe. The man asked Max to say it again. Then, when he had heard, he reached for one of his phones. 'The hotline,' he said to me, impressively.

'He'll talk to T.I.,' Max said, impressed.

He raised the receiver, and said, slowly and grandly, 'Ah yes, hello. Jonny – Foreign Affairs – here.' He was passing files off the top of his desk into the bin. 'No problem, but I've got an Englishman here who wants to come over. Yes, to you. No, from here. By canoe. Yes, yes, I know. Well, the two people he's going with I can clear from our end – I'll issue the usual Torres Strait pass. But what about a foreigner?

Exactly – but it isn't *actually* illegal yet is it? No, as I said, just a canoe! Yes I know, he must be.'

The conversation took some time.

'We're not allowing you to go,' he said, finally. 'Not unless you find two outboards – one for safety. You can't paddle all that way.'

'We'd have a small outboard and a sail, Jonny old boy,' Max said.

'And not if you call in at any Australian territory – that's anywhere beyond Moon Passage. Quarantine.'

Max said that was impossible. 'Jonny, we have to sleep somewhere.'

'If it's impossible, it's impossible. It's only because of me that Australia gave you the chance at all.' As we went out, he added my forms to the paperwork heaped in the bin.

In the corridor, Max said, 'It's his way of telling us we can go if we camp on deserted islands. I told you he was a mate.'

Max could get a dinghy for us from Yam – 'my girl there will give up hers.' But we needed a second outboard.

Between searches, we sat around Ralf's house. His garden furniture was made from plastic fishing floats which were filled with water and these supported thriving colonies of mosquito larvae. Children were playing football around the yard with a conch shell.

Ralf had once trained as an engineer in Irian Jaya, before the Indonesians took control from the Dutch. His time there had been cut short. He hadn't quite finished off the course on outboard motors. None the less, he had an apprentice. He was silent and very black, and had the looser curled hair of some of the large Torres Strait islanders whom we sometimes saw sauntering about. He watched with us, as Ralf muddled around with the gnarled components of the broken outboard.

Though Woodlocke didn't play rugby himself nowadays – not since his broken nose – he was busy coaching and we only saw him once, when he came to tell us a pupil of his had generously offered an outboard. We were saved – as long as the boy's dad didn't hear about it.

Quickly, we went along to get our passports stamped.

'Wotcha, Jonny!' Max said, walking right in.

We surprised the Foreign Affairs Officer lying flat on his desk, sleeping. He sent us out, and we waited in the corridor, behind the dappled glass screen. After a long wait, we were called back in.

I filled out the forms again, and passes were issued for Ralf and Max. My passport was stamped. We had now officially left New Guinea.

The officer said goodbye. 'Don't tell me any details. I will ring T.I. and let them know a vessel is coming through – eventually.'

But on the way back to Ralf's house, we passed an old man dragging away our outboard. He puffed and heaved, saying as he went, 'I'm not letting that madman's hands on this.' He was looking at Ralf, who had a spark plug in his mouth. He was adjusting it with his teeth.

The ancient, rusted pieces of the rubbish-dump motor were scattered over the mud lawn, children wandering off with some, playing battle tanks or stubbing their toes on others. 'What do we do now?' I said. Max and I were leaning against the remains of Ralf's house.

'No need to worry yet,' Max said.

'I did a course in engineering,' Ralf said. He was looking at the bits and pieces of outboard embedded in the mud of the lawn. 'You didn't finish your course,' I said, quickly. I turned to Max for support.

'Yes! You did a course in engineering!' Max said. Ralf was already digging out a piece of the outboard with his toe.

It had to be said, before dark Ralf *did* have the engine complete again. His apprentice looked half-dead. He had been lifting the engine in and out of a big petrol drum full of water all day as more missing parts were found and put into the mechanism. All night, they pulled the cord and the engine spurted water and shed more of its rust cake.

'Better give up, Ralf,' I said. 'Use it as an anchor – as we haven't got one of those either.'

All night they tinkered with spanners, the slave apprentice tugging the dead engine over or wailing when Ralf accidentally skinned his knuckles with a spanner. I woke from my snooze once, hearing the engine catch, somehow electrocuting them both. 'She needs to settle,' Ralf said, giving it a thump. 'That's all.' The slave whimpered.

Strangely, unaccountably, before daylight the engine was in action. A few minor adjustments with a hammer and Ralf was satisfied. We ran the canoe out with the midday tide, the two other men coming along hitched the sail, and we bobbed out to sea. Jonny, 'Foreign Affairs', looked on sorrowfully from the shore as we disappeared to our fate. The coconut palms shrank away and soon we could hardly see even the glint of glass in the white sands. Ralf started the canoe engine every so often to pull us through the currents, or yanked at the rubbish-dump engine, exploding another bad cough into the salt breeze. I slipped into a doze, rocking with the waves, happy and content. Nothing to worry about. I was on my way to Australia, and breathing in all this open air. The forest receded – no vegetation pawing at me, no ants scratching, just this open sky. It released me, gave me room to expand. After the crush of the town, the plain blue sky soothed me, the wind tasted sweet to me. This was freedom. For the first time in ages, I could clearly think out to beyond the forest. I could daydream of Hampshire, going up the iron spiral staircase to my bedroom, the musty smell of the African dance mask, supper smells following me from the kitchen, my mum trying to match a button for my old jungle trousers. 'I can't find olive green. Will your tribe mind if it's the wrong green?' Free at last. Yes, this journey to the desert was a brilliant idea.

Then the canoe was bucking. The outrigger wasn't skating over the water, it was ploughing. The water was dark and cold to the touch. 'Only Moon Passage,' Max said. 'The international border. A lot of boats are lost here.'

Then we were running along a reef, in its passage of smooth water, Australian territory. The blue dome of sky looked as empty as the seascape and for a moment I missed the life pace of the forest sounds. But in time, I saw smooth silver dugongs slipping through the waters, shadows passing underneath us like ineffectual sharks. Giant turtles sailed by, and veered from us as Ralf's harpoon chased them through the shallows. At last, one turtle was too slow, and Ralf dived after his harpoon line and lugged her up by the flippers. She came aboard, a heavy bowl looking gormless and bald, pathetically slapping her flippers and turning her head this way and that, beak open. Ralf clubbed her with an axe head, then cut her out of the shell, as if opening a can.

We headed for Tudo, a little island of sand and scrub, and at dusk moored on the beach beside the remains of a small Japanese war plane. It had an octopus living in the engine and we cooked it over a fire together with the tenderer lengths of turtle gut. All evening, a party of crayfishermen ran up and down the beach with a rifle shooting at sharks, which they said had been following them all day.

At daybreak we sat up on the beach and found the canoe marooned by the tide. While we waited, we ate dugong for breakfast with the crayfishermen. The man with the rifle was Anton, one of the local murderers.

'Max, Ralf does know the tides, doesn't he? I mean, this was just a one in a thousand slip?'

Max said he knew them all the way to Yam.

'Yam,' I said. 'Yam Island. The half-way point?' I couldn't help groaning just a little.

'No need to worry yet.'

We cut slowly through the sea towards Yam. Because of the quarantine, I couldn't come ashore, and watched from aboard the canoe while the others went off to get the boat from Max's girl. While I waited, a tractor passed with a trailer of empty fizzy drink cans. The paths were straight and white and groomed. They were combed sand overhung with flowering trees, hibiscus and pretty boxes for houses, from which came the sound of videos. Yam islanders waddled along drinking Coke, Fanta, and Pepsi. The women wore what looked like maternity outfits; they hung like loose curtaining from their wide breasts.[2]

Max came back. 'Spotless, isn't it? That's the Community Development Employment Programme. The government thinks of things for people to do, and pays them for it.' He looked up in the sky. 'If it wasn't for the spotter planes, every man in Papua New Guinea would have got here by now.'

'Where's the girl you're going to marry?' I asked.

'The one with the dinghy?' he said.

'That's the one.'

'Or do you mean the one with the canoe? Or the one on Thursday Island? Or . . .?'

He had quite a selection to choose from, but only one woman was equipped with an outboard, and it was a small one. We took it with her aluminium dinghy, slipping off into the mid-afternoon while Ralf tried to get our bigger, rubbish-dump engine into working order. I sat back again, still marvelling at the open skies.

When the winds blew up, we laughed at first. 'Hand me my life-jacket, Max!' We handed each other pretend life-jackets. However the sea changed from green to black and it spat at us; the waves tried to flip us over, and then the wind tried as well. 'Time to go back?' I said to Ralf, at the helm. But we were two hours out from Yam, and the way back was against the current. My lips burned with the salt spray on them. We rode slowly up waves, glided down their backs. The sea thumped and tossed us. The propeller roared as it spun in air, lifted clear of the water. The wind was against the tide, cutting the waves into jagged, twisting, steely ropes.

I'd never seen water like this. Not this close. It brewed, black, and then boiled over us, white. It was like saliva, the way in which it licked around us.

'No need to worry yet,' Max said.

It was all I could do to hang on, and keep low as we slid down the steep slopes, but Ralf yelled at me to go forward to help keep the prow of the dinghy down while he steered the engine. Ralf was going to try to get the rubbish-dump engine working.

I asked, 'Time to worry yet?'

Max didn't answer. His face was the same colour as Ralf's clamping knuckles.

The waves smacked us around. I held on, my face in the waves, seeing purple in their blackness, a sort of blood anger quality. A cream and brown banded sea snake was being tossed like rope; a turtle popped up its head, vertically, on a long neck, then ducked.

The rubbish-dump engine made a noise. It wasn't an engine noise at first, more like a stammering voice. Ralf tried again. The little dinghy stopped, as Max's hold on the other throttle loosened. A wave seemed to hang over us. But then we rose up the wave and it was gone. The rubbish-dump engine had stuttered its way into action.

We stared ahead, trying to will land to form out of the sea. At last we distinguished two islands. They looked as barren as the waves, black mounds between the other, shifting black mounds. Because of the currents we headed towards them sideways, and finally were in the lee of one, Nagi. I threw myself onto the coral sand. We sat together on the beach, taking breath. It felt as if we'd been swimming for the last few hours. We had only been sitting in a dinghy.

We brought our rucksacks ashore to discover that all our water and food had been washed overboard. We lit a fire, sheltering behind some large pink, granite-like boulders. Ralf told us the tall island rock next door was inhabited once. 'The people left because of bad spirits.'

'And why did they leave this island?' Max asked.

I walked off down the beach, so as not to hear the answer.

When I came back Ralf was telling Max that in the old days, old men always used to wait by the canoes, pull off the young men's *laplaps*, their sarongs, and inspect their genitals. If they didn't look quite right, the pallor was wrong somehow, the men would not be allowed out. Sharks would get them otherwise. 'You know why so many men are eaten by sharks nowadays? Because no one inspects their cocks – that's the reason.'

'I'm with two nutcases,' I wrote in my notebook. 'Never go across water anywhere again.' I watched the moon, almost half-full, a slice of coconut, horizontal, lowering, as if being handed gently to the horizon.

In the morning, we found the dinghy left high and dry by the tide. I had come to expect it now. Max walked about with a knife, opening up shellfish. We had some for breakfast, the rest we put in a polythene bag for later.

As soon as we could, we pressed on. We hadn't drunk fresh water for twenty-four hours and our lips were swelling from the salt spray.

The hull slaps and bangs on the waves, the propeller whines, coming out of the water as if to breathe and cry. The currents dance against each other. We surf with waves, they stop us in our tracks, they reach for and yank us backwards. A structural support in the dinghy breaks; another bag rolls overboard and we let it go. A petrol can leaps over as well. Now we may not have enough fuel.

At last we saw the lights of a telecommunications mast. Red and brown islands closed in around us, the water levelled out. The sun seemed to come out – up to now it had been hidden in the spray. We followed the bays around to the main harbour of Thursday Island. Max stood on the prow, supported by a rope, guiding us over the last reefs – we didn't have enough petrol simply to skirt around them. Ralf said he could hardly focus. He had been staring at the waves, not blinking for two days. We veered around a grey battleship, bobbing past its anchor chain to a stone quay, beyond a couple of luxury yachts. A fisherman watched us go by. He tugged up his line and got to his feet. We drew up at the quay steps.

'Wait down there, you lot!' A whiteman in white shorts and shirt was standing above us, looking down. The fisherman was peering more gingerly.

We waited for ten minutes in the sun, looking around the harbour, the dry hills rising around us. There were white houses on the slopes, corrugated sheds around a wharf area. No thatched houses, no buildings on stilts.

'Right. Eh, I've got the customs coming. I'm immigration. He's' – a second smart man appeared with papers – 'from the quarantine people.' A policeman, in shorts, was also here to see us.

The fisherman put down his rod and took up a better viewing position. The quarantine man said, '*I* better have a look at you first.' He came a step nearer. 'What's *that*?' He had spotted the raw shellfish. 'It'll have to go. Hand it to – no, actually, just place it on the ground here.'

Ralf's left hand was paralysed from holding the throttle, so Max and I passed the luggage forward. Ants jumped gleefully from my pack. Dry land! I knew the feeling. I watched them go, happy for them.

Max nudged me. 'Quarantine!' He began stamping on the little creatures. But now we both saw there was no need. They were doomed to die anyway – you could see it in the officer's eyes. He deftly produced a can of spray from his little bag. Some ants made a run for it, even diving onto the skin of the water. They need not have bothered. 'There's no escape,' the quarantine man said, taking his time. 'The insecticide sticks.' He put the can away. 'Resinous,' he explained.

Now it was the policeman's turn. 'Firearms? Bush knives?' I said no, not any more. '*No?*' He looked disappointed. I saw that for all these men I was a let-down; they were expecting someone more like Captain Cook, another Englishman who'd stopped off here. 'You don't carry any knife? No weapon for your personal safety? *Nothing?*'

We went along to a stone building. Another whiteman gave us a going-over. 'No alcohol on board. Are you sure?' He stared at Ralf's red, shattered eyes.

'They're the blokes from Daru,' the policeman said.

'Oh.' The new official looked a little embarrassed. He adjusted himself and shook our hands in turn.

Max and Ralf wanted to go off to meet their relatives. We agreed to meet at the Royal Hotel.

'Shouldn't meet at the Royal, if I were you,' the policeman said. 'You'll get a bottle in your face. The Torres Hotel would be slightly better. And you might not be the only black faces there.'

The policeman said he'd drop Max and Ralf off and find a cheap place for me to stay. We drove off. He told us he was from Cairns, down the east coast. He was quick, efficient, precisely spoken and in an immaculate blue and white uniform. He had a lot of muscle bulk for a whiteman, dark eyebrows that didn't divide in the middle and white legs that didn't look untidy emerging from the shorts.

After he'd dropped the others off he said he'd show me around the island. I agreed, but suspected a trap – I didn't deserve all this treatment. I noticed his strong, sensing hazel eyes. Yes, he must suspect I'm a drug runner.

He shouted, 'Hold on!' We roared up a dirt track to do a circuit of the island. It would only take a couple of minutes.

There were red and yellow forty-gallon drums every twenty-five paces, litterless mango-tree avenues; duck-egg-shell paint peeling from the metal cargo sheds of the wharf; taxis and rusty pick-ups were the only traffic. To me the main street seemed so wide you'd have to think hard before planning to trek out across it. I began to feel drowsy – the job of getting here was done and I was still being overburdened by the open spaces.

The policeman pointed his elbow out into the blue bay. 'See that red light buoy?'

'I remember it well. Our helmsman almost crashed into it.'

'It's a spare for the middle of the Gulf of Carpentaria.'

'Where?'

He looked at me, taking his attention off the road. 'The Pommy sense of humour, right?' He laughed. 'You know, it's said to be the only dangerous obstacle out there.'

We seemed to be doing a second lap of the island. The policeman said, suddenly sounding a bit boyish, 'You're an *explorer*, really, aren't you?'

'If there are any, I suppose I am. Not a "traveller" anyway. Hate travelling.' Especially water crossings.

'Is that the most dangerous journey you've ever done?'

But we had only been a few days out on the water. Without Max and Ralf it would even have been safe.

He asked what I was a specialist in.

Not a specialist in the way that any of the Kandengeis were – generalists, but in forests. Nor in the deserts. I played safe, and said, 'Nothing.'

'Sounds like you're the right man for the job.'

'What job's that?' Torres Strait Islanders stomped along the road, these again bouncy with their diet.

'The experts have failed. Why not try the naïve approach?'

'To what?'

'To *what*? I don't quite follow you. To the blackfella problem, of course. Just don't try to come away with any solutions.'

I asked him why not.

'There are too many already.'

Shops with bunches of shells, postcards. It must be a place that the other Australians came a long way to look at – 'the most northerly tip of the continent'.

I said I hadn't come here to look at Australia's problems. I had come to understand the forest.

'But the forest is back the other way.'

'Exactly,' I said. I told him how the desert would give me perspective on the forest.

'You reckon?' He didn't look as if he believed he was hearing me, seeing me even. He wanted to pinch himself. I checked my appearance in his rear-view mirror. Everything was as expected. The cracked lips, the wind-blasted skin and, under that, the yellow, sun-cheated complexion of the forest dweller.

He said he didn't want to put me off, but . . . He was about to say something, but stopped himself. Then he said, simply, 'The blackfellas are the people to show you the desert, and they take some getting to know.' Then he said under his breath, 'Even if you do find a sober one.'

'I've heard there is a problem – land rights, deaths in police custody – whoops, sorry.'

Hearing these words – 'land rights' – he had already tightened in his seat. 'Er, don't quote me on what I said about the drink. Things aren't straightforward any more in Australia.'

'Aren't they?'

He looked at me in that strange, shocked way again, as if I were an alien. 'You really haven't done much homework, have you?'

'None. I've been avoiding books – the songlines, the Dreamtime, Sydney Opera House, Melbourne Cup. You name it, I haven't read about it.'

He said he wished there was someone else to come and hear this. 'What else don't you know? Australian personalities – how good are you on personalities?'

I was not good on personalities. I said the only Australian names I knew, 'Hawke, Packer, Murdoch, Bondy, er . . . I think that's all I can do.'

He muttered, a touch sadly, 'Well, you've got the key ones.'

I was pleased with this, my first proper Australian whiteman. I had taken his hospitality for suspicion of me, but it was just the way out here. What British policeman would have picked up a stranger and given me all this advice? He was open and frank but his openness was guarded with cynicism. He was not jockeying with bush pioneer spirit, as they had been back in the Aero Club, all tribal and possessive – I could expect that later, in a remote place like Wiluna. The policeman only had a healthy touch of those outback qualities. I was an outsider, whom he'd welcome in if I wasn't a threat; he was prepared to give me a chance.

'Why did you do it?' the policeman asked, still in shock. 'Explorers carry maps, don't they? You didn't even have a map.'

'Well, you see, I have a theory,' I said. I let the poor policeman have it. 'If an explorer leaves home with a map, all he'll ever come back with is a better defined version of that map.'

'You know mate, I've always wanted to meet an explorer. Not just a traveller, I mean. A true blue *explorer*.'

I let him in on a secret. 'Explorers are oddities, that's all. They leave home because that's all they can do, you see, press themselves to the landscape, thrust themselves against natural obstacles. Otherwise they'd be travellers, people who simply enjoy the view. No, explorers are thrusters, people who impose themselves. The sensitive ones buckle and the land leaves an imprint of itself on them. Good comes out of it. Others don't buckle, they impose their own shape. They are imperialists. And, well, the West, wanting to "advance", wants people of the latter disposition. So that's what we're mostly stuck with, people who believe knowledge is rationalizing science, and who set about expanding it, the cause of the West. No one's to blame really, it's just the hard way the West is.'

Somewhere along the line I must have lost him. He turned and, apparently suddenly sorry for me, said, 'Look, some things you just *do* need to know about Australia – at least on arrival. Here's Lesson Two – by the way, Lesson Number One was that there are too many solutions to the Aborigine problem already – Lesson Two, though: Australians don't like outsiders telling them what's what. We've just been having the 200th anniversary celebrations. You just keep your head down – whether Australians, or Aboriginals.'

'Aren't Aboriginals Australians?'

'Nope. Well yes, they must be. That is, they got some of their land back in '76.'[3]

He didn't seem very sure. Yet the Aboriginals – I remembered from some newspaper article – had been here for 40,000 years or more.

He tried to explain. 'It's a matter of public perception. You see, in most people's minds you've got Australians, and . . . well, you've got Aboriginals. Not the same thing at all.'

It wasn't much of an explanation, but now it was time for me to be dropped off. 'This is the Aboriginal hostel. The cheapest place in town.'

I thanked him for the advice, and just before he left asked him if he by any chance had heard of Wiluna, in Western Australia.

'Wiluna the trouble spot?'

I said some other people had made the same mistake – actually it was only a blip on the end of a road on the edge of the Gibson Desert.

'That's the one.'

I went to my dormitory, and looked in the mirror. My lips were worse than a few moments ago – white, cracked, weeping blood.

All this exposure to open space was too much, all at once. Harried after the forest by Moresby and Daru I had sunk myself into the task of getting here, and now it was over I felt utterly drained. There was an hour to go before I must meet Ralf and Max, so I thought I'd lie down a few minutes. I lay on my bed, pushing off the pillow and putting my rucksack there in its place. It was wet but I didn't mind. I closed my eyes and smelt the woodsmoke of past camp fires. After a few deep breaths I was asleep.

Ralf and Max woke me. It was almost seven o'clock, closing time at the Torres Hotel.

I wanted to treat them and made the effort to wake myself up. 'Australia's Top Pub', the Torres Hotel said. We walked through the entrance which was through the blue jean legs of a giant cut-out, an electric-guitar-jabbing bearded hulk with shades and a purple beret.

I bought three cans of beer each. Ralf rapidly became incoherent. His eyes went from red to purple and his voice became very slow and tired. The skin tightened around his nose as he made an effort to speak. He drank two of my beers, and then wanted to sing pearl fishing songs. 'I'll sing soprano. You sing tenor,' Ralf said, hugging Max and kissing his ear.

They dragged me along the street singing. I tried to join in, but couldn't engage myself. I fell back from them and stood a while in the Children's Memorial Playground. By a pillar, 'To the Fallen', I gently pushed a child's swing. I looked up at the clear, warm sky. Such openness after months of being crowded in. I went away by myself and slept.

I woke with the smell of burnt toast from the kitchen.

It was already light, but the rest of the dormitory were asleep. I went outside and looked at the turquoise blues of the sky and sea and the bare scrub hills in between.

I was over the shock of it. All I wanted, just now, was more of that openness, that buff, exposed soil. A young whiteman in the kitchen said there was a ferry service to the mainland, and gave me the number.

I began dialling the hall phone, but the man called, 'Are you feeling all right? It's six in the morning.'

'Am I too late for breakfast?'

'What I'm saying is, you're out of office hours. Try ringing in three or four hours.'

I tried to write a letter home. Failed. I was still very tired. I looked around for the camp fire to throw the letter into. There was only a black vinyl space, a pink dustbin with a black liner.

At nine in the morning, I rang again. A voice said, smartly, 'Good morning, Pedell Ferry Services.'

'Hello. My name's Benedict, and I'm from England. . .'

'And which ferry are you interested in? Can I recommend . . .'

Soon I remembered how people, especially the whiteskins, had a way of carrying me. Now I was in their territory, I could let myself be taken.

I found Max in the street, supporting Ralf, who hardly recognized me. I gave them some money, and presents, a tarpaulin and Thursday Island sticker. They rolled off together down the street. 'I'm getting married next week,' Max said. 'I want to keep the dinghy.'

Pedells Ferry Service took me off to Bamaga, the tip of the mainland. Australia was ahead, an immense slab that began with a wooden jetty and an empty beach of coconut palms. I was dropped off at the jetty. It had red dust creeping out along it. The same red dust was painting a banana import warning board, a lone telephone box. The coconut palms were red, the corrugated sheds, power lines, the gum trees – all coated, heavily bearing a burden. I pulled at a gum tree leaf; the dust was warm as it ran over my fingers. This close, I saw the grains were not red, but ochre and umber and rust – I was fascinated, being able to handle something that was so large a part of the substance of my surroundings.

I slept on the beach, in that same dust, and in the morning walked down the road into Bamaga. Two drums of petrol clonked together in the river, the slower water stirring a skin of more dust. There was more of the dust up there in the corrugated roofs, and in the guttering more again, growing purple grasses.

School signs, bus stop signs. I've done enough, I think to myself. The

'whiteskins' can help me all they want to, from here. I feel this strongly
– that all I have to do now is sleep. I close myself over, and in this
shut-down, defensive state I allow myself to be taken out under this
intense sky, an intensity that makes me feel as if I have just stepped
onto a theatre stage.[4]

Chapter Seven

THE MOBS

A short flight, a lift from a postman, another lift from a postman, another flight. A bunk in a hostel in a town called Cairns, and then a coach to a place called Mount Isa. It went on like this, my being carried along, and every now and then I wiped the dust from my face with the paper towelettes that everyone handed out.

Outside the coach window, beyond the air conditioning, beyond the onboard video of *Crocodile Dundee*, the landscape must have changed from town lights to open fields – perhaps sugar cane, perhaps oil palm – and then to scrub. It was this scrub when I woke one morning – scattered olive and grey mulga tree-bushes on trays of oven-hot soil, pans of life reduced to dust.

In Mount Isa – clearly a mining town, though it claimed, everywhere, to be a city – I was told I had seven hours to kill. I went to a coffee bar and wrote, 'It's not that I don't want to look. Though I do feel lethargic about writing. But I'm watching Australia as it flashes by . . . all I can say is that I'm not involved.'

The roadside trees stood in soil that looked like brick. Their bark was peeling, flapping in the wind; other bark looked defended against it, thickened into plasterboard. The afternoon cemented in overhead; each day here must be like an encrustation of bleach, I thought.

The new bus-driver switched on the air conditioning and video. *Crocodile Dundee* again.

I went back to sleep, thinking over images from outside. Under the blue bowl of sky, holding rare cloud smidgens, was this empty, gunshot-blasted landscape. The jungle had closed in on you with its scent, its breath, its sounds, its life pace. But here, outside the coach there were only scurrying lizards, quick flies living off the dead and . . . well, that was about all. And this emptiness of the land magnified things, not shrinking them the way the forest did – objects were made into something by a space of nothing.

In the same way that the desert could draw forgotten images out of the back of a Western man's crowded head – the little stones were 'cannon shot', or the land a 'death cake with unforgiving icing' – I myself was being sucked out of the crowded forest towards centre stage.

In the dawn, two emus were pecking at the roadside as nonchalantly as chickens; the ground, as at Mount Isa, looked paved over.

It *was* paved over. The driver said over the microphone that we were coming into town. Which town? Now I was standing by the bus and watching the backpackers bobbing, getting under their packs. Then they were off down the road. Sparrows began picking off the fly and dragonfly remains from the coach radiator.

I decided this must be Alice Springs, the centre of the country. From here, according to the atlas back in England, I must travel along the bush road called the Gunbarrel Highway.[5] At the end would be Wiluna.

I followed the backpackers into town. Soon, though, I was getting behind, stopping to look at things. You could get 'The Total Look' at Hair Creations. 'The Living is Easy', another shop said, 'with Modern Maid.' I went by a 'Bistro' and then another. And one more. I tripped on a red boulder that had been carefully placed to interrupt the bricks of the Mall – 'Mawl' – for extra character. In the toilet, there were forty-nine air freshener blocks at my feet and the graffiti was the graffiti of any city in the world. 'I like my tea like my women. Strong and white.'

Through the night we had come through scrubby desert, and were now probably surrounded by it. But Alice Springs was just a town, just a smaller version of Cairns, a larger version of Mount Isa. I was in the middle of semi-desert, but this was a chip off some city, and it had floated out here, carried by shifting sands.

Outside the public toilets there was a strip of grass and some blackfellas having a morning shower under a lawn sprinkler. I went over to say hello; they were probably as lost as I felt. Then, nearer, I decided against. They were shouting loudly, floundering under the spray as if they were drowning. Others were not under the hose shower, but just swinging and stumbling. These had glassy flies like beads in their hair and looked at me as if they were about to beg. They had bandaged knuckles and foreheads – fight labels.

Ahead there were two whitefellas, one a policeman, another a man with a briefcase, talking to three black women. The whitefellas were acting like foreign language teachers, patiently repeating and repeating a basic sentence construction. The women said nothing. They looked as if they had all the time in the world. Not like the Kandengeis, with an eye on their own interests, but as if the whitemen were of no consequence. There was a gap between the blackfellas and the white, a division made long ago. As if the Aboriginals had been waiting around here even while the land was being made.

The briefcase man was getting impatient, but the women looked as if they might wander off any minute. The whitefella gave them a pen, and put his briefcase on his knee for them to lean on; each woman made a mark where he indicated. 'That's it then,' he said, with evident relief. 'I'll get a taxi for you.' But the women began floating away. He shouted after them, 'Oi! Which one of you's got my pen?'

Beyond the Plaza, and the pedestrianized street which had shop fronts from a Wild West movie – cowboy hat shops, cowboy boot shops – though with high-heeled ladies walking down it, I found a building labelled 'Department of Aboriginal Affairs'. A whitefella there gave me lots of leaflets – 'Aboriginal Australia', the first one said. 'Current issues; questions often asked.' All I wanted to ask was how to get to Wiluna, and the answer was, not from Alice Springs. 'Go down the Gunbarrel Highway, and you'll be fined.' Passing through Aboriginal Reserves meant getting permission from the Land Council. 'And no shooting of kangaroos or emus either.'

I looked over his shoulder trying to see a blackfella I might talk to. But there were only white people in the office, just now. The man took a book from his desk.

'*The Songlines*,' he said. 'This man got it about right.'

The book fell open at a reference to Alice Springs – the lawn sprinklers soaking the blackfellas.

Another whitefella came up and also asked if I had read *The Songlines*.[6] Everyone seemed to think I was a journalist. 'The drink problem, well, it's no better or worse than previous years.' Drugs and petrol sniffing, well, it hadn't yet arrived.

I said, 'I'm just here to listen.'

'Listen?' He had to think about it.

I said there was one question, though. 'Wiluna itself. Wiluna's all right, isn't it?'

'Not a place to bring up kids,' he said.

'Once,' he said, 'you know, it had the longest bar in the southern hemisphere. Housing for eight thousand. Peanuts grew around it. There was the Masonic Hall, Lake Violet Sailing Club, the Anglican church. Now? Now it's been demolished.'

'All of it?'

He was mulling over good times. 'St Michael and All Angels went in 1958, I think.'

I was directed to another man who dealt with claims for land rights. He was another whitefella. He produced a paperback from under the counter. *The Songlines*. I'd come all this way to be haunted by the desert, and instead was being haunted by another Englishman.

I phoned a number I was given for Wiluna. 'Ngangganawili Community,' a voice said. At last, a blackfella. But he sounded like an African, not an Australian. He said he was Kalu, the 'co-ordinator' of the community committee. They had processed my application to stay, and I was allowed to visit the reserve. They'd give me a lift there from Perth if that suited.

I saw a sign for 'disposals', army surplus, and, what with Wiluna being the place it was, thought I should get myself better equipped. The shop owner, Frank, tried to help me out – trenching spade? Tent? But I couldn't get the point. In the forest you didn't need a spade or tent, so why would you in the desert?

Frank wore a red chequered shirt and was crop-haired and broken-nosed. He was smiley, with choppy sea blue eyes. After he had duly offered me his copy of *The Songlines*, he said, 'A plastic wrapper. That's what Alice is. All glitter. They're planning a lake resort and they're putting Ayers Rock behind chains.'

I said I'd give it a miss. It wasn't what I was here for.

He seemed to take to me, at that moment. 'Alice used to be a nice little place.' Dust roads, tin roofs. Now he was selling up. Violence was up, break-ins, stealings. The blackfellas came in with no shoes on, and left wearing boots. More often, they were just drunk. Once when a man refused to leave his shop he gave him a slight push. Collapsed backwards, eyes to the heavens. Brought all the billy cans down on top of him.

An American lady said, 'You see that? He hit the black guy!'

'I couldn't leave him there. I went and got the cobbler opposite to give me a hand. Put him outside the shop. After a while, noticed there were no customers. The Aboriginal was putting them off. "It's no good, George. We'll have to move him." Took him down the way a bit. Few minutes later, saw the owners of the Gas Centre lugging him by. George's voice: "Hoi! Don't put him *here*!" The Whiteman's Burden, I called him. That's my Whiteman's Burden Story.'

When I told Frank I was going to Wiluna he closed up his shop. 'I'm not letting you plunge into Wiluna just like that.' He'd take me for a drink, he said. 'Animal Bar.'

Next thing, I was being walked along the Todd river to the bar. He introduced me to Australian slang. '"Got a kangaroo loose in the paddock." That means you're mad. You might hear that.'

Groups of figures sat in the white gum tree shade, rolling about with bottles and flasks while a police Land Rover meandered gently in and out of the trees.

Frank was saying that the judges gave short sentences to blackfellas because time away from the family, in gaol, was hard on them and also the tribes often punished severely themselves – a spear through the leg was quite common still. They used to be worse – ostracizing, which in the desert meant death. The coppers left tribal law alone – killings and so on.

We went by a shop where whitefellas drove up and were served alcohol instead of petrol, doing the transaction through their car window. But we were at Animal Bar. You could hear it – the drunken singing, and also television horse race commentary. A whitefella sat in the entrance on a high stool, fingering his hands. Seeing the bouncer my expectations were raised, but inside I saw blackfellas and white mixing amicably, and there seemed to be a private party. Everyone – there were only men here, apart from the barmaid – knew each other, and they were in the same cowboy dress.[7] Their stetsons were tipped back as they tipped back beer, thumbs in glinting belts, riding stools like ponies. The men howled their songs, and a blackfella tried a chord on his guitar but fell off the stool.

We went up to the long bar and when we'd got our drinks found a quiet corner under a sign. 'Taxi free phone – just lift the receiver.' But someone had lifted the whole set, leaving six screwholes.

I said, 'There's a racial mix in here, that's good.'

He ordered 'two handles of Four X', pulled me to a seat and said, 'Racial mix?'

'Blackfellas and whitefellas.'

'The only whiteman in here is the girl behind the bar. Though, yeah, you do get whites in here.'

I looked round the room. A third of the people here were definitely white. I said, pointing at a white cowboy at random, 'What about him?'

'He's an eighth Aboriginal. That counts.'

How very complicated, I thought. And I've come to Australia for its desert simplicity. While Frank went to the toilet, I looked around at the Aboriginals – at the bouncer, with his pale blue eyes, sandy hair, Anglo-Saxon nose. He looked up, sensing me staring – me, a whitefella: red-brown hair, pale blue eyes, Anglo-Saxon nose. He was just getting off his pedestal to come and sort me out when a blackfella woman rolled up.

The bouncer got back on his stool.

'I'm twenty-one,' she said. She was very fat, with parallel scar slashes up her upper arm and shoulder. A twisted bra strap was exposed on one shoulder. She had porky, heavy cheeks, eyes hidden between them and the heavy brow.

Frank came back saying, 'Always seems a strange habit to me after a trip to urinals.' He saw the blackfella woman. 'Washing your hands. My cock's not dirty.' Then to the woman, who leaned on the table, forcing me to lean on my side to balance it, 'Maureen, please!'

'PLEASE!' she says. 'Listen. I got something to tell you.' Her spittle sprays over us. 'PLEASE!' she repeats, as Frank tries to wave her leaking mouth away. She doesn't seem to be able to say any more, so we get on with our own drinks. Maureen slides fully onto the table, clearing the glasses with her thighs.

'Don't force us to leave the pub, Maureen.'

She asks me if I want to take her home.

I didn't really. Frank gave her two dollars. 'We want to talk.'

She went off, and, after a few more beers and still more of the advice that I hadn't yet asked for, kind Frank, now finding it hard to keep on his stool himself, says there's some 'Business', tribal Law ceremonies, going on in the Central Reserves. Probably Man-making, which mainly went on in the summer, just coming up, because in the summer people had time off from station work or, more traditionally, had gathered around waterholes at that time.

Men would gather from a hundred miles for Business, he said. Little sense of territory here. He gives me a potted account of the songlines. When a woman feels a baby inside her for the first time, an elder might examine whereabouts she felt the kick. It would help him determine the totem of the child – say, a caterpillar totem. Say it was a boy. Through the child's life he would hear stories of the original caterpillar ancestor. He would never or rarely be able to eat his totem and would follow the route the caterpillar took during the time of the ancestors, the Dreamtime, perhaps meeting men from other tribes from the same totem, following their songlines.[8]

He rationalized it. 'Of course, to nomads, learning the land, the position of waterholes, is essential.'

I imagine the old men hunching over the boys – the paint, the blood. But the boys I imagine are not Aborigine boys, with black skins, embedded eyes, but Kandengeis. Suddenly I wanted to get on, out in the desert. I shouldn't be here, in the middle of a pub, apparently drinking an Australian under the table.

'You wouldn't want to witness some of their goings-on. They have a real bad time of circumcision. Put a bone right down their cock and cut it right open. A whistle dick, we call it.'

I drank my beer, and Frank, drooping now, slowly drank his. 'Sounds more like subincision,' I said. It was said to happen on Wogeo, New Guinea.⁹

Frank explained that there were two stages, in fact. Circumcision for a boy, and later, the further operation. Until that they were considered merely 'Half-men'.

'I know the feeling,' I said, faintly.

Perhaps because I didn't sound appalled enough – but why should I be after six weeks in the Crocodile Nest? – he gave me an extra story.

'I was standing next to a bloke in a toilet once. He showed me his cock. "Look at this, mate!" Waved the ugliest thing at me!' He lowered another empty glass, and stared at the next. 'I'd be too scared to go to a Business meeting – they might want to make me a blood brother!'

I went to bed, walking out of town to a patch of desert to stay the night in. I crossed the Todd river bed, looking down on the blackfellas holding drinking parties. The police Land Rover was still travelling from group to group in a circle, seeing to a perpetual series of domestic violence. I was too tired now to do much more looking. I carried on over the bridge and found a hostel as the sun set on the bottles.

I caught the coach on down to Port Augusta, then another coach along the bottom of the continent to Perth. There was scrub and the occasional monolith – 'Ayers Rock being the world's largest', said one of the posters. In the headlights I spotted my first live bush kangaroo; a single knock on the fender announced its death. As evening went on, there were four more knocks on the roo bar. In my sleep, I counted five more.

When I awoke, we were among large sheep fields, and then, in another bus, coming to a city. We passed a gambling casino and a stadium with waffle-iron lights. I had crossed Australia diagonally in about a week. An area the size of Europe had gone by, and all I had recorded was the barbed wire shrubbery, the leaves like the peels left in the larder onion tray. Everything brittle and unflinching – shrubs like witches' brooms. These few details were all I had ever wanted – just enough for an impression of the size of space, the width of the stage, the intensity of the focus on it.

*　　*　　*

Soon I was finding a cheap hostel, and again being asked if I had read *The Songlines*. The city was bewildering to me – I still seemed to be a bush bunny and I had to be rescued by a brother of a friend from Queensland. He said I could stay while I waited for my lift.

'*Wiluna?*' Dick said over a drink, when I first broached my destination. 'In Wiluna you'll find only two tribes –' he tapped my can of Swan lager – 'the Emu and the Swan tribe.'

Like all the whitefellas, he thought I was unprepared for the rigours of Wiluna. Unlike them, he'd actually lived in the bush himself a bit.

Brought up in Queensland, he'd been a hydrographer at Port Hedland, where he'd made it a policy to employ Muslims if he could – 'Grog isn't just a black problem.' In those days the ashtrays were nailed down, tables and chairs were chained. It was the fighting; one of the best was the time the first Japanese pearl divers returned after the war. 'They took the locals snarling at them for a little time. Then went berserk. Cleared the bar in seconds.' The railway carrying iron ore in from the south, Marble Bar, was maintained by Yugoslavs. They shaved their heads to stop themselves going to Perth on spending sprees. Went mad sometimes – one man strapped dynamite around himself, lit the fuse and ran off into the desert to explode.

Dick had heard that I was An Explorer and was keen to hear the stories. He particularly admired me for my sea crossing. It wasn't the sharks, but the sea snakes.

He said that once he'd been talking to a diver in his shed. Saw lots of hand shears. 'Oh, they're for sea snakes,' the diver said. Two blokes stayed at the surface, cutting them up between them, while the diver got on with his job. The snakes were slow but deadly, Dick said. Once he'd seen twenty or so sharks circling a diver, but only when he saw a sea snake did he shoot to the surface.

He was waiting for me to begin my own yarns now. But I had had a hard time answering the demands of whitefellas at the best of times on my quest, and now, so near my destination, it was no easier. Opening up, I opened myself to be swayed by him, the West.

Then he showed me his sheath knife. 'I expect you have one like this.' He'd stabbed a man with this particular model. He'd backed slowly into another man's car, got out to apologize and was attacked with a bail hook. Dick showed me the white scars on his forearm. 'Surprisingly tough to put a knife in someone. More so than you'd think. Went straight to the police. They said thanks for letting us know. Is he dead? No? Okay. We'll go along in the morning and see if he's there.'

While he waited for me to begin, he offered more of his own adventures. He had even been mistaken for Lord Lucan. Policemen had knocked on the door one evening while he was soaking his feet in a hot tub. 'Can we see your identification, sir?'

He got out his documents. His third passport back was almost identical to the last photo of Lucan, the missing alleged murderer. They even had similar moustaches. What was more, under questioning, the officers discovered they shared the same drink – Bourbon, the same fags, Peter Stuyvesants. It had been some time before the policemen left him alone. One of them had been flown out from Scotland Yard especially.

As for Wiluna, he used to drop in there – they'd used it as a fuel dump for the helicopter. 'Used to have to weave in between all the bodies, often badly slashed. That was on "Black Thursday", pension day.'

On the strength of Dick's stories, the next day I decided to re-equip myself. I bought a lock knife, a new mosquito net against flies, an Australian army hat, and boots. The shop had a man at the door to keep out drunk blackfellas. 'They've been on White Lady.'

'Australian whisky, is it?'

It was meths with a little water and baby powder. Later Dick said *his* Aboriginals just drank half of a bottle of rum, and topped it up with meths. 'They're probably all dead now.'

He thrust his Peter Stuyvesants under my nose every ten minutes as he talked, still patiently encouraging me to open up. 'You carry a gun?'

He always used to carry a .45 in his glove compartment. A gin – he meant a female blackfella – would be in the road, he'd have to slow down. Then five 'bucks' would come from the side and jump in, wanting a lift.

He gives me a choice of belts from a hat box. All were kept supple and shining. One had a pure silver Turkish emblem on brass – found on a dead body. 'The boots were also bloody good, but I left them.'

At the start of every day it was, 'Good morning, old boy!' Then a shower, and then his stories or, as he began to suspect I was a fraud, advice. 'And never wear dark colours. Flies will settle on you for miles. And black shoes aren't a good idea. Town people wear them. Stockmen always wear brown.' And later, 'I'm not exaggerating about their dislike of the English. You're gonna see them at the bars muttering at you.'

He was perplexed. I had a track record of success – aged twenty-eight, been off alone through the world's remotest forests. Yet I didn't even have a belt or knife. What equipment I did have – the rucksack, the jungle trousers I was wearing – was a shambles. I fell short. I was not at all like any explorer he'd heard about as a boy on his station in Queensland.

'Know how you sharpen a knife? Judging by the way you handle that, you don't. Here, show me.' I began. I felt like a boy; I began trembling. 'Enough! Here, give it to me.' He did it properly. Then: 'You can crack a whip? Or not?' He was waiting. I must be good at something, he was thinking. Today he had ordered my other books from the library. He wanted to find out exactly what I *had* been doing out there.

I reassured him that I could crack a whip. He took me outside, taking the whip from the porch wall. It was a stock whip, a type I'd never tried. He cracked it – a rifle shot. I heard a neighbour run indoors. 'Good, I thought the cracker might be stuffed,' he said, running his fingers over the end cord. He instructed me. The whip must fall slowly, below the shoulder, and be brought back fast. As a boy, he used to take cigarettes from his brother's mouth. 'You can cut out what you want – piece of clothing, flesh, paintwork.' He cracked the whip at his white car. A fleck of undercoat appeared.

I didn't see how cracking a whip was going to help me. His talk was the talk of the whitefella. It was the talk of aggression, of assaulting the desert, the forest. I hadn't come to assault anything, not even all the problems there seemed to be here.

In the night, the Chairman of the Ngangganawili Community Council took me away in his Toyota.

Not to my great surprise, Herbie wasn't a blackfella either. He was a Maori, and had been in Wiluna about ten years – he came as a mechanic, just travelling, but the Aboriginals began to trust him. Now he chaired their committee and had a Filipino wife.

We saw emus occasionally – rumps like just another bush, but with leaves that would part softly in the wind, feathers peeling like petals. Our red and orange dust was spinning through the grey bushes. A wedge-tailed eagle hunched in the road on a rabbit. By daylight we had hit only one kangaroo. Herbie was relieved – only one – he'd only just straightened out the dents in the Land Cruiser.

'Are you familiar with all the problems in Wiluna?'

I thought I must be by now, but I was wrong. Herbie said the leading elder, Paddy Richards, had died. Now the tribal 'Law' had almost collapsed. Grog. 'The elder's son Graham, is good, but too young yet. I'll introduce you. Don't worry. I'm not going to just throw you out into Wiluna helpless!'

At Jigalong, further north, the elders had banned drink – people got drunk outside the reserve, then came in. 'It's helped them a lot. They have a . . .' he seems to search for a word that's not going to be too damning. It takes him a long time. In the end, there's no getting away from it. 'In Jigalong, they have a *pride* in their culture.'[10]

Herbie said, as if in a trance, 'They just think of their next drink.' He gripped the wheel tighter. 'At night they lie thinking about it.'

No doubt he was overstating the case, to prepare me. But then we passed through Cue, slowing to look at the broken hotel windows. It was the riot – yesterday there'd been the funeral of a gaoled blackfella who'd hanged himself with a belt.[11]

'While I remember, don't ever mention the name of anyone who's died, like that Paddy Richards. There's a taboo against it, right? "Christmas" is also the name of someone who died. If you last out there to December, don't say "Happy Christmas".'

At Meekatharra, we turned right off the highway. Now we were running along on dust, through sticky scrub. Bushes were like stubble on an old man's face, greens among them looking like strays among the herds of other bushes. The trees were scratched as if by a cat sharpening its claws; bark was furrowed, fallen gum leaves like curled razor blades. There were only these pictures of torment, nothing sweet and cheerful.

This wasn't desert. Not the official, proper sterile wastes of rolling sand. But if I had flown from Kandengei to the Sahara and talked to the Bedou, or to the Gobi and been picked up by Mongolians, I would have been with oasis-hoppers, people who needed tents and camels. Here in Australia the blackfellas had made a go of this land because it supported some life; the bare minimum. They could still be part of the landscape, like the Kandengeis.

Winking glass, leaves that were spindles, spokes, pins. Always with an edge, something to get back at the world with. Abandoned fencing wire looked at home here.

I expected Wiluna – Wiluna the 'trouble spot', Wiluna where you wouldn't want to bring up children – to loom. To be something substantial, robust in the desiccating lands. It did not loom. It began with what looked like electric wiring running along the road from thin tree trunks and I wasn't sure if the wiring was left from another era, or still someone's connected supply. Some whitefella might be out in the desert depending on these brittle tree trunks, the thin lines. The whole of Wiluna might be.

Now we were where the town used to be.[12] The ground was not dust and bushes, it was broken cement blocks, bricks and enamelled tiles – dust flowing over, reclaiming them all. That was the old Wiluna, the Wiluna of the good days of gold mining.[13] The first building was there on our right. It stood alone, surrounded by more foundations and a car that looked as if it had been in an inner city riot. 'You do your shopping there,' Herbie said. 'It's the community store. Owned . . . run for . . .' – he didn't seem to be able to get the right word – 'it belongs to the blackfellas.' A whitefella came out from the side office with a clip board.

Herbie said that straight ahead there had been the Lakeway Hotel. 'Pulled down last week. Too dangerous.'

The town is still falling, then, I thought.

We turned left. There was another patch of rubble on the left, then a wired-in house. Opposite was a police station, which had a lawn, the first bright green. On it were the first blackfellas. They looked drawn out of the desert just to be on this little patch of hose-sprinkled vegetation, this oasis.

'They're prisoners,' Herbie said. 'Police don't bother locking them up – there's nowhere to run to.'

On the left, more desert, bottle glass twinkling, and then an altogether more substantial building.

'That's the pub.'

All larger downstairs windows had been boarded up. The main entrance had a wooden bar across it and a protective layer of chicken wire. The back entrance was beyond a gate. I could just see the swirl of a lawn spray and a pub garden, a German shepherd dog on a long chain. Two whitemen with bush hats were coming out, talking to one another out of pursed lips, as if to keep the flies out, though there were few flies. All the blackfellas, however, were slumped in the street or among the building-site rubble of what had once been houses.

'That's what we call the bus stop. People wait there for the pub to open, then they can go and buy piss.'

There was no one waiting at the bus stop just now. Across the wide street, beer cans crunching under our wheels, was the little post office, a hole in its prefabricated wall and a note, 'Souvenir of street drinking in Wiluna'. Otherwise the bulk of Wiluna was widely spaced iron-roofed houses, and the spaces yawned open like gaps left by the fallen among ranked soldiers.

'Best not to go to the Club bar. Not the black side. The white side is all right, but on the black side, even if you're not scared, they'll rid you of all your money – take it out of your pockets; take a drink out of your hand.'

Again he must be exaggerating to prepare me. I must still look as bewildered as I did on my arrival in Australia. Putting a brave face on it, I said actually Wiluna seemed pleasantly quiet to me. A child was scuffing in a ditch, another climbing a fence into someone's back garden. A car of blackfellas swerves over the road.

'You wait till pension day, every other Thursday.'

'Black Thursday?'

'Today, they've all just taken their piss into the bush.'

The pub backed on to the desert, so we turned right, through the few rows of pretty tin housing. They ended in bulldozed rubble that merged into the desert again. That was Wiluna.

Herbie invited me in for a couple of fried eggs.

'The main rule is this. Don't intervene in any fighting. You'll see some ugly things here when they've been throwing piss against the wall – that means drinking. Just back off, right?'

That was his final advice. He'd pick me up tomorrow and take me along to meet Graham, son of the dead leader. He'd get Kalu to show me where I could stay while I got my feet.

Herbie had been good to me, I decided, as Kalu took me away. I had brought no car, or food. My face looked a mess from the forest and the sea crossing, and I didn't seem to know what I was doing here. To him I must have looked like a Pommy bludger of just about the lowest order.

Kalu, a Nigerian, took me to the store in his car, and waited outside, pacing about, bothered by the world. 'You don't seem to appreciate that you've got to look after yourself – plan. It's the weekend coming up.'

The store had meat, cheese, vegetables, cereals, eggs – everything. I filled up a box.

Drunk blackfellas were plodding around the store, men and women who were clutching at shelves to steady themselves, blood oozing from their eyebrows, crusts of old conflicts in their hair. A drunk girl had just dropped a school exercise book into the freezer and looked as if she might easily be about to have a baby. The checkout woman said, 'They can be a real delight.' I smiled warily. Was she taking the micky?

While she was adding my stores up, I noticed there were typed letters pinned up on the wall, some of them posted a month ago and still not collected. 'Sambo, Left Hand,' the computer address label said. 'Native Reserve, Wiluna 6646', also 'Teddy Bear' at the same address. 'Killer', 'Hitler'.

I turn to find my way blocked by a woman. She is purple-black. Her hair is hung as if she doesn't care, as if she's mad. She hangs in her dress loosely.

'Two dollar,' she says, closing up to me as if starting to confide a story. But she's not going to say anything more. That was the end of her life story – two dollars.

'Two dollar what?' I say.

She puts out her hand, waiting for me to accept something.

She must have just received her welfare payment. I say, 'I couldn't accept anything. Thanks anyway. I'll be all right.'

'Two dollar.'

I look at her hand. Empty. She's waiting for my money. Yet her hand is cleaner than mine. She doesn't have lips that are whitened and coming away in chunks. Her hair is fairly clean, unlike mine, with its last salty knots. Her feet aren't dusty, unlike mine. Like me she doesn't have any socks, but she's wearing good town shoes, not ones that have been carried through forest, and are held together with blue nylon that used to support Tsogamoi's mosquito net.

'Two dollar,' she says unashamed, her hand steady.

'Quite,' I reply. Luckily, the checkout woman then introduced herself. She was Nola, from New Zealand. She was tall and bright, with long, straight, centre-parted hair and a red scarf around her neck.

Kalu was waiting outside, revving the engine, so I said I'd better go. A dead-eyed black woman was half blocking the doorway. A man with one leg lay against her.

'A delight, a real delight,' Nola called after me. 'I beg you not to listen to what you might hear from whitefellas. Just judge for yourself.'

Kalu took me out of Wiluna, to the Community Office at the 'village', some Aboriginal housing twenty kilometres up a bush road. He left me to myself. I found a kitchen with an oven that worked, and – chucking aside the mattress – floor space to sleep on. In the dusk, I took a walk around the house. Dust-thick cobwebs flapped like rags in the eves. Garbage ran in the wind instead of leaf litter.

I stopped to watch a blue-headed parrot flashing its green wings against the bare sky. It was spectacularly vivid out here in the emptiness; it seemed profoundly alive. Signs of life, the parrot reminded me, were magnified by the desert. The same with my footprints in the sand that the wind had stacked against the house. They were bolder than any in the forest; in the desert they seemed as loud as astronaut prints in moon dust. The stripped cars at rest, inverted, between the scrub trees became like graffiti – cries from the unheard.

Despite everyone's efforts, I was still a *buskanaka*, an innocent from the forest. It was just how it should be. I'd arrived in the middle of Australia more or less unscathed by the whitefellas' plans for me, still much in my original dreamy state. Only now was I fully waking up.

*   *   *

The wind whistles. A rope swings from a branch, kicks to be free. Bundles of dust wheel along the road. Gusts make the sound of fast passing cars. Parrots with yellow collars and green backs and chests scrape their beaks with their black toes and flash blue feathers as they take off. A wagtail side-steps, flipping up for the insects with light tosses of itself into the air. The alien, dumped cars shine from a matt textured view – Kingswoods, Holdens, Falcons – curvaceous bodies of the fifties and sixties.

It was eight in the morning according to the clock on the oven, and Herbie was due along to introduce me to Graham, son of the unmentionable elder.

A rabbit hopped out from under the house. I cornered it, and then realized I wasn't armed. Then I remembered I'd bought food in the store yesterday. 'We're not in the jungle now, Benedict,' I reminded myself.

Herbie came in a white Land Cruiser and took me along the road to the 'village', which turned out to be a lot of prefabricated houses purpose-built for Aboriginals. They lay in an extended line, white concrete heat and dust traps. Many of them had been abandoned.

'The blackfellas won't live in a house where someone's died,' Herbie said. That accounted for some of the empty houses, anyway.

There might have been gardens once; now there were patches that blended with the scrub and beer can litter, differentiated from the bush only because they bore iron beds and bare mattresses. Skinny dogs ran in packs; fat black ladies raised floppy wrists over their eyes to look at me. The tobacco-toned, knotted hair of children parted in the cool morning wind. Men sat on plastic stools, looking as if they'd been there for days.

Herbie draws up at a house and tells me, 'Wait!' From his tone, I might be expected to draw up my windows and lock the doors. He sits down in the porch with three youngish men. Wind flaps their hair – dry hanks that have a fleecy quality from the grease.

Herbie calls me. I weave through the bedsteads, some of which are still occupied, keeping my hands up, out of the reach of the dogs that are trailing me. In front of everyone, Herbie says, 'Just be straight. Be honest. Tell them exactly what you want.'

It wasn't as easy as he thought. I had come here to show I was a Junior Man, because the desert would recognize one as well as the forest. But it was not a good opening gambit.

Herbie gave me his chair. I shook hands. Graham was big, with sideburns splashing down his face; there was Bruce, a brother, with cheeky, evasive eyes, and another, who moved his stool back. He didn't think he was meant to be part of this.

Theoretically, I told myself, I should be able to lift the tension – the Amazon, Irian Jaya, PNG, I was a veteran of the alien place. I was an expert at these introductions. But none of the usual rules were going to apply. They had seen more than enough of whitefellas. I had no novelty value, my white skin didn't promise wealth, because theoretically they had plenty of it themselves in welfare benefits. Here the white skin was just a reminder of broken promises and that they needed whitefella's rights – land rights, human rights, civil rights.

We sit, embarrassed.

Herbie says, 'Well, I'll leave you. Perhaps you could take him along to old Dusty.' He goes. The third blackfella seizes the chance and goes as well.

I made a soliloquy to cover the silence. Graham did his best as well. We have a ridiculous quarter of an hour of nothingness, talking about 'bush tucker'. I found out that kangaroo meat was plentiful out here, rabbit meat was too dry. A man called Dusty might take me out. Finally, Graham suggests he drops me at the general store. I might catch Dusty.

At the store, blackfellas are buying bananas, soft drinks, biscuits, frozen meat. An old man with a red pyjama cord around his forehead, his trouser hems in the dust, belt low-slung, puts out his tummy and urinates in the doorway. I stand about outside, smiling awkwardly at the blackfellas. They wear Wild West clothes and the men have beards like Buffalo Bill's. None of the adults walk straight. They are drunk, or have legs in bandages, wrists in plaster, babies to carry. Only the children, blowing up plastic balloons and popping them, walk upright.

A stick-limbed drunk gives a jubilant cackle – 'Hai-aa-aa!' – putting a banana at his groin and waving it up and down at the children, who laugh, their bright eyes and teeth giving off a white light from their black skin.

A man in green and brown uniform, hair silver, of military cut, olive skin, stalks about. His fringe is high, dead straight. I ask if he is a policeman. He smiles. He holds his belt. 'No, I'm with the Adventist Church.' He says the mission has been closed. He's here doing pastoral care. He bends over, and begins to bag the tin cans around the store. There must be five thousand in the immediate vicinity.

Every half-hour, Kalu goes by in his car, delivering Community mail, while I stand around waiting for Dusty and trying to be friendly. The blackfellas say hello, seeing me smile. They want to be friendly as well. But after that, after one or two words, they seem stumped for something to say.

On his fifth pass, Kalu pulls up. 'Dusty won't come now. You might as well go home.' He gives me a lift. We pass some whitefellas doing Shire Council road repairs. Kalu blows his top, biffing the steering wheel. 'What are these people *doing*?'

'Re-doing the road?' I suggest. It is the wrong suggestion.

'They're destroying the environment!' We slow to watch the caterpillar tracks biting into the dirt, and the diggers digging and shifting it a few yards, widening the road by dislodging the top soil, which looks the same as the bottom soil. 'Robbing the poor – it's always, always, the rich feeding off the poor.'

'A little simplistic?'

'It makes me so sick!'

Circuiting round to the town again, he says the soil is more fertile than you'd think. Rock melons grew beautifully here, and they had a community project growing oranges, and then there was the emu farm. 'Ozone layer, greenhouse effect. The Sahel drought, the Ethiopian famine. It's the same – the rich killing the rest.' His white teeth are flashing, his eyes small, glasses capping them smoothly. Broadly, I agree with him. But he doesn't mention other possible causes of climatic change, nor that the tribes in Africa have always made empires of each other's tribes. He is too busy with his cause; he has come here with an activist's tribal values, a warrior of the four-wheel drive.

He stopped at the post office. While he was talking to a whitefella behind the counter, I stood outside being sworn at by a chirpy drunk black lady. 'You fackin'!' Her nose has some time ago been sliced off. And put back on. The join wasn't quite flush.

I retreat down the road – men are starting to shout at me as well, now, and though I'm pleased to find I'm not exactly scared, this is my first day and I don't feel like spoiling it with drunks. But a man is coming up from the store with a three-foot boomerang in his belt. He stands in my way. 'Dollar!' When I say no, he is not angry. He says, 'Naaaa!', as if agreeing with me. It was a disgusting idea. 'Dow-nne madder.' Doesn't matter.

A few seconds later, he asked for two dollars. Then twenty dollars. He was urinating, not bothering to turn away, and rocking in the breeze because of the drink. He pulled up the zipper of his blue jeans. The entire crutch was wet. He put in more bids for money and winced, blaming himself, after each rejection. 'Naaaa!' He put his thumb to his mouth, mimicking the drunks. 'Rubbish!'

A flat-faced blackfella waves me over from the kerb, where he sits opposite the Club Hotel. I walk away, feeling tired of Wiluna. Across the road at the post office, it looked as though Kalu wanted to leave. Let's get out of here, I thought.

'Ah! So you've found Dusty!' Kalu said.

He was looking at the man on the kerb, the 'bus stop', playing cards with the drunks. I went back and Dusty offered me a space in the road. They didn't squat, the way forest people do, keeping their backsides off the damp ground, they sat cross-legged. Dusty was relaxed with me. He said he'd trained up many a whitefella as a stockman. He had pitted nose and cheeks and a good shine off the skin. Maybe he'd take me into the bush one day, he said. He got up and walked away, bow-legged, saying he'd be back soon. I was left among the drunks.

The man with the boomerang took me aside. 'Ten dollar,' he said, 'End-o-lat.'

He sat himself down on 'Glass hill', a little mound by the pub. I sat down with him. I had nothing to lose. He took off his shoe and slipped it under me as a cushion. I refused it politely, handing back the little child's lace-up. We sat in the sun together again and he talked in badly broken English and also his own language,[14] and scratched his arm with bottle glass, drawing his name on the black surface. I noticed his hands were dry, not sweating in the heat like mine.

'So what are you trying to prove here?' The question came from a whitefella drawing up in a car. He drove off when some blackfellas started to move in. The blackfellas took up the whitefella's question, surrounding me on the hill. I moved off to the protective wall of the pub, pressing myself back against the black, easy-to-scrub-down surface. 'What you tryn' ta prove?' one man shouted, more insistent than the others. After a while he stopped to vomit down the wall instead.

I walked back to the store.

A whitefella speeds up in the Health Centre car. Opens the side doors. Two men slowly get out. They are shaking uncontrollably. With walking frames, they shake themselves over to the store porch. The whitefella, the doctor, has the amazed, strained eyes of a man who has been to an all-night cinema. He says he's Dave. 'Been up all night stitching,' he says.

'I'm messed up,' one of the shaking patients says in my ear, as I lean back against the store. 'Used to drive a truck . . . before.' The words get shaken as they come out. He knows he is unintelligible. He shouts sentences two or three times, even if you have by chance understood first go. 'They've . . . go--oonn to-oo dinni--nner,' he says as the store is closed and bolted.

Rob, the store manager, came outside and said, 'A word in your ear. That's Jackie Stevens you were talking to up by the pub. A pisshead. Don't waste your time with him.'

Rob was a sharp-looking man – moustached, neat, narrow-faced, a disciplined talker. He said he was being pressured by Graham to employ blacks only. 'But I tell him, Benedict, "Graham, I'll give them a try any time, but they can't take it. One day here, and they're finished."'

He employed part-Aboriginals like Natalie, daughter of Ralf Bell, one of the police aides – at the last count, Wiluna had four policemen, two police aides. Also employed were the Pakistani wife of the Pakistani accountant of the council, and Nola the New Zealander. There was also Steve, with a weight problem. He had a centre parting in the mousy hair that hung down to his shoulders and his belly drooped to his crutch. His calves were so large he had to swing out his legs to walk. Though he was at least Australian, he, like nearly everyone else, was an outsider.

Nola comes dashing out of a side door. She's wearing flared shorts, desert grey, and her red-and-white spotted neckerchief; hair in a pony tail. 'You're not leaving for Jigalong, are you?'

'You think I'd give up half-way through my first day?'

'Some people do,' she said. 'No, I just heard a rumour.'

I told her I would hang on.

She ran to her car, apparently excited by this.

Her optimism, her faith in the blackfellas despite all the apparent evidence, spurred me on. I walked up to the pub again. But wasn't I also here to prove something? I was just another outsider, like the sociologists and missionaries, using the Aboriginals to justify my tribe's existence. Trying to prove myself for my tribe – which just happened to be a forest tribe, Kandengei of all places, not a whitefella one.

The smell of beer and urine rose in the heat. From a radio in the white bar the ABC news said that three men in a fibreglass dinghy were missing in Moon Passage. A near miss, that one, I thought.

But Wiluna was hotting up.

'Don't hit him!' A woman waddled up, shifting her fat uneasily. She screamed it again. 'DON'T HIT HIM!' She was waving at me – I was the one about to be hit.

This man was too drunk to strike. A little fly sat in the nook of his eye as he swore and waved his fists. More and more men and women came at me. They told me their names, bickered and fought over me. Then they asked if I remembered their names. 'Remind me,' I said, lightly, appeasing again. When one man or woman tried to tell me, they were lost under the deluge of other blackfellas, each interrupting and irritated if I didn't reply. Men hit women, women hit men. Sometimes they used their fists, making loud thumps, other times iron fence posts. The faces came at me – a round face, dark eyes deep under a brow like a thatched eave, old eyes like burnished leather. As another woman screeched, I watched saliva trickle down her lips, and turn red as it picked up the dust towards her chin. How much more independent the women were here than at Kandengei, I thought. Would Starlight ever have approached me like this?

'Hello darlin'. Howa you goin'? All right?'

'All right,' I replied to them. 'And you?' They were taken aback that I asked.

'Yes,' they'd say. 'I'm all right.'

There was a woman with educated English who had a face with flesh creased in two spots around wounds. I will call her Rose, because I can't remember her name – maybe it's as well. She was plump, in her teens, but with a wispy beard below her chin, growing like moss in a cool, shaded niche. 'People have written bad things about us. They are saying that we fight white people. But no one has hit you yet, have they?'

'Not yet, no.'

I spotted the Adventist man far off, collecting flattened beer cans into a bag. He looked like a beachcomber, lonely. She laughed, and her accent relaxed. 'He been here three weeks only,' she said.

She told me that whitefellas were always getting lost in the bush. 'We go and get the dead bodies.'

I said I was sure the next of kin appreciated it.

Rose nodded. 'We are good people.'

The little girls were telling their mothers not to swear, the next age group up were rolling around the porch posts, incoherent, draining another can. By their teens they were punching the men. By adulthood they were fighting their own toddlers.

A whitefella drew up. He had a licence to shoot kangaroos and was selling tails off the back of his van, his 'ute'. He stayed in his car, as the previous whitefellas had done. The blackfellas went over to buy the tails, carrying them away in newspaper on their shoulders, eating into the raw meat which smelt strong in the dry air. Then they regrouped around me. 'I'm a Lawman. I've been through it,' a youth said, and stumbled away to begin a fight.

Another youth walked out into the road and faced him. They both yanked their cowboy shirts off, and squared off in mid-street, just like the Wild West. They boxed in classical style, looking noble with their Queensberry stance and posturing fists. Jackie Stevens was at my side. 'Pllleeee-eeeess!' He nudged me. Gave a soft wink. He was shoved out of the way by other, less polite beggars.

A voice shouted at me. 'Hey!' He rocked the sentence up and down, giving it the local rhythm. 'I was talkin' to you!' It was the youth who had gone off to fight earlier. The other was lying on his face in the road. No one had picked him up. The youth had a curly mop of hair. He jabbed a grey-haired man who had a red band around his forehead. 'Aborigine style,' the youth said. 'He's from the Ward mob, like me.' They stand together, both missing an upper front tooth – knocked out during a Law ceremony.[15] The old man, taking a prompt, gave me a genial smile and said, 'Dollars!' Sorry, I said. The youth said, 'I've felt all the pain.' He pulled his father's shirt up. The drunk man grinned foolishly. I looked at the scars across his black chest, horizontal bars that were neither as pretty nor as extensive as my nice crocodile marks. 'They've ripped off my fackin' foreskin. They've cut my cock open.'

I went to the whitefella's bar, round the back of the hotel. I needed peace, just to gather myself. There was only one other customer. He sat on his stool, his hat down, almost touching the bar. He looked fresh from the desert, although not so fresh, perhaps. A television set rambled on. Here the air was cool and static. I glimpsed through to the blackfella's bar, saw Jackie Stevens, and felt like a traitor. The barman said, 'Fishing for stories, eh?'

'I only arrived yesterday afternoon,' I said. 'Everyone seems to know about me already.'

The man on the stool said, 'What do you know about anything here? You were asking for Dusty at the store, weren't you? Biggest bullshitter in town. You'll be on to the sandalwood mob next! Yeah, you're going about this all the wrong way, mate.'

'I've only just arrived.'

'You're a rubberneck,' the man said, under his hat.

The barman said to me, softer, 'That's a tourist.'

'A blow-through,' the hat said.

'That's a –' But I wasn't listening. I left after one beer, passing old black and white photos of Wiluna – camels, aloof, carts of sheep wool bales. Tired, wrung-out lands, empty then, empty now.[16]

Rose was now getting herself involved in her own fight. She was accosting a woman who was lolling on her back between two men. 'You fackin' drunk. Why don't you fackin' go home instead of fackin' showin' what you've fackin' got. Put your fackin' dress down!'

The women went into a bit of unoccupied road and wrestled over an iron bar. Rose got the worst of it, but took the blows in silence. A passing police Land Rover stopped. The whitefella, again remaining in the car, took the metal stick in through the window and drove off.

Dave, the health man, swerved up in his car. He looked out through the waving sticks and fists, through tonight's patients. 'Just a word. Watch yourself next week. After pension day. OK? This is nothing.' He drove off.

At last I found a haven. I'd spotted a large man with placid eyes who didn't drink and who pushed the drunks off gently with his large forearms. He was Cyril Claw, he said; I sat beside him on a crate. He had a bobble hat and sideburns that were grey along the fan edge. He said maybe I could come along and visit him, some time, for a yarn.

Unfortunately, his brother Eric was with us. He was on crutches and looked like a cowboy cult exhibit – the hat, the moustache, the chequered shirt, jeans. 'You here to cause trouble?' he asked. Cyril said, 'Don't be like that. Let the whitefella come along for a yarn.'

A truck went by. On the back amongst a heap of blackfellas a three-year-old slashed at an orange with a carving knife. A fat girl threw an orange at the chasing dogs. Everyone else began throwing oranges too. A thought crossed my mind. Nomads revelling in the lack of desert shortage, I thought. Wiluna suddenly was that – not simply the hellhole the whitefellas found it but a fantasy, one big feast in an oasis.

'Cyril,' I said. 'By the way, what's a "blow-through"?'

'He's a passer-by, innee?'

Eric said he thought he was.

'Just wondering.'

Rose was standing over us. For no very good reason, she lifted out one of her breasts. It was very full and long, tubular, with a sausage's firmness of skin. After a while, she squeezed it back in.

'Can I come along tomorrow?' I said.

Eric Claw said I'd best be careful if I was going to write a book. They were going to give the last man who came a rough time if he ever came back.[17] 'If you want to learn from us, you gotta become like us,' Eric said. Both men agreed. It sounds like a joke – all around were blacks laid to waste.

I walked out of Wiluna, back towards the village, through the bush. It was sundown. There was about twenty kilometres to walk, but I didn't care. The desert was quiet, the desert was calm. I listened to the wind, and my feet on the dust, happy to hear the screams of Wiluna recede behind me. I walked past the last iron roofs. After the rust on the roofs, the rust on the sand.

Wiluna was a focus of loose tribal energy, forces that could work for me or against me, I thought. That might be useful at one stage, but I wasn't ready to handle them yet. I could be pleased that I wasn't too afraid of the other Junior Men, and their sticks. I thought I might be able to handle them. But at the moment I'd be wasting my time here. I didn't even know my surroundings, these sands that had produced the blackfellas of Wiluna. I'd go to the desert, understand that first, I thought. I had seen the blackfellas drinking and eating as if at an oasis, and I had seen the men and women playing cards and drinking together as if in foraging groups, back from hunting berries or lizards – the only difference was that they had benefit money in their hands.

Further out, as the sun went down in the bush, a car screeched up. Kalu. '*What* are you doing? It's twenty kilometres to the village.'

I said I knew. And I had fifteen to go. I wasn't scared of the dark.

'What happened to Dusty?'

'Oh yes, Dusty.' I'd forgotten about him. I said, 'I left him gambling.'

'Your behaviour is not really rational,' Kalu said, waving me aboard. 'What precise arrangements have you made with him?'

None, I explained, succinctly. Kalu looked ready to despair. 'No car, nowhere to stay. What else haven't you got?' Luckily, I could say I had boots and a water bottle. He dumped me back at the Ngangganawili Community Office, where the only sound was the wind and the lawn sprinkler that had been left on.

The next morning, a Sunday, I had a chance to use my water bottle and special desert boots. I took a short cut through the bush to Wiluna. Not having forest trees to block the sun, it was easy to navigate.

So I was alone out here in the desert, at last. I looked around at it – leather wallets that were the carcasses of birds, lizards that ran high off the hot sand. Despite my clanking water bottle, and my thumping boots, I surprised two groups of kangaroo. What I later learnt was a spotted nightjar, a grey speckled bird with an owl face, eyes with a predator's lustre, rose up and dropped to the stone litter. I was charmed.

But the charm was an impulse, nothing sustainable, I decided, putting away the water bottle and changing back to my light shoes. The desert had a feeling of aftermath, of violence done. In the forest this feeling would have been seen in something more tangible – the signs of a scuffle, of distress, of leaves ripped off, of a scene abandoned.

Looking around, winds desiccated anything not tightly sealed. Links between the living were unpredictable – there was waste here, dead ends. The desert was a land of food chain breakages. Species at the beginning of the chain – insects, sedges started from scratch, with hardly a soil, occasionally in the right place at the right time to catch a casualty to the elements. I stared at the land, ran my fingers over the rocks – the rough side, then the wind-polished side – or cracked open a leaf. From the forest I had come to a land of stones, the same objects that gave Kandengei time, a sense of permanency, the same objects that

I had collected as a boy. The barren territory was the right place to be. Its dry air was going to be good for the memory; I could feel it chasing out the clinging forest, clearing my head.

I remembered, as a boy, the smell of oil shale on my fingers, the brittle clatter of pebbles running down a blue sea-cliff as I scurried with my hammer. In choosing this land of stones, I had come to the right place.

Chapter Eight

A TASTE OF THE WIND

Cyril Claw's house had a bad view. That is, it looked out on Wiluna – the scenes of refuse, the landscapes of decay. Beer cans rocked in the lee of the bashed-in fences. Cars sat here and there like crushed beetles. Dogs clambered in and out; upholstery spewed into the wind.

Over by Cyril's house, a woman was sitting on a bed in the sunshine, a man beneath her. Cyril was sitting in the porch, waking up. 'The dogs'll skin your legs,' he called. I came through unscathed, swinging my special desert boots in my hands – the only use I ever found for them. We sat together, around us graffiti which was just lists of signatures in felt tip – the clans, family groups.

Red-dusted cobwebs slapped like human flab as the breeze took up. I knew Cyril wanted to help, as Graham Richards had, but there was the same shyness between us. And, I was sure, there was something else.

Cyril yarned with dedication, aiming to please. First, memorable times he'd had in the bush – a snake that went up a man's trousers as he lay asleep by the camp fire. No one would help. 'Weren't game, see.'

I quite saw. And the man had to wait until the sun came up – the snake came out with the heat.

Then, memorable times in Wiluna. These led up to the present – last night, when some blackfellas broke into the pub. Children were fed through a broken window to pass the drink out. Cyril himself had got three months for doing that, once – Whitefella's Law.

I looked around this gypsy camp – the blankets flapping, the Emu cans rolling in the wind. The unculled dogs mewed and fought and whimpered and ran with passing cars as men and women slept off yesterday's booze.

In the old days, Cyril said, starting up again, his father's time, they would cut off an enemy's head, bury the body in a pit, pack sand around with fire at the base. He was cooked and ready to eat when the blood boiled out of the neck stump – that was how you knew.

A man with a red cowboy hat, 'SAM' written across it in capitals, came to yarn as well. He had a stick, with which he pressed my leg, gently, for attention, and told me half stories. 'That's it,' he said, half-way through each. He tapped his ear. 'Memory gone.' It was the grog. He had drunk two flagons and a case and ended up in hospital for four months. When he 'woke up' an Adventist friend by his bedside said, 'Don't thank me, thank der one on top.' That was how he got converted. He gave up kangaroos – unclean – and used to attend the Adventist church every Saturday. The missionaries had even given him a date of birth – 1 January. It was same with all the old people, here: 1 January.

On TV, it was Bugs Bunny. Men got out of bed to come and laugh at the cartoon rabbit. Children ran in as well, looking in at the fridge as they passed. In it there were kangaroo quarters, not yet skinned, a large block of ice, and an emu.

Sam showed me the bisymmetrical stitching up the centre of his chest, like a zip. He had been fed through a throat hole and it had ruined his voice box. 'I can't even sing now,' a sad little voice said.

A whirlwind blows cards from a woman's lap. She picks up most, and I run off to stop more, stamping on them. But when I come back she's carrying on playing. She thanks me, but then lets them fly free. Other household items follow the cards – buckets, the flour tin seats, cushions. Everything gallops off and they let them.

More blackfellas were waking. They dreamily chucked biscuits at the kangaroo dogs. When the police came to round them up, they hid the dogs away, Cyril said.

I wasn't going to get anywhere. I'd sensed it before. There was somewhere a division between us. Cannibals, head-hunters the New Guineans might be, but they weren't so different from Westerners. The Kandengeis balanced themselves with nature, that was all. They had a mixed market economy, they had buildings, relied on trade. But these hunting, gathering wanderers were different. Almost all they had was in their heads – their entire history and impression of the world. I saw that they were kindly telling me stories because they wanted me happy. It was a bush welcome for a stranger. But there was somewhere a deeper division to cross, perhaps their Law, but certainly into the world that nomads had to carry around in their heads.

'What are the chances of me getting a blackfella to show me around the bush?' I asked Cyril.

He suggested Dusty. I said Dusty hadn't seemed all that enthusiastic. I sat some more with Cyril and Sam, blown by the wind, smelling the reek of meat and blood from the fridge, until Cyril said that the man living opposite – beyond the bedsteads, ruptured cars and children and adults lying like tramps in blankets, he meant – was in charge of the project to gather sandalwood from the desert.

I walked over. Kenny Farmer's house was much like Cyril's, a relic of the whitefella days, probably with another overhead fan not fixed since it broke a generation or two ago. However, the garden fence was still standing in place, and a lot of children wearing bright new clothes were running about, pulling each other's hair out. A white truck roared in as I came near, distracting the dogs. The driver looked a clean-living man – an Adventist, I decided.

He jumped down from the cab. He was a short blackfella, dressed with none of the cowboy gear. We introduced ourselves, and I asked if I could go with him. I didn't give a reason. He prodded the bunch of small warts, black polyps at the crook between his nose and brow. He wasn't suspicious, wondering if this was worth it to him – so far here I had never been aware of the *payback* system of the forests. He was just seeing whether it was practicable. 'Yeah, come along. Learn a bit about the bush tucker.'

The bush tucker was his idea. He had decided I must be going to do something, and learning about food in the bush was as likely an objective as any other.

And so the desert, opposite pole to the forest, drew me out to it.

On the Monday, Kenny Farmer loaded up fresh supplies for the sandalwood mob. I bought my own food, and at the checkout Nola mentioned that on Saturday she'd woken up and found a child curled up asleep on the floor of her house, a six-year-old boy. He'd been left for the weekend with no food or parents. 'Happens a lot, like that,' she said. She went outside with some food to give to some of the oldfellas, whose pension had long since been utilized by the younger men.

I climbed into the cabin with a squat, amiable man called Albert – 'Albert Jonathan Charles Ingram' it said in biro across his denim jacket, and Jonny Long, who spoke good English and was handsome and tall and had a friendly beard of silver and black and a little horseshoe in his left ear, attached by a large clip. Last in was a stumpy, groomed dog called Bruno. Kenny was at the wheel.

We drove off down the Gunbarrel Highway, passed Bondini, the reserve, passed the turn off to the Village and on towards Mungale, the sandalwood camp.

A wedge-tailed eagle lifted from a fresh kangaroo corpse on the road; a large gold and black lizard, its skin looking thick and dry, like a worn tyre tread, ran across the ruts, the two barrels of the straight road. An oil patch deepened the colours in the dirt, and firmed up the car marks, giving an illusion of water, of life.

This is an old place, I thought. I get the feeling it is a root, a stump – an old mountain ground down to nothing. That's how it feels, very ancient and probably wise. It's going to be extremely broadening for me. But still the desert was a remote thing – it was alien and sterile, and unlike the forest, which thrust down on you, it gave off nothing. It sucked on you. I could feel this through the windscreen, the pressure difference between the jungle and so much barrenness. I so wanted to be released out there.

The men sat in silence looking out through the window. Sometimes, when we saw an animal, they made a little sign in their lap, a hand signal such as a person stalking game might make. A kangaroo – palm upwards, end two knuckles curled in, forearm waved up and down. A turkey – a curled finger held up; a hand wiggled for a snake.

The sun set, flaring into a yellow dust, dying into a blue band; then there was just the immensity of the sky and the studs for stars.

'We'll camp here,' Kenny said. It was a simple matter, with nothing more said. We pulled over to the side and laid ourselves out on our bedding.

In the morning the wind was bitter. Walking around I saw a dead cow. Her skin was as dry as clay. Her eyes hadn't been pecked out by birds, they were still looking up, like stained glass. The tongue was out, brown with dust and stretched into the sand as if she had died licking.

Coming back to the truck, over the hoof-compacted ground, the other three men were gathered around an empty cattle stockade, fighting to free a kangaroo from the metal bars, yanking it out by the tail. Albert chased it into the shade. 'Git owd of it, you bastard!' He was desperate to give it a chance. In New Guinea, in Sumatra, in the Amazon forests, you'd have walked right on by, or else eaten it.

We came off the Gunbarrel Highway and along a side track. We must be nearing Mungale now, and I said to Kenny, 'You sure no one's going to mind me being here? I mean they don't know me.'

'You're all right.'

In the road there was a beheaded snake; it looked like an oily tow rope. 'We only eat the large ones,' Jonny said, as Kenny pulled the truck off the road. 'Python, ya know?'

There was a lone windpump and a water tank that had broken open. The debris had flooded out and long since dried into a sludge of small bird skulls that looked like lost golf balls. Further off was a large new metal shed and, in between, the camp, an open space with a crowd of about twenty men and women rising from a fire. The stark trees around the camp were hung with inverted tin cups and hunks of emu – I recognized the yellow bubbles of emu fat from Cyril's broken fridge. Canvas sheets flapped from a few trees as windbreaks and even where securely fastened they had an untidy lean; there were no neat sapling-string knots, no thatchings, just the odd branch pulled over.

The crowd came up, half-running, as I jumped down. They ran right on by, stampeding to the back of the truck, and the stores. 'Cordial! Cordial!' Two youths and a young woman grabbed the lemon barley water and raspberry concentrate. 'Weeties!' And they swiped the breakfast cereal. The older people were ripping open cardboard boxes of fruit and vegetables – tomatoes, apples, pears.

Every member of the camp now had his pile. They gathered them up – Fray Bentos steak and kidney pies, tomatoes, flour, onions, apples, eggs – and took them back to the fireplace. Next they shared them all out again.

They had been about to settle to a vast afternoon meal – a kangaroo had just been brought out of the ashes. We had interrupted them. And before Kenny could introduce me they began on the kangaroo. We stood around waiting, Kenny rolling his thumbs over his tummy, smiling at me every now and then, awkward at the lack of welcome for a whitefella. Now Jonny had joined in and now Albert and they were adding more food to the menu – 'weeties' were tipped out, steak after steak went on to the fire. They didn't want to be rude and both women and men did look up and smile, but it seemed it couldn't be helped. I had called at a vital moment. 'Come to the camp and read the papers!' laughed a youngish man to me. He favoured the wispy Spanish type of Wild West beard. He wore a silver ring in one ear, and one long curl at the nape; he had lost both front teeth.

'Noel,' nodded Kenny, standing by.

'Salt, salt!'

'Sugar, sugar!'

The sandalwood mob sat on the flour tins, Albert was getting puffed even carving up his chops. A clown-nosed man, with a deep double chin, the roll of fat rolling, unrolling, said to Albert, 'Give yourself a shave, clean yourself up, then women will *like* you!'

Kenny said, 'That's Simon.'

Albert gave back a heavy stare, like a show wrestler, and the men and women laughed, and he scowled, and they laughed again.

Another man, whose face was set in a sly squint, only one eye fully open, said, pointing an elbow at Rusty, the little pet dog,

'Brought that mongrel with you, have you? Good, he'll do as a rug.'

'Russel,' said Kenny. As the meal broke up, Russel was the first to come to shake my hand.

'Any strangers in town?' he asked Kenny.

'Only me,' I said. At that moment everyone, it seemed, looked up. They smiled – not mocking. Theirs seemed to be the white Australian type of humour, but a squeeze less dry. And they felt happier now that I'd made a contribution. Far from ignoring me, they'd been waiting.

Looser about talking now, they went on to tease Albert about the hotel drink robbery, and the forlorn efforts of the police. 'They can always get you for *receiving*, mate. Stealing is only three months!'

In the afternoon, I walked about camp and, guided hesitantly by Kenny, made notes on the bush tucker. Then I drifted about, trying to learn my surroundings. I found the feet of the emu they had recently shot and made footprints with them across the sand. The sandalwood mob left me alone – Kenny had said I was here to learn the bush tucker and they let me get on with it. But all the time I knew I had to learn through the blackfellas and was wondering if the whitefellas back at Wiluna in the bar were right to laugh at me. Soon you'll be out with the sandalwood mob! they'd mocked. They thought they weren't traditional blackfellas, because Kenny was a churchman and the men with him had got themselves into action like whitefellas.

But I had seen them in Wiluna – the foraging behaviour of the drinkers, I had seen the disregard for housing, their gypsy camp manners – and I bided my time, watching the sandalwood mob settle down to work, chipping and clunking bark off the wood while it was still soft with sap. They sat in a circle, in the shade of the shed. With axes, hammers, spanners they clubbed away, and days passed while I watched them, seeing them in their whitefella shirts and with their truck and whitefella business but still hunters and gatherers, the men leaving to hunt down more sandalwood trees and the women in camp cooking or pottering off to look for fruit and insects.

Their story, unwritten for the forty or fifty thousand years they'd spent here, was now being written in the litter scattered downwind. The *Woman's Weeklys* that everyone liked to flick through, some wind-shredded cotton, a plastic bucket, a spare tyre. They stretched for miles, these bits of whitefella society, fewer and fewer items the further out you went until there was nothing – just the bush, their previous life, which had been stored in their heads, leaving no evidence but a few stone chips, perhaps the odd skeleton killed by a trained dingo, fur peeling off a kangaroo skeleton, a spinal column turning to chalk.

The first night I watched the grey-pink cockatoos, galahs, flock over the water pump. 'Good feed,' the men said, encouragingly, but not coming over.

'Kangaroo better,' said Russel, stirring another meal on the fire. This was only shyness, I hoped. Given a day or two we'd be over this. At dusk, Kenny tried his best to include me. He sat with his legs apart, a pudgy hand on his knee, other hand around a mug. He scratched his neck, looking for something to say, and when I said I'd lived in New Guinea he said 'Oh yeah?' Then we had to face the silence again.

So they then told me the names of the birds – the red-headed parrots, 'manjinjara', the topknot pigeon, 'koromidgi-midgi', the 'ganga', crows. They used to trap all these by placing bushes over the drinking holes to slow the birds' escape when startled.

The conversation couldn't be sustained. They told me about bloodsuckers, the March flies. Russel, the skew-faced man, chipped in, whistling past his single front tooth that burning dung kept away mosquitoes. The conversation wouldn't stretch further.

I sat beside Kenny, with his fists on his knees and his good-natured, implacable face suggesting fun another time, and looked at the group.

These women were fat – at least on first appearances. But actually the fat was distributed mainly on the shoulders, the bust and bottom, the low tummy. But though their heads were swallowed by their necks, Malala, on her knees clearing an oven space in the ashes, burrowing like a mole, had thighs like slack inner tubes. Her lips were moist lozenges; she had a mouth bowl the size of a bathroom sink plunger. Her creator had pressed his knuckles either side of her nose, squelching in the eyes, ejecting the brows, cheeks. She got up, walking unstably – too top-heavy. She urgently needed a third, tripod leg. She wore loose, sockless football boots, and at each step locked her foot flat down onto the ground. Her shoulder-fat mound swung like a camel's hump, riding loose as she walked. Around the fire, everyone gave her a good two feet clearance.

And while Malala ate and ate, gaining weight, being bound harder and harder to the earth, Margaret was, by contrast, verging on a doctor's recommended body weight. Given a balanced, moderate Western diet, she would have looked a skinny, fidgety type of person. The other two women were both young. Rhonda was a mother with a black eye and one entire leg in a plaster; her toddler child's footprints showed up their little creases and wrinkles in the sand. Then there was Elaine, a teenager who kept giving Jonny looks, up through her fringe. It was some time before I saw she was doing the same with Russel, even Albert, and in fact myself and all the other men.

The windpump slowed as the wind died, clanging, cranking slower now. The water ran away, pulsating from a hose, overflowing from a bathtub.

Michael, a youth trying to train his hair flat with water, said there had been another whitefella who had been interested in bush tucker. Clive.

The thinner woman, Margaret, who'd had one arm covered in flour all day, said to Jonny, 'Clive. Where ee from?'

'From the madhouse!'

Everyone thought this was very funny. 'He got nuttin' up 'ere,' Margaret said, pointing sharply at her head.

Clive had run a station nearby. He spoke the language and the elders had 'learned' him. He used to make tea from gum leaves; also sandalwood – certainly not *their* custom, Russel said, 'Tastes funny!'

Clive had also buried himself up to his head in sand. Meant to protect against the heat, Jonny said, shaking his head. Outside his station he'd put a collection of tall boulders to mark a sacred site. 'We walk right over it.'

The next thing, all the other men – all but Kenny and a couple more – were walking off, spreading out into the dark. They were lighting fires as they walked – not bending, just chucking matches blindly into the spinifex and grasses. An orange, leaping floor spread out from the men, illuminating the trees. Silently the space around us was growing as they flung matches.

I went to Jonny, by himself at the fire. 'Why do you do that?'

'For snakes, or something.'

'And to encourage new growth for kangaroo feed?' I said, finding myself slipping over to the blackfella slang.

Jonny didn't reply to the right question. He said, distantly, 'Albert was bred out here.'

'They'll have been through the Law then?'

Perhaps Jonny tensed a little – I wasn't sure in the dark. But he was quiet, not stirred to answer for a while. I watched the light on the men's silhouette, something ritual about their spreading out into the bush, a cleansing movement. Then Jonny said that Albert had been through the Law so young that the gap where his tooth had been knocked out had closed over.

An ant, on its way back from the stores left lying around, and now painted with flour, crossed my foot. Jonny said, 'The dingoes will be in tonight, for live or fresh meat.'

I was looking at the men, the quietness over them. Buffalo came up. I'd become wary of this man – his right hand looked as if it had been crushed; the thumb was stiffly cocked, and when pointed, his hand was a pistol. His behaviour was bullish; he might be a bully. His hair hung down about his hard nose and drunken-rage eyes. I said, 'The dingoes hunt in a mob?'

'Naow,' Buffalo said quietly. 'Dey hunt alone. Unless dey have to feed der liddle ones.'

The other side of the fire, Albert is cuddling Elaine. 'I'm your sweetheart, don't call me "old man".'

I was still watching the men, mainly with their shirts off, some of them sparkling with sweat, the raised ritual scars on Russel's shoulders catching the firelight. The men were turning back in, not conscious at all of being watched, and not clubbing together but taking their own paths back through the flaring grasses.

The men laid out their swags, and I unrolled my sleeping bag. I asked the youth called Michael why no one slept out of the wind, in the shed. 'Perhaps it got a snake in it,' he said, as though he'd never thought of the idea of shelter before, the warmth in cold, the coolness in heat.

I lay down and stared at the sky. I had never seen stars so low, perched on the land. Another thing. It was silent out here – but not the silence that I'd been expecting of the desert. The wind was always somewhere, licking the scrub, parting and reparting your hair with dust. Approaching from downwind through this openness, I felt, you could creep up on someone unawares.

Once, years ago at school, we had done a play, Beckett's *Waiting for Godot*. This camp had the same emptiness as the set, the inaction of the characters. 'Well, somebody could wash all the plates up,' Kenny says. No one moves. '*We* godda *warder* de *treees, tidy* de *camp*,' Michael says. No one moves.

The expectant stage, the barren set – theatrical symbols again. But it could not be helped in a place that was a stimulant – where life and thoughts were magnified by the scale of space around them.

Days follow a regular course. In the morning, no one wants to get up to make the fire. When they finish eating, plates are left and within moments the remains harden in the wind. The axes are sharpened with files in the way Dick told me not to sharpen blades, and then the blackfellas begin, they begin bashing the bark off the sandalwood. Russel or Michael or Jonny might get up, volunteering to come and tell me a bit about the bush – the gidgi tree of thick, clumped foliage that could burn for weeks along the roots underground, or other trees blackfellas burnt at the base to fell them for firewood. Then my guide leaves me, goes and makes tea or returns to sit in the circle, knocking at the wood.

Sometimes they do have sessions with the rake, clearing up the litter as if housekeeping, but the litter piles are left to blow away, and possessions, burdens for a nomad, blow away, freeing them again.

They asked my name sometimes – 'Your name again?' – but soon forgot it. They were self-contained in a way that a community of settled, housed people, with their supply needs, could never be. After Kandengei, the women by night, men by day – *this is the way we make your spirit strong* – I felt the absence of forest pressure so keenly I was dizzy out here.

However, I believed the sandalwood mob did like me, and this was partly because I was always ready to share out my own meagre food – potatoes, tinned fish, sugar, tinned milk, tea. So, in this neutral, impassionate way, we got to know each other's habits, and on their part, they were happy to leave it at that, just asking my name from time to time – 'Your name again?'

At the end of each day, the men came in silently from lighting up the bush. In the camp, they were back to what I regarded as normal – a settled person's normality.

'Crikey! Move your fackin' feet. Dey stink!'

'I washed 'em!'

'Yeah, but dey're still powerful.'

In the night, ants plundered the camp, exploding with an acrid pong when I rolled over, accidentally crushing them. I would lie awake, looking at the bristling stars.

The fifth day, the blackfellas got up as usual, hunched in the cold, then made the fire and feasted – 'Hey, that's naughty!' Albert said, as Michael dipped his bread in the oil of the egg pan. Buffalo growled, 'You snore like der pigs goin' ta market, anyhow.'

Elaine was always last up, appearing dopily from the women's group, and today as usual sat getting warm with knees together, quiet, cheeks full and a little red, burnished, craning her thick, short, soft neck down to drink from her cup, her bleached hair in corkscrew curls, her toes turned up, her child's feet out.

The wind was from the south, what, in the camp, they called *Yulparira*. The flies rested still, on the lee side of our bodies. From out of this wind, now and then, we heard a dog howl. Russel said that they must be pups if they were dingoes. Adult dingoes didn't howl. They were out to the west, probably out along by some waterholes a mile or two off.

As the wind dropped I left the camp to find them, the early sun on my back, the shadows long on the wind-tarnished rocks. All I had to do, Russel had said, was to follow the truck tracks out there. Behind me the sounds of the camp faded into the wind. I could hear Elaine dilly-dallying and dreaming – she was playing her fingers along the zinc shed.

'You workin' or *whaaat*?' I heard a man say, whipping the end of the sentence. They told her to fetch some water, put on the tea. She must now have brought water from the wrong petrol drum. '*We* down *wan* dat,' they said, the sentence rising. And then, swaying the sentence, and allowing the second syllables to fall, '*Dat's* der *funny warda*.'

Ahead, I heard the dingoes again, a soft whine that was ruffled by the wind. They were still there.

The crickets, which had the wind-burnished dark glaze of small rocks, jumped up and were taken away by the wind. Otherwise I saw no movement but the rattle of the bare shrubs. I passed lizard holes, the sand entrance piles carved by tails, and also the pronged tracks of kangaroo feet.

Something gathered in me. It was like this before, walking through the bush to Wiluna, noting the focus the desert gave to the living, the magnitude given to beings, to simply Being. Any moment, you thought, might come a pulse of clarity. But I was chasing too hard. I knew I was. The whitefella questions were welling in me again.

Now the wind was fouling my hearing sense. I could not place the distance to the howling, though I could see the rock holes, five feet across, four or five of them in the hard rock, clustered in a westerly line ahead.

I left my water bottle on the track, and moved around to the north, downwind. I took off my shoes, crept to the nearest hole. I could see the bottom of the far side – moss, four feet down. I snaked forward, veering to come in from the west by a route clear of small stones. Next thing, without warning, a head shot up. The dingo hadn't seen me and I found myself with the view of the white underside of a muzzle. I could see the shine of saliva on the black lips. It was a howling stance, the foxy head back – but the pup stopped before he let out a sound. Suddenly, alerted, he dipped down. And shot up again. The dingo hadn't known where the danger was but now found himself caught, looking straight into my eyes. We were only a breath apart. The low sun behind me was shining straight into the pup's eyes, the gold irises. The little dingo jerked down again.

I retreated, wanting to leave the place as far as possible as I'd found it.

*　　*　　*

The blackfellas and I might have carried on in our fixed relationship for an eternity. They might have learnt to trust me, and told me a bit about their Law, but the closest I would ever really be was friend. And there was more; I was convinced. There was the divide I had sensed ages ago between the three women and the whitefella with the briefcase in Alice Springs. No doubt I was going to be shown more desert tricks, more of what they had already told me – that sandalwood could be boiled into a scarlet dye for your beard, or as a tan for leather. That the first clothing here was from the rabbit the whitefellas introduced – women made little aprons. But I would get no further, I was certain of it. However, five more days on, an event, minor in itself, marked a change, a conscious effort on their side to begin to look closer my way.

Russel was taking me a few paces from the camp to point at the yellow sawdust at the base of the *kurutanpa* shrubs, a sign of edible grubs in the tap root. 'Good tucker, that.'

The last time I had seen a grub like this I had eaten it raw. It had been what you did in New Guinea. So now I did the same. Seeing the little grub in my hand, my fingers closed so it couldn't escape, I was again back in the forest. I took the little pale, wriggling larva onto my tongue and swallowed it down. I didn't give it a second thought.

Russel's mouth was hanging open, I noticed. He looked at my hand. For a moment he had no squint at all. His weaker eye, normally almost hidden by the sleepy lid, was regarding me suspiciously. 'You cook 'em up,' he said, slowly, looking at the grub in his own hand, then his eyes brightening and settling on mine. 'Least, I do.'

'In New Guinea, you have them fresh,' I told him. Inside, my own excitement was growing at his eruption of interest.

Russel, still with this look on his face – the weak eye out of recession – trotted off, leading me along the main track to the Highway to a large tree. He played wire that he'd found somewhere in his pocket down a little hole in the bark, and fished enthusiastically. He plucked out a witchetty grub – fatter than any sago grub, a fat, white, twitching finger. 'And you can eat witchetty grubs?' he asked. 'You down' mind 'em?'

'Well . . .' It was bigger than anything I had eaten alive, far fatter than a healthy sago grub, and there *were* limits.

He saved me. He pocketed it, saying, 'Like 'em on toast, I do.' I felt proud. Something from Kandengei began to blaze in me. We had many sorts in New Guinea, I said.

'In der bush?' He was standing facing me, grave with attention. He asked me what I had eaten. I said, working through the animals in size order, and the light in Russel's eye egging me on, 'Grubs, frogs, snakes . . .'

Suddenly we were comparing notes – the juicy chicken meat of the lizard, the gelatinous strings in the kangaroo tail, the knuckles of tender, beefy turtle flesh . . .

In the camp, everyone was head down, clonking at the sandalwood.

Russel said, 'He can shoot a bow 'n' arrow!'

Michael got up from his pile. 'Like de Red Injuns? You shoot bows and arrows like der Red Injuns?'

I said I could, though not quite as well. 'Not at all as well, in fact.' Shame was setting in. I hardly ever actually killed any of the animals myself. Johnson and Spencer, anyone who had been unlucky enough to be off in the bush with me, knew only too well: I was a rotten shot.

Other men gathered round, including Buffalo, with his Bill Cody chin beard and riding boots. 'Where'd they do dat?' he said.

New Guinea, I said.

Michael said, 'Dat's up der top.'

Buffalo said, 'Dat your place? Wid der Red Injuns?'

'I've lived there a bit.'

Russel said, 'Shootin' bows 'n' arrows!'

Noel, the same age as Michael and myself, with the earring and missing front teeth, said, 'Dey got cowboys as well?'

'You stupid or sumthin'?' Michael said. 'Dat's the Wild West.'

Buffalo raised his stiff, gunbarrel fingers. He said, 'New Guinea. Dey a bit like us – blackfellas. Dey not Red Injuns.'

I was given a mug of tea – it was mostly sugar. 'What's der name again?' they asked.

'Benedict,' I said, nodding confidently.

'Whaaaat?' Margaret said, screwing up her face.

The other men didn't hide their disappointment either. They wanted something short and snappy. But more than anything, they wanted something from the 'motion pictures'. Clint, Doug, a name along those lines. One or two said, slowly, 'Benny dik – t?'

Russel suddenly said, 'We can call you Dick?'

Before I could hastily interject an alternative, Michael said, 'Dick, you can come huntun' wid us, anyway.'

I would have liked to have gone off with a boomerang or spear, but instead we sat with a rifle on the open truck, holding Bruno, who would have to do for a kangaroo dog. And the wheels of the truck made their mark on the desert – compacted lines that would later hold moisture and trap wind-blown seeds of low golden grasses, leaving the indelible stamp of the whitefella's technology.

Kangaroos fled, emus ducked, turkeys swerved. It was late in the afternoon – not a bad time to hunt because a turkey only flew when it wasn't hot. It wouldn't fly either if there were birds of prey around, so the first thing to be done was to scare the local eagle into the air. Russel pointed out an eyrie. 'Eagle nest.'

An adult circled, screeching over its single chick. '*He* gettn' wild.'

The truck stopped. Michael turned the palm of one hand upwards, knuckles curled in. Kangaroos. Russel said, 'Dey're heaps of 'em out dere.'

I saw them now – ears cocked on narrow, rabbit heads in the silver-headed grasses that they called *windulga*. Some kangaroos began to pitch up, smelling us. It was no good stalking kangaroos, even by foot, because you might startle others along your path, Russel said. We waited for the shot, hearing the wind sweeping over here, then over to the left.

Bang! The bush kangaroos bounded away – all except one. We let Bruno go. Michael followed with a heavy spanner.

The truck thumped along; we stood on the back, holding on to the cab. Michael swung the buck kangaroo up by the groin and leg. 'He goin' along wid his missis.' When Michael had chucked Bruno aboard, he said, 'You know what a *yakiri* is? Dat's a headband der old men wears.'

Russel said, 'To keep your brains cool!'

For an hour, the men potted away at the kangaroos, mindless of how many they needed. And now it was the turkeys' turn. They had freckled grey and brown body feathers, an arm's worth of tubular neck and a beak at the end that was a sharp wedge. They trotted away from us, heads high, not a flustered feather as their partners went down.

While we'd been hunting, the women had been foraging. As we arrived, Malala was walking in, plonking her feet down as she came, soles dropping flat, leaning back on herself, hauling back her stomach, her breasts floating on her. Dragged in her wake was a lizard, a 'goanna'.

I went over to see the other women tapping the soil for the tunnels of 'orkada', honey ants, these huge women wielding long bars with the sensitive fingers of safe-cracking criminals. I ate one of the ants on the way back – and then two more. They were so much better than sago grubs; you held the ant by the front and bit off the abdomen, which was swollen into a translucent sack of fluid honey.

By now, Malala had the goanna pegged through its front and back

legs for easier tossing in the ashes. Michael was skinning the kangaroos from a branch, flaying deftly, leaving only the head and feet.
Michael said it wasn't the traditional way; they were meant to be
cooked in a fire pit without being skinned. 'So as not to lose water?'
I suggested.

Russel commented, 'Dey used to shoot fellas in the head for doing
dis.'

Jonny said, 'Still do, Warburton way.'

Russel said, 'Yeah, stay clear of the Warburton Mob, Dick.'

Jonny said they'd be coming in from Warburton, which was further
out along the Highway, during the Law time, a bit later. 'I'm just
saying – in case, you know?'

But the two of them were now addressing me, facing me square
on. 'They Lawmen,' Russel said. His kindly, hidden eye appeared,
skew-whiff in the squint, a mismanagement under the dark brow.

Jonny was more to the point. 'You're a whitefella, dat's all we're
saying. It's blackfella business.'

The line was neatly drawn for me. Bush tucker was one thing,
the Law, another. Law Business, they were saying, was blackfella's
business. It was a fair point, but where did it leave me? These people
were part of the land, they were my access to the desert. I sat with
the others in the camp, but feeling apart from them, wondering if this
journey must fail.

The kangaroos were eaten – even Kenny the Adventist ate his share
of the 'unclean' beast – then lizards. Then on to the turkey. Plucking
it, roasting it. They worked through everything except the feet. Brains,
stomachs, tails, they were all gone. The next morning, the kangaroo
'runners', the lower guts, lay about in desiccated strings, sausage beads
hard from the wind. I think Russel must have noticed how quiet I had
been during the feast. He came to me while I was by the windpump,
doing my teeth. Large pale green dragonflies were coupling over the
water as it wasted away.

'In your place . . .' Russel said.

'England?'

'Wid the bows 'n' arrows. They got a Law, there?'

I said yes. Russel had walked over because I'd felt left out. He was
making a move to me. My emotions gathered and rose. He was going
to make an effort to help. We'd get to know each other over a week
or month and eventually I'd understand whatever divided us. I wasn't
asking to see their Law, just to understand them, their countryside;
we'd find a way round.

'You been through it, ain't you? I can tell.'

But how could he tell? I said I had been through a New Guinea Law, yes.

'Here, Dick,' he said, 'we got a different one.'

He ended our conversation there, with those few words, even before I had tried to show off my crocodile marks. He was carefully re-sealing the differences between us, reminding me I was an outsider.

Suddenly, two days later, without discussion, we were going. There was no reason that I could see – the act of moving was enough pleasure in itself. Easy come, easy go. It wasn't just a poor regard for schedules; it was the value to them in randomness. They feared growing roots. They wanted to be with the land as a whole, not one piece in particular, and they moved quickly, signalled as if by a changing wind. One moment the women were making dampers, a flour and water bread, while the men were out hunting sandalwood, yanking roots up with chains, the next the camp was being abandoned. The fresh dampers were being left to burn in the fire ashes and it was time to go. No discussion, just the rolling-up of swags, the rolling of a water drum onto the truck, and away we went, and that secret, invisible thing connecting these people had worked its magic.

We lay on our swags, going back along the Gunbarrel Highway on the open rear of the truck. If anyone said anything, it was 'wandee', at the doe kangaroo we saw, or, at the boomer, the buck, 'moodeela'; mostly, though, they restricted themselves to hand signals, sexing the animals as well – a waved little finger for a girl, a wagged chin for a boy. They were obsessed.

We stopped at 'Sydney Head', a grove of gums below low red escarpments. Through the afternoon, while the three hill kangaroos shot en route were cooked up, the men smoked their Log Cabin and played cards. 'Fack face!' Albert said, playfully. 'He trai-in' give me dee tain.' He's trying to give me the ten.

'Four, indee?'

We were invaded by bull ants, which had the sting of a bee and were an inch or more long with sloe-berry rear ends and heads. Jonny lit a fire on their nest – it would keep them quiet; they buried down and waited for the fire to pass over.

'Hey, my buddy is coming!' Albert called out. It was the sound of another vehicle but it hadn't come into full view yet. However, he was right. Mrs Farmer had had the same impulse to move. She was bringing a whole lot of children out into the bush.

We shifted again, this time in a convoy. I rode in the cab, where there was a slab of kangaroo meat on the dashboard and live bullets in the ashtray. 'This meeting was prearranged?' I asked Kenny as he steered, body splayed over the huge wheel. He said no. 'We got lucky.' We made one stop on a sheep station to look at a balling shed where a cousin had worked, then another at Windich Spring. Here we had another meal and the children played football with an old kangaroo head, a skin pouch with empty, dry eye-sockets.

The men wandered off, singly, drifting quietly through the bush, becoming reflective in the way they did at bedtime, setting light to the vegetation. There were pools of green water with long-necked tortoises bobbing in them and a white gum tree with two scars on its side. The first scar was old, a huge gaping navel made by a whitefella called Forrest, Russel said. The whitefella had come through here and shot at a few blackfellas attacking him, the invader. 'They cheeky, sometimes.' Russel was like the others, he showed no malice at the incursions or killings, he was just perplexed. They stacked up some stones to show me how some whitefellas had made a little battlement.

'Dey only comin' to drink warder,' he said.

'What was Forrest doing here?'

Russel cheered up suddenly at the thought. 'Lookin' at der good country.'

Buffalo smiled, contentedly. 'Yeah, it good country, dis is.'

'He was important, was he?' I asked Jonny, who was wandering near.

'The whitefellas's got a statue of him in Perth. St George's Terrace.'

I decided Forrest must have been important. And the second gash in the tree was made during the erection of a plaque to mark the centenary. It was hand-punched with the letters: 'Forrest 1874 F41. Geraldton Historical Society 1974.'[18]

After some dampers, tea and a monitor lizard, we were off to 'Number Five', the fifth well out from Wiluna on the Canning Stock Route, a route for cattle from the north down to the booming goldfields of the old days. There, where what had been good country had now been trampled into ground made of bricks, we turned off to Blue Hill.

Time for another feast. There was a barbecue atmosphere – chops, margarine, tomatoes. Mrs Farmer had even brought a collapsible formica table. The children knocked a tennis ball about with sticks, not allowing it to stop.

'Stap!'

'Naa-gk! Still roalin'.'

They wore the latest day-glow orange and yellow singlets and Bermuda shorts. Stewy, Jonny's son, was eleven or twelve years old. His shoes were large and loose on his skinny feet, shoulders narrow, hunched, like his father's. He sang pop songs or pretended to throw a spear when the ball was at the other end. And when the ball finally came to him he ran with his wrists limp, forearms high, hands horizontal, flapping, making his glorious advance up the pitch with the sun flashing from the stark black skin of his back.

The girls cried out. '*He* stap *ov*-er *der*-er.'

Stewy shouted, 'He *nev*-er.'

The girls cried out, 'He *chead*in'.'

Stewy got bored with the shouting; he trotted off into the bush to fire stones with a ging, a catapult which he'd made from car inner tubes and which he kept hung round his neck.

The girls dispersed back to camp to circle around on a tyre-less bicycle left from a previous visit. I went off to write notes. Stewy found me. 'You storyin'?'

I said I was. 'Have *you* had a *turn?*' He was offering me his ging.

I tried my best – not very impressive. He skipped away to the camp, brought back a brand new mirror as a proper target. Before I could stop him, he fired. One shot and it was beyond repair.

The next morning, Mrs Farmer walked onto the hockey pitch, interrupting a game.

'Sorry bout dat ladies an' gents, we gotta clean up.'

'We d'winner!'

I helped pack up. Mrs Farmer gave the commands. 'Ged dee warda for me!' or, 'Take some eggs for de road.' And we were gone, moving again, leaving the formica table exactly where it stood, the bicycle where it happened to fall. Off we went.

Brumbies, wild horses, ran with us along the track, until we came to some salt bush, heathy clumps on spreads like tidal flats. We went around a vertical-sided valley, along an escarpment edge. Apparently there were water marks on the cliff. 'Must have been made at the flood time, or somethun',' Russel said. 'Noah's time,' Albert said. We watched a 'giddi-giddi', a hill kangaroo, slice straight up the white and red layered cliff sides.

Their old men had stories of the flood as well as the Bible. Russel said to me, 'In New Guinea?'

'Oh yes.'

Albert nodded. 'He shoot wid der bow an' arrow.'

'Too much wind here. And dere ain't der straight wood,' Russel said. 'But if you been through der Law out dere, we'll see you right.'

We'll see you right, he said. I decided I'd stick with the sandalwood mob, hanging on to that phrase for all I was worth.

*　　*　　*

Back in Wiluna, screaming Wiluna, Kay, a veteran of thirty-five years' worth, with curly, urban-tidied-up hair and staid spectacles, added up my stores at the till. She said Dusty had left for Mungale, the sandal-wood camp. Nola, the New Zealander, was away in Perth. Her house had been broken into at the weekend. I said, 'Who would do that?'

'She's too good to them,' said the wife of a road maintenance man. She was new here and stocking up. Apparently unable to find a relevant story about robbery, she told another. In Tennant Creek, she said, the Aboriginals didn't walk down the pavements at night because they were scared of spirits coming in from the roadside. So they walked down the middle of the road. 'They prefer to be run over!' At night, she continued, they locked all the doors of their houses and kept the lights on.

'*That's* Tennant Creek,' Kay said, punching the till. '*This* is Wiluna.' She totted up my supplies – just piles of potatoes, sugar, tea, baked beans.

The road grader woman said, '*We* get fined thousands for killing kangaroos and yet now they're running all over the place. And why are there so many? It's the whiteman's boreholes. And what Aboriginal ever thought of putting them in?'

I supposed I wasn't meant to answer, so I didn't. She gathered up her frozen meat and said it was only a fifty-dollar fine for killing a sheep. I asked how much a sheep cost.

'Twenty-five dollars – I've just bought one for a barbie.' She swept from the store and into her Land Cruiser.

'She's just a blow-through,' Kay said, waiting for my money. 'Me? Thirty-odd years here and I offer no solutions.'

By her tone she might have meant to the whitefella problem.

Outside the store, five flies were conferring in the nook of a blackfella's eye. A bearded lady in a bobble hat shuffled along with her shopping; in Tooting she'd have been an out-of-sorts eccentric lone widow pushing a supermarket trolley, a whisky comforter under her jacket. Here, she was any one of twenty women.

By the kerb, Steve, the vast whitefella who worked for the Ngang-ganawili Community, was lowering himself into his green car, hanging on to the roof while the seat took the weight and the car listed and settled.

Sometimes I saw Kalu racing by, fighting his fight. Later, Herbie saw me and stopped his car. 'You making out all right?' I said I didn't know.

'It's like that,' Herbie said. He drove away.

Bill, a young American gold prospector, came up. I'd met him before, just as I'd left with the sandalwood mob. 'Aristocrats of Humanity,' he'd said. 'That's what the Aboriginals are.' It sounded like something from the *National Geographic*, to me.

'Saw that in *Time* Magazine,' he said.

Almost right.

But this morning I saw he'd been out in the bush with his pan and he looked as if he was needing to talk to someone. He looked weaker than when I'd last seen him and his feathery blond moustache, always frail at the best of times, this morning seemed to be coming away. He said he'd had a rough night. His van had got stuck near 'Number Two' – the second well out on the stock route. He had burnt the only wood in sight to keep warm – a convenient heap of it – and in the morning found out it was sandalwood being stored by Kenny's mob. His eyes had a desperation about them. 'You heard about how tough the Law is?'

I said that their law was only for them as far as I could see. Whitefellas were judged differently – to such a degree that out here they didn't even seem to resent the whitefellas killing them. 'By the way, have you heard of a man called Forrest?'

He didn't hear. 'Like, it was either light that pile or die of cold. Don't tell anyone, right. They'll be after me!'

I said again that their law wasn't our law. He said he wasn't talking about *their* Law. He was talking about whitefella's law. 'It's anti the whitefellas.' He said the settled, Westernized Aboriginals in the towns caused all the protests, the riots, not the genuine bush men. It was apartheid – fines for going on their reserves, fines for shooting their kangaroos. 'You're catchn' on kinda slow,' Bill the American said, apparently having even caught the blackfella's version of his accent.

More blow-throughs passed by – Max, a part-Aboriginal shearer, whose sister had been chopped up and put down a well by her husband, and whose brother had been given six years for thumbing a lift with a gun into Wiluna. His hazel eyes would open out and pivot, wickedly. He had sheep's hair and a wicked, roving brown eye, 'If my wife doesn't give me some cash she won't get a naughty tonight.' Road graders, pile drivers, poisonous spider sprayers . . . These were the nomads of Wiluna. The blackfellas had found their oasis long ago.

I was staying at Kenny's house, with the sandalwood mob. I walked back there with my box of stores past the Club Hotel. A whitefella: 'Still with the sandalwood mob? You Pommies learn slow, don't cha!' And a blackfella: 'Lend a dollar!' And on past the Shire, that is, local government, caravan site. It was a wired-off green sward with a shower block and the caravans of the blow-throughs.

On a bit further, and I was in the open rubble – Cyril Claw's house out on the left, Farmer's on the right. Further off, more houses, the few leftovers of the whitefella days, now with flattened gardens which were dormitories. On the rise to the right was a house with camel wagon wheels in the fence and walls fortified by corrugated iron, plates and plates of it. It was owned by Peter Burns, who was a professional dingo hunter, dingoes and wild cattle-dogs being a pest to livestock. By the look of the garden, of claimed territory behind the wire fence, of energy put into the land, I guessed Burns was a whitefella.

Kenny was just leaving with his wife. He was keen to go to a church meeting – 'They got some negro from America coming' – and she wanted to go shopping. She tucked some dollar notes into her bra, and they left. She loved shopping, just as Kenny liked the sandalwood mob enterprise. I had now learnt that far from being an example of Adventist diligence, the business was soaking up money as quickly as whitefellas poured money into it.

The sandalwood mob were glued to the television set. They sat with the children and an assortment of drunks and stared and stared. The commercials reminded us it was getting near Christmas – the forbidden word. Santa Claus got a laugh when he appeared on the screen. Men with shaggy, uncombed locks who had been menacing me outside the pub walked up to the screen and pointed at the bearded man and laughed at his fur-lined red coat. When Santa waved, the thugs, like the children, happily waved back.

I had a shower, and regretted it. Though Kenny's house had no graffiti, the house, SDA or not, was treated as much like a piece of outdoors as the other blackfella homes. In the shower passage, there was excreta from Bruno's furry friends – Ice-cream, Jelly, Spot and more besides. I dealt with the razor blades in the basin but kept tripping on clothes on the floor. And the rusty dust was everywhere – in the sink, coming from the shower, on the shower curtains. I went to fix myself something to eat, but the kitchen table was underneath flour, milk, sugar, damper pieces, onion skins, hummocks of used tea bags. I opened the fridge to put my butter away, but all available space had been taken by a kangaroo. On the TV set were the leftovers of a cow. The dogs were fighting over the hide on Kenny's bed, strips of the fat clogged the sink. A baby's feeding bottle was melting on the gas stove, and there was more, much more.

Later in the afternoon, most adults had gathered enough energy to go off drinking again. Abandoned children from all over Wiluna crowded into the house. Excreta accumulated in the toilet. Children chucked bread crusts over their shoulders, as they sat goggling at the telly. It grew dark, the grown-ups came back, puking and bellowing with the dogs. The children had to lock out their drunken elders and betters – fathers, uncles, mothers and aunts – who were wheeling about in the dark, unable even to support each other's weight.

Buffalo, for example. He stomps around with an axe. As he runs about the garden, a few protective arms go up – stiff, like salutes. But it is Malala he's after. He gets her on the leg with the blunt side of the axe. The same blow would have shattered my leg, but she's still standing. The second blow gets her on her neck hump. She grabs a stick of firewood and harangues the air space between them. They lock together, come apart, weapons swaying high. They stand off, go in. It's an insect ritual. They make mock swings at each other; they turn round, offering their heads to be chopped open.

Meanwhile, the children are transfixed by the TV, oblivious of those adults who find a way in and lurch and grub for food, hitting their heads on the floors as they fall. What kind of generation were the blackfellas rearing? The answer was, one that took fighting and neglect as normal, yet went to Jonny, who was still quite lucid, to ask me to move my chair. 'They're scared of you, Dick!'

I was disquieted and sad, surrounded by these violence-adjusted children and their parents – the slobbering mums and dads. By dusk I was so angry I even wanted their destruction. The 'settlers', the whitefellas, were the original cause, I knew, but on the face of it all you saw was blackfellas ruining their lives, disgracing their heritage. The New Guineans might be a bore if you shared their village, the *avookwaarks* might ruin your sleep, but they struggled to die with some dignity. What comfort could I draw here? That they were using the wealthy whitefellas as a resource as only nomads knew how? It did them no good at all, preying on settled people. I shouted at Albert and Michael, as they pressed me to lend money. I wanted them to be angry. The only stand their old men had made against their destruction was to stop spirits being sold at the pub. I said, 'You're drunkards! Can't you see the whitefellas are killing you?'

They ignored me; they only said it was tax rebate time coming up – last year they had drunk the bar dry. 'You call that clever?' I said to Michael. Daring him.

Albert wandered off, looking at his feet. He was not angry, not even remorseful, just in a direct line to the pub. Michael said that Charles Perkins, of the Department of Aboriginal Affairs, had come to Wiluna and told the *West Australian* it was the worst town in Australia. 'People pissing on the walls,' he apparently said. 'It's a disgrace.' Michael reported this without comment. Just the way it was.

I said I had a good mind to go down there and take a few photographs of the fights. If half what I'd witnessed was written up – a child sleeping in a dustbin, women hoisting themselves onto drunk men who might or might not be dead – I could sell my story to a magazine. Someone could make a name for himself. This place ought to be exposed.[19]

Michael said, 'The ABC crew came once.' He added, dreamily, 'We had to smash up der cameras.' Then he went all quiet on me. Though still sitting with me, he was suddenly gone, taking the world a nomad carried about in his head with him. But after a while he began speaking. He spoke seriously. Later, looking at my notebook, I found he'd apparently spoken in standard, not broken, English.

'I took an M16. I came to Glass hill, by the pub . . . I took the M16 and began shooting all my brothers and friends. I went to that hill and I put the gun to my head. I shot myself from the front. Like dis. And the first bullet went straight through. And then another. I felt nothing. Then I took a knife and did myself in – in der ribs. Then I woke up, hitting myself. Like this. Again and again.' He beat his chest hard, really wanting to hurt himself all over again. 'I woke up.'

There was nowhere to sleep indoors. I lay in the porch, sheltering with dogs in the sweaty, hairy smells, locked out with the drunk adults. Women screamed, gurgled. 'Goo-aaawayeee!' 'Ya fackin' shit face.' 'Naow!' 'Get out, ya fackin'.' Men stumbled around, whirling sticks. Dogs that had been my greatest enemies were suddenly my friends – they went at the strangers coming in. I could see their teeth showing in the last light. Then it was too dark to see the dogs or the strangers and whether they had bars. I just heard them, the swearing, the screaming, the sickly coughing.

Across the rubble, one of the blow-throughs was singing from his caravan. It was along the lines of:

Chorus: Oh I abhor the Abos, they don't know what they're doing,
They've wandering pricks – whistle dicks – but we're the ones
   they're screwing.

Now last week I was huntin'
out Hill Creek way with Bruce,
who saw a gin [black woman] worth twenty shillin',
so I let old Joe lose . . .

Oh, I abhor the Abos . . .

Well, some gin mew, others howl,
some kinda squeal, like a fowl,

this one hollaw-ed, when Joe followed
and it lasted quite a while . . .

Oh, I abhor the Abos . . .

Well, Joe's a chaser, through and through,
knows the emu, plains kangaroo,
now he knows the Abo too,
and if you don't know, I sure do!

Oh I abhor the . . .

A blackfella was coming through the dark, beating back dogs. He was
shouting that he wanted to fight 'Farmer'. He whacked his bar at the
house. He shuffled past me as I lay in my blanket, trying to hide in it. Dogs
circled the man like sharks. He beat at the back door. Again and again.
'Farmer! Farmer!' As I listened, I heard clearer. 'Foreigner! Foreigner!'

Heck! That's me, I thought.

'You're a spy. You're nuttin' but a hound dog. You clear out!'

He was coming this way now – to me, under the blankets. I had
my eyes closed; I was like a child, hoping the ghoul would go away
if I kept him out of sight. I was expecting the crack of a bar on my
head, and from all I'd seen, my skull wasn't going to be as strong as
the Aboriginal one. I was afraid, but also, suddenly, angry again. So
angry! This is a mess! I thought. These children shouldn't be here!
You men are drunken yobs, you women are sluts. Your children queue
up in the school library for sex, half are pregnant and you're all on
whitefella's charity. My God, don't you have any pride?

'Who's dat?' The man prodded my back. I turned round violently
at him. I was angry at the waste, the stupidity, the smells. The man
jumped back.

I can't see who it is. I close my eyes again, thinking of that stick.
I wait, wait for the stick, and then hear him shuffle to the door, and
beat it. The door is opened – light spreads out over me. A boy's voice
timidly says, 'Yes?' The man pushes in – 'Where's der whitefella?'

There is complete silence for me in the world at this moment.

'Where is ee? He been spying on us. Writn' stuff. WHERE IS EE?'

The boy says, 'Gone to the bush.'

Who was the boy? Who would do this for me? Stewy? But this boy's
voice had broken. Why should some stranger do this for me?

The man stumbled back past me. Another man blundered up to him
– he was a friend of Farmer's because the dogs had let him through. A
sandalwood man. He said, 'You fackin'. What you want?'

The stranger says, 'Der bar is for the dogs.' Now the new man is making the other shuffle back. He's probably shoving him. 'You not gonna touch him. You not gonna touch him! You understand? You gonna fight me first, buddy.'

Albert? Russel?

The stranger goes off, whacking his way out through the dogs.

I look carefully, and the newcomer – 'saviour' doesn't seem too dramatic a word – isn't anyone I've ever seen before. Later I'm to know him as Maurice Wongawol, a relative of Mrs Farmer. But for the moment I'm confused – all I know is I don't know him at all. I'm stunned and sleepless. What have I done to deserve protection?

Later, as the night cooled, dogs came to share my blanket. I shifted them off me – but softly, not wanting them to have to go altogether. Some of the blackfellas were treating me with respect, as a close friend. I was happy at that, disappointed in myself – I'd acted like a boy, someone who needed to be protected. I was meant to be good on the physical side of Junior Manhood. So much for Benedix the *geenjumboo*. And then there was Michael's dream, and how badly he had taken it. '*I took an M16. I came to Glass hill, by the pub. I took the M16 and began . . .*'

At dawn, a chill wind blew over us – me, the dogs, blanketed men and women. Dogs limbered up in the shattered cars. There were sporadic shouts from the figures filling the space between the litter. Youths fought in the soft, sweet, early light – a mop-headed man tackling another from the 'Dudley Mob' with an iron bar. Women watched from where they lay, letting out aggressive, throat-ripping roars at them to stop. After a while other men, still tottering from drink, split them up. As the Dudley Mob man leaves, he shouts over his shoulder that he will be back to kill our man. The sun waits, the wind blows. We lie back. At last the Dudley Mob send a man. He comes up behind our man with a new bar. He raises the bar. I'm about to close my eyes, so as not to see murder – had Herbie meant me not to intervene in domestic disputes like *this* one? – when a woman dives in, blocking the blow with an arm.

She lies on the ground a bit, silent, then limps off. Now, as I get up, the first Dudley man is back again. He is short, a weed, but he engages our man, who is chunky, tall.

I gather the Dudley man is a brother of the other, whose girl was taken for the night; this is a matter of honour, though I'm not sure how this can be, when everyone seems to sleep with everyone else. Then I find I'm supporting the wrong side – the Dudley man. He's a foot shorter and he's putting up a good effort against our man, who is a thug. All power to his elbow if he can gain his Junior Manhood against this opponent. We watch this duel at dawn – graceful fists bobbing into each other's faces. It goes on lightly for quite a while in the golden light, foreheads inclined, fists up, a brisk dance of gentlemanly fisticuffs which is oddly beautiful.

'First up, best dressed,' Kenny's wife says, struggling to control what to me feels like half of Wiluna's children asleep in her kitchen.

'What do you do for a crust?' she says as the morning wears on, and jabbing a lounging kid, making her join in the token housecleaning.

Kenny, in the sandalwood truck, is gathering together the drunks from the streets and pavements. Michael, Buffalo, Jonny, Russel, Malala . . .

Malala swings her fat over to vomit in the sand. Then she is given a chair, and climbs up. The last aboard is the brutish man who has just been fighting the Dudley Mob. His hair is rippled with blood; he has a long since broken nose, thick-fleshed cheeks, unintelligent eyes. He also has a Cro-Magnon brow, a slut's shoulders, clubbing hands. I keep my distance. However, he is kind to me, gently taking my baggage. He lies down gently beside me. Just like the others, in the desert, away from the excesses of Wiluna, I'll find him with always the kindest of intentions.

At the dingo hunter's house, the one with the garden remaining, we take on board an older blackfella called Micky Wongawol, a brother of Kenny's wife. I've heard from Kay at the store that Micky walked out of the desert as a lad, bringing with him his sister Dara. Now, going by Burns's house again, she waves us off, standing by the camel wagon wheels, sporting a new pair of sun-glasses.

We take the truck out to the farm, Desert Gold, for some oranges and go up and down the rows, pillaging them for free. But before we're finished, half our men have jumped off. They've caught sight of an abandoned 'six pack' of Emu.

We set off for Mungale again, leaving a man to watch the wood at Number Two. Jonny said, without feeling, 'Some whitefella set light to that pile.'

I said, 'You know it's a whitefella?'

Michael said, 'It's der white van. Bill. We know all der tracks.'

They weren't going to complain. 'A month work, that,' Kenny said, but he was speeding off happily into the bush to start all over again.

Micky Wongawol reviewed the land that shot past. He had a proud smile, and a tongue that was not only pink, but also blue and black. All under control out here, his eyes were saying, looking out. He never leaned back, propped himself, but sat alert, content, entertained by the bush as if watching the telly.

His wife had a very round face and a yellow, red and black bobble hat. Her eyes were smiling eyes; her left brow was creased forward, as if heavier than the other side; she looked at Micky, her view of his back, rather reverently; on occasion, she prods him with food she has unwrapped. Both are very quiet; they have a granny and grandpa contentment with each other, their eyes steadily lit.

The rest of the mob were sobering up. They discussed the latest pregnancy. 'Sybil's gone three months . . .'

Elaine said she knew the father. 'She *punch* him *in* de *gut*-ers.'

Michael said he'd missed that fight. 'We was *waatchn' Tee*V.'

We stopped for the night where we had camped before on the way out, at the stock fence just short of the station called Glenayle. For the first time, I got out my camera. Everyone was instantly on the alert. 'Photo comin' up!'

I put the camera away. I'd never liked photography anyway. Instead I asked the old bloke, Micky, if I could join him. He didn't mind. He said he had 'learned' many whitefellas before, including Henry Ward, the oldish whitefella from Glenayle whose family name was shared by blackfellas all about here.

'You're the whitefella wid the bow 'n' arrow,' Micky said.

'News has got around, then.'

'Hard to pull, ind-ee?'

I said it wasn't too hard.

'I could give you some yarning. Good time.' He chuckled. He was coming out with us to make spears, he said, especially spears with lots of barbs. 'Good money!' He didn't like towns. 'All dem cars – brum! brum! brum! I down' like it. And when the wind gets up the smell of dog shit turns me, ya know? I like to siddown in der bush.'

He had built the old cattle holding fence – the wooden, disused one. Camels had helped lower the posts in, and they also used them to heave the canvas buckets up from the well. The second, metal stockyard was built by Buffalo – he was born under a tree near here, at Nimanga. Micky goggled. It had taken Buffalo, a tractor and a whitefella only four days!

The stockmen, all blackfellas, took it in turns at night to circle the mustered cattle. It took two hours by horse but Micky preferred camels. They were 'good-uns'. You broke them in by smoking them, tying up the front legs as they knelt, lighting the fire upwind. After two days the smell of the camp fire was home. They pegged the nose, made a harness in the bush, with a girth strap either side of the belly. Each morning, Micky said, the camels would lie down beside their packs, and wait for work in a row, talking – 'Blub, blub, blub' – especially about any stranger in the camp.

Now Micky had a car. It was being fixed, back in Wiluna – which he referred to as 'the camp'. He explained that the 'dadiator band' was broken. 'I gotta licence, everyding!'

The journey continued, everyone quiet, looking out over the land, spreading fingers, curling them, as they saw a kangaroo, a lizard, a turkey.

We arrived to find Dusty and his wife had been through the stores, pillaging, scattering. The sandalwood mob accepted their loss without a murmur. They came to see what was missing, what not, then buckled down to work. The journeying was over, and so was their dreamy state.

Dusty and Sunshine were camped under a bush a little off from the camp. She had gathered a bucketload of berries like raisins – '*wamula*' – while he had hunted out spear wood. He made himself busy in the camp, using his stockman's training, his voice blaring from his beaten-about face, and sitting like a grand old duke, presiding over the 'yarning' in his camp.

Micky settled with his wife under another bush. He had a little lizard which they were going to share. 'He's a good cooker, you know.' Another of their favourites was 'cocker'. 'Make a soup – good one.' Also turkey: 'I like to get dem fellas.' He'd also had quite a few dingoes when he was a boy. 'Speared 'em.' He talked as if he thought I used only a bow and arrow to catch my supper. 'By jingo, I gotta learn you,' he said. I should try a gun one day. You could shoot kangaroos. 'You can knock 'em clean off.'

He began working a boomerang, holding it against his bare foot and shaving it with a metal file. There was plenty I could learn from this man, but he wasn't often in a talking mood. Often, in the early days, he sent me over to 'the old fella', Dusty. Dusty was never prepared to spend the time and sent me back to Micky. 'Try the old fella.' Micky would get up, seeing me coming back. 'I'm gonna have a wee-wee.'

So I didn't pressure Micky, and he gradually accepted my visits and began to set me straight, as he put it, about the bush tucker. There were wallabies in this area, 'no worries', despite what younger men thought. Hunting a kangaroo, you bore in mind that the kangaroo faced downwind – otherwise he 'burns' his nose. 'Come in at his elbow, then you're der winner.'

I wrote all this down, and if he ever made a mistake, he carefully corrected me. 'Oop! sorry. I ran over der line.'

Bilbakáru wood, from sandy areas, was what I needed for my spears. If there was a shortage of this straight wood, there were roots I could use instead. Anything, it seemed, but carry on with the bow and arrow. I wrote it down. 'You got 'im?' When hunting, men and women spread out, coming together if they found something. He named fruit – *kulieu*, the potatoes on a vine that you spotted by the crack they forced in the ground as they swelled. 'When dere ripe, coo! Den you can have a good feed!'

In his bush days, summer had always been spent near the well at Nimanga. 'Got to have water 'n' feed.' Other times he used to 'travel up an' down'. He looked back fondly. He had travelled in a group of about fifteen, others coming to join them every once in a while. 'When we got a big emu, we light a fire, send a signal, dey all come in, den. We got meat, see.'

Finishing the boomerang, he slipped it under a few inches of sand. It would stop the boomerang cracking. 'It going to be hot.'

I noticed that what might have started as stories of the past often ended as stories of the present. This was mostly just a yarner's trick, a way of including me, carrying me back in time. But if we talked a long time, it was more than that. It was his own mind losing its feel of whereabouts.

A tar from the base of old spinifex, he would begin, could be kneaded and plugged into holes in boomerangs, car batteries, water bottles. Then, his time sense showing signs of slipping, 'Emu fat is good for your sore. Rub 'im in.' Slipping further, he was telling me about a poison for a spear. And then it was *my* spear. He was mixing me into the yarn, giving me a momentary place in his history. How I should brew up plants until they were 'nice 'n' black'. I should put them in a rock hole and poison the kangaroos that came to drink. 'Take out the runners [guts] quick. Poison, you know. You'll be going up dere.' He pointed to heaven.

I walked out to visit the dingoes again. Going by Dusty's shelter, he called, 'Morning, boss!' 'Just off to see the dingoes,' I said. Dusty said he had brought a whole kangaroo out to the rock holes so they didn't starve with the summer coming on. Suddenly he said, '*Poor* old dingoes.'

He gave me a lift out there in his Toyota. 'Kangaroo been fightn',' he said, perusing scuff marks ahead. By the holes, Dusty got out and pottered around. I did the same, wondering what he was looking for among the scattered little stones. They were rusty, brown chips that were light and couldn't have been knapped into blades. Underfoot, they made a chinking, broken porcelain sound. 'I been a kid runnin' around here with no clothes on,' he said.

The day before, I'd been out in the truck with the mob to Walawaro, another rock hole, and found myself looking at the ground, and Micky doing the same. There I'd spotted stones with a simple, unworked blade and also a boulder with a wave in it, once used for milling wild grasses, *wangunu*, into flour, then a more portable grinding stone, a long, delved-out slab.

But if Dusty was looking for something like these, he lost his purpose. I tried to rekindle his enthusiasm. 'Was this a place you drank from in the old days? On one of the songlines, perhaps?'

He cut any further talking right out. 'They're kinda secret, those tales.'

We went to see the carcass; it had gone. There were only some guts in a beaded chain. However, now there was also a dead pup in one of the holes. I was struck by the moment. It was the first time I had witnessed something rotting out here – my first smell of decay. The breeze was no longer empty. Chemistry was at work here; these weren't just water holes, these were cauldrons, places mixing juices, compounds fusing.

'Poor old dingo,' Dusty said again.

The men had killed an emu, and were cutting it up with an axe, splitting open the rib-cage and the huge shoulder of lamb legs. Malala was probing for honey ants, her heavy earlobes flapping in the wind as she scooped out the sand. Margaret was trying to get Elaine away from the fire, where she was whispering with Noel. 'Start ya bloody brain!'

Micky frowned, seeing me come his way, but then seemed to remember he'd enjoyed the last yarn and nodded that I could sit down with him.

'When dey is liddle, you can eat 'em,' he said, pointing at the crows overhead.

Only two things did Micky ever tell me that were incorrect, and even then perhaps he had again lost his bearing in time. He said them both on this day.

'We not allowed to play wid food,' he said that afternoon. 'When we see kids playing, we tell 'em to eat it all.' This wasn't accurate – without even looking around I could see spare damper loaves rolling in the sand, flies pitching on spare ribs. But perhaps his mind was on the past.

And how, I asked, did you get help if you needed it, in the bush? You lit a fire?

If you wanted help, you lit a fire. It worked beautifully. 'Every time!' he exclaimed, thumping his chest. This, as things proved, was the other piece of information that he got wrong.

His original name had been Woopa Wongawol. Woopa was his first name, Wongawol his place. Nimanga, near where we had spent the night on the way here, was where he saw his first whitefellas. He had had no thought of attacking them. 'We got wise, by dis time!'

He had his first chin hairs; he must have been a bit older than Stewy. Even from far off, the whitefellas were a strange sight. 'He a little bit scarey, you know? We look eye to eye. Dey smell a bit different. We were a liddle bit strong. Kangaroo, he knows your smell too. Round der body.'

He had crept up 'windside' of them, and watched from behind the bushes, as the white men dug a well, 'bucketing and shovelling' soil out of a hole. Whenever the whitefellas picked up anything, Micky and his friends ran off. They thought it might be a gun. At the end of each day they crept away, hiding their tracks by dragging a branch between their legs.

However, one day he did meet them. 'When I heard about dere tucker and dere tea, I woke up! Good one!'

Finally, he had touched a whitefella, rolling a fold of skin in his fingers. 'That's a soft one, all right.'

He looked at the boots. 'Hey, that's a marvellous! All stepped up – a funny one, in ee?' He had never seen shoes. Older people had sandals. 'Dey plat 'em right back to the foot.' You made them from trees. 'Take off the bark, just under. I'll *show* you, by and by.'

I wrote down all he said. Micky watched the pen. 'You got 'em? You *must* have got 'em. He trick you a liddle?'

He dug a lizard from the sand beneath him. It had a large head that was designed for burrowing, rather than sensing. It was poisonous; he carved it to death with a pocket knife.

Come summer, he said, he used to leave this area and go to Carnegie, Nimanga or Jangera, where there was a good tortoise creek. 'No car stealin', no store-feedin'.' He saw Dusty sometimes when the old men had meetings, though Dusty was from further north. So they wandered, and all the way they lit fires to encourage grasses – '*kandeelou*, that one, after a fire, he'll come up quick.'

They made bowls from the wood of gum trees for carrying water, they had a club, the nulla-nulla, the womera, a spear thrower, the spear and boomerang. That was all. Like that they walked from hole to hole, through the world provided by the dreamtime. This barren place that was like a rack – a theatre, like all art forms, an instrument for extracting truth.

Somewhere far off, a sweet smell. I thought it must be from gum trees, but how could such sweetness be carried on arid air? It was a rich, fine smell that carried me home to my little bedroom in Hampshire. Among the relics – the Yeti charm, the African dance mask, were some joss sticks. Incense. Sandalwood.

I walked out towards the rock holes, just enjoying the smell. I stopped along the track in the twilight, and looked around – the tufts like toothpaste, silver wig grasses, anthill bolsters, mounds like seal pups; sofas of spinifex, others like old heather rugs; a pair of warblers rocking above a twiggy nest; biscuit soils. It was enchanting, this soft light falling on so much uncovered land.

Back in the camp, I went to see Micky. He said if I ever got crook, sick, I should sit downwind of a sandalwood fire to clear my head. 'By jingo I'll learn ya,' he said.

Herbie came out to check on how things were going. Kalu, the Nigerian, came in his own car, and was followed by Max, the sheep shearer. They set up a barbecue for themselves away from the camp; Kalu had brought a tent and a plastic bath to wash in. 'You laugh at my tent, but I was brought up with six in a bed.'

'Twelve,' Max said, topping him.

Max checked over the windpump, and Herbie fixed up a radio set. Through the afternoon, the sandalwood mob came up to talk on it. They talked into the airwaves without discipline, hearing voices out there and breaking through other conversations to get to them. Five or so conversations were going on, hacking into each other. 'Anyone read me from der workshop? I'm here at der sandalwood camp,' Michael said. Out there, on a variety of frequencies across the outback, scores of blackfellas were blindly knocking, pressing their transmitter buttons and calling across the airwaves.

Dusty had been out in the bush over the last few days. He had been 'bogged' in sand for two of them. No food, only a pint or two of water. Herbie turned another chop on his barbecue. 'If that had been a whiteman he would have left his car. He'd be dead.'

Then it was time for the Nangganawili Community team to pack up, and Kalu was gone, careering away ahead of the others. Margaret said, 'He got all dat smart talk.'

'He's *chee*ky,' Elaine said.

'Yee-er.'

'Walkin' along styley way.'

Michael said, 'All dat loot.'

Herbie wished me luck. 'Probably even more unlikely that they'll open up for you out here. Their traditional grounds. *Someone* might hear them.'

'They do a lot of hunting in night. In the day, Mummy will wait over dere. When someone is coming, she will run off – der baby one will stay in the rock hole. That's a cunning one, in ee?'

The dingoes hunted in a mob, but weren't afraid to tackle anything alone. 'He's as good as my bigfella kangaroo dog! *He* can roll 'em.' Micky acted a kangaroo, half-hopping himself: 'Daa-da, daa-da, daa,' then 'BAM!'

He sat again. 'And when the belly is full, dey go back to camp.' He made as if to regurgitate food like the mummy for the pups. 'Spew! Dat's a funny one. The pups sing out,' Micky raises his chin. 'All tail waggin'!'

The men had lit a bush fire in the afternoon. I followed it to see what animals would run from the blaze as it swept along. None. There were hardly any out there.

I wandered with the other young men, watching the fire move, mesmerized by it in the way you can be by flames or the rhythm of waves – the way the blackfellas were by the fires but also by the view of passing countryside from the back of the truck.

The fire was eating vegetation into the wind, as well as with it; it was feeding off the spinifex resin, raising blackish smoke. I watched the ashes lie down afterwards in a fleece that was gradually disassembled by the wind. While I was still half hypnotized by the flames, my shirt must have flown up, caught by a gust. I didn't notice until I heard Michael whisper, 'I think dere Law is tough.'

'It's kinda tough all right,' Russel said.

I showed the marks a bit, then tucked my shirt in, self-consciously. Michael waved at Noel, laughing and saying to me, 'He'll be going through it this year!'

Noel grinned to me, patting his trouser zip. 'Already done.'

Kenny had seen the dingoes come in last night – 'their eyes like red coals'.

I went out to the waterholes. Overhead there were *gan-ga*, crows. Micky had said this meant it was going to be hot. The only sounds were my feet on the lightweight, rust-tanned stones. Finches streamed in strings from the holes – this told me the dingoes were not at home.

I walked round in a circuit, coming back through the bush and down the main road track, with dozens of thorn balls in my socks. For a while, I found myself continually pulling to the side, getting out of the middle of the road; I did this several times, instinctively veering to the kerb side to get out of the way of traffic. Why should I do this in the middle of the desert? I listened. I looked around. No vehicle coming. Further along though, I had a clearer view of a white car abandoned near the horizon – it had taken only this to trigger my road sense. The desert really is like this, I said to myself – expectant, waiting for an act.

'What now?' Micky asked gruffly, as I came to him again. But he made a space.

It was after dark. He was on his knees, swathes of grey chest hair from his boiler suit, straightening spears with his weight, rolling them, returning them to a heap of ashes.

He remembered another whitefella he had helped: Len Beadell, while he was surveying the Highway. 'Showed him der country. That was about five years behind when we all come in from the bush,' Micky said. 'I been losin' mate. Can't say name.'

He was filing down his spear with a stone. 'He comin'!' He patterned it with parallel lines, then rubbed it over with fat. He thought about adding a barb – 'cunning one, ain't ee?'

'Can I ask about the time you were walking in the bush?' I asked. He took my enquiry literally. After a lot of walking on hot sand, the soles of your feet cooked and hardened. If you sat in the camp too much of the time, 'Ow! Too sore.'

He gave me a spear-hunting tip, forgetting it was no longer done, losing his time sense again. 'Chase a kangaroo when it's hot heat and his foot come off! Finished! Den you can cheat im.'

The spear was finished. He put it to one side. He looked around to Esta, his wife. Her beard was showing in the firelight. She got up, understanding she had to go. I didn't fail to register the significance of this. We were about to talk in private.

He said, quietly, 'The marks you got – here the same, only you got cuts.'

'Someone told you,' I said, opening my shirt. I showed him front and back.

I said, 'You use what? Ochre?'

'Okers. That's right.' He chuckled, echoing my statement. He stopped. 'Who been tellin' you?'

I said I was just guessing. He said the ochre was for the grabbing time. 'Law, ya know?' He was tugging his chin. A boy. 'Dey straight 'em.' He flicked his fingers in his lap.

Shoe-lace lizard tails were shooting from the track, down holes. The white plastic of an old margarine tub was breaking underfoot like an eggshell. Under the tree, bird droppings that were as hard and tightly curled as snails. A lizard was battling with a cricket – the sound of a foil sweet wrapper being undone slowly and clumsily, perhaps with one hand . . .

I looked up. For crying out loud, what was I doing out here? I was half-way out along the track to the dingoes. I'd walked half a mile from the camp without even knowing it. What had I come out here for? There must have been a reason. But I couldn't remember.

I walked back to the camp. I thought: when they grab a boy for initiation, it's from out of the gutter nowadays. They seize him, and before he's sober he's taken away in a pick-up, off into the bush. And the desert's trying to do the same to me! Doing my grabbing.

Elaine was giggling with Michael in the shed as it creaked under the sun. 'If ya wanna jiggle,' Jonny said, 'there's a lot a bloomin' room outside.'

He was feeling crook, and was staying back in camp. I made him some tea and we got talking about Wiluna, the state of things. I was treading carefully – rumour had it his wife had died during a drinking bout. He said, 'When I was a boy they'd rub soap in my mouth for swearing. "Fack" is the first word the kids learn, these days.'

Elaine was now chasing a wild chick through the spinifex tussocks. 'Leave it!' Jonny shouted. She went away to add her name to the graffiti, 'Elaine Jones only, 89', overwriting another entry, 'Sarah Kelly only, 88.'

'The Law is all the rearing they get nowadays,' Jonny said. This was Law Business, but it was he who'd broached the subject. 'When you've been through the Law, they've got a right to punish you. They're hard. Two times I've been whacked by them with a tribal thing.' He went on without any prompting. 'There's Blackfella Law, and Whitefella Law. The oldfellas came along to the gaol a year or two ago, and asked for some blackfellas. "Him, him and him."'

The police let them go. They took them away into the bush and punished them. 'Blackfella's Law is harder than white,' he said.

I went away, happy to leave it there. Suddenly I was deemed someone who could be told things. And this land had a way with itself, I was starting to feel. If I could hold off my whitefella questionings, if I could only wait around long enough – here, or Wiluna – it was going to enact everything for me.

I told Micky my yarn – the story of the Torres Strait crossing, the black waves, the tossed sea snakes, the waterless islands.

'Oooh,' he said. He didn't like water. He didn't like the sound of the canoe, either. 'Oooh. Never been in them thing. We frightened – all them war-da.'

Buffalo came up. He asked Micky to go off with him to 'see der country'.

'I don' like a running around. *I* like sidding down.'

Buffalo swore loudly. The windpump pigeons rose. 'Wild talk!' Micky said. Micky began giving me spear-throwing instructions. He was enjoying himself. 'You can spin 'em. Yeah! The spin will carry 'em. Dong!' A spear would go straight through a turtle's back, he said, 'and come out dis way'. He pulled an imaginary shaft through his back.

Buffalo marched off.

Micky had had spear fights in his time – even trained for them. 'I've train. We'll be the winner. Dodge 'em, dodge 'em.' Until, finally, 'Hook 'em. Follow 'em up.'

While we talked, Esta shuffled around their little camp, or sat facing downwind, looking out at the bush.

'Old time, you know? When a man goes after a woman. We bring him back to de mob. Stand 'im up, give 'im a boomerang and shield. We start chuckin' spears, then! Dodge 'em, dodge 'em . . . Swish! If he's a man, he'll fight 'n' kill him. Jealous fight, you know? They'll hook 'em. Woman too – she'll be punished. Hook 'em. The woman will fight her. Woo!'

Micky waved a finger at a cloud fleck on the southern horizon. 'Lookin' like rain is coming!'

The clouds swelled into discs like knots in blue wood. By the afternoon, they are feathery wands, by dusk, grey turkey plumage lobes.

'By an' by, I'll learn you more,' Micky said that night, almost to himself. 'When dere no ladies present.'

In the camp they were 'meat hungry'. However many 'weeties' they had, it wasn't enough. For the last two days the men had wandered the area with metal bars, goanna-tracking. Now they were desperate, flinging them at the 'cockies' – or the *yaralapulpa*, pigeons with tidy, thin tufts on their heads and flute-whistling wings. The blackfellas plucked the cockies down to their blue and purple skins and had them on the fire. But it wasn't enough. Soon they couldn't stand it any more. They upped sticks.

I joined them on their journey to Sydney Head; six kangaroos, two turkeys – they hardly counted the killing. They made a fire and Michael went shooting again.

Russel showed me how to cook the Law way. He bent over a kangaroo, his tribal shoulder slashes like rain splashes, and cut the animal's belly open, hauling out the guts, pegging up the slit with a sharpened twig, and winding the guts round the peg to help seal the slit.

The other men were leaving, wandering into the bush in a mob. I recognized the drifting faces, the airy manner, from the truck rides, the absorbed look they had during the night fires. I asked the women around the fire. 'Men's business,' they said.

Russel said, 'Go along, if ya like. Might pick up something.'

'You think I'm allowed?'

'You all right.'

There was no alarm from the men as I came to walk along with their group; they seemed half-expecting me. We stopped by a bush; Jonny bent under it and brought out a short wooden panel. He said nothing, the other men said nothing. They traced out the whirling lines marked on it – indented, I found out later, with a kangaroo bone. He held it to the back of Simon's round head, showing how it would have slipped into the headband.

'Mind if I come for a yarn?'

'No. I don't mind.' Micky sat up, enthusiastically placing his hands on his knees. Esta, the smiley old biddy, is absent. That is why I've chosen this moment to call in.

He wanted to know when I was going. I said I was learning to be a man the New Guinea way. 'It's a tough one,' I said. 'For me, anyway.'

'You not a man yet?' He was dabbing his breast, indicating the crocodile patterns.

'It's a traditional journey. Like a young man going off to follow his songlines, perhaps.'

That seemed to make sense to Micky. 'Dat's when we finish 'im off.'

I told him about Kandengei, how I was tasting the wind. When the wind was good – and even if it wasn't – then their New Guinea spirit was meant, if it was still in working order, to guide me to strike. '"Strike" meaning I'll go all out for my Junior Grade manhood, I suppose.'

'You testing the wind then?'

'Tasting, yes.'

'Den what?'

'Then – well, in the olden days you used to kill someone and take the head back.'

'By jingo!' He giggled and listened for more, pop-eyed. But it was mostly finished now, I said. He shrugged. 'The same. Killing over now.'

I retold Cyril's account of how you cooked up a body in the sand. You watched for it to boil. He laughed. 'Shovel Stevens's time. Wooo!'

He described a meal he'd had once on a pretty hill. It sounded like a picnic. 'I was given a arm to eat,' he said proudly.

'Well, my journey isn't like that. I just look for manhood without eating anyone. Even without fighting, if I have anything to do with it.'

Micky was getting quite excited. I was going to see him chuck a boomerang one day, he said. And I was going to learn to say some of the important words. Malu, gan-ga – he greedily hisses and chews the syllables. I must get my mouth used to them.

'There . . . Nu Guinea. You got one?' He waves his little finger. A woman. He circles his breasts with his fingers. 'You got a woman?'

'Two!' I said, happily.

'Ooh! Dey good ones? They dress up smart?' I said that in the old days, ladies used to rub their breasts with pig fat to make them shine brightly – 'still do in the Highlands'.

'Here we do paintin' instead, ya know?' He kept an eye out for his wife, puffing a little. He wiped his fingers on his chest – a wiggled line.

He said, 'Some stories a liddle the same, I think. Some a liddle different.'

I told him the story of the time the water came up, drowned everyone in the world, except a canoe load of forest creatures rounded up by two men and a woman. The crocodile spirit let the water down.

'Flood time,' said Micky, sighing. It was just as he had suspected.

His wife was pottering back. Micky said to me, 'After, you know?'

One of Dusty's puppies disappears in the night. All the next day he's wandering about, calling for him. A dingo might kill a domestic dog if the dingo was in season and tense, Dusty said, but she wouldn't have taken a pup for food.

'Did you hear about the Chamberlain case?' I asked him. A white woman near Ayers Rock had claimed that her baby had been snatched by a dingo.

'That's not a dingo. I told the police. That's a spirit thing. That's a *Wonggai* [people's] place. I told them.'

'And what did the whitefellas say?'

But Dusty was too busy worrying about his little pup. 'He won't be comin' back now,' he said, looking out into the dusk.

It was nearing the grabbing time, Micky said. Ooh! They had such a big meeting. Old women cooked up big dampers – he was drawing it out – and the kangaroos were all got ready. They strung up the boy using a rope made out of hair. They carted him off to Jigalong or Warburton. They took him all round the neighbourhood. The journey ended with him going through the Law. Oh, the singing that went on.

Esta was stirring, coming nearer. She was wearing his green balaclava, dry grass on it. Micky rubbed out his picture – just three parallel lines, the kangaroos, and two circles, the men and the women. 'By an' by,' he said, quietly.

The camp is quiet. Rhonda, the young mother with her leg in plaster, spades out the ashes and digs a boulder-sized damper into the fire. The baby girl toddles around the woman's back, pulling her mule mane of hair. Rhonda's floury handprints are all over the girl, mottling her black skin.

The spongy cirrus clouds fatten up then disperse, raked out over the sky, at last taking the sun from us.

I make myself some tea over the fire, and write in my notebook and talk to Russel. The sandalwood mob were being far more open with me and a lot of this seemed to be due to my having been given so much time by Micky. Micky was well regarded in Law circles, I'd decided.

Noel is scooping water over his head. Now he's pouring a box of 'Fab 3' washing-powder over himself. Elaine is looking up through her fringe with soft eyes, wiggling her finger, trying to entice him round the back of the water tank.

I ask Margaret when the dingo waterholes were made. 'The Dreamtime?' she says, pausing, as if awaiting an answer from me.

'At Kandengei, they do a lot of carving. They use shells for eyes.' I drew the shape of the cowries in the sand. He redraws the shell for Esta. 'That's a clever one, in-ee.'

He wants to know about marriage. Bride prices, arranged marriages, cross-cousin marriages, we talk it all through. He asks, 'Dey fix a girl for you?'

I sigh heavily. Don't ask.

He asked, 'You pay for 'em?'

'Through the nose.'

'*We* have 'em – the same! We have a big meetn', you know? All der brother-in-law, father-in-law on dat side.' He draws them in the sand, just a circle. 'And all *us* on dis side. With all the heap of boomerangs, spears in front of the girl. Whole bundle of 'em!' The bride seemed to sit with a bunch of women, the male relatives in line in front, facing the bridegroom's family. The picture – just circles and lines – was finished. 'The women, they got more of a smell, you know. If you go windside, dey can burn your eyes. I down' like it.'

He changed the subject. In the 'old men days', if you wanted to kill someone, you could do it from Perth. You drew the figure of someone – Micky drew a beetle-like figure – and you put a stick right through it. They would sing the song, all the men. When the person had died, you knew. The stick fell over. He drew a line from the male group, a half ring or circles, to the stick, lying in the middle of the beetle, a scientist's pinned specimen.

I sat in silence, hardly believing it, the way he was confiding. While I gaped, he carried on, telling these and other things as if it was his duty as an elder.

Buffalo, Dusty, Micky and Esta were packing up. Apparently a lot of Warburton men were heading for Wiluna – Dusty had heard it on the radio. Something was afoot. Sunshine, Dusty's wife, said it was Business. 'Maybe a boy has hung himself up in a gaol. Maybe a spearing. Or they just walking about the bush.' Then she remembered. 'Though that doesn't happen now.'

They were gone. I didn't have Micky to learn from any more, and I felt listless. I worked out the date in my notebook: 23 November. It grows humid. The wind blows, the pump clatters madly. Flies swirl over us and the moist air clings. Later, rain dashes down; there's lightning. In the night, over to the south, we see two fires, signs between Dusty and Micky.

The next morning, Elaine notices snake tracks. I can't see the slightest sign. Rhonda plants her plaster-cast leg and probes the sand with a bar. The snake finally writhes out. It is only a little shorter than me – and I am six foot four. I am expecting a desert snake to be the ochre of the sand, but it is a moss green, black flecks giving a burnish to some scales.

While I'm busy admiring the snake, the men and women are screaming. They bombard it with sticks, poles, clubs. Finally it is pinned
down by a rock. It swings and bites its own back repeatedly. Soon it
is dead.

When everyone is calmer, Michael shows me the snake tracks, alternate raised creases. He walks around, flinging a casual hand along them
as if scattering corn, hardly a look down. He's following a smell, you
would have thought.

Is it the close weather? Or is it the snake? Whatever it is, everyone
else is distracted. All day I feel as if I'm the only person out here.
Heaven knows where everyone else is.

I remember something Kay told me at the store. Nola took some
children out into the bush. One child began teasing another, saying
the name of the dead man, Paddy Richards. There was hysteria. It
was like nothing she had ever witnessed before. 'Horrible,' was all she
could describe it as.

In the evening the sandalwood mob were standing around the
fire with their mugs of tea, worrying each other with ghost stories. Jonny said that a Dangara, a giant man, was seen around
here once. Russel said he'd seen a footprint more than 'a foot or
two' long. 'He had five toes. *Like* a man, but . . .' Russel stopped
himself.

Jonny said, 'At Sandstone, you got the little man. Not round
here.'

Buffalo said that when Left-hand Sambo was a boy he was chased
up a tree by Bomba, a monster emu. His father killed it with a spear.
During the telling of the tale everyone grew steadily quieter until Buffalo himself was quiet. After a while, Jonny finished the story. 'Burnt
it in a fire.'

Then Margaret suddenly said to me, 'What you *really* want out
here, Dick?'

Kenny agreed to drop off a barrel of water for me by the rock
holes. I wanted to be alone, get to grips with what was going on
around here.

Kenny warned me. A dingo would last three days without food and
water. A man who knew the bush, not half so long. 'You gotta be
careful.'

I had a good breakfast. The blackfellas waved me off, casually. I
was reassured by this, the looseness of their waving. 'Bye, Dick!' 'See
ya, Dick!'

I walked into the wind.

As I came near, finches rose from the rock holes. No dingoes for company just now.

I made my camp at the base of a tree on a slight rise. I hauled in firewood, then watched ants set up supply lines to my stores. Somewhere near, a bird chirped like a cricket. The flies on my back played.

I followed fresh dingo tracks, lost them; made a camp fire for a picnic. It flared up. Suddenly it was a huge blaze, and before I could do anything, the sandalwood truck came charging in from nowhere. Russel leaned out of the window. 'We seen ya signal. You all right?'

I said I would try not to do it again.

I waited for the dingoes to come in. One day, two days, three. I improved my camp, pulling off dead sheets of bark from a gum tree for extra windbreaks, cutting kangaroo skins left by the dingoes for rope. The fourth day I woke under velvet grey, heavy cloud. There was no sunrise. I washed. The cool air flushed around my bare skin, catching hairs, sparking.

Still nothing out here – dingoes, spirits, nothing that I could sense. I listened to the wind, the breeze-shattered trees, the sand scuttlers. I was not getting anywhere. But would it always have to be like this? Hadn't I, through my white skin, been the *racionale* in South America? Wasn't I the one who couldn't see the hairy angel, the Gugu in the forests of Sumatra? Wasn't I the bandee in the Crocodile Nest who kept morale up with 'Old MacDonald had a Farm'? And now, was I never to feel what gripped the minds of these blackfellas?

Certain birds called by regularly – finches with an orange beak, white belly, grey back and throat and black collar, whistling a single sharp note; others that looked better suited to a back garden. Warblers like sparrows with cumbersome tails – the spinifex bird, I'd heard it called – a strinted grasswren, they were after the black beetles in the folds of the hard kangaroo skin, or the insects running from the termite-riddled tree stumps that composed my firewood.

I woke, hearing a growl. It was a territorial sound, a warning, but out here the doggy sound was homely. The dingo would be a companion.

In the morning, down by the rock hole, I saw her, a mother with stretched teats. She looked at my camp, a stone's throw away, and at me; she was cautious but unafraid. In the far distance, at the edge of the open field of stones around the rock holes, crossing east to west, was another dingo, apparently on a different mission.

The bitch also went off hunting, and I tried to stalk after her, scratching my progress behind me with a stick. I wasn't difficult for her to lose.

The following morning, she was back. I filled my water bottle, made myself drink a litre more water and set off after her again. She went the same route, west. Soon, again, I was far behind, and I made my way back, following the line I'd etched in the ground. I found a crop of *goondong* – the fruits like small tomatoes. Peeled, Micky had said, 'he come lovely, sweet.' Then some *tordor*, pods like hazelnuts that he'd hunted as a child. I sat down and ate a few, noticing that my grazes from the wiry branches had stuck over with a hard dust layer. Six days alone out here. Isn't something more exciting going to happen?

In the evening, sitting by the fire, I heard a roar. It must be a gust of wind, but it was gathering, shaking through the brittle trees. I stood up. I could no longer pretend; it wasn't the wind. I was trembling, certainly feeling haunted now. Was this it?

But the next moment, I saw light down towards the rock holes. A beam. Headlamps. The truck – the sandalwood mob checking I was all right.

I had spent nearly a week in the bush and I felt cheated – who knows, even I might have sensed something out here eventually. I had not been allowed to escape; I felt contaminated, past-hugged.

It was the plump Junior Man called Simon, also Elaine and Michael and the hairy thug. They had news from Wiluna. 'Two boys have been grabbed, yesterday. Dere's a whole mob of dem dere,' Michael said.

I gave up nearly all my precious pears and apples to my guests. They took everything offered. Some they took away with them to hand round the camp.

Alone again. I lay near the fire, a fast cricket chorus of ten notes in my ear, feeling a bit of a failed Junior Man. Micky was out there, at the centre of the rituals, the enactment of the songlines, the struttings and frettings. Alone out here, in this vacuum, it was easy to feel the tug of any energy that they were building back there near Wiluna.

I stared at the flames, depressed. I ate half a damper, drank some tea. A half moon came up late. In the night, the fire was hot in my face, the wind cold on my back. Crickets with starched, tight collars made backflips towards the fire, gradually making it to the flames. Then frying, poor things, one by one.

I walked back into the camp at breakfast time. I felt weary, as if I'd been travelling a long, long way.

Everyone was ruddier-skinned that I remembered, perhaps because of the cloudier sky and less of the burning wind that could even blacken the stones. No sign of Micky or Dusty. I sat around camp, writing notes, listening to the clank of the windpump, the thudding of the sandalwood mob working on the bark. A day of it was enough. I'd been affected somehow by the amount of space out there. I missed it.

This place could haunt you, if you let it, I thought. Yet the view is openness and light. Little finches swirl through it. The moon came up around midnight, and I watched it whiten from orange. The sky was cool and clear. Then, still in the night, I walked out; the dogs didn't bark, they wagged their tails, letting me go.

In the moonlight, there were shapes, no textures. The rock holes were ahead of me. I found myself saying that the timing was right; as if I knew something was going to happen. Though of course it wasn't. Nothing was going to happen and I knew this perfectly well. However, as I grew cold and woke fully, I was slightly taken aback by my having got up at this hour. I was thankful for the approach of dawn, low shelves of cloud beginning to be underlit in yellow. The rare objects in the dark out here were haunting me, jumping out at me. I was startled easily by sudden clashing branch sounds from the unsteady wind.

I was relieved at the first birdcalls. A peeping, single tone on an ascending scale. Then a melodic chit-chat warble.

Details budded from the night as the sun rose, beginning to light the scenery, light playing on the handful of perfectly smooth rock holes. The dingoes were not in. However, I walked up to my old camp and found they had taken the borrowed kangaroo skin back to their hole.

The sun is an orange yolk just clear of the horizon, over by the blackfellas' camp. I jump at the sound of a bird chirp. I see the ashen grey finch's mascara eyes, fawn chest, fruit-cracking beak. I want to set myself free out here, to know this place, but how can I ever do that? Everywhere I go, I have to drag a stick, mark a trail.

I walk from my camp across the rock holes and straight on, north, into the bush, drawing a line with a stick behind me. I do not mind where I end up. I can't get lost, as long as I keep drawing the line. Nor can I have freedom; I'm on a lead. It's an irritation.

I draw my line. Over the dust, over the round pellets scattered on it like burnt-out crystals, through tuffets of needle leaves in scorched yellow. And hearing the stick scrape and jump against the stones, I get more and more annoyed. I want to be able to wander free, I want to be rid of that line, but what can I do? Without the line, I'd be lost. I cannot take part in this place; not for the first time on this trip, I notice that while I'm after this extremely elusive title of Junior Manhood I'm not so very different from a Westerner. I'm striving, proving, cutting, drawing maps, carving through nature's nations. With the stick I'm breaking a crust of kangaroo dung, through volcanic craters of ants, their spewing turrets that look as if they're from dead planets, the last blips of the living. On, cutting up geyser pillars, globular stumps, stiff grasses, sea urchin spindles, coral tube passages for soft insects.

On and on; linear exploration – conquering, dividing in the manner of a whitefella, unable to let go, having to stay safely on the end of the safety line.

Cobweb tissues, locust wing leaves, bark rains, fire assemblages of branches, surf clouds, dust cakes, used-Elastoplast bark strips. A dead lizard – its tongue-twisted desolation, bark-dry lips, brittle tail.

I was on the ground. I must have fallen. I must have tripped, hit my head and stunned myself.

I stood up, fell to my knees. I was light-headed, nauseous and weak. I must get to the shade. I reeled. The colours around me were gone; I could see only heavy contrasts, blacks and whites. I felt heavy, dragged down. I wanted to sleep suddenly. Then I was scared; I wanted to sleep too much. It couldn't be right.

How long had I been here? The sun was up, and it was sunrise when I started walking. An hour had passed? Could it have? I was confused.

My water bottle. Where? It should be hanging from me. But I see the bottle, also a shoulder bag and the stick, some ten paces away. Already I am wondering if there is a clear line back to the rock holes from the stick – my safety line. I rise. Again my head is swimming. I feel sick – the blood leaving my brain. I bend my head, walk with it low, as if I'm wading. Crack! A blow to my forehead. I'm sure someone has hit me. But I find my face is in the dirt – it was just the blow from the fall. Then a flush of clarity – adrenalin from the fright. I find I've got to my bag.

I drag myself to a bush and lean against it, slumping against it hard. I drink, make myself eat the dried fruit I've brought. Check that I've brought some matches out with me. Thank goodness for that, at least. 'I'm in trouble,' I say aloud. My head is so heavy; I can't walk back yet. I can't even sit up. I have to lie horizontal. I'll wait for the heat to go. Summon energy later. With the cool, I should be stronger.

I wait, dreamy, trying to remember. I was walking out, north from the rock holes. How far? A mile or two. Three, four? No more than three, probably. And then I fell. But my water bottle and stick weren't beside me, why was that?

All day I fight against sleep, squeezing a sharp pebble in my hand, thinking of some of my other notable catastrophes – canoe upset alone in the Amazon, stitching myself up while alone in Sumatran jungle, you name it. I'd survived those – an average of one per trip. But this time I was a witchetty grub whiteman, who had come from the trees out under the blue sky that pales everything to dust.

Wallace, Nightlight, Stars, Daniel. I haven't even made the Junior grade.

The sun starts to turn down. I get up, fall. My God, I'm in no better condition than before. Now I know I'm in trouble. All that bother to get over the mountains, that extra thought, taking along a map of the forest for my mum's sake, and now I'm lost in a desert. Sorry about this, Kandengei. Let's hope it's only a temporary fault.

Time for the signal. I must light a fire. Micky said it works every time.

I throw a match. The first three do not catch. Then I wait as the grey oily spinifex smoke rises. The wind gusts, the flames rip. Soon, I have to crawl away so as not to burn. I'm left with a low shrub to lean against and it has no more shade than chicken wire. While the fire gushes, the sun moves, and I shift to keep in the shade of the bush, such as it is.

But no one has come yet. Fear takes hold – I'm to die out here. The desert has grabbed me. And I haven't even finished my journey. This place had tricked me. It has drawn me into the middle of nowhere, and now it had dumped me.

I look at the damage my fire has inflicted, and am pleased. The lust, joy of destruction in those flames – their dazzling appetite. I've put up quite a fight . . .

The sun is weak. No one has come from the sandalwood camp. It's up to me. One pint of water left. No more fruit. My God, all the people I'm letting down. My family and friends in Britain and then there's all those teeming Smaarks.

Around me, destruction. The flames have died. My fire has eaten trees whole, or sometimes just their roots, felling them. Red dragon tongues stretch over the blackened sand – paths of underground fires. There are spouts of escaping air from cooking roots. The soil has risen like pastry, into orange, Vesuvian cakes. Sticks smoke like fag ends, ash tailing to them. No survivors . . .

319

Dusk arrives. They aren't coming now. A small scorpion emerges from the sand near my face. Then another.

I daydream, imagining voices from the camp.

Michael is talking about petrol-sniffing at Dock River – 'The girls don't sniff any more. Only the boys sniff. It shrink der brain.'

Later, Albert says, 'That knife in't yours. You didn't breed 'im.'

Jonny: 'You'll give me that knife back even if you swallow it.'

I hear Malala's grunting as she cooks. I picture the caption on her T-shirt, 'Di's 24 hr. fast food'.

The same pictures, the same words, the same puzzles revolve round and around my head.

Then I imagine the sandalwood mob jumping to their feet, as Max, the sheep shearer, comes with a truck of fresh supplies. The boxes are unloaded. It's night-time. A video recorder has arrived; everyone gathers round, faces glowing blue and white from the TV, the generator racket rendering the sound unintelligible – however, I can discern that it's a Western. Surprise, surprise.

My head clears. I'm surprised to find it's daylight still.

Can I make it on hands and knees to the rock hole? I think so. Someone might come to check on me there tonight. I should manage it, if only by tomorrow. I summon myself, rise . . .

And I'm lost! Where's the big tree? I've burnt down everything around me. I've been the instrument of my destruction. I've knocked all my own signposts down. Typical.

I crawl around and around. I have to lie down again. The ground here is hot from the fire. I push myself again, circumnavigating the biggest tree. Yes, it must be this tree, but where it once had a thicket I have created a field, another void.

I have my orientation: the fire-smudged line. I have to take the tree by the hand for support. I circle the tree, looking for the line out. Catch it. I'm on my way. Walk slow, slow, my head down by my knees, staring at the ground. As I leave, I catch a movement in the soil. No survivors, I said? A bull ant cautiously pushes open a tunnel. It has the mandibles and head of another small black ant clamped on a hind foot.

I leave the smell of burnt cake. I sight the water drum; I slump there; hide in its shadow. I haven't the energy to suck water from the pipe to start the flow into the water bottle. I lean on the drum; push it over – fortunately the drum is empty enough to be shifted. I roll the drum from side to side, catching the water as it swashes out.

I push on to the camp; a silly, limp walk back. Straight into the shed, where I've left my sleeping bag. And onto my back, in the dust. But no one has even noticed. I have to tell Margaret. 'I'm crook,' I say. Sick.

I ask her to boil water, trying to hold my voice level, trying to play down this rather embarrassing drama. Kenny comes with some tea. He hangs there, fingers tightly wrapped around the cup. Dusty has come. He says, 'You might as well go back with Max.'

Max is back? But that was just me daydreaming.

Dusty repeats what he's been saying. I find it's an order. 'We can't look after you here, see. So you might as well go back.' His punchbag face is evasive.

A moment later the men crowd around me and ask how I am. Then Max is fixing up a video machine. The sandalwood mob grow silent; I watch their blue and white faces as they goggle at the screen.

I see all that, and don't understand a bit of what went on out there today. What made me go out there? What happened? I only know that the desert got to me after all. Who could deny it?

I drag myself off into the open air and lie down. Much later someone is leaning over me. 'By jingo, you're a funny one!'

Micky. He thinks it's amusing. He's giggling, his stubbly, bear's face hanging over me again, blocking the stars. 'By *jingo* I gotta learn you!'

Chapter Nine

THE WATERHOLE

Dismissed by so many whitefellas for its waste and decay, Wiluna had the power of focused energy. It was a focal point of dreams – for the blackfellas dissipating themselves at this everlasting waterhole, but also for the nomads of the present – the Black Consciousness movements of Kalu, the head-huntings of the SDAs, and then the Pakistani accountant, Kalu the Nigerian, Herbie the Maori, Nola the New Zealander, her husband Charles the Englishman, the doctors, the teachers, the blow-throughs. I sat with the blackfellas in the road dust and I watched them going about the day-to-day running of the waterhole. All those new nomads coming to join the old.

A whitefella, Jim, stands holding his belt, thumbs tucked behind the buckle. Above him, the hotel sign, 'Licensed to sell Fermented Spirituous Liquors'. He's holding tight to a post.

'He's a drinker, that one,' says Rose, pulling a beer from her bra. She hands it to me for a first swig, the flesh on her shoulder blades wobbling. 'He likes girls,' she says. 'Young ones.'

'Doesn't his wife know?'

'Yeah, she caught him in bed with one.' The wife sleeps separately, Rose says.

'I think I would,' I say. Jim, the whitefella, comes away from the post – someone else is in need of it. And he stands laughing with the other blackfellas, legs apart, his hands by his hips like a gunman, the only white among blacks. 'At least he's good at mixing.'

Rose takes a second can from her bra.

Past the school fence, through which some men are urinating – a teacher looking up from his class just now would see a long line of genitals poking through – there's the caretaker of the caravan site, Cora, from the Philippines, her hair plaited to mid-thigh. There's also the post office lady, who always has a story for the newer blow-throughs – 'Somedays you can hear the children coming – the smashing window panes.'

And George Quinlan, the priest, now plodding alone back to his house. A plastic bag catches his ankle, pinned there by the wind. He fights to get it off. In a minute he'll be in his kitchen, looking out over the blackfellas, from whom he's separated by his efficient-looking guard dog. Quinlan has been here only a couple of months, but his walls are draped with all his knick-knacks – a french-polished boomerang, a charcoaled, slightly cross-eyed, Lawman, Testament quotes, gilt-edged Bibles, glass cabinets full of cut-glass ornamentation. He housekeeps all this finery, all the delicacies, staking himself against the dust, against the bush. And when he isn't out collecting beer cans, he sits indoors in a grey tweed jacket, his heavy black boots clacking on the kitchen floor, rereading the Bible, perhaps trying to understand why Leviticus 11 apparently forbids the eating of the kangaroo, staple food of the bush.

Rose now takes a tobacco tin from her bra. David, the doctor, whirls by in his white car. Stops, reverses, asks how I am. But I should be asking him. He is red-eyed. He's been up all night again, he says. 'Stitching.'

There are two children alone on the kerb. The older one, a young teenager, scratches her fingernail clean with a slug of glass. The little boy threads beer can rings on to a stick.

Rose says, 'I haven't been inside for a whole year.'

A man is stooping over me in the road. 'What . . . are you . . . here?' He's struggling with his consonants, unable to say a word more. We ignore him. He stumbles off, trips over another blackfella.

'My sister got a H.H.,' Rose says, pointing at the girl picking her nails. An H.H., a Hot Hole.

Sam, the man paralysed down his right side, goes by. Holding down his red cowboy hat he hobbles as fast as he can after a mob with a carton of beer. His thin walking stick clinks on the glass litter as he goes.

A boy is walking down the street, smashing the lights, one by one. He raises his ging, fires. Smash! Moves on. A policeman happens to be driving past. He orders him to come to the car. 'How old are you?'

The boy smiles brightly, not hearing properly, thinking he's being asked how's he doing. 'Good!' He says. He doesn't even know he's committing a crime.

After a while, I leave. It's still early in the day and most blackfellas won't arrive for a bit. The pub hasn't opened yet.

Back in Wiluna, then. In my eyes, no longer Wiluna the scrapheap, a rubbish dump, but instead Wiluna the waterhole, the pot of moisture in a desert that allowed decay, the breakdown of matter, but was also a source of life. I had been out in the bush, tasting the wind, you might say. And that had been enough of a taste. *Whether it tastes good or not, the spirit comes to you and guides your hand to strike.*

However, for now I must wait. The sandalwood mob were still not back from the bush, and there was no sign of Micky either. Some blackfellas said he was at Bondini, the reserve where the grabbed boys were, others said he was with the Warburton Mob further out in the bush.

I was camping at Kenny's house. During the day I sat yarning with the blackfellas, trying to make friends. But without the sandalwood mob, I had no allies. Cyril was nowhere to be seen and I was back to square one; just another blow-through.

By afternoon, drinking would be well under way. A drunk woman fawns, swaying, smearing me with her damp dress top. A white-stubbled blackfella bends over me, his hand in my face. 'Hey, I wanna talk wid you. You can't write Law.' They had all heard I'd been writing in the bush. My neighbour raises her head from the depths of her neck and says, 'You takin' our names down? Give me dat book.' A small party stands up to harangue me. I stand up as well.

Threats with iron bars, threats with fists. But I was finding that if I shouted at the mobs, they backed down. I was allowed to go. They seemed affected by my white voice, as if the town was my territory, a whitefella's domain.

Not before time, after ten days, I saw Jonny Long by the store. The sandalwood mob must be back. Reinforcements.

But Jonny said, 'Naagk, just me and a couple. Micky's out still in the bush somewhere as well.'

'Is it Law Business? No one's very clear here.'

'They're scared to tell a whiteman. But it's Business, all right. He's out with the boys they grabbed.'

As I left, Jonny called after me, 'Bad time, coming up.'

'Oh?'

'Warburton Mob gonna be comin'.' People were not going to yarn, he said. 'Law time. People can get hooked.'

'Being speared really does happen still?'

'With the Warburton Mob coming into town it does.'

There was a new blackfella among those here. He stood in the road, trying to keep his balance. He was a sad man, he said. He had given the community assistance, he told me, waving grandly at the school, as if he had paid for it. But the other blackfellas were only interested in the bottle. 'This makes me so sad.' He levers the words out with his tongue, as if they are too heavy.

'I have to fight,' he says, and now the words are indeed becoming too heavy – he has begun his second can of Emu. 'Three years I been away. I'm a rich man – I been to High School. But I come back to Wiluna because of the Law.' Another man wanted his woman, he explained. 'I must fight him. This is our way. I will show that I am a man. I have killed eight people. You hear that? *Eight*! What do you say to that?'

I didn't know what to say to that. 'Well done?' I suggested.

'Later, there must be a big fight. Men are waiting for me.'

He fell back into the dust.

I waited, every day or two hearing that another few boys had been grabbed and taken off into the bush. Off to Micky.

Perhaps Micky hadn't meant it. He wasn't going to teach me how to be a Junior Man. Or perhaps he was caught up in other affairs. This was a busy time. But I needed to know one way or the other. Time was passing and I was meant to be on a quest here.

Meanwhile, the atmosphere was getting tighter, the currents of tension around here stronger. A steady trickle of strangers were arriving from Jigalong and Perth, all of them with their status to prove; this was the 'Bad time', the Law time, coming up.

One day I caught sight of Cyril at last. 'Hello, Cyril. Where've you been the last two weeks?'

He was distant. 'Off in the bush.' I decided to leave him be. He tugged me back, feeling bad. Without me asking, he drew snake tracks in the sand by the store and explained how you knew which way the snake was going. Then, about starting a fire by hand. You needed good lungs to blow the smouldering nest you'd made. 'Run out of wind, run out of fire . . .'

'Cyril, you don't sound happy. Is there something wrong?'

Nothing wrong, he said.

'Is the sandalwood mob coming soon?'

'Must.'

'Micky?'

He pulled down his bobble hat. 'Must.'

In the night, men chased each other round the caravan site with bars. Men and women were armed even for the early afternoon fights.

'Here, I wanna say somethun.' A Jigalong man was trying to take me aside. I let him take me a little way. 'You, I wanna talk with you. Why you here?' His neatly scarred arms showed from his sleeveless jacket. He walked off, waving me to follow. He had an iron bar.

A boy I recognized as Kenny Farmer's son said, 'Don't go wid him – he gonna hit you wid a stick.'

He bellowed some more. I carried on walking with him. The prickly pear cacti of the beer garden, whitefella's property, was getting further away but I reminded myself of my little theory; this whole town was a whitefella's oasis; they wouldn't touch me here.

Now the man had me to himself. He got all excited, and shouted in my face. If I wrote about the Law, he'd give me a whistle cock. 'You better fly like a bird, I'm tellin' you.'

I said I'd bear it in mind. I walked away. He stared at his iron bar, bemused that he'd let me go, but letting me go all the same.

Down by the store, men were jumping down from the back of a truck. They had their shirts off and at first I thought they were covered in dust. There was no shine to their skin. Nearer though, I saw it was ochre; and their upper arms were painted with black bands.

Jonny was in the store. 'They been out at Bondini,' he said. 'Law.' He took me along the supermarket shelves to one man, Geoffrey Stewart, who was scratching his chin with a packet of instant cake mix. He was a skinny man with dreadlocks and a snappy, quacky voice. There was a lump like a bee sting on his forearm and mud had been pasted over it: a blood-letting point.

Jonny said Geoffrey Stewart had been brought up at Ululong, near a rock hole I'd visited once with the sandalwood mob. The oldfellas grabbed him and walked him off to put through the Law over Warburton way. When he'd arrived back at Ululong, walking across the bush, he'd got clothes on. Hearing Jonny say this, he said, 'Maan!' He tugged his hair-fringed jaw. He spoke to Jonny, framing his head artistically with his thin arms. 'He was one of the last in from the desert, he says. Seeing Wiluna was like looking at a garden of paradise.'

Charles, Nola's English husband, was outside in his car, wearing a tan hat. I'd heard it said he had an MSc in something and was helping out at the mine that was out of town.

'You could do with a break,' he said. He had pale blue eyes and a strong voice with a whistling resonance.

He took me up the road for a coffee. The Robinsons had a house and caravan on the road in from Meeka – once the 'brass quarter', Redhill, a hill where all the government employees had been. You could still see the quartz pathway entrances, street lamps. We had our coffee in the caravan. Outside, crows were raiding the dustbins.

I told Charles about my little incident out in the bush. I said I didn't think it could have been anything obvious – heat exhaustion, sunstroke, dehydration. It must have been just the knock on the head.

'I've found bodies over the years – one of them half-eaten by dingoes.' They'd been a whole family once. You could see the father's tracks.

How he'd stumbled along, going for help. 'Took off his clothes to keep cool – usual thing.' The mother had died only a few hours before. The child was still just alive.

'Do children last longer?'

He wasn't sure. 'Probably the mother gave up her rations.'

I stayed for a second coffee.

Down the road, a willy-willy, a small whirlwind, was clanking the cans it lifted up, throwing crows around with the puce dust and flashing silver debris.

Charles had another thought. 'There was another man who died out there once. But he'd somehow decided he wanted to be out there alone. Water was brought to him occasionally, but no one saw him. They heard him laughing and howling. Like a mad dog.'

I was spared that one, anyway, I thought.

Charles took me back to the store. I had a good talk with Nola. 'There's someone I wanted to ask you about,' I said. 'He's called Micky Wongawol. He seems to have taken me under his wing.'

'Truly?' she said. She'd given a lift once to Nellie, one of Micky's sisters. They were caught in a sudden storm; but then Nellie had said she could see a light ahead of them through the dark. '*Micky's* light,' Nola said. 'It was guiding her.' Nola wasn't sure but she thought Micky was regarded as special. Just a feeling she'd got seeing him with the other blackfellas.

I walked over to see Peter Burns, the dingo man. It was where Micky was said to stay whilst in Wiluna. Dara, the sister whom Micky had brought out from the bush as a little girl, was sitting on a bed in the living room, staring at TV with her blue plastic sun-glasses on.

There was a silent dog, a smell of talcum powder and of blankets. Dust lay on the uneven plaster of the walls and along the framed black and white photo of a dingo. On the mantelpiece, over a wooden fireplace with a brick Roman arch, were some daffodils and freesias. They were plastic; someone had recently topped their bottle vase up with water.

'He's still out in der bush,' she said.

She went next door to wake Burns. He came, after a while. He was a little shaky. It was too early in the day for him. 'Want any breakfast?' she asked him. She had onions frying on a gas stove. 'Can a beer,' he said. I thought it was a joke. He looked at me. 'You want one?'

He drank his down.

He had nicotine fingertips, grey stubble and eyes that were clear blue. He had made an effort for me – he had combed his hair through with water. I asked if the dingoes out at Mungale were safe.

'Should be, if they stick where they are,' he said. 'Is that all you've come to ask me? Whether I'm giving strychnine to some mongrels out there?'

I said I was after Micky Wongawol.

'Better try and find him before the Law gets under way proper.'

I went to the whitefella's bar – through the beer garden, past bar towels out on the washing line, wagon wheels, prickly pears, a grape vine decorating the barbecue area. All this was patrolled by Max, the German shepherd, who seemed only to know how to attack blackfellas. The bar was beyond the lobby, where the main door, now barred up, had once looked onto the street. Now the only light to the interior was provided by a delicate glass flower lamp left from a previous, happier era.

'They're animals,' said the barman, reaching up to adjust the volume of the wall TV with one of the battery of weapons confiscated from the black bar. He had just finished fishing out knickers from their toilets. He showed me the stones thrown at him last night. He said, knowingly – he'd been here a month – 'I keep one step ahead. Need to.'

Merve, the hotel manager, said, 'Never had a riot here, so don't go saying that in your book. Never been a riot. Not unless you count the stabbing down the street once.'

Outside, a woman screamed, then groaned. Merve seemed to be handicapped in this way; he had trouble hearing certain things. His shiny face was grumpy, superior. 'Never had any trouble like that.'

Through at the black bar, I saw a face, more gory locks.

The man who always looked fresh from the desert was here. He was always here, on his stool, under his hat. He said if I was *really* interested in writing about the community I'd spend my time at the emu farm – 'biggest in Australia' – and not messing with the drunks.

'Their skulls,' said Jim, the one who liked black girls, 'are about that thick.' He measured a space with his fingers, as if ordering a shot of whisky. Their brains had no room to expand with alcohol, he explained. 'Read it somewhere.'

'There's something different about them, all right,' the barman said. 'They're on another planet.'

'I've seen them play football while drunk,' Merve said, slowing. The barman turned down the TV, giving me the impression that these moments from Merve were well worth hearing, or just plain rare. 'They were playing football,' said Merve. 'Out on the street here.' He stood behind the bar, marvelling out of the netted window at some vision.

*　　*　　*

Nola said I looked tired. She wanted me to know that I could call at her house if I ever wanted something. 'Wiluna gets to you somehow.' She had been stuck eight years here, Herbie more, Kay and her husband thirty-five years; none of them had intended it that way.

And now Wiluna was getting to me.

I wandered out to the bush, over the remains of Wiluna and to the tall creaking sheds that stood alone at the end of what had once been a railway line. From a distance the sheds looked like something dug up, old seashells perhaps. Closer at hand, there was a rusted crane, with its hook still swinging where it had unloaded the last cargo; bolts left after the line itself was ripped up. A broken coffee cup, a petrol funnel, brand new Emu beer cans in a huddle.

Then back into town. I could see a new vehicle in the caravan site, and headed there.

The lawn sprinkler man got off the tractor as if it were a horse, adjusted his hat, and started up the spray. Wagtails rushed to the water. A yellow-headed, black-eyed little bird, later found to be a white-plumed honeyeater, ducked under the water with a dragonfly fizzing in its beak. Another, a singing honeyeater, a grey masked bird striped white under the eye, a pale yellow band flowing with the body line, threw back its head under the shower and trilled softly. A passing dog, doing the circuit of town bins, stopped a short moment in the lawn spray, shook, trotted on, drawn like everyone else around here to an oasis.

'Mobile T-shirt Printers serving outback Australia', read the sign on the new vehicle. It was a white truck with folding steps and shutters and five spare tyres on the roof. 'Hutchinsons – licensed hawkers'.

Ray and Gordon had come to Wiluna for the peak spending season, the time of the annual tax rebate. There was going to be cash everywhere before it was gone on booze. 'Mother's milk to them.' Gordon had a duff right eye, closed during the heat of the day, and a forehead which was a bed of black spots waiting like overripe potatoes to be dug up. He moved on, he said, when he'd made his buck. He had a Thai wife on order.

Most of their trade was trinkets, but they specialized in personalized T-shirts. I wanted to know which the blackfellas liked best – motorbikes, cars, animals, flowers. Ray, who ran the operation, showed me the bestseller. It was glitter-laid palm trees bending to rippling waters.

Time for another coffee with Charles, I thought. I waited half a day, and caught him at the store. 'Everyone seems to be getting more distant to me, instead of less. I'm going backwards.'

'It's going to get increasingly difficult. Around summer, their whole mood changes. It's the weather, apart from anything. But the Law as well.' Now was the time the blackfellas were vigilant, looking about to make sure they weren't being sung or bone-pointed to death.

I said, well they were certainly swinging their iron bars a lot, anyway. I'd had a theory that they wouldn't hit a whiteman in Wiluna. Now I wasn't so sure.

Charles said he'd tell me something. One man here once punished his wife by spearing her three times in the leg. 'Must have hit an artery, air got in. She died. Taken by whitemen, put in gaol for three years. After that, on release, the Lawmen broke his spear-throwing arm.'

I couldn't see the moral to his story. Charles said, 'I don't know how far you've got with them. I'm just saying there's a law for us, and a law for them, and you're only really going to get in trouble ever if you come under their law.'

All evening, youths strolled around town with weapons stuffed down their trousers. Jonny said they were looking for Malcolm, one of the two half-Aboriginal police aides. The whitefellas in the pub were saying that Malcolm had gone to the reserve this evening to have a word with a blackfella. He went off to Bondini, the reserve. 'The boys were still out there, being put through the Law, and he walked right in on it.'

The discussion was interrupted by a blackfella woman screaming at another next door. 'You're just *good* for *walkn'* around and *shown'* off your *figure!*'

The whitefellas were getting drunk themselves, now. While men were being carved up next door, they threw out a scruffy blow-through for swearing. I decided to leave myself.

Outside the black bar, a youth said to me, 'I'm a maaan!' He placed his fist in front of me, in a pledge-of-allegiance poise. 'You stay out of my way, or your dick will be like a shovel.'

He was another man from Perth, back here to prove himself at Law time, and I retreated to the whitefella bar again to see how fast they were learning about Malcolm. They were filling out the story. Normally the policemen went round in pairs, in cars, but Malcolm must have gone alone, they agreed.

Rob, the store manager, the whitefella with the clean-cut moustache, said, 'Benedict, this was heavy stuff he walked into.'

They think I've learnt nothing in the last couple of months, I thought.

'You've got to be careful too,' he said.

They think I'm a fool, I thought. I do hope they aren't right.

Jim said, 'They mutilate the boys.' The whitefellas gave me details of blood-lettings, whistle-cockings.

The barman, who had Irish red hair and a dry skin, said one of the Richards family was going to kill Malcolm. 'He *will* do, as well. Somewhere, some time.' He wiped the counter deftly, using his dramatic skills, the yarning tradition that this theatrical countryside seemed to have landed everyone with. He repeated, 'He'll kill him.'

Time to go outside again. An iron bar spun down the street, off a woman's head. She hopped away – the leg was a previous injury – towards the police station. Women screamed, encouraging her on, but a man snatched her before she reached safety.

The battles raged.

It was sunset. Soon it was going to be impossible to fight properly. I went back to Kenny's house. Alone with Jonny in the garden, I asked if he had any ideas about my sickness. A school principal jogged by in a track suit.

'You got crook.'

The teacher was scaring the crows from the caravan site gum trees.

He said, 'You were in a *Wonggai* place.' An ancestral place. 'You got dreaming, or something. You better ask Micky that one.'

The school term broke up. Herbie helped erect a Christmas tree in the garden, while the sandalwood mob children put their sports prize shields on top of the TV. A softball statuette for Tiana, another statuette for Stewy. 'It's for footy.'

I sat in the pub garden, writing a letter home. What could I tell them about Wiluna without worrying them about me? I sipped my ginger beer and began 'Wiluna is unique in many ways, really . . .'

A swarthy man in a singlet parked his truck. He had missing teeth and black body fur on his arms, throat, shoulders – probably it was all over him. 'Know where I can get a beer, mate?' Max, the German shepherd dog, rose, taking up his chain. His large ears pricked; this man with all his black body hair was, without doubt, a sort of blackfella. Max couldn't believe his luck. A blackfella in broad daylight! A blackfella he had been waiting for, and now, at long last, here he was. Max drew back his gums, flashed his teeth, and charged.

Tables flew as the leash strained. My ginger beer was gone, my letter soaking, the sunshades spinning.

The whitefella was leaving. 'Catch up with ya later.'

A new day dawns in Wiluna. The wind roars, the sand hisses; among the swish and tremor of the caravan site gum trees, a Dobermann puppy yaps inexpertly on his chain; crows quack.

Stewart, a teacher, is leaving after three years. 'Don't want to see his ex-pupils killing themselves.'

He said goodbye to the pets' corner, posters, handiwork with names and ages of pupils, a brand new American system of discipline – bad marks for swearing, good marks for work – 'if the whole class gets over fifty we take them off trailbiking.'

But it didn't seem to be enough.

I'm standing with Jonny Long over a fire in the Farmers' garden. A car draws up with Cyril at the wheel.

'Where we goin'?' Jonny says, getting into a car which already had five men aboard.

'Bondini,' Cyril says. The reserve. Where the grabbed boys lay.

'Any sign of Micky?' I called. But they were driving off. I had breakfast alone, cooking over the fire in Kenny's garden, feeling unwanted.

Stewy came up. 'Plate!' he ordered. I handed my enamel dish over, thanking him. But he didn't wash it up with the others, he took it away to chuck as a frisbee.

I was left alone again. Stewy could at least have asked me to play.

Half an hour later the car was still circuiting the town, letting off some men, who'd seen unfinished Emu cans, and gathering up others, who had finished theirs. Cyril drove up again. I was by Kenny's garden fire, playing with a bug that had a black back embossed with yellow, musing that it was like a New Guinea war shield.

'You been through the New Guinea Law? Jonny said you been through the Law.'

I said it was different.

Jonny poked his head out of the crowd in the back seat. 'Come along anyhow.'

'Are you sure? I'll get fined. And they might do other things to me as well.'

'Naagk!' Jonny said. 'You're all right!'

'Cyril?' I said.

'Yeah, all right today.'

Bondini was out on the way to the village, on the Gunbarrel Highway. Whitefellas had assisted them to build standardized white bungalows in a 'V' formation facing a spread of broken glass and dust to the road, along which rumbled road repair tipper trucks with red dirt tails.

We drove across the middle of the spread, into the middle of the blackfella's place, passing a group of oldfellas, the Lawmen, and right up to one of the houses, where there was a looser cluster composed of both men and women. We drew right up. Everyone was talking in loud whispers, a whistling that was almost lost in the wind. I was used to these same blackfellas screaming and bellowing, but here there was a church hush.

Jonny and Cyril sat down with them, so I did the same. I now noticed that three of the women had taken off their blouses. Their chests were smeared with oily ochre; it shone from their flab and where it had been smudged over their bras.

Cyril and Jonny and some other men, all fairly junior, I guessed, rose. They were walking off, leaving me. Best to stick with them, I thought. They had given me the invitation to come here. Now I was following them into the open space towards the older men. I caught up Jonny and asked if I should be following. He didn't reply.

We went past a youth who was by himself in the middle of the open space, head down. His shirt was off and he was covered in grease and ochre – it was in his hair as well, forming clots that shone like blood and trailed heavily in the wind. He was in jeans, cross-legged, his elbows on his knees, leaning right forward, as if very tired.

Nearer the Lawmen, I saw some of the sandalwood mob – Russel, Michael, Albert. But they didn't give me a welcome, they were distant in a way that reminded me of the time I'd seen them on those nights walking out into the bush. The faces here were transfixed, the stark, uneven pallor of the sand itself. They talked quietly, and sometimes laughed, but I'd never seen such distance in people's eyes.

'You siddown silent,' a younger man said. I sat behind Jonny at the edge of the group, which I saw now was a circle, those forming the inner ring all older men. I tried to take in their faces – these were the men of power – but they were mainly strangers, twenty or more of them, some talking but all of them reflective. Dusty was here, in his chequered blue shirt, centrally placed. Micky also – more modestly, I rather thought, on the edge.

I was surprised when Dusty called out, 'How ya going?'

Since he felt he could call out above everyone's heads, I thought I might. I asked if I should leave.

'I down' know.'

I called to Micky, who was sitting tight under his Paddington Bear hat. I had to ask twice. He said, 'After.'

Men rose, sat down. At times it was a tidal flow, men following each other, talking in whispers and looking suppressed by the dignity they were giving this moment. There was no obvious discussion; men rose up from outlying groups and came over; men from our group did the opposite. There was no debate, not by the standards of the Kandengei spirit house, just a welter of cross-cutting conversations; it was more a shuffling of a pack, as if they would see what sort of hand they came up with, but I supposed there must be clan organization here somewhere. All rose, finally. The meeting was over – the cards laid down, as it were.

A yellow Toyota cruised up. The Half-man was led to it. I was about his age. Two Lawmen manhandled him aboard.

The men were talking naturally and louder now; they were suddenly back with me again. The distance had closed up. Graham Richards, son of the late Paddy Richards, came straight over. He ordered me to sit down over by the houses. Other men, young, town-educated blackfellas, circled round me. 'You're a whiteman. This isn't a place for you.'

'Fair enough.' I had told Jonny this might happen. I started walking back to the houses. Back to base again. Life isn't easy sometimes when you're an explorer, I thought.

Before I had gone far, an older man beckoned me back. 'You been through the Law?' I said New Guinea Law. I showed some of my collection of scars. Everyone dashed around me, for a look. 'What about the foreskin and undercut – you got one?'

I told him no.

He decided to check. He said, 'Any ladies around?', then shuffled on his knees, and drew out from his flies what looked like bacon held in a thick black rubber sandwich. 'Can you show me yours?'

I said no, I couldn't.

Another Junior Man in a shooting jacket with an expensive cut said, 'The New Guinea Law is different, mate. You better go quick – you heard Graham.'

I decided to. I went over to Micky and said I was going.

'They from the towns,' he said. He seemed surprised I felt I should listen to them. I consulted Dusty. Dusty said ask Morgan. Morgan, an old man in a baseball cap, said, cheerily, 'Whitefella! It's all *right*!'

He pointed at the ground. I sat again. 'You can stay for now. Ask Micky.'

'Micky?'

I asked Micky.

'Dere's not so much happenin'.' He touched my sleeve, remembering. 'Ladies dancin' later.'

'Later today?'

'Today, tomorrow, 'til der boy come back. But down' madder.'

It sounded interesting though, I said.

'You gotta learn some things wid me first,' Micky said, rising, puffing a bit. 'I'll see ya bit later.'

Things are beginning for me, I thought. At last things are beginning.

Micky strode off towards a car that was leaving for the bush. I sat with the rest of the men, watching the yellow Land Cruiser set off, the boy in the back between two men holding nulla-nullas, the clubs, and fingering the hair belts, the belts for tying the boy up. Off along the Gunbarrel Highway, circling around the bush – Warburton, Laverton, wherever, alerting the Lawmen, all their *avookwaarks*, rousing them all to come to Wiluna, where the act would be performed.

The youth, the Half-man, begins the circuit which will end in his attaining Junior Manhood.

The Lawmen disperse into small groups and drive or walk away, mainly back to town.

I sat in the shade of Dusty's house on the reserve, wondering what would happen next. In the evening Dusty said, 'The old fella must be drinkin' or somethin'.' He gave me a lift back into town.

I passed Eric, outside the pub. He was out of his leg plaster-cast now and able to fight properly again. He said, 'You been through New Guinea Law? Dat's what they sayin'.'

I said I had, yes.

'You must live straightway. No pox, the straight way. Otherwise get a hook through you. They'll knock you in the bloody head quick.'

I said the Law I had gone through was different.

He thought, and then swigged and said, 'Den dat's all right.' He looked steadily into my eyes. He looked as if he had been told otherwise.

The following morning at the Farmers', Cyril pulled up. Jonny climbed in, saying, 'Micky said you been through enough Law to come, or what?'

I said only what I knew. That my Law was different.

'Better not to risk it,' Jonny said. The car left and I stayed where I was, standing on the morning pools of shining dried blood. I sat down against the house wall, and waited for someone to come and tell me that Micky had somehow sent for me.

Beside me a centipede like a child's plastic necklace flicks on the concrete. Twenty or more little ants come in at it, darting in and then out. A small red ant lifts a ladybird by its rim, alive, and carries it off.

In the afternoon, the sandalwood mob were back; but no Micky. I tried Peter Burns's house. Micky's van was outside. He had roofed over the back of the vehicle with corrugated zinc sheets; underneath was a gypsy assortment of mobile home accessories – blankets, cups, firewood, spears, boomerangs, odds and ends, even the many-plaited ropelets that composed a hair belt. And all just left lying about.

'Excuse me, any sign of Micky?'

Dara, never one to drink, was drunk. 'I'm only having some Christmas cheer.'

Taking it that we were all allowed to say Happy 'Christmas' now, I asked when Christmas was. No one knew.

The dingo man, Burns, was on the same bed. On the other was Glen, of mixed extraction, with a very new baby on its back between himself and the mother. Both were glued to the telly.

'Excuse me, any sign of Micky?'

But it seemed that Burns was in a temper. I had interrupted him raging against the blackfellas, and now he started again. 'I don't want you fackin' cants camping here anymore. This is my house. This is a whitefella's house. Straight out – old Burnsy's tellin' you.'

I refused a beer. It set Burns off. 'You're standing in the door, whingeing, the whole fackin' Pommy bit!' Glen laughed – some American junk on the telly. Burns said, 'You mongrel bastard!' And back to me: 'You're a Pom. A fackin' Pom!' I'd only come in here to ask for someone. He broke into song, rhythm tapped sharply with his boots, clack-clack. 'Oh I am a whingeing Pom, you can guess where I come from . . .'

However, I saw now that a lot of the insults were meant with affection. He accompanied many with a right-eyed wink. He stopped, fixed it, like a long exposure, then carried on. He drew his head down into his neck, raised his shoulders as if bracing his face and then grinned.

I noticed there was someone else in the room – Bret, a silent mixed-race boy who sat in a chair by the door. He was about ten, a son of Marjorie, a blackfella who, it now turned out, was also in the room. She was on the floor asleep with a can of beer in her hand, a disposable nappy stuffed in her bra. Burns said it was her toddler who was outside in the road crying.

I had got no answer about Micky's whereabouts and so I went down to the store. He was there, strolling from drinking party to drinking party along the supermarket shelves. He was jocular, excited to be back. 'How you doin'?' he asked me, but I needed to catch him alone.

The afternoon wore on. Around the town strolled bare-topped Junior Men, dusted with ochre and wearing a mantle each of dried blood, a lacy ring around their shoulders. By now, customers at the store were unsteady. The signatures they made, signing for their provisions at the till, became less and less like X's, and more and more like wiggles.

In the whitefella bar, the new barman is getting some advice from the man fresh from the desert. 'Don't serve the Warburton Mob, when they arrive. They'll cut your throat.'

There's other news. The garage has been broken into again. The mining company has sent out their invitations to the Christmas party. The police will also be doing the same shortly. Blackfellas get invitations, 'but only whitefellas want to turn up'.

Another news item. George, the postmaster, a bone and gristle man with white side-cropped hair, was spreading the news that there was a cyclone coming. It was up in the north, just now.

I can't find Micky, so I try Peter Burns's house again. Bret, the small boy, is there in his silent world, washing up, sweeping, sitting on a bed, lying on his stomach, feet drumming as he hums a song. I ask him the date. 'December the wonth.' Burns thinks it must be later than that. We listen to the news on TV; it's the 12th.

Micky comes in at the doorway. I'm saddened. Somehow I'd hoped the drink wouldn't affect him in the way it did the others. He is an intimidating bulk, swaying his weight over each of us in turn – Glen, Burns, myself. 'Give me a dollar!' I find some loose change. It's about the first time I've given out money to anyone. I tell myself this isn't a bribe.

When he's gone, Burns says, 'Micky's stuffed.' His brain's gone. Too much booze. Once Burns had told him to leave a woman alone – Micky was beating her.

'Poor old Esta,' I said.

'Wasn't Esta.' He winked mischievously. 'Remember, they jump from woman to woman like dogs.'[20] Burns concluded his story. 'Micky wrestled Burnsy to the floor. Pinned him down, strangled him to death, almost.'

Glen concurred. Micky had almost wrung Burns's neck. 'He been like one of them kangaroo dogs fed gunpowder to make 'em more mad.'

Well, even gurus had faults, I supposed. But when I told Burns I was depending on Micky, he'd kindly promised to teach me things, Burns said, 'I'm telling you, he's stuffed.' His son was serving a ten-year sentence. Pack rape. 'How can you rape a girl here? They line up for you. When he gets out he's not coming here. Straight out. He's fackin' mad.'

Burnsy told me I'd best move in here, if I wanted to catch Micky sober. I came back later with my rucksack. Burns was upside-down in his bedroom asleep. I sat by myself in the living room. Bret dived in from the dark. He was panting. He sat down beside me on the bed and started talking fast. 'We been fast walkin' along and seen the devil!'

'What did he look like?'

Bret's eyes stared out from his buff face. 'We been feelin' fresh wind.

Been see the chidee-chidee cross.' It was a black and white bird with a long tail, he said. 'A willi wagtail.' But this was a Mamu – the desert version of the forest spirit, the Wunjumboo. Bret said he had a whitefella name – Featherfoot. 'He a Jinakarlipill. They can be makin'-up dead. He trick you. The devil – he'll block you off. Change.'

I said, so the black bird crossed the road, and you felt a cool breeze. And then what happened?

'He after Ned Abbot,' Bret explained, simply. 'They come here to kill people and eat them. Some fella at the [Warburton] Ranges – they been drinkin' at der rock hole. Mamu came. Thousand been come. Hundreds and hundreds and hundreds. Too many. Jesus help them. Save their life. Hide them in the tree. Der Mamu had a good drink. They went away then. They can tie you up 'n' skin you 'n' eat you. Lucky they not seeing 'em. Otherwise they been killed. Maybe die one million years.'

It was straight on to the next story. 'When Wilson 'n' Killer went –'

'Killer? That's Wilson's kangaroo dog?'

'Naagk! Dat's Killer Jackman.'

I hadn't met the man – at least I thought I'd have remembered him if I had.

'When they were young. Thousands and thousands of Mamu came. They chuck spears. Too many. You can't dodge them all. One will get you, go right through. But Jesus helped 'em – heap 'em up and burn 'em up then. You can see them all standing up. They still there. Standing up. They sticks.'

'So are you afraid of going out at night?'

'They'll grab you. Block you on the road to Bondini. Change into somebody and grab you.'

In the morning, Micky was leaning against the store, his head back, eating a strawberry in his fingertips, holding it by the stalk. He'd been away on the back of a truck somewhere. Dust streaked to his temples, showing where the wind tears had blown. I asked where the Warburton Mob were now.

'We listening.'

'Micky, you'll still find time one day to teach me about the bush or whatever, like you said. To finish my journey, I mean?'

'We *listening*,' he repeated.

I didn't want to nag, but that wasn't enough information to go on. 'Is there anything I should do?'

Micky said, 'You stay in camp. I'll holla for ya.'

He went off to get fixed up with a drink, one more nomad, his world unattainable to settled people.

In the post office George said it was a Thursday. He had heard that the cyclone now had a name, Ilona. The first signs would be here in a day or two.

Cyril stopped at the store with his car overladen with drunks. He was on the way to the reserve, and wondered if I wanted a lift. Micky was out there, and there were now lots of camps along the main road – the Jigalong Mob. But I said I'd best wait for whatever Micky had in mind for me.

I went into the store to buy something. It was an excuse to talk to Nola. Nola said she had heard that Malcolm the police aide was back in town. 'They must be fairly forgiving, now.'

She said she'd been to Warburton once. The children greeted her with 'cold black staring eyes'. In the old days, she said, when the missionaries had more power, they put knickers on the people. They forgot to tell them to take them off when they went to the toilet, and so everyone 'smelt bad'.

She remembered the pus oozing from the infected ears of kids. Every now and then, maggots dropped out as well. How could they withstand the pain, she wondered, and not do anything about it? And how could they not want to take off their knickers?

I said I didn't know either; they weren't with us, some of the time, that was all I felt.

As I left the store, Nola said she'd try and get me out of town if the Warburton Mob chased me with spears. We both laughed, after a fashion.

The wind blew in gusts. Bushes ground their twigs in the soil, scratching circles as they bent and swerved. The cyclone was coming.

'Hi, Dick!' The sandalwood mob were wanting to buy me drinks. I sipped beer with them a little bit, allowed them to waylay me, walking around with a towel around my neck, in case I was socked from behind, and visiting Dusty, who was playing cards. He said if I were him I'd leave before the Warburton Mob came. 'They're wild.'

Mid-afternoon. A man buckled backwards off the kerb, slammed by a man beside him. Another was bumped on the skull with a rock. Women yelled as they advanced on each other, men raised their fists in the street.

A Jigalong man, who had been trying to pinion me for days, said, 'Now, I wanna . . . what you doing . . . work here?'

'Ee all right,' Russel said, intervening for me.

I said, not sure if I meant it, I'd be okay.

'Yeah, you been through your Law,' Russel said. He left me.

'Siddawn!' the Jigalong man cried.

Nowadays I'm not so sure I'm afforded the safe status of a whitefella. I play a mixture of challenge and evasion. I keep the towel tight around my neck.

'I'm not going to talk if there's fighting,' I told the man. 'You like fighting?'

No, no, he said, hastily. 'I down' like fighting.' He wandered away, following a passing Emu can.

Russel and I sat together against the post office fence, opposite the pub. Jackie Stevens, the man with the yellowish beard who'd taken me aside once, and given me his little lace-up shoe to sit on, came up. Now, like then, he asked for dollars, strumming his fingers on his lips, and later, drunker, sang 'Waltzing Matilda' for me.

The Jigalong man was back. 'I wanna talk! You wan an undercut? That what you want? You're welcome! Say Yes or No. You're gonna tell me now.'

It was time to call at the post office, I decided. In here, the whitefella, George, was having a peaceful Friday, pigeon-holing mail. He said Ilona had been off the north coast, around Dampier and now coming down; so far we had only had the beginnings of it.

Outside, the Jigalong man was waiting for me. He was blocking the path. He took down his trousers and showed his penis. 'You want one like this?'

I didn't, and I walked away, but was soon trapped again. Jackie Stevens, the yellow beard, sang on my left, while this man stood in front of me, his trousers undone. Margaret was on my right, gripping my hand with lust. 'Shud up! I wanna talk wid my friend.'

The afternoon turned to dusk. Men and women brawled, children played with toy trucks around the lamp posts. 'You okay?' I asked one little boy. He looked up, smiled beautifully, and carried on playing.

How could these children afford to smile? I couldn't afford to smile, how come they could? However, at the far end of the street, by the playground, I found other children who were crying. Drunks were on their swings.

'Here! I wanna talk with you.' The Jigalong man has an iron bar. This time, he's coming at me with a thoroughness that doesn't look a bit like the empty threat to a whitefella on his own territory. I'm beside the hotel, trapped against it. I step back, and feel the wall, sticky and wet, against me. The man comes in with his bar. He's running. A woman screams.

Then Micky jumps up from the pavement. I hadn't even known he was here. His huge hands are in the air, and he drums at the stranger. 'Fack off! You down' know anything.'

The Jigalong man turned. 'I wanna see *you* tomorrow!' He was walking away. 'You're a newspaper man.'

Micky said, 'You been through more Law than he has.'

In the dark a long-haired man with blood drying on his nose in the wind introduces himself as 'Killer'. Killer Jackman – the man Bret told me about, who was almost caught out by the local Wunjumboo. I'm about to ask him the details when the Nangganawili Community Toyota pulls up. It's enough to stop any conversation.

A man circles the vehicle whacking a woman with a baby in her arms. She gulps each time the bar hits her; the baby sleeps. The women are wailing together and the men are chasing the man round and round the Toyota. The driver is getting sick of this by now and gets out to urinate, slamming the door so hard the window smashes. The explosion appears to make no sound. The shattering glass isn't audible above the screaming.

Micky strides by. He looks gruff, in fact dangerous. I saw now what Burnsy had faced once, when he was being strangled. He pushes Killer, putting his stomach out and nudging him back. '*Wama?*' Booze?

Micky turns to me next. I face him, angry. But he doesn't ask for money, or push me with his stomach. 'You gotta start actin' like a man,' he says. *Maan.* It sounded a loaded word, the way the blackfellas used it.

I tell him I'm trying. We stand in the street in the dark some more, while he tells me, 'We waitn' for the Warburton Mob still. He not ready yet.'

'You want me to be at Bondini when they come?'

'*You* been through der Nu Guinea Law. You come. You *gotta* come, if you're a man.' Micky looks over his shoulder every sentence. Children skew away from us. With his elbow, he fends off Judy, who has a thick, flat lower lip that points upward to my face. Killer stands by. Apparently he's allowed to listen.

I say that the younger blackfellas didn't want me here. Micky doesn't seem to care. 'You gotta come.' He turns on people gathering to heckle me. 'Fack OFF!'

He says he'll pick me up tomorrow. I could stay at his place on the reserve. 'When they cut der boys they do this.' He was meant to be drunk, but now he nimbly squatted, feet on ground, legs a little open, and made a slight bound. A kangaroo. 'I got to learn you. Watch me tomorra.'

*   *   *

In the morning, though, there was no Micky to be seen.

I waited for a while at Burnsy's house. With all the grabbing that was going on, Dudley and Rodney, a part-Aboriginal from Dusty's mob, were hiding in the kitchen. 'They'll have to catch me first.'

The women were laughing. There was only one window for the two to escape by.

Outside, some of the sandalwood mob – Michael, Russel, Albert – were coming by from the reserve. Each had a broad band of black over the shoulders. It was outlined in white which was drying and flaking in this fierce wind, like old toothpaste. I caught Russel's eye and he smiled. 'Sorry you can't be there, kind've.'

The wind was still up and it was beginning to drizzle. Out on the Meeka road, a frog hopped from the creek; it had been waiting in the ground since the last downpour, eight years ago.

I went to wait for Micky at the pub. By dusk, I had got myself into trouble again, and was surrounded by armed Jigalong men. Max, the sheep shearer, came by in his car and stopped to pick me up. 'Are they after you or something?'

'They're just getting more familiar with me,' I said.

He asked where he should drop me. I said I had to find Micky. 'We could try the reserve, perhaps.'

'Bondini? No way. That's a Law place.' He wasn't going to allow me to go there. I said I had been before.

'Well, I haven't and I don't want to get whistle-cocked, mate.' Finally he agreed to drop me on the road, if I was sure.

There was a relative of his lying in the back seat – Gloria, who had a fat, uneven, punched lower lip. 'You'll get crook,' she said, pleading with me, eyes like Max's – dead drunk and floating. 'They'll cut you up!'

Max dropped me off. 'Sure you're all right here?' I said yes, I should be if I stayed with Micky. Max raced away.

There was a steady, cold drizzle in the twilight, few people about. Micky's van was on the edge of the clearing on the near end of the line of houses. Micky was asleep in the back, under the corrugated iron sheets. Esta was shuffling around him gently, rearranging blankets.

There was nowhere to go, with Micky not up yet. But to my surprise a skinny boy came from this end of the line of houses and ushered me to the second one along. It was a 'rubbish house', abandoned when someone died. In one of the two rooms, I found a gnomish man with a flattened nose and one eye that was immobile. He was balding, like his dogs. The other room was clean and empty, and with a light that worked. There was a toilet at the back.

I settled in, and talked to my neighbour, the gnome. I'd thought he must be an outcast of some sort to be living here, and now he lent weight to my thought by telling me about life in Fremantle Prison, where he'd been sent for a couple of murders.

An oldfella was coming from next door, the end of the line of houses. He looked disturbed, likely to be violent; I tried a disarming smile and it seemed to work. He relaxed the muscles around his eyes, and smiled back. I told him that Micky had sort of said I could come and visit him.

He said, 'And I'm tellin' you too. You are welcome!' He was leaving. I realized he had come just to tell me this. 'Whitefella,' he said, looking back at me, then turning round fully. He half reached out to me, and dropped his hand softly between us. He said, grinning, 'It was my boy dey took to Warburton!'

Later, a handful of blackfellas from the town gathered round me, and I braced myself for the usual round of abuse. But strangely, again it was as if I was officially expected, and they wanted to be welcoming. They wanted to yarn, they said – Sheila, who had grey hair, casually chopped, and a small face with low sideboards of white, a few weeks' growth from shaving; Geoffrey Stewart's brother, George, usually a belligerent man with two fingers in the air – he had actually lost some of the remaining fingers, once getting petrol on a hand bandage while filling up a truck, then lighting a cigarette. Also a second man, who'd lain down drunk on a railway line one day and lost an arm and foot. And a woman who had been stabbed in the hand by her husband. That was why her hand was bandaged. Now he'd been grabbed – just walking with her to buy some 'Log Cabin'. He couldn't run from them 'because of his knee trouble'.

Next morning, it was cold and wet again. Micky was at his camp fire, mouthing sweet nothings at the dogs.

'You're a long one, in-ee!' he said when I appeared, and measuring my height with his hands.

We drank tea together. He said, 'You had a dreaming?'

'Last night?'

'Out there. Mungale. You had a dreaming?'

I said I think I just fell over, and got crook.

'That's a *Wonggai* place you in.'

A youth came up quietly. He wore a shirt but had heavy daubs of greasy red ochre on his face, like a clown. He said to Micky that the Warburton Mob had radioed. They were on their way.

I was expecting the man to throw a glance my way, challenging a whitefella's presence. Again, it seemed to be all right that I was here. It was enough that Micky had sponsored me. However, to a second Junior Man, Micky said, 'He been through Law in New Guinea. Same, see.' The man went away, accepting. But could he really accept this, I wondered? The Law was *not* the same, any fool could see that. And these Junior Men might not be so generous as Micky in their opinion of me.

While I sat there, and Dusty drove about in his Toyota talking loudly, men, Junior Men like myself, came up to see Micky. He mumbled at them or merely nodded and then they went on their way – perhaps to grab more boys, perhaps to order tea and dampers from the women. I saw how near I was to the power base here. And because Micky thought he could help me, and he was a desert type of *avookwaark*, I let things take their course.

We talked most of the day about Kandengei – the Crocodile Nest, the Wunjumboo, the division of the village into two political halves, one Niowi, the other Niamé. However different the customs were, he closed his eyes and said, happily, 'Same, same,' or 'Dat's it!' and twice, 'Good enough.'

'This man feels he knows what I'm after,' I wrote later. 'I'm sure of it.'

That night I saw the ladies dancing in the open space. I did not go over, but watched from Micky's camp, at first unable to hear more than a whisper of them in the wind, seeing only their feet and legs in the light of their fire. When the wind blew, sparks ran from the fire and I could see the shine from their arms, breasts, chins – the ochre stage make-up. Then the wind dropped, the light died, the last sparks were veering into the dark.

Next morning, the ground was rich and dark and heavy from last night's sprinkle of rain. I had my morning tea with Micky again. Geoffrey Stewart strutted about, head up, his slender limbs angular, cutting the air around him. He came to speak to Micky, went away. Came, went. He, like most men now, wore no shirt, just the ochre make-up.

Dusty hurled down some spear wood for some oldfellas camping behind Andy Campbell's house – Morgan and a couple of Jigalong men. They began carving the bark off the spears while Geoffrey Stewart was strutting about, his voice charged. He was organizing, using his high chin and long, bony right arm to span the camp as he directed people at the different camp fires.

Out of the bush behind Andy Campbell's house came a line of Junior Men. I hadn't seen men walk in single file out here – there was no need, in a place of open space – so I noticed them immediately. They were tapping the shoulders of the men who were carving spears. Just that, a slight tap with a twig. No one looked up to see what was happening; they carried on with their spears.

But it was like the touch of a wand whose magic takes a while to take effect. After a minute or two everyone was leaving their morning tea, coming away from their fires and wandering off. They were going into the bush in the same direction, going past Micky's camp, away from the open space. Esta and the other women were gathering around the houses. Micky hadn't moved off yet, he was still cooking his damper, but the surroundings were fast emptying and I looked at him for advice. Perhaps I should leave. 'We goin' bush,' he said.

'"We" – is that me?'

'Yeah, you're comin' along.' He looked at his damper, about to go to waste. 'You go wid him.' He pointed to Campbell, whose grey beard was a little sticky with blood this morning. I followed after Campbell, but he passed me back to Micky. 'Go wid der oldfella.'

Micky began walking out; I tagged behind.

The men ahead were walking loosely, talking in whispers, stilled in the way I had seen so many times before, lost in a distant place. Micky had all but forgotten me. I was walking behind him as an apprentice – unsure, alone and out of my depth again. Something was about to happen out here, and I felt the dreadful anticipation of an initiate walking in to the Crocodile Nest for the first time. Now again I was an outsider, a novice being brought into an exclusive society.

We were coming to a clearing; the others were quiet, demure, sleepily slow in their movements. Overhead, the sky was fairly clear, just high cloud veils; the sun was coming out, the shadows darkening.

Graham Richards was here. Last week his brother had wanted to kill a police aide for coming to this place. Or maybe not even as close as this. I looked to Micky – but he was sitting down with the older men. I heard Graham's voice. He said, sharply, 'Siddown, and no buggering about.'

I sat where he pointed.

Looking about, I was with a youth who was lying in shorts on a blanket, partly under the thin shade of a bush. He waved a leafy branch absently to keep flies away from his groin. He was an initiate, only just becoming a Half-man, someone who at Kandengei would have been junior to me. Around him were other men, probably his sponsors, people like my wau. I had come walking to this clearing like a boy, not like a man, and it was a boy's place that had been given me.

Graham told me to lie down and cover myself. Why 'myself'? It was as if the energy of the ritual, the equivalent of ones I had helped administer in my time, might be too much.

But I closed my eyes and covered my head with my shirt like the Half-man, the merely circumcised. Soon the Senior Men were clunking hand clubs on the ground in their circle; I put a hand on the ground feeling their double beat – the pulse of themselves in the desert as the clubs thumped into the sand. I was happy to know only this, their rhythm. I didn't want to *see*, take mental photos, capture them. From Kandengei I already had more than enough secrets.

I listened to the beat of the thumping clubs, and laid on top of it the dancing rhythm of the men from the Crocodile Nest; the sounds of the feet of the Senior Men on the ground, the shells around their legs, the feathers in their hair.

I heard someone say, 'Whitefella.' Micky's voice. Graham then said, much softer than before, 'Open your eyes.' I blinked and saw the Junior Men in rows. Not crocodiles, swaying in a line in and out of the Nest, but kangaroos bounding in a line. The men had painted themselves with a black band around the waist; they wore a loop of fresh blood on their shoulders, some splashes from their groin. I was dizzy, opening my eyes into the bright light and seeing them – the oldfellas dreamily beating their clubs, and the Junior Men hopping, more blood speckling from them to the sand.

'Good enough,' someone shouted. It was over. We were walking back. The men were quiet, the mesmerized manner that I'd only experienced looking into a fire, but that these people adopted, it seemed, whenever they were feeling bonded to the land. I myself felt fresh, and immensely excited seeing these Junior Men here as part of their place, as others had been at Kandengei. Micky walked with me, looking straight ahead. 'Up there, ee the same?'

No kangaroos, only the crocodile, I said.

He was not looking at my gestures, but looking forward, back to his camp and the line of whitefella housing beyond, as if he knew enough anyway. 'Good enough, no worries!'

Micky sat down and had a breakfast. Graham came up to check with me. He wasn't angry any more, he was pleased for me, smiling. 'You okay?'

The other men acted the same. Even the young men who had come in from Perth and Jigalong.

It was cold and wet in the afternoon. Micky packed up. 'No play,' he said, showing me the rain. I jumped onto the back of his van and had a ride back to Wiluna, running my hands over the hair belt.

Under the cyclone drizzle, wagtails pranced and flipped around the town. A large plastic container of meths, stolen from the police station, was being passed around. Kitty, widow of Paddy Richards, a large woman whose mind was always turned by drink, ran about naked, chasing men.

In the whitefella bar, a Ngangganawili Community Council woman was yarning. She had to get a signature for a cheque, she said, brandishing her drink for attention. She told her tale; she'd driven to the reserve, stumbled across a corroborree, a dance. 'I got away with it,' she said, tossing the sentence out, gravely but proudly.

I said, 'But that was only the women's dance. The proper business goes on in the bush, not by the houses.'

'What do *you* know about it?' a little man said behind his drink. He had a rat face, sharp red nose and addled eyes.

I wanted to say that I was there. But it wasn't something to brag about, it was a privilege. While I was deciding what to say, the man, who was fresh from the desert, said, 'If ya want to yarn, yarn. But down' bloody whinge.'

The rains became torrential, washing out the roads. Trucks tried to make a last-minute dash and ruined them further. Blackfellas sighed and moped – there'd be a delay in the annual drinking extravaganza, tax return day. The Bell's weekly delivery truck was stuck in Meeka. The Warburton Mob wouldn't get through, either, for a while. All day it rained. I stayed at Burnsy's house, hoping for a sight of Micky. He came late in the evening and sat me down in Burnsy's garden; 'I'll take care of you, no worries.' He seemed to enjoy being in the chilly damp wind, out by the fence with the wagon wheels and the old kettles that were flower pots. We sat on chairs with our hands over the oval bathtub fireplace.

There was a special cave where he would take me, one day, he said. He could bind people up with magic string from there, point the bone and they would be 'shot' inside. He'd cook kangaroo the Law way for me, five minutes in the sand, then drink the blood pool.

His eyes were watery from the wind, and dull from the drink. But he was not muddled in his mind, just slurring his words. I remembered how Merve, the hotel manager, had said the drunks had played football, while drunk. Micky was like this now – always able to finish his story, always alert to being overheard by Esta, who was pottering around.

Micky put his head right to my ear sometimes, telling me how he was grabbed, how he wasn't scared, how they'd painted his chest and face with spots. He explained some of the things I'd seen the day before. A line of women had walked out into the open space to present tea and dampers to the Junior Men after the dance. These were the grabbed boy's 'mummy, sisters and aunties'. He told me there were eagle dances, emu dances.

Esta approached, flapping her hand for attention. He gave a vigorous shake of the head, telling her he wasn't ready.

He carried on. He hadn't liked me lying down during the kangaroo dance. 'I felt sorry for you, liddle bit,' he said. 'You gotta tell 'em "I'm a *maan*".'

Micky shook in his seat with the emotion of that word, the dead weight of it.

All very well, very pleasant to hear it, but I was not convinced. Leaving aside my spiritual perception, with which I had made slow but probably significant progress, and the physical, with which I scored highly because of the discipline of the Crocodile Nest, I could see a very obvious difference between me and the Junior Men here. I had no actual interest in fighting. I avoided it. There was no emotional commitment to 'my' people, and, as a whitefella, probably there never would be.

I tried to get some of this over to Micky – my failings in commitment; the mental and spiritual tribalism.

'You good enough for now.'

'That can't be right. I've got heaps to learn.'

'You learn enough.'

I said, 'You've seen me in the streets. I'm not interested in bashing people.'

He laughed. 'You won me.'

I didn't understand. He said, 'You won 'im – the sandalwood mob, the Jigalong mob, town mob. What else you won? Your mob up there, Nu Guinea.'

Micky and Kaavon, back in Kandengei, shared the same confidence. They had the confidence of travellers, and seemed to be able to under- stand me, a traveller. I supposed there might be a thousand or more shamans like them out there talking tonight – the Hmong priest in Thailand, a Tirio Indian in the Amazon, a Siberut healer in Sumatra, Kaavon – all talking together. Micky seemed that confident in the way he judged me.

'I telling you, you won plenty. Where you begin travellin' in the world?'

With my rucksack in the Orinoco Delta, before crossing the land of El Dorado – my first independent expedition. The Indians took me in. My innocence was too much for them to stand, I'd thought. They didn't want my death out there among the mangroves and mosquitoes on their conscience. It was the same right across the Amazon – picked up, dusted down, and taken in.

But after the Amazon, Irian Jaya, Papua New Guinea, Sumatra. It was true – I had risen up through village after village. Kandengei, the Yaifos, the whitefellas. It didn't count as having a working knowledge of Junior Manhood though. I told Micky that. He said, patiently, 'I'll learn you by 'n' by.'

The wind howled, Wiluna screamed.

'Warburton Mob, comin' up now,' Micky said. 'You win 'im?'

With Micky, I was beginning to think, all sorts of unlikely things might be possible.

Then he seemed to change his mind. He said, 'You got a revolver? Or two? No need to show 'em – hide 'em under your clothes.'

But I hadn't got a revolver.

In the reserve the women chanted, shuffling in the dirt by the fire, rain running from their chests like beads, over their margarine and ochre make-up.

Here, life seemed to go on with little regard to my intentions. Events were out of my hands, out of everyone's hands. It was a feeling I had had in the bush at times, and now it was the same in Wiluna, only more intense. I watched the world, and we all watched the world, and it did things to us.

I was caught up in something here, wanting at times to leave Wiluna for a few days' break, but, like the whitefellas who had found themselves staying here for years, unable to pick myself up and go. The whitefellas, the blackfellas, we were all bubbles floating in the winds of the Dreamtime.

In the post office, George said it was 19 December. There had been four and a half inches of rain yesterday.

In town, the sandalwood mob had their dance paint on. They wanted to buy me drinks. They called me older brother, 'gorda', and even relative strangers said, 'You seen der dancin' now,' and 'We makin' you feel at home.'

However, when the evening violence was under way, I left. If I was getting close to these people, and it seemed I was, my companions might be as unrestrained in drunken violence as they had been in praise.

The floods around us were the worst for many years. We were cut off. We were alone out here, all of us nomads and dreamers.

The women danced, the Half-men circled far out in the bush.

*   *   *

Micky was drinking with Esta and other women, by the hotel. He had his hat on, chin strap tight. He was puffing a little. 'He's a Maan!' he shouted, as I walked by. The women stared, seeing it was me referred to. Micky lobbed an Emu can my way. It fell short, into the road. A car passed, bursting the can and creating a trough in the bed of empties along the kerb. The other drinkers were still looking at me – they knew I had the crocodile marks, had been with the men dancing, but that couldn't be enough, could it?

I could only agree. When had I shown the manly attribute of fighting? I said nothing, though I knew Micky was waiting, along with the women, for a response. I walked on.

Micky called after me. 'He's a Maan.'

The roads were open again. Now it was tax return day – Thursday 22 December. Herbie sat at a table outside the store, doling out the annual rebate to those finding themselves told they were eligible.

Twenty or so groups on the immediate fringe of the bush sat with their cans. 'Not a spare tree to piss behind,' Herbie observed, as another drunk put his mark opposite his name.

Michael was drinking alone; he called me to his tree. His girl-friend had gone 'cos she things I'm going wid another girl.' His teeth whistled in the wind as he talked. Rhonda came to join us. She had just hit her sister. The flying doctor was on his way – seven stitches.

Heads to the sky, lips to the can, the blackfellas drank and drank, sharing their beers. 'We call you *gorda*, down' we, Dick?' One by one the sandalwood mob came up and handed me drinks, and even cash.

Kitty, the woman who had earlier been running around naked, was now dressed but still running around. She was known, when drunk, to have an obsession with whitefellas, I'd learned. Cyril said she had once gone up to the kangaroo meat man, and socked him in the jaw as he turned round. Then she picked up an axe and chased him round and round his car. 'I went to my car then,' Cyril had said.

Dusty said, as I hid, crouching down among his card game, 'She got on top of you yet?' He was wheezing with laughter. I said I'd be scared of hitting a blackfella. I'd be put in gaol. Dusty said, 'If you hit her I'll be right behind you.'

'Ee all right,' Russel said. 'Self-defence.'

My back received a sharp blow and I found Kitty coming at me for a second swipe with one of her great fists. 'You're a spy! You're a spy!' She put a finger up into my face. I swung it down with my hand. She resisted. Fired her other hand at me. 'You're a spy.' She took a stick from a nearby fight and trotted at me. What could I do? Sock her one?

Wrestle her to the ground? I would never get used to violence, it was infuriating. Down her green T-shirt, and flowery skirt, ran the spittle. 'I'm gonna shoot you, you fackin' mongrel spy!'

I walked backwards to avoid the lunges and blows better, and found myself being run out of town by the woman. Explain this, Micky, I thought. Some man.

Now the proper fighting had started. The duel's between the true men and true women. The strangers, more of the Jigalong Mob, and some Warburton early arrivals as well, began their haranguing. 'We don' need whitefellas! None of you.' 'You piss off out of town mate, we don' wan you here.'

All day they drank the whitefella's money away. They shouted, they waved a stick or fist in my face, often with no fingers, perhaps only a thumb. Friends of mine – the sandalwood mob, Killer, Cyril – stepped in, disarming my attackers. 'Dat's a pleasure, you're my *gorda*.' Their older brother. I didn't deserve it, I really didn't. I felt ashamed.

And I wondered if any fight would come between me and these people who were calling me a brother of theirs. That would be a real fight, one of the good old showdowns between Junior Men.

I walked to Nola and Charles's house to say goodbye – they were leaving for a Christmas break.

Charles said, 'Only seven stitches Elaine got?' There was a nurse who came here, he said. Her third day: a woman came to her with a headache. The woman was drunk so she sent her away. As she was leaving, though, the nurse saw a fleck of blood. She brought her back and began taking off the patient's clothes – 'gave up after the first three layers.' Then just put her in the shower. She began the inspection. 'She'd been scalped! The skin was hanging like a cat flap – cut across the top, right the way back. 113 stitches.'

Nola gave me a slice of Christmas cake and a mug of tea, and took me back to Burnsy's in her Toyota. She told me to take care. I said Micky had asked if I had a revolver. She said I ought to take a cricket box at least.

She hooted the horn as she left.

Dawn breaks on Christmas Eve. The Warburton Mob is a long way out, at Dover Creek, but the word here on the reserve is that they are heading this way now.

The Campbell family, my neighbours, mope and wail at the news. They've been racking themselves all night for the agony of their son. Andy Campbell has a badly swollen left cheek. Fluid weeps from it as if from an extra eye; the last crisp flakes of blood from yesterday's cuts wash away. Geoffrey Stewart pulls off his clothes and walks around naked, crying like a child. Passing me, he pulls my hand to his face. He holds it against his soft beard and cries. Campbell beckons me next door, into his house, into the stink of dogs, urine, bad meat, cat's blankets. One dog has its head in a sugar bag, another has been at the flour – there's dough in its saliva. With his hand, Andy scoops spaghetti from a tin into his mouth. It splatters down his beard. A woman does the same with a tin of braised beef and onion, losing half in her own lap.

Outside, dogs are copulating, bitches whimpering but submitting. Jane Wongawol goes behind the nearby car, half pulls down her knickers, then half squats, and urinates.

The latest news is, they're coming on Wednesday. More wails, duets from the men and the women. No one seems to notice Geoffrey's nakedness, that we're not in the desert nowadays.

I sit with the family, moved by their passion, but also increasingly horrified. They pick up a pan from the fire, beat themselves over the head with it, letting the food fly. The old marks of mourning they once obtained in the desert, made with stone knives, bound open so they would scar well, are now being remade with frying pans, breeze blocks, sticks from the fire, whatever will hurt them.

This is as bad as the day they buried Yargee. They took her from us at Kandengei and buried her at our sister village, and the Junior Men buried her, and women dashed themselves against the orange clay, and fell into the hole with the coffin, wanting to be buried with her. I remember her, Yargee, and mope as well – her real death, the symbolic death of boyhood, they become fused.

While I'm sitting with the blackfellas, trying to reach out to them, a stranger strides over from his camp by the road. He shouts at me, and looks around, pleased with himself. He has shaved this morning; no one else here has shaved for a week. The man starts pestering me over a permit for the reserve; he says he's on his way to the police. I say I am assuming I didn't need a pass. I've been invited here.

'Where's your permit?' he repeats. Micky gets up from where he's been with the Campbells, and pushes the man over. 'Where's yours?'

Micky says to me, 'You *got* a permit.'

'The papers? No, I haven't.'

'Papers are whitefella's business,' Micky says to the man, who's still on the ground, wondering what went wrong. The stranger gets up, pushes me. He thinks it was me that knocked him over.

Micky gives him a second knock. The stranger falls backwards again. Micky says, 'Come back 'ere!'

The man does what he's told, getting up and looking bewildered and very unhappy. Micky taps my chest. 'Show 'im.' I undo my shirt.

The man says in a faint voice, 'That's not our Law.'

I say, 'Well, you're right, but Micky said –'

'He's a Maan.' He'll punch anyone who threatens me, Micky says.

Michael, from the sandalwood mob, comes to see what the fuss is. He says he'll do the same. 'Get 'im in der guts.'

I'm grateful to Micky for all his help, of course, but I realize then how much it meant Michael saying this. I'm aware that it's my peers whose opinion will count most. They are the ones who will judge me most harshly about my Junior Manhood.

In the town there was a significant heightening in energy. Fighting, shouting. Everyone seemed to need to release themselves. The blackfellas seemed to have expanded their Law area from the reserve. The town was no longer a clearly whitefella domain. I wanted to write more than ever, empty some of my thoughts, my own gathering energy, but couldn't risk producing my notebook on the reserve and spent as much time as I could at Burnsy's house, trying to write. But even that was hard, with so many people milling about, unsettled.

'I'm Benno the whingeing Pom, guess where I come from,' sang Burnsy as I walked into the house with Micky on Christmas Eve.

Micky walked straight on through to the kitchen, where there was a leg of mutton on the gas stove. '*Meelka*,' he said. Food. He picked the mutton up, tested its temperature, and ate the lot in his fingers. Then he tipped back the giant saucepan and drank the juice.

Burns was badly drunk, and in a tantrum about the blackfellas who were all over the place, raiding his house – sheltering from the Lawmen who might grab them, or collapsed from drink, looking for drink, or outside siphoning his petrol tank. 'Bludgers, the whole fackn' lot of 'em.'

He thumped Bret, who was asleep. He continued to sleep. 'You're not getting any fackin' feed or soft drinks, tomorrow, straight out.' I pleaded for him. It would be Christmas Day.

'He'll get 'em – Burnsy's soft inside.' He ducked in his head and winked. Later he was in the middle of the room spinning in circles, sparring with imaginary blackfellas. He fell over and his face went blue. 'He forgets to let out wind,' Glen said, taking him off.

Burns soaked his head in water, and came back. 'You all right?' I asked.

'I'm not going to fackin' die on you, if that's what ya mean.' He winked again. 'Compliments of the season.'

Burnsy went to sleep, Micky and the other blackfellas wandered off into the rain. Glen was slumped on his bed, his slumped wife and slumped baby beside him. He told me that Micky gave him 'the willies'. He said Micky had two revolvers. 'And a red crystal. And a blue crystal. And ee got two horses.'

I asked where all this was? Where were the revolvers? He patted his heart. That was all the indication I was getting. Perhaps Micky had been referring to some sort of spiritually protective revolvers. There was certainly a magician in him; like Kaavon, he didn't seem held by his people's bond, restrained in the way of the others. He had, or had the bearing of someone who had, a different reality in which he could travel, some way of orbiting the cosmos which was God or the spirits around us.[21]

'He get the wind up me, sometime,' Glen said.

'Yeah?'

'I seen the blue crystal comin' through the bush,' Glen said. 'That was *him*.'

The ladies danced, the Warburton Mob brought the Half-man nearer.

The town was taut, crying for action.

Twelve bodies lay on the pavement along the hotel. 'I'm dreaming of a white Christmas' sang the TV in the whitefella bar, but outside Micky was whacking a man to the ground, Dusty socking a youth. 'They been teasin' Rodney,' Dusty said. I looked for Rodney, the part blackfella who hadn't been through the Law; he was pulling a lady's hair, dragging her into the road.

I went to the Robinsons' empty house, made myself a cup of coffee, and drew up a chair. I began writing in my notebook, and tried to release some of the tension, let out my thoughts.

> There is a lack of free exchange in this desert, everywhere but here, in these waterholes.
>
> Every creature out here is a specialist in the water line. The predators and predated, they pass the water between themselves, keeping it from leaving the living cycle.

It was the custom that whitefellas bought in old cars and sold them for a fortune to the drunk blackfellas. It was said that there were two cars out there in the bush, side by side. The first had been driven out on an almost empty tank, and when the engine stopped the blackfellas walked back into town and bought another one. It ran out of fuel right next to the first. Both cars were still out there, somewhere, side by side.

Now, Christmas Day, the money was gone, the whitefellas' cars had been bought and probably lay ruined. Gordon and Ray, the trinket and T-shirt hawkers, had gone back home happy with their profits, and there was no more money around for anyone to spend. It was less than a week after tax return day.

All the other whitefellas were eating or drinking, gambling away the night under their tinsel Christmas trees. I sat alone in Burnsy's garden, not wanting to hear the sound of Glen beating Denise, and afterwards the sound of her feet as she limped around, hugging her baby, not answering Burnsy, myself, or anyone else who called in for a drink.

Burnsy found me out there. 'Come indoors – I can put up with the blackfellas, so you can.'

Micky, Burns, Glen and I sat together, having a Christmas drink. 'You had any feed?' Burnsy asked me. He told Glen, 'I've taken a liking to the Pommy bastard.'

We watched the TV – the Munsters, Alf, Neighbours. There was an advertisement for a new Japanese car. 'Hasn't got a roo bar, even,' Glen said.

A series about a dolphin, Flipper, came on. 'Wad that?' said Micky. I grew bored. So did Micky. We drank another can.

Micky was puffing; his eyes almost dead. He got up, shuffling to the door. 'Here, come outside.'

It was dark now, the wind strong, rapping on the metal roof, sucking up, blowing out. There wasn't much light here. We stood in the shelter of the veranda, holding our cans. I wondered how much his eyes took in. He was swaying a lot, and it wasn't the wind. 'I wanna talk to you.' He sat down on the ground, by a crumpled mattress.

Micky said, 'You said up dere, they don' give you one?'

'One what?'

On the veranda, where once a goldminer might have enjoyed a yarn, leaning back, eyes out to the stars, Micky unzipped his trousers. 'Undercut.'

I looked at what he showed me, out of politeness. Then I said, 'Sorry, what was the question again?'

'You'll come to Bondini and get one?'

I said it just wasn't the custom. It wasn't a question of fear, it was just not what I was here for. Around us, the bare yellow doors and frames, green walls, all dabbed with rain. Burnsy's hard boot-heels tapping on the cement floor.

He said, the blackfella way to greet a man in the bush, 'Law time' was to hold him.

'Him?'

''im.' Micky was looking at his flies.

I said, coughing, 'Haven't heard that one.'

'Not the same your way – Tootin'?'

Tooting, London SW17? Did he really mean Tooting?

I said it wasn't what they did in Tooting. Or even New Guinea. He said to me, 'If you're a man, dere gonna let you do that.'

'You're kind enough to do that, but you have nothing to lose. No offence, but let's see what the other young men think.'

'You done enough. I keep tellin' you.'

I had come some way along the spiritual front, and perhaps understood all I could for a whitefella, but there were other basic problems. I was the man who had to be protected because I didn't want to hit anybody. 'Sorry, but I can't take myself seriously enough, yet,' I said.

'You stick around.'

A poisonous centipede that's bigger than my biro is on the floor beside me. It is alive, but stuck to the cement floor by its dried juices from a minor injury. I sat writing my notes out of sight amongst the capsized cockroaches.

'It's *my* fackn' house. Spot on.' Burnsy gives an inverted thumb sign, slowly, meaningfully bringing it down. A man you wouldn't want to bump into after dark cowers in the doorway.

'You haven't got the decency to knock on the fackn' door. Where are you from, anyway?'

'Warburton.' He must be in the vanguard of the party.

'Well, I don't want any Warburtons here.'

'What *is* the Warburton Mob like?' I asked. The Warburton man had sloped off.

Burnsy said, 'They're mad.'

Micky woke up and asked to be dropped off at Bondini, the reserve. But Burnsy wanted to know if there was any trouble for him there.

Micky said, 'No trouble – and der whitefella's comin' too.'

'I'll take my 303 and dog anyway.'

The ladies shuffled in the sand for the Half-Man, in the bush Junior Men went through the movements of the animals, bounding in the spirit of the kangaroo, running as the emu . . . The boy was on his way in.

Back in town, I wrote for hours, unloading my mind – chain after chain of dialogue, images I'd snatched from the winds blowing through here.

Each metabolism is a sealed unit, a moisture envelope. They keep the water from escaping by wearing cutaneous skins; they don't sweat, they try to move slowly. Otherwise they have to live underground, the secretive life of the moist.

I stumbled into the daylight, on the way to the outside toilet. A man was in the way with a torn shirt and three rocks in his hands. 'You seen my missis?'

'What?' *It's the scavengers that have the speed – flies and ants speeding out of cover for the pre-desiccation plunder,* I thought.

He was tetchy this time. 'No – I'm askin' *you*. You seen my missis or *what?*'

Whenever excreta is dropped, it is already dry, like a breakfast cereal husk. No water waste.

I pushed on by to the toilet.

Back in Burnsy's house, we had our own fight going on. Greg was yelling at Denise, his wife, 'I gonna give you a *hide*-in.'

Her face was already puffed up. Burnsy said, 'She used to be a pretty thing.'

'I write a pass,' Micky said. 'A letter up to them thattaway.'

'For New Guinea?'

'You can take something I give to you.'

'A gift for the headman there?'

'I'll give you something, by and by. You take 'im to 'em. You bring some here.'

'That would be good,' I said. A bridge between you. Yes, I think Kaavon would like that.

'He a good fella?'

I said he'd been good to me. But their Crocodile Nest had been dying and I did so much that was wrong – in the end I'd been too much to handle.

'You all right now.'

'You've seen it for yourself. You call me a man, but I do it all wrong. I do it all sneakily. I get to the top all the wrong way. I never stand up and fight – I'm not interested. And what's more, however much I fling myself around the world – Orinoco and so on – I always get away with it. As you pointed out, I get to the top.'

'I been tellin' you!'

'Yes, but what sort of warrior is that, who doesn't actually do the fighting? Sounds a lukewarm warrior to me.'

He said, 'You a lonely one, in ee. You got to der top. You a king one. Dat's a good one to be.'

'I had persuasive qualities, Kaavon said.'

'You're a king one, all right. You're a king without a chair.'

'A throne?'

'Dat's im!'

Once down in Hampshire a gypsy had said, while making polite conversation at a barn dance, there were types of people. There were Rainbow Warriors, Priests, Earth Mothers, Kings. She had a whole range of categories, but my one was a natural ability to wield power. I'd laughed a little – she'd also asked me to kiss her – drank down my cider, and moved on to the next small talk. Years later there'd also been a 'Neo-pagan' who had a job in accountancy. He'd diagnosed me the same.

I thought to myself, 'Orinoco, Amazon, the rest – Kandengei, where I'd convinced the village to take me on. And all because I'm a king, for heaven's sake?'

Micky drove to the pub, and on the way I sat in the back of the open van, watching the stars, thinking, I've learnt a lot; I've come a long way from Kandengei, whatever the root cause of my apparent progress.

There was drinking, there was beating. Taking me back to Bondini that night, Micky crashed the car off the straight road and into a telegraph post. We walked the rest of the way. Dogs howled, hearing us come; men snarled. There were lots of bodies about, filling up my house and much of the open space of the reserve.

In the morning, my neighbours, the Campbell family, had fresh grease and ochre over them – lugs of it in their hair. Andy Campbell pressed a fistful into my hand; he almost ruined my shirt as he tried to spread it over me. I took my shirt off and Russel rubbed it over my back while water boiled in great vats, dampers rose out of the fire ashes. We were expecting the Warburtons for tea.

The men, the women cried. A brother of the grabbed boy, Andrew, whirled a burning branch around. I didn't have my towel around my neck now for protection, not even a shirt. I was seated on the ground beside Killer, wondering how everyone could sit like this with their backs exposed, while the man whirled the burning stick around. He dashed it against a wall, threatened us all; embers sparked off and stung my back, making me jump up. No one else bothered much with their burns.

The Warburtons drove in – Toyotas, trucks, they curled in from the road, circling like a circus troupe. But these were only the front runners. Alice Springs, Dock River, there were people from all over the Western Desert.

In the afternoon, Killer said, 'It's sprinkling.' The rain came. Cold showers, just as the bulk of the Warburton Mob were sweeping in. They were not fiery, or loud, but quiet and sullen from the cold. Dusty said nothing might happen for days.

Now, wearing the ochre, I felt more at home here. I had a badge, a stamp of approval – the ochre and, more suspect, the crocodile marks. But I did not feel safer. Charles had warned me that the closer to their Law I was, the more vulnerable I'd be, the more up for grabs, and all the evidence did point that way.

Vehicles ran up and down the road into town, swaying as the passengers took another swig, or the driver simply lost control of his faculties. I put my shirt back on and walked into town – there was a continual stream both ways, men wandering along like vanquished footsoldiers. I bought some last supplies. The whitefellas in the store were saying, weightily, 'There'll be one and a half thousand out there, now.' Five hundred, I said to myself.

Dusty was at the store. 'You want a lift back? They're wild, I told you. They might cut you up – you know that?'

I said I'd be staying next to Micky. He said, 'You bedder.'

Dusty stopped before the reserve, on the main road, got out and asked again if I wanted to be here – 'You might not get out again,' he said. Then added, 'All that easy.'

He told me to take off my shirt, to allow people to see the ochre. All the Warburtons were setting up camps along the roadsides and later they'd close the road to whitefellas. He drove me right to Micky's camp, by the Campbells. I got off, with my cardboard box of food. Sunshine gave me another warning, and Dusty checked that I had the situation clear in my mind. If I wanted to leave, he said, I should tell Micky. Micky would try and get me out in one piece.

They watched me set my box down at my house by the Campbells, then drove along to their house. I sat at my house, Micky nowhere to be seen, as stitches of tension tightened around us, the first fights breaking out by the road.

Bones sink into the sand, I thought, *keeling as they crumble away.*

Splashed water runs far on the dry soil unabsorbed, independent. Dust cases it as it rolls, hardening around it.

From now on there was a stream of visitors, men and women shaking my hand along with all the Campbell hands. There was no sign of Andrew Campbell, the Half-man.

The Campbells moaned and groaned, sitting cross-legged, hugging each other, bashing their heads with billy tins. Malala waddled by, naked. Towards dusk the drink took hold. 'You wanna get burnt?' A man stumbles over our bare backs, forgetting who his fighting partner is, and threatening us all. Killer stays by me – I wonder if he's been posted to look after me by Micky. Now I come to think of it, he and others, such as two men called Frank and Maurice Wongawol, have been around me, arriving in the nick of time to push off drunks, for the last month. I watch Killer, his back exposed, not caring about the embers flying against him, treating them like leaves in the wind.

A man in jeans comes from across the reserve with a spear and womera, spear thrower. He is calling at the Campbell family, 'Come ere, you fackin' . . .' No one goes, they are busy moaning and groaning for the Half-man. And when Jane, one of the younger Wongawols, is being beaten with the firewood, chased around the nearby car, no one hears her, or the thumps of the wood on her. She sits in the car, waiting to go to hospital. Killer, after some prompting from me, murmurs, 'The car's crook anyway.'

In and around the bush, there are hundreds of camps now. It's like the night before a pitched battle, the eve of Agincourt. I listened to the keening of the Campbells and felt for that grabbed boy who was somewhere out there in the bush. I'd been through all that myself, the 'night before' nerves.

If I wanted to leave to avoid bloodshed myself, I should go now. And of course by now I saw it wasn't just the fighting I was in line for. Micky was expecting something of me, to be with the other young men as they danced their dance for the boy, spilling their blood for him, loading the ritual with power.

I saw this, and there was still time to leave. But I was caught up, as I had been for weeks. I didn't move.

I cooked up some noodles, and a tin of braised steak and onions on the Campbells' fire. Children, up to now running in and out, between the fighters, rolling tin cans on strings behind them, circled round, smelling the meat. I gave it to them. Afterwards, they went around telling the grown-ups, 'He gave us feed.' But the grown-ups were in no state to listen; few were in a state even to hear. The children kept moving, safe as long as they were on the wing.

Sounds here are sucked, as in the forest, but actively, by the wind, I thought.

Dusk. A fire was lit out in the bare, central space where the ladies had danced all night. For the first time today, I saw Micky.

Finches bursting by look like us, a lonesome crowd.

Men with red wool headbands, *yakiri*, gathered in around the central fire – only a score of them, mostly from Wiluna. Women went out, and clumped around them. The breeze raced over the lone party, over the land.

Dusty, Micky, Morgan, they thumped the ground out there. Back here, at the Campbells, Geoffrey Stewart pranced naked, still bashing himself. The men were chanting now. The sound came and went, brushed by the wind, picking words, skewering them, rifling them.

Stones burnt by the wind are overheated scones, marzipan slithers, cakes – all tempting, as Jesus found.

Killer was leading me over. It was dark. Skirts flapped in the firelight, cracking louder than the flames. We joined a line of men and women, the Campbells. We were adjacent to the oldfellas, who were still beating the ground in a small circle, their headbands loosening with the sweat and shake of their bodies. Four women on the far fireside were kicking their feet in the sand and singing out a refrain, 'heeee!' a lower 'Waah!' and higher 'heee!'

Ants erupt from the ground
– sudden lava from ancient planet craters.
Next, crows go towards the carrion, hopping with the ant tide.

Some time, the men's chanting faded; they were only beating the ground now, just marking. *Ants using a dead cockee beak as a hatch entrance – the tongue as a doorstep.*

A word must have been said, a signal given. But I had seen nothing; I just understood it was over. Killer said to me, 'It will be tomorrow morning.'

We were dispersing. *Old trees die upright in this baked soil. They fill with the sand carried in the wind. Falling, they shatter like stone columns, spreading into dust.*

I am walking back with Killer, who is silent. *Termites, scattered from the fallen tree, regroup. They come back to the remains in five-lane ordered agitation.*

One of the Campbells had stopped me. I moved sideways to let the firelight onto his face, and off mine. He wore red cotton around his head, the mark of the Lawmen. He was short, curly-haired, the Junior Man who had hurled the burning stick about earlier, and beaten up Jane Wongawol. 'Your Law good enough?'

The fitful winds here like motorway side lashings, setting a death pace.

I said the oldfellas seemed to think it was.

I walked on, catching up Killer. The Junior Man had me by the shoulder. He hoiked me around. I was more insistent, knocking his arm up, and off. I checked: I wasn't afraid. 'Ask Killer,' I said loudly, pointing over my shoulder. Killer didn't respond. 'Killer?'

Killer was walking on.

The wind blew over us; I was a little scared now, but of the place, the strangeness of the violence around me in the dark, not so much of this man.

The man said, 'We'll fight about it.' He had my right wrist in his hand. I wrenched free, but he was looking around, not finished yet. I understood he might go for a weapon. Unfortunately for him, I had a knife in my back pocket. But I was quivering now, very alert. For weeks I had avoided a fight and now was I going to prove my physical bravery? Did I have to? The Korogo *banis*, the New Guinea mountains, the ghastly sea crossing. No, was the answer. I did not. Spiritual bravery was something of a greater priority and tonight I was sensing the spirit around me. I was able to feel it, be in fear of it, yet stand here. This was the bravery I was more interested in.

But there might be no avoiding a show of physical bravery. I recalled that Dick, down in Perth, had said it was surprisingly hard to stab into someone.

I pulled him along with me, trying to get into the light coming from the houses. Was I going to wriggle out of it as usual? Was I going to do that, not try and be brazen, like a fighting man? Yet again?

His pockets looked empty. I didn't think he had a hand knife.

'How we know you're a Maan?' he asked. 'If you're a *maan*, you'll do it – fight me.'

He probably had a point. Looking around now – for an excuse not to have to try to clobber him – I saw men were all around us, fighting. They had sticks, they had spears, they had clubs, they had the last available garden fence posts. Any man worth his salt was pitching in. They were Men of True Men.

So I should now have a go at whacking him with a spear. I should now stand like all the other men, in the night, ripping at my opponent. This was proof of Junior Manhood if I wanted it: clonking this thankfully short bloke on the head.

The sky cleared. In the soft moonlight, he said, 'I can kill you.'

That's as maybe, I said, and stood there confusing him – neither running away, nor diving at him. I didn't need to respond to him; Micky was saying I had done enough, and I could believe him. I had learnt I didn't need to fight. I could get by in other ways. He had a term for it, being a king type who instinctively knows the methods taught in the Crocodile Nest, Koran and Bible. 'Whose service is perfect freedom.' One way of gaining power was being humble, submissive, vulnerable. Bottom could become Top, according to the Law of Polarity.

So I stood there feeling in control, feeling sensitivity to the night around me, feeling its resonance. I let it blow through me, hot in the wind. I had come a long way from Kandengei. The forest. *Spine mounted sago palms; marshes that are sumps. Up above, in the clouds of branches, folded-up bats, down below, pipe-cleaner feeler roots and myself, with my questions.*

'You've been through the Law? Show me the Law you been through.' I walked to the pale bath of whitefella house lighting, not looking back. He had to follow if he wanted to see. Alone with me in the night, it seemed, he put out his hand and fingered my chest. 'Dat's not enough. Dat's not our way.'

In the forest, empty biscuit packet wrappers were often picked up by guides, spiked onto foliage or displayed on their headdress. Here in the desert they are left to blow away; no claim is made – to the wrapper, to the land.

His accent was slipping, and by his stillness I knew the extensive crocodile stipples had set him thinking. I think he thought that my Law looked rather tougher than his.

'Dat's a different way,' he said. Before he had sounded full of drunken bravado, now he was calm, speaking steadily. I said I knew it was a different Law. He said, 'Der Warburtons been drinkin'. Dey might not allow you off dis place, without you fightin'.'

'Then I will have to fight, I suppose,' I said. I accepted that. Would it be worse than six weeks in the Crocodile Nest? No, Benedict, I answered myself, it would not.

'If you stay, you gotta dance wid der other men. You down' mind 'em takin' blood from you for der boy?'

I saw the scene – lanky whiteman bumbling his way around the sand, copying the other men, not knowing his part in the ritual. But I'd have to get by, if necessary, I supposed. I told the man that if it was good enough for him, it was good enough for me.

He waited, looking at me, studying. 'Dat's all right, then.' The house lighting went out. I looked at him in the bare moonlight, this Junior Man, and he looked at me and understood that I didn't need to fight.

'You ain't scared much, are you?'

He took off his headband. He put it around my head and I let him. He said, 'I'm gonna greet you der Law way.'

'You are?'

'Man ta man.'

I heard a zip being undone.

Oh God, I thought, as he gently reached out for my hand.

I walked quietly to Micky's camp, letting the *yakiri* Lawman's head-band slip down around my neck.

Micky was tucked up with Esta a little further out into the bush than normal, a little further from the danger zone.

'Whiteman coming!' Micky chuckled at his use of the whitefella's word, 'whiteman'.

'Hey! I think I've got somewhere!' I showed him my headband.

'Good one!' Micky said.

Strangers were scouting around us with their armaments. 'Too much *wama*,' Micky said. He himself hadn't been drinking. 'I'll watch over you.'

'I'm sure I can cope.'

'Tomorra, you gotta be a Maan and help der boy.'

'You mean?'

Micky was indicating a flow of blood down his trousers from his groin.

Yes he did.

But it was an unnecessary act. I had done enough – Micky had said it himself. I had been as far as I could go, for now. I was beginning to want to go home again, back to the village, the sticky air wrapped in forest.

'Come mornin' dere goin ta be wild,' Micky said, settling back to bed. 'You ready yourself for fightn'.'

Strangers who managed to blunder on through the front line defences – the dogs – probed around our camp, jabbing us with spears. I lay still, like a dead sago grub in my sleeping bag, trying not to roll and catch the light. From time to time, Micky chased off men. Women shrieked as they attacked, coughed as they were beaten. I lay thinking of Kandengei, wondering if I would get a better welcome, this time round.

I watched the dawn burning away the soapy sky. The stars were awash, fuzzy. Geoffrey Stewart was walking about briskly, his fingers closed tight, and his arms stiff, telling everyone to get up. 'Geddup!' Micky told me to pack up. Women were already drifting away, to the road.

'What now?' I ask Micky.

'Too much *wama*,' Micky said. 'Der Warburton Mob gonna kill you, if dey see a whitefella and down' stop to ask if you been through der Law.'

'Kill me? Oh, I don't think so, do you?'

He did.

I was already packed. I sat on the ground waiting for Micky, who was feeling around in his scattered clothes. He brought out a stone blade. He plucked at it with his front teeth, notching an edge to it. He shuffled up to me on his knees, puffing and pouting, contemplating. 'I down' wanna hurt.'

I looked at this blunt-looking blade. 'Er, how do you mean?'

'You ain't goin' out there, into der bush. Too much *wama*. You done enough.'

'I'm glad you said that,' I said. 'That I've done enough. I thought that you were going to have a go at *me* with the blade, for a moment.' Looking around I see Esta has gone. The men are rising, gathering in the open area. We are running out of time.

'Hold on a liddle. I wanna try somethin'.' Micky then takes my hand, and there's so much gentleness from the man just now, this man who can kill, I don't mind when he starts for some reason rasping the blunt blade across my thumb. It is Micky who winces, not me. He's worried about hurting me. The thumb bleeds a little, and he stops immediately.

'What was that for?'

He said, giggling, 'Just testin'!'

'Testing what?'

He said, 'You're a Maan, no worries!'

Micky wasn't to blame. He had seen me dodge so many fights now. I could easily have been a wimp after all.

I stood up to go. 'Time's up,' I said.

Micky brushed his sleepy early morning eyes. 'You missing out on today.' He splashed his fingers down his crutch. 'I feel kinda sorry for you.'

'Don't worry about it unduly,' I said. But I felt the pull of those other young men now heading out for their ritual and I wasn't all that happy, watching them go – Russel, Alfred, Michael, Jonny – slipping into the trance state, beginning to travel . . .

'Now I gotta show you I'm not scared.' No, he didn't have to. But before I could stop him, he took the blunt stone and rubbed it across his own thumb.

He takes me a few paces off, among the bushes, and sits me down, with a little bag. He puts two incised oyster shells into my hand; they're for a man to hang over the pubic region. He also has a rectangular one, 'for womans'. I chose the smaller, more modest of the men's discs. Micky approved of the choice. 'You can put it in pocket, den!'

He produces a yellow stone shaped like a crane hook. 'Dis one I carn' give you. It too strong. It make rain come, see?'

We have only a few moments longer. Suddenly, there's so much to ask this man who was beating men back to keep me safe all night, but who was scared to cut me. He says, 'You take 'im to Nu Guinea. They happy then.'

I pictured Kaavon on his stool, his cobwebs, his sacred stones. He would be. He was a well-travelled man. He'd understand.

Micky had gone off a little way. He was scratching in the sand, and came back with a small panel for a man to wear in his headband. 'You show 'im.'

I would. I'd call a meeting in the spirit house and show it and its circular patterns off.

'You come back later. Bring something nice from Nu Guinea.'

'There's so much to ask you, suddenly,' I said. 'Micky, I've come right across the world, and do you know what I've found? Something obvious. That the world is the same everywhere. It doesn't change. It cannot. There are fixed rules governing us – I should have learnt it back home. The Law of Polarity – you have power in being the opposite. Sympathetic Magic – like attracts like, hence the missionaries over here, tribes drawn to other tribes. Or isn't there any truth in that? But anyway, we – humans, I mean – don't seem to have got anywhere. Everything has been said long ago. Did Homeric Greece discover the creative mind, philosophy? Perhaps, but what does it count for? There's one basic plot, one Love Triangle, one golden triangle. There are said to be seven different jokes, twenty-seven Ken Dodd says – he's a British comic. He's studied the subject – 10,000 books.' I talked on like this. Such feelings, such entanglements swilled around my mind.

Micky said, one day he would show me something he has for me at Mungale. 'We got big place, over there.'

He had this taproot strength in him – no need to ask, just be. His questing was over. He knew enough of the human condition.

But for me, time was too short. 'Micky,' I said, 'this law of polarity. If we are slaves to a master we have power. So why do we not rise up? Why do we not take power? Why, as powerless humans to an infinite God, are we not able to make our God our slave? Are we not of the same potential power as God?' This, and so many more questions.

But time has run out. All around us now, men are whacking at each other, taking out hanks of hair. Others have already left for the bush and the Law.

I shook Micky's hand. He said he'd see me again, some time. He laughed, 'Some time, when you wanderin' the place, looking for an empty seat.'

'Throne,' I said.

'Dat's 'im!'

Him and his kingship notions. I found I couldn't speak. He chucked my chin, flipped it up with his fingers. I did the same to him.

Suddenly Maurice Wongawol, a small man with a moustache and startled hair, was standing by me, magically knowing I needed an escort out. He took me along the line of the house to Dusty's mob. On the way I passed the Campbells. Andy said, 'It's all right. You come back again.' I heard this from other mobs along the line of houses, people giving me permission to go. 'You can go.' It made the leaving harder.

The women walked out of the reserve, and I went with them. 'You goin' for goods?' they asked. I said I'd probably be back. Some were still drinking. I took a toddler from one. Put him on my neck. Two yellow-haired twins ran along with me.

We sat down, as if for a picnic. We must wait while the Men got on with their business. A child playfully settled a spiky mountain devil lizard on my neck, another little girl slipped onto my lap, drawing pictures in the sand for me. The sun whitened. In the road, a man was being jabbed at with a spear. He was having to dance. Another lady was smacking a man with a club. Finally, this man, like the other two, walked away from their fight and into the bush.

A hijacked truck from the emu farm crashed through the scrub nearby us, chased by the Community Toyota. A fight on wheels – another duel between True Men.

And I was walking out not with the men but with the women . . . I was going out by the back route. And when I might have been witnessing the Law as a Junior Man, kicking the sand, I was in Wiluna paying for a lift down to Perth by unloading beer cans from the Bell's delivery truck. Instead of the privilege of shedding my blood as a Junior Man, I was handling crate after crate of the Merchandise, stocking up the deadly waterhole.

Then, feeling sick at the thought of all I had missed out on, I was aboard the truck, and the dark-glassed, silent, hard youth taking me away, borrowing my last $25 from me, leaving me at midnight at Guildford, outer Perth, the middle of nowhere and with my baggage frozen from the truck cooler.

Some man I was. And it took some time for me to gather myself, look back and know what I had done. I had come so far. I needn't worry that there was some mystery left over. I had already learnt that without mystery there couldn't be truth, that in nature truth didn't come direct and pure, that you had to be a specialist, a shaman, to interpret it all, straining it from what the rest of us see – the world coloured by the juggling elements. But ever since the Crocodile Nest, the ritual rebirth, I had been learning, growing up again, this time in the eyes of nature.

I thought this through. And as coaches took me back across the continent, and I caught a flight, and another, and a truck to Pagwi, and a canoe from Pagwi, my thoughts rose. I smelt the forest, humid air, it embraced me and there was a kind of song of celebration in my head. Benedix is back, I thought.

The lake opened out in front of Kandengei, and this time I did get a welcome. Spencer and Errol were running along the waterfront with the children, Nightlight leaving her hopscotch, running indoors. It was good to be back. Wallace was no doubt happily sliding another fish onto his plate, Nathan turning another Bible page, Stars out there, somewhere, hearing the stampede, smiling to herself, perhaps rearranging this evening's schedules. I felt the village reacting to me – nesting movements; my pride rose. This was what it was like to feel victory.

Soon my wau was off in the forest, killing a pig. Spencer was trying to put me in some smart clothes the village had assembled together, and then we were trying to fix the zips and buttons that I broke as I squeezed them on. I was sent to wash in the lake; the jigging pale light of the water danced on the pig as it came into the Smaark territory hanging from a pole; a Wunjumboo face was drawn on a piece of precious cardboard, limbun flags hung around it, and these posted above a stool, which now was to wait empty at the bottom of Wallace's house. All day, while the stool waited, Wallace was sending Errol up and down coconut trees, Nightlight and Songbird were chattering as they ground the coconut, mixing it with sago into leaf parcels, *bangor naow*, a meal for the women of my wau. And in the softer light of dusk, when I had been forced into the tight clothes, and we had abandoned the battle with the broken zip, I was at last wearing the parcel around my neck, and sitting on the stool, my wrists all decked with kina coins from my wau. Above me was the Wunjumboo, the yellow palm flags blowing across me. A last reminder from Wallace to keep my eyes to the ground and not to smile, then my wau called out, his clansman beating a hand drum, his women in thick sago skirts, fanning me.

> *Nian na nian yagwa ra ra*
> Child, child, you come, you come . . .
> *Bandee-a bandee-a yagwa ra ra*
> Novice, novice, come, come . . .

I feel the wash of the women's sago skirts, the breeze of their leaf fans, I hear Errol lightly calling my name and the older women sighing, seeing me, and all the time I look steadily at my white feet, trying to quash my fears that I might not get through this without ruining it by smiling. Or, I begin to feel as the ritual goes on and on and on, I might fall asleep.

My wau calls my Smaark clan brothers,

> *Nian ee giran gurur nee-a-rok . . .*
> *Giran* [bird], come, come . . .
> Where is that tree? Come, come . . .
> Coconuts come . . .
> Sun, moon, come . . .
> Stars, come . . .

And now he is calling all the ancestral haunts, villages before Kandengei. *Tunbungoo and Mandangoo . . . Swapmeree . . . Nyaurengei . . .*

And finally, an hour or half-hour later, the end comes, and a stick tapped on my right shoulder and left, and I can stand up. I am back, Wumvunnavan, Spirit of the Saltwater Breeze, *geenjumboo*. And I know the most exciting thing in the world for a young man. That, while the world is now small and exploration for the whitefella is over, for anyone who can leave their maps at home, it has only just begun.

Epilogue

NOTES, EAST SEPIK PROVINCE, PAPUA NEW GUINEA

Kandengei Village, 28 January 1989, and the succeeding two weeks.

I tell them the story of the journey again and again, and I don't see why they aren't sick of it. Quite often I retire to my mosquito net to avoid having to tell it again. Tonight, they even assembled everyone to get me to give one of the grand speeches they are so fond of.

'And now,' Kumbui said, standing up in the middle of the *geygo*, the men high on their benches, barracking and spitting, 'Wumvunnavan will tell us the story of his journey.'

'Oh God, Wallace, is it time for my big speech?'

'Yes.'

'Wallace, can I stay sitting?'

'Only if you are sick. Are you sick?'

'No.'

'The old men are waiting . . .'

I leaned back against the bench and looked at my audience – the rows of old, dopey faces, some of them dribbling, earlobes empty of shell earrings and noses empty of bones, pretending not to want to listen to a mere Junior Man.

I sit in my mosquito net, and sometimes Daniel comes. Or I go over to the lakes and talk to my grandmother, or just lie or sit in silence, looking out across the water, skimming my gaze through the heads of the purple lily flowers, reminding myself I'll be heading home soon. Tooting, my room on the third floor.

Things have changed in the six months I've been gone. Metal houses have sprung up everywhere, strangers wander through the village and it's not safe to leave my rucksack around. There's more and more bickering between the village and local politicians as they fail to deliver the gold and wealth everyone is expecting from heaven knows where. But there have been changes on a more personal level as well. I've been expecting Nightlight to come to me, but not a sign.

In the village, as far as my role is concerned, there's the feel of a job done. Kaavon simply isn't around at all and my wau shows only a polite interest. Stars is still served up to me, but she's just a companion until I leave, a courtesy gesture. She's often too busy to come, singing with the church most nights.

The *avookwaarks* were true to their word. They didn't want to trap me and what more can they do with me without doing just that? I can never be one of them, *their* Junior Man.

I must leave them to it. Kaavon must get on, transfer the reins before the village dissipates. The AOGs are, after all, more than willing to have a go.

A note today from Daniel. 'I woke up this morning and saw tears on the face of [Nightlight]. I said what is wrong and she said nothing is wrong, I am just remembering Benedix.'

They all seem to think I've left! They are already mourning me. Telling me I'm gone. But I'm still here!

Stars on the Water was at the AOG service yesterday. She joined up while I was away. She said she may not come as often. Our nocturnal get-togethers are wrong, she says. They're unchristian, apparently. And I haven't even kissed her yet.

In two weeks she's off on what she calls an AOG 'Bible improvement' course. Good luck to her, I say.

I don't have much difficulty remembering home now – the oppression of the village has gone. My thoughts wander out of here, out of the forest, with freedom nowadays. The Tooting pond, the Hampshire bedroom with the African dance mask.

In South London once, I remember, just before I left, I was out searching for party candles – a farewell supper party. Woolworths didn't have any. I chanced on a shop just off the Clapham end of the High Street – it had no sign up, but a yellow window poster said, HOUSE OF THE GODDESS.

They had candles, all right. Peering through the window I could see nothing else. Then I saw bookshelves, a poster of a half-man, half-leopard, and a nose-ringed young woman with volcanic purple hair, her mittened fingers around a statuette of a squatting, generously proportioned woman who was giving birth. Then I saw a broomstick and a black cat.

I was apprehensive, I don't mind telling you. Hidebound by super-stition the Kandengeis might be, but they have cultural taboos, 'dos' and 'don'ts'. This was Christendom, where Witchcraft was perceived as an evil – it might attract bedsitter weirdos.

The atmospheric conditions were hazy: an oriental temple cloud of incense sent me into an allergic sneezing fit. My head struck a mobile of a pretty witch taking off over a full moon, and I knocked over a figurine of Isis as I tried to remount the witch on her broomstick.

But Shân, the witch in charge, was a pleasant enough woman with a cotton plait in her hair. I quickly gave her my credentials – write books . . . adopted by New Guinea village . . . got a crocodile cult . . . privileged to be put through their initiation . . .

She only laughed – it could only be a joke. So that was that, on this occasion – I was too shy to peel off my shirt, revealing my crocodile initiation marks, and anyway, she might be a weirdo.

Christians, I later heard, said Shân did sacrifices. I imagined babies and virgins, but the truth, I found out, was less interesting. There were no sacrifices, no blood. It was middle-class magic. She danced on Clapham Common quite a lot. The police had once floodlit a coven with patrol car headlights, one Member of Parliament occasionally proclaimed them Satanists, and many local churches included them in their prayers. However, many Clapham Common dog-walkers were better informed. They saw them as part of the local scenery. Like the trees they talked to, the witches were a friendly part of the common, and they didn't drop litter.

Shân's politics were Green, her favourite company women. The second time we met she had been up all night doing 'cleansing rituals' in her temple out the back. She had some crusty excretions around her overtired eyes and she picked these off and licked them from her fingers. It was natural, she said, and exactly what her black pussycat did.

Why am I recalling this? The point is that Kaavon and Micky, those travelled warriors, would have been scared a little – the House of the Goddess, the incense and candles and, of course, the women. True Men Micky and Kaavon may be, but there were limits to their Manhood as well as mine.

Lately, I've been thinking what a lonely place the forest is. In the desert, you had God – he might be awesome or pitiless but he was a companion none the less, and there was a kind of solace in him. But here God is lost among the life around you, splintered into an infinity of leaves and invertebrates, this grinding system which fast includes you. Before you know it, it becomes a simple matter of fighting, of mucking in. These forests are closed circuits of living electricity – sparking, ruthless, but contained, exclusive. You bid to become that élite by head-hunting, or whatever other means nature counts fair, or you fail – and the ants come, dismantle you, then take you away.

I see Daniel a lot nowadays, but today he has gone off for a week in Wewak, leaving me a note in my mosquito net. It is not the substance of the message – a request for sleeping pills from England – but the tone.

Simply it is that they, the Niowra, have taken him . . . Loyalty to the tribe; submission to the collective.

'MY EYES ARE CLOSE NOW AND THE PEN IS FALLING OF MY HANDS NOW READY TO SLEEP NOW SO GOOD BYE.'

He really *is* saying goodbye. My final connection is broken. Daniel has done his duty to the Niowras – fallen in love with one of them. It really is time I was going.

GLOSSARY

AVOOKWAARK Bigman (Pidgin), elder statesman, literally 'ancient' or 'revered' crocodile and here titled Reverend.

BANDEE An initiate, boy being schooled as a man in the confines of the 'Crocodile Nest'. He is shown the men's secret/sacred objects and thus in religious terms is a novice. Various other objects will be shown him during his youth after the ceremony, so in some respects he might be regarded as an 'initiand', someone being initiated, throughout his younger years.

BANIS Pidgin for 'Crocodile Nest', the coconut/banana leaf screen built around the Spirit House during an initiation, and secluding the initiates.

DREAMING/DREAMTIME An Australian Aboriginal concept: the unending period (inhabited by spirit beings) which saw the creation of the world and, when respected, sees to the continued empowering and magical sustenance of the world. For fuller explanation, see Part III, note 15 below.

GEENJUMBOO 'Junior Man', the first rank a male achieves after his initiation.

GEYGO Spirit house, in Pidgin *haus tambaran* or *haus boi*, the building which only initiated men may enter; a religious building, also a debating chamber.

JINBUNGOO 'Senior Man', the second rank of a male after his initiation – one less than an *avookwaark*.

KANDENGEI Said to be the founder village of the Niowra group (of Iatmuls) on the Middle Sepik river.

LAUA Protégé of a wau, who is his mother's brother and who acts as guardian to him.

NIOWRA Group of villages forming the western dialect portion of the Iatmul people of the Middle Sepik. Includes Nyaurengei, the near neighbour, and Korogo, on the main river. Either the Niowras or Iatmuls could be considered a 'tribe'; however, I have tried to avoid that word, except where making use – ironic or not – of its 'primitive'/wild overtones.

PIDGIN *Tok Pisin*, a language of some seven major ingredients developed since European contact for communication between peoples in a highly 'tribalized' country.

SEPIK 'See-pik'; one of New Guinea's major rivers, supporting the freshwater and more aggressive saltwater crocodile; because of the river's wood-carving tradition, it is known as the artistic heartland of PNG.

SHAMAN A so-called 'witch-doctor', or medicine-man; a person with special powers that enable him or her to enter the spirit world, communicate with the spirits and even battle with them in person, thus restoring harmony in the world/a sick individual.

SMAARK The clan to which I was allocated as a consequence of Wallace, the Smaark Catholic Church leader, adopting me.

SONGLINES A term denoting the paths taken by spirit beings during the Aboriginal Dreamtime, an unending period of magical Creation. Boys would be sung the stories of these journeys at initiation, and later go out into the bush following the trails of magical essence left by particular

spirit ancestors with whom they were associated. See Part III, notes 6 and 15 below.

WANBANIS Pidgin for a male who shared the same banis, Crocodile Nest, or initiation with you: therefore a person to whom you owe special allegiance.

WAU A Guardian uncle figure of almost sacred status to his Laua, male protégé. He holds the boy between his legs while he receives the crocodile markings, emphasizing the Laua's ritual 'rebirth'; after the initiation, the wau in effect takes over the role of the boy's mother.

WUNJUMBOO One of the most pesky of forest spirits; like all the spirits, only usually appearing when an ancestral law, or taboo, has been transgressed, threatening the community's balance with nature and the cosmos.

NOTES

PART I: THE NEST

1   These and other speeches from the more senior men were translated from a mix of Pidgin and Niowra with the help of Daniel and several other younger men, and edited from the notebooks I was allowed to take into the *banis*, the initiation compound or 'Crocodile Nest'.

2   In references to my participation in the initiation I try to avoid giving the impression that I myself have 'been initiated' – I have merely been through an initiation ritual. The coming into power was not something that I could fully take on, as a passing member of the community, and one striving to learn experientially yet having to maintain a notebook. It might have been easier had this been a mainly spiritual initiation: the ceremony could be more accurately described as a 'ritual of manhood', one where boys learn to exercise physical and social power in and around the community. Here, as in the Aboriginal community I was to visit in Australia, full priesthood is acquired in later life and only certain individuals achieve shamanic powers. Kaavon and Micky may fall into this category. For full accounts of Sepik initiation in its traditional form, see Bateson (1958), note 5 below, and for a wider context *Rituals of Manhood: Male Initiation in Papua New Guinea*, edited by Gilbert N. Herdt (Berkeley, University of California Press, 1982). Also, of course, my own account of the Kandengei initiation itself in *Into the Crocodile Nest* (see note 3 below).

3   Exploring ideas generated by this and each other forest journey, I came up with *Mad White Giant: a Journey to the Heart of the Amazon Jungle* (London, Macmillan, 1985), then *Into the Crocodile Nest: a Journey inside New Guinea* (London, Macmillan, 1987) and *Hunting the Gugu: in Search of the Lost Ape-Men of Sumatra* (London, Macmillan, 1989), followed by the present book. I approached the task of writing about

376

the forest differently each time, giving some symmetry to the series by passing through the four elemental 'quarters' or categories – successively Fire, Air, Water and Earth. *Mad White Giant* was written in a fiery, passionate vein, *Crocodile Nest* was in a more cerebral mood and so forth, this book completing the cycle.

4   A sizeable, original and incisive examination of Hmong shamanism is Jean Mottin's *Allons faire le tour du ciel et de la terre: le Chamanisme des Hmong vu dans les textes* (Bangkok, White Lotus, 1982). A useful, if political, survey of present-day Hmong culture continues to be Nicholas Tapp, *The Hmong of Thailand: Opium People of the Golden Triangle*, Anti-Slavery Society Indigenous Peoples and Development Series Report No. 4 (1986).

5   Several individuals have been involved in initiations among Sepik cultures, though none in the Niowra group of Iatmul villages and all incompletely. Deborah Gewertz gives a thorough cultural background and general environmental description based on her work with the nearby Chambri communities in *Sepik River Societies: a Historical Ethnography of the Chambri and their Neighbors* (New Haven, Yale University Press, 1983). However, while the Chambris are to some extent 'Iatmulized', they are not of the Iatmul group, to which the Kandengeis belong. Gregory Bateson gives a detailed account of traditional Iatmul culture in *Naven: a Survey of the Problems Suggested by a Composite Picture of the Culture of a New Guinea Tribe Drawn from Three Points of View* (Stanford, Stanford University Press, 1958); see also his 'Social Structure of the Iatmul People of the Sepik River', *Oceania*, vol.2 (1932), pp.245–91, 401–53.

6   When I arrived in Papua New Guinea, doubts about going with few maps, or indeed plans, surfaced fully. My state of mind – doubts concerning the technique of plunging wholeheartedly into a society and out again before the clarity given by freshness is lost and the physical and emotional effects of abandoning my own habitat tell – is shown in a diary note I have just found dated 6 June and given here in edited form. 'Feel hollow, fraudulent. I'm here for months [the whole expedition was to take nine months]. Matthew [Jebb, Director of the Christensen Research Institute] will be here for five years. I'm tempted to burrow for more maps, flip to Goroka where Meg Taylor is preparing to retrace the steps of her [explorer] father. She has plans; I have nothing. I have Australian dollars in case I end up there, dreams of returning to Irian Jaya. But I must hold tight. It's not for me to decide. I must feel my objectives from here, no longer play on my white skin.'

7   Most Pidgin, which at Kandengei includes most conversation with me
    – though not that with Daniel, Wallace, Nathan and other Town
    Kandengeis – I have rendered into English to avoid the unsophisticated
    impression it tends to give. However, where individuals spoke in broken
    or dialect Pidgin I have translated it as such, using the models provided
    in English by Daniel, Wallace and Nathan. The spelling of *Tok Pisin* is
    generally consistent with Father F. Mihalic, *Introduction to New Guinea
    Pidgin* (Milton, Jacaranda Press, 1969). Place names are more or less in
    line with the current (undated) map, *Wewak; Gateway to the Sepik*
    (Wewak, Wirui Press).

8   Michael Somare. See *Sana: an Autobiography of Michael Somare* (Port
    Moresby, Niugini Press, 1975). John Ryan's *The Hot Land: Focus on
    New Guinea* (Melbourne, Macmillan, 1969) is a detailed account of the
    time leading up to independence (with Somare as first Prime Minister),
    and Sean Dorney, *Papua New Guinea: People, Politics and History
    since 1975* (Sydney, Random House, 1990) is a thorough, up-to-date
    volume.

9   This was the conclusion of *Hunting the Gugu* (see note 3 above), in
    which I was following up stories of an elusive 'mythical' ape-man.
    Also interesting in this context is Robert A. Brightman ('Primitivism
    in Missinippi Cree Historical Consciousness', *Man*, vol.25, no.1 (1990),
    pp.108–28), who finds that dwarfs and hairy peoples (perhaps mythical)
    are used to embody notions of a state of progress – that is, a movement
    away from nature. Brightman discusses how 'traditional' societies (such
    as Kandengei's) are cited by outsiders as 'ahistorical'. 'History to them
    is the recital of sacred meanings within a cyclic as opposed to a lin-
    eal perception of time' (S. Diamond, *In Search of the Primitive*, New
    Brunswick, Transaction, 1974) – which accords with my attempts to
    approach exploration from a non-linear, that is, non-Western, perspective.
    Also interesting, with regard to the ferocity with which the Niowras
    maintain their taboos, is Brightman's reference to C. Lévi-Strauss, *The
    Scope of Anthropology* (London, Jonathan Cape, 1967): the Niowras
    would be one of Lévi-Strauss's 'cold societies' which 'resist desperately
    any structural modification which would afford history a point of entry
    into their lives'.

10 Deborah Gewertz states that: 'every adult Chambri and Iatmul had to
    commit homicide and take the victim's head to achieve adult status'.
    While in the village I argued to myself that the head-hunting expeditions
    were times when individualism and forward thinking were 'allowed' and
    that, as these were typical Western behaviour characteristics, I might at
    last 'legitimately' do an expedition without imposing the West and my

'self' too strongly. However, as Gewertz points out ('From *Sago Suppliers to Entrepreneurs: Marketing and Migration in the Middle Sepik*', *Oceania*, vol.48, no.2, December 1977), much head-hunting behaviour was very disorderly: 'The bush-dwellers [usual victims] endeavoured to satisfy this need by selling their own infants as victims'. Margaret Mead also comments, 'my Iatmul informants assured me, however, that they too [as well as the Chambri] frequently bought bush infants to be ceremonially slaughtered' (*Sex and Temperament*, New York, Morrow, 1963). However, even in the 1930s, patrols by outsiders were noticing head-bagging on an apparently widespread scale (J.K. McCarthy, *Patrol into Yesterday*, Melbourne, Cheshire, 1972); and it would also seem that the status of a kill was to some extent commensurate with the initiative of the killer and the scale of his exploits – or so the *avookwaarks* maintained to me. Given this, and the fact that present-day expeditions, to the towns, appear to have lengthened, I feel with hindsight that my idea of using the national or actual 'head-hunting' ritual of manhood as a tool with which to explore the forest genuinely had a base in local culture.

As regards my claim that the Niowra gained a kind of immortality through the balance of their community with Nature, Bateson (1958) argues that the intensity of inter-male competition might lead the villages to self-destruct; but the system is still more geared towards sustaining the environment than is ours – which must inevitably fail.

11 The question of whether, or how much, the women were behaving in a decadent, or more Western, less taboo-restrained, way by asserting themseves kept me busy during many a long day, and indeed night. Certainly the women's nocturnal visits to me in later weeks were acknowledged as exceptional behaviour, while the 'traditional' courting males must have at least been encouraged by the increasing presence of promiscuous Town Kandengeis. During the course of my stay I was increasingly under the impression that the women held a deep-rooted, if concealed, power base that might be at least a match for that of the males. I now find that among the neighbouring Chambri, also people who rely on the women's fish for food and trade, Mead (1963) found the same. 'For although Tchambuli [Chambri] is patrilineal in organisation, although there is polygyny and a man pays for his wife – two institutions that have been popularly supposed to degrade women – it is the women in Tchambuli who have the real position and power in the society.' (Gewertz discusses this further in 'A Historical Reconsideration of Female Dominance among the Chambri of Papua New Guinea', *American Ethnologist*, vol.8 (1981), pp.94–106.)

12 Gewertz writes on male and female perceptions of their own power in 'The Tchambuli View of Persons: a Critique of Individualism in the

Works of Mead and Chodorow', *American Anthropologist*, vol.86, no.3 (September 1984). 'Many Iatmul . . . have told me that women are in need of careful watching, for they once owned the men's houses, sacred flutes, and other accoutrements of culture and threaten to someday regain their lost possessions.' Much of the 'insecure' behaviour of the men seems to have stemmed from the 'inequality implied by their very existence' – through women's reproductive capacity.

PART II: FIRST STEPS

1   The *Post-Courier* did a special 'mining and energy' report (23 August 1988). Fresh finds of gold were reported constantly around this time (in, for example, the *Niugini Nius* and *Post-Courier*), particularly around Porgera and Mount Kare, perhaps ultimately adding to the feelings of frustration among freshly Western-educated youths arriving in towns that had no jobs to offer them: 'PROVINCE CALLS FOR RULE OF LAW' (*Post-Courier*, 15 August 1988); 'LAE IN RUINS AS YOUTHS GO WILD' (*Niugini Nius*, 4 August 1988).

2   There have been many published accounts of the Cargo Cult activity, some of the most spectacular stories coming from the first white men seen by locals. For example, *First Contact: New Guinea's Highlanders Encounter the Outside World* by Bob Connolly and Robin Anderson (New York, Viking Penguin, 1987) tells the story of the 1930s gold-hunting expeditions by the Australian Michael Leahy. The Whitemen were believed to be ancestral spirits (probably complete with a Paradise of goods), and one of the porters was thought to be a dead son returned. However, just as extraordinary is the way Western expansionism, with 'scientific exploration' its inevitable spearhead, has been and is conducted with little respect for philosophies beyond those of our own (linear-thinking) Western tribe. Mick Leahy might symbolize 'the ruthless impetus of Europeans to appropriate the goods of the earth wherever and however they could be procured' (James Griffin, *Hemisphere*, vol.29, no.1, July/August 1984); however, prospectors and other such obvious Western pioneers as evangelical missionaries (see note 9 below) are merely the most obvious, and convenient, 'imperialists' for us to target.

3   To give some uniformity, I have used traditional stories concerned with this district based on those gathered later at the settlement often known as Mahaba, although at the time I knew it as Bikaru. Many are common to the whole region, and all have their parallels.

4   Jakob estimated infant mortality at 60–70%.

5 'RELIEF AID NEEDED FOR FLOOD VICTIMS' (*Niugini Nius*, 7 October 1988). 'About 400 people have been evacuated to higher ground . . . East Sepik Bruce Samban who went to make a personal assessment of the flood damage on Wednesday was forced to stay overnight at the camp with the missionaries due to bad weather . . .'

6 Don Kulick and Christopher Stroud give a fascinating anthropological analysis of how such 'kits', and indeed the introduction of literacy itself, have ironically enabled cultures in the region to expand traditional requests to Supernatural Powers for goods. As I found in the course of the journey, far from wiping out cultures, as Western 'tribal rights' activists often feel, missionaries frequently replace old systems in little more than name only and give valuable stability to communities vulnerable to other outside pressures. In the same article, 'Christianity, Cargo and Ideas of Self: Patterns of Literacy in a Papua New Guinea Village' (*Man*, vol.25, no.2 (June 1990), pp.286–304), Kulick and Stroud also touch on a tension felt in their (Sepik) study area, a tension I myself felt in Kandengei: 'no one ever knows exactly what others really think or intend to do about things,' they write, 'because their statements on any matter are expected to reflect not their thoughts, but rather their willingness to exhibit their [understanding/knowledge] and to agree.'

7 Almost entirely because of the publicity generated by the 'tribal rights' group Survival International. However, the Summer Institute of Linguistics (whose primary aim is simply to translate the Gospels into local tongues) might be considered much less 'thorough' in its apparent destruction of local culture than other missions I have stayed with – for instance, the Regions Beyond Missionary Union, who stay on longer. See also note 9 below.

8 By Hal Lindsey (Michigan, Zondervan, 1974). To me, more interesting reading is a missionary guidebook, *Before All Else Fails . . . Read the Instructions: a Manual for Cross-Cultural Christians!* [sic] by Kevin G. Hovey (Brisbane, Harvest, 1986):

Allegiances

Western missionary
a) Primary allegiance is a faith allegiance to God.
b) Secondary allegiance is to oneself.
c) Third allegiance is to the sanctity of human life.

Papua New Guinean
a) Primary allegiance is to one's group (clan/village), including all members both living and yet [to be] born.
b) Secondary allegiance is a fear allegiance to the super human of the clan for the sake of the clan.

9 The first thorn in the NTM's side was an article by Norman Lewis, published in the British *Sunday Times* in 1968 and entitled 'Genocide in Brazil', which led to the foundation of Survival International. Since then, Lewis and Survival International have inflicted fresh wounds, most recently with his retrospective account *The Missionaries: God Against the Indians* (London, Arrow Books, 1989). As a direct result of their activity, the NTM international headquarters issued a directive warning staff not to allow strangers on to missions. As NTM's policy is not to respond to criticism, according to Bob Kennell, now Chairman of the Field and based at the Goroka HQ, I will quote from my notebooks:

> Bob: See, we've been burned real bad by writers and anthropologists. We've allowed them in, made them welcome. Then they stab us in the back. You've heard of Survival International? Well, they've been running a war against us. Saying we spread disease to get them [South American 'uncontacted' peoples] in from the forests, rounded them up.
> Me: They are not a rich organization. It would be difficult for them to get their facts absolutely right. I'm sure they mean well.
> Bob: There is no way that this is accidental. It's a deliberate campaign. We're not afraid of the truth.

Lewis is a distinguished writer, and he presents what must be intended as the necessarily romanticized view of a Western outsider – talking in terms of 'unspoiled' communities, people who lose their 'desire to produce beautiful things' after sustained mission contact; certainly his publications have been acclaimed by an outraged outside world. However, whatever the picture may be in South America, in New Guinea – basing my opinions on weeks spent at the Summer Institute of Linguistics (Irian Jaya) and NTM (PNG) missions – locals would not recognize the alleged goings-on, nor his statement that 'in another thirty years no trace of aboriginal life anywhere will have survived'. My experiences on this expedition strongly suggested that indigenous peoples are not necessarily at the mercy of missionaries who decide to attach themselves to them – or not as much as might at first seem. My former, contrary view (and one that is apparently prevalent in the West) I feel now was at best ill-informed and probably actually racist. In Paraguay, too, Indians in regions where both the NTM and Lewis are at large are found to be adept at using imposed (missionary) religious models to their own ends, even keeping their original belief systems intact beneath a Christian veneer (personal communication, Stephen Kidd, South American Missionary Society). By labelling indigenous peoples 'helpless' we are maintaining the Western myth of the 'noble savage', the 'innocent' of some imagined Eden. However imperialist a missionary organization may be, it is all too easy to make them scapegoats while, for example, logging and mining continue wholesale. And yet the forestry and mining companies in turn are all too convenient as symbols of the destruction of the natural environment: the threat, both physical and spiritual, has its origin here at home, in the very nature of our Western demand for Progress.

PART III: MEN OF TRUE MEN

1 One of the most famous accounts of the early European travellers is Frank Hurley, *Pearls and Savages* (New York, Putnam, 1924), which tells of 'Adventures in the Air, on Land, and Sea', during a journey up the Fly river and along this coast.

2 A recent thorough survey of the Torres Strait society, their past, present and future, is Jeremy Beckett, *Torres Strait Islanders: Custom and Colonialism* (Cambridge, Cambridge University Press, 1987).

3 This was the Aboriginal Land Rights (Northern Territory) Act 1976. My story looks at Australia from the point of view of someone fresh from a community within New Guinea, and the questions I ask are limited to my specific quest. John Pilger has recently put the Aboriginal land rights issues into a wider political context in *A Secret Country* (London, Jonathan Cape, 1989). *Frontier* by Henry Reynolds (Sydney, Allen & Unwin, 1987) is one of a batch of books published in connection with the 1988 bicentenary celebrations. 'This scholarly treatise will shock anti-land rights lobbyists,' writes Roberta Sykes, who thinks the author should have gone further, talking of the white invasion in terms of outright genocide (*Sydney Morning Herald*, 25 April 1987).

4 Paul Carter, I now find, uses the same metaphor: 'Australia was always simply a stage where history occurred, history a theatrical performance' (*Road to Botany Bay*, London, Faber & Faber, 1987). Later he states: 'The Aborigines . . . were not physically invisible, but they were culturally so, for they eluded the cause and effect logic that made the workings of history plain to see.'

5 For a light account of the bush road construction, see Len Beadell, *Beating About the Bush* (Adelaide, Rigby, 1976).

6 Bruce Chatwin's *The Songlines* (London, Jonathan Cape, 1987) seems destined to become a classic. As the *Sunday Telegraph* put it neatly: 'The Songlines emerge as invisible pathways connecting up all over Australia:

ancient tracks made of songs [taught to boys at their initiation] which tell of the creation of the land. The Aboriginals' religious duty is ritually to travel the land, singing the Ancestor's songs: singing the world into being flesh. *The Songlines* is one man's impassioned song.'

7   Cowboy cults among both Aboriginal and White Australians are observed in the more modern of the anthropological literature mentioned in note 8 below.

8   For better informed accounts of totem allocation and the passing on of ancestral 'songlines' at initiation, see note 15 below and the early but classic accounts by B. Spencer and F. J. Gillen, *The Arunta: a Study of a Stone Age People* (London, Macmillan, 1927) and *The Native Tribes of Central Australia* (London, Macmillan, 1938); also Géza Róheim, *Australian Totemism: a Psycho-analytic Study in Anthropology* (London, Allen & Unwin, 1925); and G. Horne and G. Aiston, *Savage Life in Central Australia* (London, Macmillan, 1924). Richard A. Gould, *Yiwara: Foragers of the Australian Desert* (New York, Scribners, 1969) has an excellent annotated bibliography which 'includes nearly all available sources on the Gibson Desert Aborigines [the main centre of my attention] and their Pitjantjara-speaking neighbors'. He gives a general survey of Gibson Desert people and their traditions; more specific aspects are also looked at elsewhere: a standard work now is R. M. and C. H. Berndt (eds), *The World of the First Australians* (Sydney, Ure Smith, 1964), a general but comprehensive survey of Aboriginal groups throughout Australia. Daisy Bates, *The Passing of the Aborigines; a Lifetime spent among the Natives of Australia* (London, John Murray, 1938) is a first-hand account of life among Aboriginals from the Victoria Desert, although Gould questions some of the author's conclusions, particularly about cannibalism. A useful collection of papers by various authors on burial, initiation, mysticism, revival of tribal Law, world creative powers, etc., is M. Charlesworth, H. Morphy, Diane Bell, K. Maddock, *Religion in Aboriginal Australia* (St Lucia, University of Queensland Press, 1984).

9   See Ian Hogbin, *The Island of Menstruating Men: Religion in Wogeo, New Guinea* (Scranton, Chandler, 1970). The practice is not an isolated one in New Guinea, but whereas the Wogeo (off the Sepik coast) and also the Mountain Arapesh 'bleed' their penises and are said to equate the act with menstruation, the Gnau, a people of West Sepik Province, apparently do not. In *Day of Shining Red: an Essay on Understanding Ritual* (Cambridge, Cambridge University Press, 1980) Gilbert Lewis, while discussing what interpretation to put on the act, found close parallels with Iatmul (Niowra) rules and practices at initiation.

In an Aboriginal context, numerous anthropologists have put forward reasons for the practice, which is rarely conducted with the amount of ritual accorded to the earlier circumcision stage even though it marks the male's final attainment of adulthood. 'Vagina envy', 'menstrual envy', imitation of kangaroo (male) organ, contraception and other theories are discussed by H. Basedow, 'Subincision and Kindred Rites of the Australian Aboriginal' (*Journal of the Royal Anthropological Institute*, vol.57 (1927), pp.123–56) and more recently by Philip Singer and Daniel E. Desole, 'The Australian Subincision Ceremony Reconsidered: Vaginal Envy or Kangaroo Bifid Penis Envy' (*American Anthropologist*, vol.69 (1967), pp.355–8). If the operation is intended to be a contraceptive device, it fails; of the other theories, those favouring a connection with the taking on of female attributes are now generally deemed most likely. See for example Ronald M. Berndt (various papers in *Oceania*, commencing with R. M. and C. H. Berndt, 'Preliminary Report of Fieldwork in the Ooldea Region, Western South Australia', *Oceania Bound Reprint* (1945), pp.102–3), and also M. F. Ashley Montagu, 'The Origin of Subincision in Australia', *Oceania*, vol.8, no.2 (1937–38), pp.193–207.

10 Robert Tonkinson, *The Jigalong Mob: Aboriginal Victors of the Desert Crusade* (Menlo Park, Cummings, 1974) is a clear, pithy description of Jigalong and contemporary Western Australian Aboriginal culture. The settlement is renowned among aboriginals for its success in maintaining their 'Law'. Tonkinson traces the community's rejection of the Christian mission they were based at, plotting their survival and lack of compromise from the time the settlement was boosted by a final immigration from the desert in the mid-1960s.

11 'RIOT IN CUE DEEPENS ABORIGINAL-POLICE DIVISIONS', reported the *West Australian* on 2 November 1988. '. . . The Cue attack [on the police force, a police car and the local hotel by up to forty Aboriginals] follows violence earlier this year in Geraldton, Moora and Northam.' Police were now being issued with batons, riot shields and helmets for the funeral of Graham Walley, the man who had died in Greenough regional prison on 23 October. In December 1987 a Royal Commission into Black Deaths in Custody had begun enquiring into 108 Aboriginal deaths since 1980. Hal Wootten QC, a commissioner, found on 11 September 1990 that the death of one 'Clarence Alec Nean' ended 'the stress of growing up as an Aborigine in a society in which Aborigines were marginalised, denigrated and denied dignity and control of their lives by a racist bureaucracy and community'. The Commission was due to conclude its investigations at the end of 1990.

12 In 1892 an explorer named L. A. Wells found this to be auriferous land;

a minor gold rush began and soon a town was established and named Wiluna, supposedly from the Aboriginal for 'place of wind', Weeloona. By the mid-1930s the community was eight to nine thousand strong; there was an Olympic swimming-pool, tennis courts – illuminated by night – paved streets, a fire brigade. However, the population fell rapidly as men departed for war service, and although Wiluna was the only place in Australia where arsenic was produced, and Tokyo Rose broadcast that the town was Japan's No. 1 target, gold production was becoming unprofitable with the loss of much of the workforce. The mine, once 'the largest in the southern hemisphere', was closed in 1947 and the town fell into rapid decline. In 1963 the white population was reported as 90.

By the end of the 1960s almost the last Gibson Desert Aboriginals had come in from the bush and their population was already many times that of the whites (by 1980 they numbered 400 compared to some 30 whites – mainly government employees and their families). In 1974 the 'Seventh Day Adventist Native Mission', situated some seven miles east of the town, closed, and the following year the Ngangganawili Community (of Aborigines) was formed. In 1977 the Department of Aboriginal Affairs initiated a village building project on the mission site. Self-determination was the watchword, and the Aboriginal population itself constructed houses that were, in theory at least, suited to their own needs. The Community had already taken over the nearby Desert Farm citrus fruit enterprise (from Golden Mile Orchards), and in 1976 an emu farming project was established, also partly with the hope of providing employment for the black community. However, drink was now a major problem: in 1980 the Court of Petty Sessions managed to hear 1500 drink-related offences from among the 400 Aboriginals. H. H. Wilson and A. S. Hill have written a thorough account of the town's history, 'Weeloona – Place of Winds', *Western Australian Historical Society Journal and Proceedings*, vol.4, pt.2 (1950), pp. 48–62. See also G. H. Topperwien, *The History of Wiluna* (unpublished ts, Library of Western Australia).

13   A detailed picture of the region's goldmining boom is Geoffrey Blainey, *The Rush That Never Ended* (Melbourne, Melbourne University Press, 1963); see also James Doughty, *Gold in Their Blood* (Adelaide, Rigby, 1977). C. T. Stannage (ed.), *A New History of Western Australia* (Nedlands, University of Western Australia Press, 1981) is an incisive account in more general terms, including the demise of Aboriginal culture.

14   The Aboriginals of Wiluna are migrants from the Gibson Desert, mainly Mandildjara, but also Gadudjara, Budidjara, Bidjandjadjara, Giyadjara and Wanman people, who all share a common 'Wonggai' language and generalized tradition. Brief guides to the tongue are W. H. Douglas, *Illustrated Topical Dictionary of the Western Desert Language*, Warburton

Ranges Dialect, W.A. (Perth, United Aborigines Mission, 1959) and *An Introduction to the Western Desert Language of Australia* (Sydney, University of Sydney, 1958), the spellings of which I generally adhere to in the text.

15 Until recently anthropologists have tended to focus their attention on male ritual and what appeared to be male dominance. Diane Bell, *Daughters of the Dreaming* (Melbourne, McPhee Gribble/Allen & Unwin, 1983) challenged many established notions of the female role: '. . . I have argued that women are not pawns in male marriage games and are not the uninitiated of their society. We have seen that women are autonomous, independent ritual actors who actively participate in the creation, transmission and maintenance of the values of their society.' See also Phyllis M. Kaberry, *Aboriginal Women: Sacred and Profane* (London, Routledge, 1939). In Aboriginal society there is little or no female initiation ritual as such, though in some groups, for example, the vagina might traditionally have been incised at puberty (some 'whitefellas' at Wiluna incorrectly talk of there having been female circumcision) and, as with the men, an upper front incisor might be knocked out during early adulthood. However, as noted at Kandengei, women may come into power in ways that do not seem obvious to the outsider.

But the very purpose of my journey concentrated my interest on man- rather than woman-making. Male initiation at Wiluna might appear to have been reduced to truncated rites, as elsewhere in Western Desert societies – as noted by A. P. Elkin, *The Australian Aborigines* (Sydney, Angus & Robertson, 1964) and others. Certainly the initiand does not undergo the lengthy training and indoctrination that once constituted his passage to manhood, and at Wiluna the availability of drink further interferes with tradition, but the ritual has not degenerated to the extent that an outsider might think. In initiation the boy undergoes a symbolic death (and rebirth) and so his initiator – his 'killer' – is someone he must avoid afterwards. For this reason he tends to be from a different community: in the case of Wiluna, this will mean a more traditional community such as Warburton or Jigalong. Ironically, Wiluna has in fact become one of the most popular initiation sites because of the easy access to alcohol there. Lee Sackett ('Punishment in Ritual: "Man-making" among Western Desert Aborigines', *Oceania*, vol.49, no.2, December 1978) also finds initiation used as an important disciplinary tool by older men brought up to a nomadic hunter/gatherer existence and now with little day-to-day influence in a society oriented around pub opening hours.

At Wiluna there are six major rituals of initiation (Sackett, 1978). Circumcision, performed in emulation of Malu, the kangaroo-man ances- tor, starts the youth on his progression towards full manhood and the title 'Law man', that is, one who knows and follows the Dreamtime (ancestral) precedent. A boy will be 'grabbed' from the town, taken to the reserve, given a hair belt and club to symbolize the manhood he is about to begin to attain, and led off to a secret place. There he is kept in seclusion and kinsmen of two groups (a 'sun-side' and a 'shade-side', composed of alternate generations) dance and sing to him, recounting among others the *milgu* songline, the tale of the travels and exploits of the kangaroo-man ancestor. After he has witnessed the re-enactment of Dreamtime events over what might be days, though with intervals spent alone with his guardians, the boy is brought back to the centre of the camp and in the company of the women the men set about choosing circumcisers. After further business the sun-side and shade-side groups sing and dance, performances which eventually end with the women wailing then leaving, and the circumcision of the boy. After weeks of seclusion, during which he is sung portions of a further animal-ancestor songline and also reminded that he must now observe the (traditional) Law, he is released as a 'semi'- or 'half'-man. During the next few years he will witness a rainmaking ritual, one associated with carved boards, and two involving polished stone objects, but he is regarded as fully a man only on completion of the subincision rite. This, contrary to popular opinion among the white community in Wiluna, is comparatively straightforward, even though it is the stage which confers full adulthood. The youth is once again 'grabbed' and, in his own or another community to which he might be taken, once again a songline is sung to him, sun-side and shade-side groups dance, and he is secluded, this time for only a few days, for the subincision and recovery. The cut at this time is usually only a short one, about an inch long; it is gradually extended during later ritual performances, such as the re-enactment of the Dreamtime events for the circumcised, until the whole of the underside of the penis has been fully opened.

To explain the Dreamtime, *djngurba*, further: Aboriginals traditionally did not feel themselves as separated from either nature or deities. The forces of nature were expressed symbolically through mythic beings and because humans were associated with these spirits, through the use of ritual they could gain access to those forces (R. M. Berndt and C. H. Berndt, *Aborigines of the West*, Nedlands, University of Western Australia Press, 1979). The Dreaming was where the spirits or forces lived, a period of timelessness which saw the shaping of the world by the spirit and mythic beings, humanized creatures who moved across the land, over 'tribal' boundaries, leaving trails of their spiritual essence. But this 'period' had no end. The creatures of the Dreaming – for instance, Wadi Gudjara, the two lizard-men ancestors – often had powers that could be used by humans, and it was this magical power that was released in ritual and could be directed at people, the land or animals. At initiation, boys would be sung the story of the journeys made by Dreamtime beings; later each boy would set out across the land, following a route with which he was particularly associated, perhaps through having been born on the track or site of a specific spirit being. A child came into the world when a wandering 'child spirit' at last found a mother, transferring life from the Dreaming into her womb. Ideally this occurred in a place linked to his or her father, so that the child inherited the father's spirit associations and also the same personal ties with certain 'agents' attached to that line of land – maybe a crow or hill kangaroo, that acted as a totem intermediary with the Dreamtime and symbol of the relationship between human beings and the supernatural beings manifested in the land.

Robert Tonkinson, *The Mardudjara Aborigines: Living the Dream in Australia's Desert* (New York, Holt, Rinehart & Winston, 1978) discusses ritual and life stages of peoples related to the Wiluna Aboriginals, and puts their cultural background into a historical perspective with the reaction of the first explorers (Giles, Forrest, Warburton, etc.) to them and the bush. Norman B. Tindale, 'Initiation among the Pitjandjara Natives of the Mann and Tomkinson Ranges in South Australia' (*Oceania*, vol.6, no.4 (1936), pp.199–224) is a rather early but specific account of initiation. For a detailed study of the association between Aboriginals and the land, see Nancy M. Williams, *The Yolngu and their Land: a System of Land Tenure and the Fight for its Recognition* (Canberra, Australian Institute of Aboriginal Studies, 1986).

16 They were not, of course, totally empty, except in the imaginations of whitefellas who came to this alien place and naturally felt alienated. The people of the Gibson Desert, groups of nomadic hunter/gatherers speaking a common language, wandered the bush with little disruption from the outside world until the early 1900s, before which the only whitefellas they saw were the first passing explorers: Warburton (1873), Forrest (1874), Giles (1876), Wells (1896) and Carnegie (1896). Then Alfred Canning, surveyor to the state government, was chosen to seek a cattle route down from Kimberley to the thriving goldfields at Coolgardie, Kalgoorlie and elsewhere in the south, and in 1906 set about sinking wells through the Great Sandy and Gibson Deserts to Wiluna, from which livestock could continue by rail. The first cattle came through in 1909; Aboriginals were drawn to the sure water supply provided by the wells, and with increased contact with drovers over the years began to leave the bush for mission stations and fringes of towns such as the fast-emerging Wiluna. In the 1960s there were still small groups of Wonggai (the general name) living in and around the Gibson Desert with little or no contact with whitefellas, but by the mid-1970s all but a handful of the original population had

left. In August 1977, W. J. Peasley led a party from Wiluna to bring in the last two people, a couple ostracized by the Mandildjara dialect group (*Last of the Nomads*, Fremantle, Fremantle Arts Centre Press, 1983). Geoffrey Blainey, *Triumph of the Nomads: a History of Ancient Australia* (London, Macmillan, 1975) is a general history; Penny Hardie, *Nor'Westers of the Pilbara Breed* (Port Hedland, The Shire of Port Hedland, 1981) is a 'story of brave ancestors who pioneered the outback Pilbara in Western Australia' and, although geographically removed from Wiluna, gives an idea of Aboriginal adjustment to whites and of station work, also including the Aboriginal strike assisted by Don McLeod.

17 This was probably Lee Sackett, who has even written an academic paper on Wiluna and its drinking habits: 'Liquor and the Law: Wiluna, Western Australia', in *The World of the First Australians* (see note 8 above). He comments that, while drink is destructive in many ways, it also gives the location attraction as a Law centre for other 'dry' communities.

18 The shooting occurred at Weld Springs, approximately 60 miles to the north-east. John Forrest was engaged on an expedition to cross from Champion Bay, on the west coast, to the centre of Australia, 'the telegraph line between Adelaide and Port Darwin'. Windich Springs he calls 'the best springs I have ever seen'. At Weld Springs he was 'attacked by fifty armed natives . . . They seem determined to take our lives.' He had already shot one man, but appears remorseful: 'We could follow the blood drops for a long way over the stones. I am afraid he got a severe wound.' See John Forrest, *Explorations in Australia* (London, Sampson Low, 1875). Having labelled various landmarks (e.g. Carnarvon Range) with the names of his friends and acquaintances, Forrest went on to become Surveyor-General and the first colonial Premier. Another classic of the period is David Wynford Carnegie, *Spinifex and Sand: a Narrative of Five Years Pioneering and Exploration in Western Australia* (London, C. A. Pearson, 1898).

19 The nearest that Wiluna has come to it is, I think, an extraordinary article in *The Spectator* (21/28 December 1985), 'Australia's Human Zoo: Hal Colebatch finds horrifying mutilation has been re-introduced among the Aborigines'. The reference is to subincision, which he fears represents the spread of a new 'Stone Age' cult and an apartheid loaded against whites. 'Already there are white men on town leases in the Northern Territory entirely surrounded by land given to Aboriginal groups where anyone may be fined $1000 for setting foot without permission.'

20 This is not altogether hyperbole. Sackett (1978) discusses the Wiluna life-style of drink and 'highly promiscuous sexual encounters' – rape is virtually unknown and it is fully recognized that 'females are as likely as males to initiate advances leading to sexual intercourse.'

21 Regarding my suggestion that Micky might be a shaman, an individual who finds himself with, or learns, powers that allow him to travel into a spiritual dimension, '[Shamans] are of immense social significance, the social health of the group largely depending on faith in their powers . . . The various psychic powers attributed to them must not be too readily dismissed . . . for many of them have specialized in the workings of the human mind, and in the influence of mind on body and of mind on mind . . .' A. P. Elkin, 'Aboriginal Men of High Degree', *The John Murtagh Macrossan Memorial Lectures for 1944, University of Queensland* (Sydney, Australasian Publishing, 1945).